Government of Paper

Government of Paper

*The Materiality of Bureaucracy
in Urban Pakistan*

Matthew S. Hull

UNIVERSITY OF CALIFORNIA PRESS

Berkeley · Los Angeles · London

University of California Press, one of the most distinguished university presses in the United States, enriches lives around the world by advancing scholarship in the humanities, social sciences, and natural sciences. Its activities are supported by the UC Press Foundation and by philanthropic contributions from individuals and institutions. For more information, visit www.ucpress.edu.

University of California Press
Berkeley and Los Angeles, California

University of California Press, Ltd.
London, England

Library of Congress Cataloging-in-Publication Data

Hull, Matthew S. (Matthew Stuart), 1968–
    Government of paper : the materiality of bureaucracy in urban Pakistan / Matthew S. Hull.
        p.   cm.
    Includes bibliographical references and index.
    ISBN 978-0-520-27214-9 (cloth : alk. paper)
    ISBN 978-0-520-27215-6 (pbk. : alk. paper)
    1. Government paperwork—Pakistan—Islamabad.
2. Bureaucracy—Pakistan—Islamabad.   3. Capitals
(Cities)—Pakistan—Planning.   4. City planning—
Pakistan—Islamabad.   5. Public records—Pakistan—
Islamabad.   6. Municipal government—Pakistan—
Records and correspondence.   7. Islamabad
(Pakistan)—Politics and government.   I. Title.
    JS7093.A6R425   2012
    352.3'8709549149—dc23   2011042373

Manufactured in the United States of America

20   19   18   17   16   15   14   13   12
10   9   8   7   6   5   4   3   2   1

In keeping with a commitment to support environmentally responsible and sustainable printing practices, UC Press has printed this book on 50-pound Enterprise, a 30% post-consumer-waste, recycled, deinked fiber that is processed chlorine-free. It is acid-free and meets all ANSI/NISO (z 39.48) requirements.

Contents

Illustrations

TABLE

MAP

Acknowledgments

This book has benefited from the insight and support of a number of extraordinary people. I would like to thank first of all those who provided intellectual guidance for this project when I was a graduate student at the University of Chicago. John Kelly introduced me to anthropology when I was an undergraduate and has been an imaginative, rigorous, and encouraging mentor to me ever since. Through brilliant teaching Michael Silverstein introduced me to the social study of language, and he creatively helped me develop my approach to documents and government. After inspiring me with his insights into colonialism, the late Bernard Cohn sparked my interest in urban planning and encouraged me to pursue its study in the postcolonial period. Arjun Appadurai deepened my understanding of South Asia and vigorously encouraged me to connect my research on contemporary Islamabad to other disciplines, times, and places. I would also like to thank William Hanks and Nancy Munn, whose understandings of the role of language and materiality in social life have guided this project since its initial stages. Early on, Seteni Shami helped me cope with the complexity of cities in an anthropological framework. C. M. Naim opened the world of Urdu to me, enduring my grammar and accent with good humor. I am grateful to Webb Keane for his early encouragement to pursue my passion for documents. Anne Ch'ien's unflagging encouragement and preternatural management of practical details was an invaluable support throughout my graduate years.

Friends provided community and intellectual stimulation during my time in Chicago: Asad Ahmed, Rizwan Ahmed, David Altshuler, Bernard Bate, David Ciepley, Adi Hastings, Heather Hindman, Tatsuro Fujikura, Jim Kreines, Mithi Mukherjee, Omar Qureshi, James Rizzo, Jennifer Tilton, and Rachel Zuckert.

I am deeply indebted to friends and colleagues who have read this manuscript at different points and given me encouragement and insights: Kamran Ali, Geoff Bowker, Markus Daechsel, Patrick Eisenlohr, David Gilmartin, William Glover, Andreas Glaeser, Trevor Goldsmith, Zeynep Gürsel, Maya Jasanoff, Paul Johnson, Naveeda Khan, Martha Lampland, Paul Manning, Faiza Moatasim, Hajime Nakatani, Rob Oppenheim, Mark Padilla, Laura Ring, Paul Ryer, the late Leigh Star, Peter Van Der Veer, and an anonymous reviewer for the press. The book has greatly benefited from the comments of numerous audiences, but particular thanks go to those of the Michicagoan Conference in Linguistic Anthropology and other forums at the University of Michigan and the University of Chicago.

Colleagues and students at the University of North Carolina and the University of Michigan have provided me warm and stimulating environments. Special thanks to Sepideh Bajracharya, Juan Cole, Tom Fricke, Judith Irvine, Stuart Kirsch, Alaina Lemon, Michael Lempert, Bruce Mannheim, Barbara Metcalf, Farina Mir, Erik Mueggler, Julia Paley, Peter Redfield, Patricia Sawin, Lee Schlesinger, and Andrew Shryock.

I am enormously indebted to Margaret Wiener and Christopher Nelson who inspired me with their own work and helped me understand where to take this book over the course of many lively discussions. Through many exchanges of our work, Elizabeth F. S. Roberts insightfully, intensely, and tirelessly engaged with the manuscript, for which I am immensely grateful.

I am grateful for the enthusiasm and insights of my editor Reed Malcolm, and for the efforts of his colleagues at the press. I am indebted to Faiza Moatasim, who kindly interrupted her own research in Islamabad to take several fine photographs, including the one on the cover. The copy editing of Ellen McCarthy and Robert Demke greatly improved the text. I wish to thank the Social Science Research Council, the American Institute of Pakistan Studies, the Charlotte W. Newcombe Foundation, and the Committee on Southern Asian Studies at the University of Chicago for generously supporting my research and writing. The staff of the United States Educational Foundation in Pakistan provided important support. Thanks are due also to the National Documentation Center of Pakistan for the use of its archives.

Those in Rawalpindi and Islamabad to whom I am indebted are far too numerous to name. I am grateful for the kind assistance of many current and former employees of the Capital Development Authority and Islamabad Capital Territory Administration. I would like to thank especially Zubair Osmani, Khaled Khan Toru, Zaffar Iqbal Javed, Rawal Khan Maitla, and Amjad Farooq for their assistance, friendship, and insightful observations. Mustafa Kamal Pasha, Saeed Anwar, S.A.T. Wasti, Waqar-ul-Islam, Ayub Tariq, and Rehmat Hussein, Shakir Hassan, and Colin Franklin all enthusiastically gave me invaluable assistance and insights.

My time in Islamabad was enriched by the friendship, observations, and assistance of numerous individuals. I would especially like to thank Ayesha Mahmood, Babur Khan, Amjad Farooq, Ghazanfer Dada, Mohammad Idrees, Rashid Ahmed and his wonderful family, Sajad-ul-Hassan, Tariq Yousef, Patris Gill, Mukhtar Ahmed, Saleem Uddin, Chaudhry Hansa, Chaudhry Gulzar. Farukh Rauf and the late Fazal Ali Khan were wonderful companions and unsparing of time despite the press of other demands. Melodia and Tony Drexler provided a warm home to me and my wife for a brief period. The late Aftab Shah, Misbah Shah and their children Mustafa, Murtaza, and Tanya befriended me early on and happily welcomed my presence day or night. Finally, Mohammad Qasim Shaffi, his brother Asif, sisters Ghazala and Farzana, and his parents opened their home to me as family and supported me in ways the word hospitality doesn't begin to capture. My gratitude to them is profound.

I am grateful to my mother, Ann, and late father, Stuart, as well as Lynn, Jonathan and Mark for their support and for their unspoken conviction that some day this book would emerge. My children Alex and Zsofi graciously accepted my nightly departures for the office despite their pleas for just one more bedtime story. Most of all, I have depended on the practical support, encouragement, criticism, perspective, and love of my wife, Krisztina Fehérváry, who listened to, read, and edited this book countless times.

Preface

The bulk of the ethnographic research for this book was done in Islamabad in the late 1990s, before the onset of what David Gilmartin has called a "climate of alarm" about the Islamic world. Much has happened in Pakistan since. Not long after I left, Pakistan conducted its first test of a nuclear device. The military dictatorship of General Pervez Musharraf has come and gone. The American War on Terror has roiled the region for a decade.

Academic and popular American discourse today overwhelmingly characterizes Pakistan through Islamist militancy, nuclear weapons, and political instability, the latest episodes in a long-running story of Pakistan as a "failed state." The problems highlighted by this trope are real. However, this trope draws our attention away from other significant dimensions of life in Pakistan and, more importantly, leads us to disregard what state institutions actually do and how Pakistanis engage with them. Research in the summer of 2007 confirmed to me that such engagements remain at the heart of the tensions and crises of the Pakistan state.

Portrayals of bureaucracy often exaggerate stability, overlooking how bureaucrats and bureaucracies respond dynamically to events. However, bureaucrats struggle to respond using well-established implements of documentation and deliberation. This book focuses on continuities in the bureaucratic material infrastructure while attending to how that infrastructure plays an unexpected part in change. Although this book is ethnographically grounded in the recent past of Pakistan, an account of bureaucratic infrastructure has much to tell us about its present and future.

December 2011
Ann Arbor

Note on Translation
and Transliteration

Unless otherwise noted, all translations of Urdu conversations and written materials are my own. For the sake of readability, I have employed a simple transliteration system for Urdu and Arabic words that does not use diacritics. This system does not distinguish between long and short vowels (e.g., *a* and *ā*, *i* and *ī*) or between dental and retroflex consonants (e.g. *t* and *ṭ*; *d* and *ḍ*). For proper names and Urdu and Arabic terms commonly used in English-language speech or writing (e.g., *purdah* and *mohalla*), I have adopted the most conventional English spelling. Urdu terms are pluralized in the English manner, by adding an *s*.

Introduction

In the electronic age, documents appear to have escaped their paper confinement. And yet, we continue to be surrounded and even controlled by a flow of paper whose materiality has vast consequences. What are the implications of such a thorough paper mediation of relations among people, things, places, and purposes? *Government of Paper* addresses this question by showing how the material forms of documentation and communication, the things I gather together under the term "graphic artifacts," shape the governance of the planned city of Islamabad.[1] Governing paper is central to governing the city. And paper is also the means by which residents acquiesce to, contest, or use this governance.

My research began as an exploration of how the Pakistani government shapes social life in Islamabad through its planning and regulatory control of the built environment. However, I gradually came to understand that the modernist program for shaping social order through built forms had expanded a material regime of another, equally significant sort: a regime of paper documents. My conversations with residents about their patches of the built environment of Islamabad quickly veered from family, architecture, and law into stories about the trials and tribulations of their documents and files. Some months after I had arrived, for example, I talked with Ahmed, a driver who was about to move to a small house he had built in a new area of the city. Sitting on the floor of his one-room apartment behind the office building where he worked, he replied laconically to my questions about how he thought his life would be different in the new place, the design and construction of his house, and zoning and building codes. When the conversation lagged, he got up, went to a cupboard, and pulled out a thick gray file folder like those used in government offices. He had never been allowed to see the official file the government maintained on his house, but he had made himself an unofficial replica. As he opened the file, he became talkative, enthusiastically narrating his house as episodes of document acquisition: the transfer certificate giving him title to the land for which he had passed 5,000 rupees (Rs.) to an agent to save the Rs. 8,400 official fee; the form generated by the surveyor showing where the plot was (it had been an achievement to get the surveyor to show up); a possession certificate a friend of his, a fellow ethnic Gujar, had facilitated; the house plan that his architect had illegally copied from a house file maintained by the city government; the "No Objection Certificate" approving the house plan; and many others. As his story arrived at the end of his file, he smiled and tapped his finger triumphantly on the last document, recently obtained. He had finally negotiated with a city inspector for a "completion certificate" that allowed him to occupy the house legally—the paper crown of his undertaking.

Until this point, I had been focused on records at the other end of the documentary spectrum, namely maps. My initial encounter with Islamabad was through the mediation of a map showing a monumental national administrative area dominating a numbered and lettered grid of sectors (each 1¼ square miles) that extended boundlessly to the west—as far as the paper would allow anyway (fig. 0.1). Drawn in 1960, this map, the work of Costantinos Doxiadis, a Greek modernist architect and the planner of the city, was also the first vision of what was to become the highly planned national capital of Pakistan, established under martial law in 1959 and situated on agricultural land several miles north of the large existing city of Rawalpindi.

Over the last five decades, the sector-by-sector construction of the city has gradually transformed Doxiadis's map from utopia to ideology. Versions of it are now found on roadside billboards, on posters on office walls, and in newspaper advertisements. A translation of this map in poured concrete lines is the focus of the garden in Shakarparian Park to the south of the city. The carefully pruned rose bushes in sector squares iconically figure Islamabad as a giant, well-ordered garden. In contrast, Rawalpindi, the older city to the south, is represented by an unruly mass of unclipped bushes covering an irregular area in the midst of the grid.

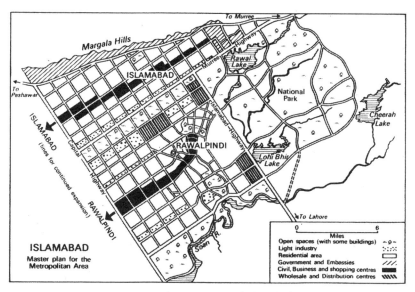

FIGURE 0.1. Constantinos Doxiadis's 1960 map of Islamabad.

Before the city was much more than a map, the Pakistani government established the Capital Development Authority (CDA), giving it complete administrative and judicial authority over the planning and development of the city. Given the comprehensive scope of planning and the clean, centralized command structure of the CDA, I had expected to find a wealth of official documentation on the city as a whole—reports on population, housing, roads, building regulation, and so forth. But what I found—or rather, didn't find—surprised me.

The once-celebrated Master Plan had no other comprehensive and unitary embodiment than the old reports of Doxiadis, reverently collected in a bookcase in a CDA library, away from the main CDA offices, and almost never consulted. I was told the last person to look at them before I came along was a curious British diplomat some years earlier. The official in charge of CDA employee housing had no comprehensive documentation on how many housing units were under CDA control and where they were, though he managed perhaps as many as twenty thousand. A former CDA chairman told me that "there is no one who can tell you what [the] CDA owns. . . . [P]ieces of land were acquired years ago and no one even knows we have them." CDA board decisions, the main policy of the authority, were dispersed in files and not available for reference since no one had compiled them. What general reports had been produced in the 1970s were out of circulation and hard to find. Later, I sometimes found whole reports inserted in a file, localized as part of a particular case. The CDA did not even have a unitary set of representations of land areas. The department handling land acquisitions used the Urdu revenue record, generated with chains and pacing and calculated by *kanal* (one-eighth of an acre); in contrast, planners relied on maps produced by modern transit–stadia measurements in units of square kilometers. These two land reckoning systems are difficult to correlate. Aside from city maps, more often found displayed on walls than in the hands of planners, there seemed to be no representations of the city as a whole.

I spent several frustrating months trying to get hold of the sort of comprehensive documents I thought planners should use before I began to try to understand the genres they actually were using, like those Ahmed had shown me. What I discovered is that even synoptic maps and reports are most efficacious not as what Bruno Latour (2005:187) calls "panoramas," big pictures weakly connected to what they show, but rather as artifacts entangled in the prosaic documentary practices through which the city is constructed, regulated, and inhabited. Order and disorder on every scale in Islamabad are produced through the ceaseless circulation of millions of maps, forms, letters, and reports among bureaucrats, politicians, property owners, imams (prayer leaders), businessmen, and builders. The larger crisis and the persistent endurance of the Pakistan state are usually understood only through high politics and the broad institutional relationships among bureaucrats, elected politicians, the military, and more recently, militants. However, the stories of documents, from humble completion certificates to broad sector maps, help explain both crisis and stability in Pakistan.

In comparison with the modernist new city projects of Brasilia and Chandigarh, which James Scott (1998) has characterized as failures, Islamabad has been a success. The population has grown at a steady pace to nearly one million, and though there are perennial complaints about the city's lifelessness, many Pakistanis consider it to be the most beautiful and livable city in Pakistan. Picture books feature its architecture, and even poetry has been written about it. Nonetheless, all has not gone according to the Master Plan. In most neighborhoods, unauthorized mosques built by different sects abound. The planned correlation between state-owned dwellings and the government rank of their occupants is often weak or absent. Most dramatically, the boundless westward expansion envisioned by Doxiadis stalled, perhaps forever, in the

11-series of sectors, just six miles from the president's house. The ways the CDA governs its paper and governs through its paper has played an important role in these developments. Bureaucratic writing is commonly seen as a mechanism of state control over people, places, processes, and things. But the political function of documents is much more ambiguous. In Islamabad, a high-modernist planning project typical of the postcolonial world, paradoxically, has been partly undermined by the very semiotic technologies that made it so quintessentially modern: its documentation and communication practices.

This book tackles the epistemological and ontological problems of documents, problems raised by the recognition of the relative autonomy of objects. The producers of government documents, much like scientists, claim to represent, engage with, or constitute realities "in the world" independent from the processes that produce documents. And yet, recent scholarship has shown how bureaucratic texts are produced, used, and experienced through procedures, techniques, aesthetics, ideologies, cooperation, negotiation, and contestation. Most existing treatments of documents separate or even oppose these two aspects of documents. I argue that we need to address both. In addition to describing the logics, aesthetics, concepts, norms, and sociology of bureaucratic texts, scholars also need to account for how documents engage (or do not engage) with people, places, and things to make (other) bureaucratic objects: as Annemarie Mol (2002) puts it, how bureaucratic objects are "enacted" in practice. Practices of enacting bureaucratic objects are as complex, variable, and illuminating as more traditional anthropological subjects such as rituals and myths. Without adopting a naïve postsemiotic approach, we can confront an unproductive dichotomy between the constructed and the real. A planning map is not only an ideological projection of a bureaucratic vision of the city; this vision is embedded in the technical and procedural processes that link a map to roads, structures, streams, and documents.

WRITING OF THE BUREAUCRACY

Mohammad Waseem (1989) has aptly called the state of Pakistan a "bureaucratic polity." The central role of civilian bureaucratic state institutions in Pakistan is captured in the way Pakistanis refer to them simply as "the bureaucracy." The bureaucracy is recognized in both academic and popular discourse as a more or less independent political actor alongside the army, elected governments, and political parties. The contemporary position of the civilian bureaucracy grew out of colonial history and the early decades following Partition in 1947, when the new Pakistan state was created in two territories, West and East Pakistan (now Bangladesh), separated by over one thousand miles of Indian territory. The administrative system reassembled by the new state of Pakistan was well established compared to other political institutions in the country.[2] The advantage of this early institutional capacity gave the bureaucracy a central role in the political process of the new state.[3] Nationalist historiography portrays Pakistan independence as a transfer of power from the British colonial government to that of the leading political party, the Muslim League. It was equally, however, a transition between the British bureaucracy and the emergent Pakistani bureaucracy.

In portrayals of postcolonial governance, the continuities between the colonial and the postcolonial are often exaggerated, even as they are underspecified. The postcolonial is often figured as a "legacy" of the colonial; the colonial is seen to "haunt" the postcolonial. In contrast, much of this book is devoted to showing how colonial practices operate in new ways in the postcolonial era. However, the process of decolonization has perhaps proceeded most gradually in the area of civilian administration. The continuity of personnel and ethos within the early postcolonial Pakistani bureaucracy is obvious, especially at the senior ranks. Former members of the Indian Civil Service (ICS), the elite members of the professional class of Muslim bureaucrats that Hamza Alavi (1983) has termed the "salariat," led the establishment of the Pakistani bureaucracy alongside British nationals, some of whom were retained until as late as 1957.[4] One British former colonial officer signed the first of Pakistan's currency notes as finance minister and led the Reorganization Committee formed in 1947 to establish the Pakistani bureaucracy. Another British officer was appointed as the first head of the newly established Pakistan Civil Service Academy, tasked with training the elite civil servants of the Civil Service of Pakistan, modeled on the ICS. The Civil Service Academy emphasized Western dress and cultivated British social graces and manners. Shakespeare, Locke, and William Blackstone were part of the required curriculum, and English language was prescribed for all conversation during the training period. After completing the program, officers were sent abroad for a year of study in Oxford, Cambridge, or another Commonwealth country.[5]

The continuity of the colonial bureaucratic material infrastructure, much like that of roads and bridges, was more obvious, unquestioned, and profound. If documentary writing has long been recognized as an essential element of modern governance, it has been seen as an especially central component of colonial government in South Asia.[6] The British colonial government came to be known as the "Kaghazi Raj" or Document Rule. In 1852, a Parliamentary Select Committee asked John Stuart Mill to explain the good government of the Indian territories. He replied:

> I conceive that there are several causes; probably the most important is, that the whole Government of India is carried on in writing. All the orders given, and all the acts of the executive officers, are reported in writing, and the whole of the original correspondence is sent to the Home Government; *so that there is no single act done in India, the whole of the reasons for which are not placed on record.* This appears to me a greater security for good government than exists in almost any other government in the world, because no other probably has a system of recordation so complete. (cited in Moir 1993:185, emphasis added)

This complete system of records developed from the documentation and communication practices of the English East India Company, the quasi-governmental trading corporation that eventually transformed into the government of colonial India. The most common explanation for the pervasiveness of writing within the colonial government is that practices of written accountability designed for the management of far-flung and unreliable commercial agents were carried over into the operations of territorial rule as the Company gradually assumed the form of the colonial government of India.[7] Accountability at a distance was certainly a major factor. The directors of the Company in London distrusted their faraway agents, who routinely served their own interests alongside or even through their work for the Company.[8] The centrality of writing in South Asian governance, however, has more to do with the fundamental problematics of the corporation as a social form than has been previously recognized.

Three decades before Thomas Hobbes famously argued that the lack of a final, absolute authority led inevitably to a war of all against all, the Company had worked out mechanisms for the accountability of all to all. The Company was constituted as a "body politick" by Letters Patent (or charter) of Elizabeth I in 1600, which laid out a structure of governance strikingly similar to today's modern corporations, with an elected governor, officers, and "committees," individuals who formed a body operating much like a contemporary corporate board. The charter specified who was a member of ("free of") the Company, what the offices would be, and how individuals would be elected to them. Still, the problem of regulating day-to-day actions of officers and employees remained.

The Company solution was to create a social organization constituted by the movement of paper. According to the *Lawes or Standing Orders of the East India Company* written in 1621, an early ancestor of today's corporate bylaws, only through a connection with a piece of paper (a bill, warrant, note, book, and so forth) could an action be construed as an action of the Company. A cash payment made without a warrant was not a Company transaction, and an individual who made it was required to reimburse the Company. Goods transferred without a receipt were still considered to be in Company possession. Even cooks on Company ships had to produce accounts and receipts for the bursar or repay the funds extended to them. The *Lawes* expressed a thoroughgoing rejection of trust in people.

> And forasmuch as the affaires of the Company are so contrived, that there is now little or no trust imposed in any particular mans accompts: But that he hath also some checke by Warrants, Bils of parcels, or the accompts of other men. (East India Company 1621:70)

Vouching was done by artifacts, not people. The *Lawes* specified a kind of documentary buddy system in which every document was to "be vouched" by another, produced by a different person. The book recording the payments to workmen on the docks, for example, was "to be vouched by the Notes of the Committees" (East India Company 1621:79). Not only signatures but also autography was required to ensure the connection between a document and a particular individual. The accomptants general was instructed as follows: "you shall digest and enter all Accompts into the journal your self with your owne hand, For we will admit no diversity of hands" (78). This solution took form within the horizon of the empiricist metaphysics growing in Britain: a practical attack on the problem of words and things, an attempt to make discourse into actions definable through a trustworthy material order open to the witnessing of members of the Company.[9] It was precisely the materiality of graphic signs that made them useful as a palpable sedimentation of the real.

This method of defining Company business was the germ of the practices that by the late seventeenth century would come to distinguish Company business from the "private trade," business carried out by Company servants on their own accounts in India. As Miles

Ogburn writes, an office manual published in 1675, *Regulating and New Methodizeing*, "sought to institute writing practices that, in their repeated performance and reinscription, were intended to constitute a distinction between the 'public' world of the Company's business and the 'private' actions of its servants" (2007:71). From the late seventeenth century, such reforms effectively reorganized the Company not by redefining duties and offices, but by instituting new forms of documentation.

Prosaic documents were central not only to the constitution of the Company but also to its infamous transformation into a territorial power. The "Revolution of Bengal" through which the Company became the de facto government of the region in 1765 was provoked by conflict over routine customs documents.[10] From the 1650s, in exchange for lump-sum yearly payments, the Company had been given an exemption from tolls and other duties on goods it transported for export from its port in Bengal. Even as the Company was using documents to distinguish between Company and private business, it was using them to blur the division between the Company and the Mughal imperial government. In 1717, the Company persuaded the Mughal emperor to grant the Company the authority to issue passes (*dastaks*) that could be presented to customs authorities to exempt particular shipments from the assessment of duty. It is likely that the emperor and the nawab of Bengal (the regional ruler) considered this new authority merely a new means of implementing the long-standing arrangement of duty-free export of Company goods.

But what might have been seen as relatively minor administrative change had far-reaching consequences. The imperial duty-free policy was gutted by the Company's ability to produce the documents used to implement it. Company officials soon began to issue passes to its officers for their private trade and to sell them to Asian merchants, depriving the government of tax revenue and undercutting many native merchants. Disputes over what the nawab considered an abuse of passes culminated in his military defeat in the Battle of Plassey in 1757. Subsequent nawabs installed by the Company proved equally intransigent on the matter of passes, and, following another decisive military victory for the Company, Robert Clive forced the weak Mughal emperor to grant the Company formal control of the area in 1765. Several years later, the Company tightened its control over customs revenue and its own officers by eliminating passes altogether.

As Company territorial rule expanded from the late eighteenth century, administrators recognized that Indian functionaries, like their

English counterparts, were often more committed to their own interests and social institutions than to the Company or government. Longstanding debates about the propriety of Company officials gradually transformed into a discourse about "native corruption." British officers in India were frequently transferred among different posts. They lacked knowledge of the locales they administered and of the permanently posted native functionaries on whom they helplessly depended. In response to these uncertain loyalties, the British, building on the elaborate written procedures of the Mughals, expanded their graphic regime of surveillance and control. Official discourse was anchored to people, places, times, and artifacts through an elaborate use of signatures, dates, and stamps. Like Mill, officials transferred from London often noted that the Indian colonial government used written documentation far more extensively than its metropolitan counterpart did.

The mid-nineteenth-century British colonial administration, as Smith (1985) argues, was not an organization simply employing various written genres (reports, records, and manuals) but rather an organization whose overall structure and practices were constituted in large measure by this "genre system" (Yates, Orlikowski, Rennecker 1997). Normative procedures were laid down in hundreds of manuals produced for every sphere of administration in the late nineteenth century. Manuals for village-level revenue staff (*patwaris*) instructed them on how to carry out field measurements and draw up records of rights. Office manuals, which I will discuss in chapter 3, stipulated the forms that office communications and records should take and specified in meticulous detail how they were to be stamped, registered, accessed, transported, stored, and destroyed. Positions within an organizational division were defined in relation to genres of papers. Rules prescribed what genres officers and staff of different ranks could read, draft, write, and even the means of inscription they were authorized to use. An office manual published in 1891, for example, required a senior clerk to write in pencil in the margin of a "paper to be dealt with" but in ink on the notes section of a file—red ink when referencing another file (Government of India 1891:42). Officers were required to use a full signature to approve some documents, initials for others. These manuals distributed influence within the office and articulated a paperwork ethics through the specification of the care and duties owed to different genres of documents. Rules prescribing what documents could be exchanged between organizational divisions and the protocols for doing so were a technique of social analysis that defined relations among divisions—even constituted them as different divisions (Strathern 1999). Such manuals also engineered the hierarchical relations between district-level administration, staffed by Indian Civil Service officers working in English, and village-level administration, staffed by provincial and local cadres. Regulation of the subordinate staff through manuals allowed the district officer to remain aloof from the details of land revenue and "free to assume general charge" (Smith 1985:160). District officers prepared a variety of kinds of reports, censuses, surveys of land tenure ("settlement reports"), and "district gazetteers" that described the history, social composition, economy, and administration of a single district. The reports promoted the synoptic view of the district consonant with the district officer's remove from local knowledge that was enabled by the manuals. Discursive and material features of these different genres shaped knowledge of village society and participation in governmental processes.

Bureaucratic continuities from the Company and colonial to the postcolonial can be overstated. A contemporary Pakistani clerk would probably consider the colonial practice of attaching white, "emerald," "vermillion," and "sky" colored reference slips to papers to index their urgency to be as antiquated and impractical as donning a Victorian woolen waistcoat.[11] New kinds of documents—such as completion certificates, "Out of Turn Allotment of Accommodation" forms for government housing (chapter 1), and "demolition certificates" documenting the destruction of houses on expropriated land (chapter 4)—have been invented to implement the project of a new city and deal with its contradictions. However, though they are part of new projects and repurposed in novel ways, many of the bureaucratic inscriptional practices from the colonial period have remained vital in the contemporary period.

SIGNS OF PAPER

The centrality of writing to formal organizations has been recognized in Western social thought since long before the mid-eighteenth-century French political economist Jean Claude Marie Vincent de Gournay coined the derisive term *bureaucracy,* or rule by writing desk. Most works on writing and bureaucracy quote the same passage of Max Weber:

> The management of the modern office is based upon written documents (the "files"), which are preserved in their original or draught form. There is, therefore, a staff of subaltern officials and scribes of all sorts. The body of officials actively engaged in a "public" office, along with the respective apparatus of material implements and the files, makes up a bureau. (1978:957)

Writing and documents have long been of interest within sociology studies of the internal workings of formal organizations.[12] But Ben Kafka's observation regarding historians is equally true of anthropologists: until recently they have "discovered all sorts of interesting and important things looking *through* paperwork, but seldom paused to look *at* it" (2009:341). Documents have been out of the sight of anthropologists for a few reasons. The traditional social science division of labor left formal organizations to sociologists, political scientists, and economists, while anthropologists concentrated on nonmodern, small-scale societies that were seen to operate without or independent of formal organizations.[13] When anthropologists turned to the investigation of formal organizations in the 1920s and 1930s, they brought with them the analytic tools and empirical emphases developed through the study of lineages, clans, age-sets, chiefs, and big men. Lloyd Warner, as a student of Radcliffe-Brown, contributed to the extension of ethnographic methods to industrial organizations as well as to the discovery of "informal relations" in the famous Hawthorne Western Electric study in the 1920s and 1930s.[14] In the 1980s, ritual, informal relations, and more recent concerns like gender, anomalous classification, attitudes, and bureaucratic ideologies were bundled together within the concept of organizational culture.[15] As the main mechanism and dominant emblem of the formal dimension of bureaucracy, documents received little attention.

Another reason that anthropologists have overlooked bureaucratic paperwork is that we produce and use documents in much the way the people we study do.[16] It is easy to criticize Gerald M. Britan and Ronald Cohen's recommendation to depend on organizational records for ethnographic documentation: "Unlike traditional field subjects, formal organizations generate large quantities of written records-logs, calendars, memos, minutes, plans, reports. . . . This record is the observer's basic account of social life in the organization. Its analysis and comparison with other documentary records and interviews about organizational activity provide the basis for an ethnographic depiction" (1980:23). On the other hand, rare is the institutional ethnography that doesn't draw on reports or organizational charts for insight into the workings of bureaucratic organizations.

Documents have also been overlooked because it's easy to see them as simply standing between the things that really matter, giving immediate access to what they document. Although the denial of the mediating role of documents, what William Mazzarella calls the "politics of immediation" (2006), may be a tactic of power and authority, their invisibility is also a phenomenological quality of mediators. As Patrick Eisenlohr has written, there is a "tendency of media to disappear in the act of mediation. In fact, media can only function as such if in the act of conveying something they are also capable of drawing attention away from their own materiality and technicality in order to redirect attention to what is being mediated" (2011:44).

To analytically restore the visibility of documents, to look *at* rather than *through* them, is to treat them as mediators, things that "transform, translate, distort, and modify the meaning or the elements they are supposed to carry" (Latour 2005:39). Just as discourse has long been recognized as a dense mediator between subjects and the world, we need to see graphic artifacts not as neutral purveyors of discourse, but as mediators that shape the significance of the linguistic signs inscribed on them.

One of the most fruitful insights to emerge from the general rehabilitation of materiality in the social sciences and humanities is that representations are material. Anthropologists have long recognized that things are signs, but until recently they have often ignored that signs are things. Within anthropology, the problem of the materiality of signs has been constructively developed within a Peircean framework. In contrast to a Saussurean semiotics that spirits signs from the material world into systems of ideation, materiality is at the heart of Peirce's approach to signs.[17] He argued that a sign must have "qualities independent of its meaning" (Peirce 1986:62). As Keane observes, "representations exist as things and acts in the world. . . . A medium of representation is not only something that stands 'between' those things it mediates, it is also a 'thing' in its own right" (1997:8).

The material qualities of graphic artifacts are mobilized in signification, but they also allow them to mediate many other processes besides semiosis. In the next section, I discuss some of these other processes and their relation to communication, but in the rest of this section I concentrate on the role of the material properties of documents in their semiotic engagement with their users, that is, how their material qualities contribute to their meanings.

The insight that representations are material encourages a shift from semiotic structures (texts) abstracted or abstractable from their material vehicles to the relationships of material forms and texts. As Roger Chartier writes, "The significance, or better yet, the historically and socially distinct significations, of a text, whatever they may be, are inseparable from the material conditions and physical forms that make the text available to readers" (1995:22). Even the concept of writing as inscribed signs, though a convenient shorthand, abstracts from the concrete material forms through which inscriptions reach our eyes and hands.[18] People don't read writing. They read (and do much else with) files, road signs, forms, computer screens, reports, and visiting cards.

Webb Keane (2003:419) poses the problem of the interpretation of signs in general terms, arguing that it is governed by what he calls— generalizing the concept of linguistic ideology (Silverstein 1979)—a "semiotic ideology," "assumptions about what signs are and how they function in the world." The semiotic functions and nondiscursive uses of graphic artifacts are partly shaped by semiotic ideologies specific to graphic artifacts, what we can call "graphic ideologies." Graphic ideologies are sets of conceptions about graphic artifacts held by their users, including about what material qualities of an artifact are to count as signs, what sorts of agents are (or should be) involved in them, and what the roles of human intentions and material causation are. Graphic ideologies are obviously tied closely to linguistic ideologies but include notions specific to graphic representation. At the most basic level, such ideologies include conventions for the interpretation of graphic forms, determining, for example, that a page is scanned from left to right or that the size of characters is iconic of importance. Graphic ideologies may also include views about how artifacts are or ought to be produced and circulated, such as those embedded in Euro-American copyright laws or Mughal sanctions on the production of the imperial calligraphic mark (*tughra*). Graphic ideologies also define the normative relations between discourse genres and graphic forms (for example, that an official communication should be presented on letterhead) and the sort of person associated with a particular graphic form (a citizen is embodied in a petition with a distinctive graphic organization).

Graphic ideologies may also include more general conceptions regarding the ontology and authority of graphic artifacts and their capacity (or incapacity) to represent or produce truth, spirit, presence, life, and so forth.[19] Mark Lewis describes early Chinese writers, for example, who conflated what we would consider sign and object, crediting lines, trigrams, and hexagrams of central texts with vitality and generative powers (1999:260–62). Brinkley Messick (1993) describes orthodox Muslim views of writing as a questionable, even dangerous, though indispensable medium; the truth and authority of a written text can only be ensured by its animation in an oral-aural chain of transmission through men of good and pious character. Graphic ideologies range from widely held cultural assumptions to refined understandings elaborated in technical works such as exegetical guides and office manuals. Some of these ideologies may offer competing interpretations and enjoin different uses for the same graphic genre or artifact.

This book describes a great variety of graphic genres in use within the Pakistani bureaucratic arena: files, office registers, minutes, organizational charts, plans, elevations, maps, visiting cards, "chits," petitions, powers of attorney, memos, letters, revenue records, regulations, reports, policy statements, and office manuals. While there are some commonalities to the use and ideological constructs related to most genres within Pakistani bureaucracy, each genre has its own pattern of use, distinct formal discursive characteristics, graphic conventions, material form, and interpretive frameworks through which readers produce and make sense of it. As I describe in chapter 3, the interpretation and use of most of these formal genres is governed by an official graphic ideology, elaborated in office manuals, which regulates the production and circulation of official artifacts, views words as corresponding to things through acts of reference, and identifies autographic authorship with agency. More diffuse understandings of these genres, of course, diverge from this official ideology.

Graphic ideologies mediate the significance of a variety of material qualities of graphic artifacts, most prominently organizations of graphic space. The graphic organization (along with other material qualities), functioning as an interpretive frame, may be a basic determinant of what discourse genre the inscriptions are taken to represent. In the case of filling out forms, as Donald Brenneis (2006) has shown, graphic organization is especially important in shaping responses because it may remain below the level of consciousness, an aspect of material qualities that Daniel Miller highlights as the "humility of objects" (1987:85–108). As we'll see, most documents within the Pakistani bureaucracy have their own peculiar spatial organization. Conventions of graphic organization, however, may hold across different genres, and even languages and scripts. The common format of books in many different European languages is an obvious example of continuity across languages. The continuity across scripts can be seen in the Pakistani bureaucratic arena, where English-language genres provide the paradigms for their counterparts in Urdu. Business cards, letters, legal documents, and entries on file note sheets written in Urdu maintain the organization of graphic units of corresponding English-language genres, even though Urdu is written in the right-to-left Perso-Arabic script. This suggests a distinction between a language community and a "writing community" analogous to the distinction between a language community, a group of people sharing a linguistic code, and a speech community, which shares pragmatic norms across two or more languages (for example, ways of greeting shared by speakers of French and Italian). The graphic norms of the Pakistani bureaucratic writing community, defined through English-language genres, are shared by functionaries and clients writing in different languages and scripts.[20]

Discourse genres tend to be associated with a particular graphic organization, but in practice they do not always coincide, which creates a bivalent significance. As I'll show in chapter 2, for example, petitioners enact an ambiguous political subject by combining the discourse of a supplicant with the graphic organization used by bureaucrats in their memos. In other cases, the graphic organization and discourse can be in outright contradiction, as in the unusual case when a printed form was allegedly used to inscribe the discourse of a unique personal recommendation (chapter 2).

The significance of a particular mode of inscription varies with any number of contextual factors. Within the Pakistani bureaucratic arena, typing usually indexes the importance of the artifact, though this varies with the genre and the position of the author. The typing of note sheet entries in files usually indexes the importance of the matter, though the informally known inscriptional habits of the particular officer may make this association stronger or weaker (some officers are known to have most entries typed). In contrast, a request from a senior official or politician handwritten on the back of his business card indexes his personal interest and may be dealt with more speedily than a typed letter from his office would be. The availability of instruments for different inscriptional modes is another important contextual factor. That is, the significance of any particular mode is shaped by the options presumed to be available to the principal, much as the significance of phoning has changed with the widespread use of text messages. Handwritten petitions index the low status of the petitioner and are therefore treated with less concern than typed petitions, since Roman-script typewriters and computers are widely available. In contrast, handwritten Urdu petitions, while generally not accorded the same importance as English-language ones owing to differences in the status of the two languages, are not as devalued since Urdu typewriters are not in common use.[21] Returning to the business card example, since a senior officer, with an office staff at his disposal, obviously could have had the request typed, the handwriting is not seen as an index of lack of sophistication or economic inability, but of personal attention.

Photocopying is another important mode of inscription with indexical significance. Contrasting print and handwritten manuscript copies, Messick observes:

> As a "copy" [a manuscript] is virtually the same thing as the original, not because it "looks like" the original in the photo-identity sense accomplished by mechanical reproduction, . . . but because it has passed through an authoritative process of human reproduction and collation. Although they apparently accomplish the same task, manuscript and print copies work with differing technologies and epistemologies. (1993:240)

This is an important insight, though the relevance of actual photo-identity to the social determination of a photocopy as a copy is probably overstated.[22] Such a clear contrast cannot be drawn with respect to photocopies within the Pakistani bureaucratic arena at least, where copies must be authorized as copies to be given official status. Since the use of a copy implies the (at least local or temporary) absence of the original, making visual comparison between original and copy impossible, the practice of human authorization is fundamental in most practices. Even authorized photocopies, such as those of file note sheets, may not be given the official standing of the original, since the "original" signatures of numerous officials are inscribed on the original, but only that of the single authorizing official appear on the copy.

The surface of graphic artifacts can also serve a range of semiotic functions. The material qualities of the artifact surface such as size, color, shape, and basic material can index the discourse genre that its inscriptions represent. Colored foolscap paper (8.5" by 13"), for example, frames writing as internal "notes" of the Pakistani government. Costly surfaces can indicate the importance of the communication and the wealth or high status of the principal. Certain kinds of legal representations in Islamabad have no legal standing unless executed on stamp papers of various rupee denominations. The physical composition of artifacts, how the surfaces are ordered and physically linked to one another, may also shape the significance of the discourse they carry, for example, by determining which graphic forms can be seen together. Assistants sometimes dupe their own officers into signing a file note by placing the part of note the officer would object to on a different sheet folded over, and then presenting the rest to him for a perfunctory signature. The detachability of Post-Its, artifacts rarely used within

Pakistani bureaucracy, was allegedly used by Asif Ali Zardari when his wife, Benazir Bhutto, was prime minister, as I discuss in chapter 3.

ASSOCIATIONS OF PAPER

Thus far, I have discussed how graphic artifacts convey significance in encounters with individual users, how they form associations through semiosis. However, graphic artifacts are simultaneously constituted by and constitutive of broader associations (Latour 2005) of people, places, and other things. We can distinguish two related ways that documents build on semiosis in composing associations. First, the circulation of graphic artifacts creates associations among people that often differ from formal organizational structures and draw people outside the bureaucracy into bureaucratic practices. Second, as they participate in the enactment of bureaucratic objects, that is, of their "referents" (legal houses, deserving petitioners, expropriable plots), graphic artifacts draw these objects into the associations formed through document circulation.

I will return later to the question of the relation of documents to their referents, but now I'd like to consider circulation and the question of how documents relate to formal bureaucratic organization. Situating writing entirely within the dynamics of administrative control is an example of a tendency "to excessively sociologize transaction in things" (Appadurai 1986:5). Over the last decade, work in diverse fields, including the history of the book, material culture, and science studies, has criticized the view that artifacts are simply reified social relations, that the forms, uses, and meanings of objects are simply a function of "social relations" or expressions or reflections of social orders and processes.[23] Latour argues that this view "is unable to explain why artifacts enter the stream of our relations, why we so incessantly recruit and socialize nonhumans. It is not to mirror, congeal, crystallize, or hide social relations, but to remake these very relations through fresh and unexpected sources of action" (1999:197). Rather than trying to abstract relations among people, Latour argues that we should replace the study of social institutions with that of "associations" (2005) or "object institutions" (1999:192) composed of humans and nonhumans.

Max Weber came close to this conception of bureaucracy when he wrote, "The combination of written documents and a continuous operation by officials constitutes the 'office' (*Bureau*)" (1978:219). But Weber characterized documents as the passive instruments of bureaucratic organizations formed through norms and rules rather than as constitutive of bureaucratic activities and the social relations formed through them. Consider how he explained that bureaucratic institutions often remain stable despite, perhaps even especially, through changes of regime.[24] He identified the "system of files" as one source of this stability, but made the sociological argument that it was mainly the effect of norms inculcated in bureaucratic functionaries (Weber 1978:988). Weber rejected the view of the anarchist Mikhail Bakunin, who argued that the French Revolution ultimately failed because it focused on eliminating people rather than records. Weber dismissed this "naïve idea of Bakuninism" because it "overlooks that the settled orientation of *man* for observing accustomed rules and regulations will survive independently of the documents" (1978:988 emphasis in original). We don't need to follow Weber in distributing explanations of bureaucratic order to one side or the other of a divide between the sociological and the technological. The "orientation" of bureaucrats is in part a bundle of habits of documentation and communication shaped in relation to the material intransigence of bureaucratic records. To characterize government by association is to describe how graphic artifacts translate and displace social relations within government and how they do not simply reproduce them in another media.

The idea that artifacts are constitutive of forms of sociality has been most developed in the study of consumer goods and technical artifacts, but it has also been productive in recent reconceptualizations of publics. Chartier describes how earlier scholarship on the history of the book in Europe concentrated on the distribution of different genres of books among the various groups that made up the society of the ancien régime. The assumption behind this focus was that social divisions—classes, professions, religious affiliations, and so forth—determined the production, circulation, and reception of different genres of works, which were viewed as reflections or expressions of those social divisions. Chartier criticizes this assumption, arguing that "works and objects produce their own social area of reception much more than they are produced by crystallized and previously existent divisions" (1994:14). Chartier argues that an understanding of the book must reverse the previous perspective by beginning with objects rather than social groups and designating the "social areas in which each corpus of texts and each genre of printed matter circulates" (7). A new public was created in France when existing texts were published and circulated in the format of thin blue chapbooks (the Bibliotèque bleue). Similarly, Michael Warner conceives of a "kind of public that comes into being only in relation to texts and their circulation," a "space of discourse organized by nothing other than discourse itself" (2002:50). As an ideal-typical sociocultural form that is organized by discourse and no other "external framework" such as a state or kinship, a public is a form of sociality that is especially dependent on the circulation of the artifacts of discourse (52).[25]

These insights on publics and circulation can be extended to other graphic artifacts and broadened from forms of socialty to associations. The public is merely a theoretically specified limiting case where discourse mediated by graphic artifacts is postulated to be the *only* determinant of social form. But all forms of writing contribute to their own unique forms of association, though not with the same liberty from other social processes as Warner's theoretical public. Even in bureaucracies, which have organizational determinants that compete with those of written discourse (hierarchies, divisions of labor), a similar though less influential function of written materials can be seen. As I discuss in chapter 2, a visiting card with a note from a patron knits together a network of affect and influence. Thus, even "face-to-face" relationships, conventionally conceptualized as the most unmediated form of social relationship, are the product of associations mediated by visiting cards and chits. Likewise, a file draws particular bureaucrats into a matter or excludes them as the file moves across their desk or is routed around them (chapter 3). A list of names entitled to compensation for expropriated land engenders an alliance (in legal terms, a "conspiracy") between senior bureaucrats and villagers, crossing the antagonisms between the state and the village (chapter 4). Unlike a public, these associations are not easy to identify and generalize about, partly because, being irregular and often relatively short-lived, they are rarely culturally typified like more common or stable forms of sociality that have labels such as "directorate," "family," or "*biradari*" (kinfolk or community). They are often much more transient and always more particular, irreducibly dependent on the peculiar characteristics of the graphic artifacts around which they form and the milieu in which they are taken up. The significance *and* function of bureaucratic inscriptions are heterogeneous. A property document and a government file may inhabit the same world of bureaucratic inscription, but they circulate differently and gather around themselves different people and things.

In scholarship on bureaucracy, *writing* has remained the very image of a formal organizational practice, the central semiotic technology for the coordination and control of organizations. This portrayal follows the instrumental orientation of practitioners of bureaucracy themselves. Weber, for example, was well schooled in the administrative sciences (*Polizeywissenschaften*) that developed in early-nineteenth-century German universities to train government functionaries. The organization and circulation of written materials is conceptualized as isomorphic with formally structured social organization and interaction. Cases in which this condition is not found are seen as dysfunctional and therefore not properly bureaucratic.[26]

Although forms of sociality that are gathered around artifacts in the Islamabad bureaucratic arena are shaped in part by institutional structures, kin, friendship, and financial relationships, they are not merely materializations, projections, or realizations of these relationships constituted by other means. In other words, graphic artifacts are not simply the instruments of already existing social organizations. Instead, their specific discourses and material forms precipitate the formation of shifting networks and groups of official and nonofficial people and things. A methodological focus on associations formed around and through documents (rather than socially defined organizations) helps us address a classic problem raised by scholarship on the state: the difficulty of defining a state in organizational or institutional terms presents challenges to ethnographic study.[27] Rather than trying to define an institution and a terrain of operations, I describe the heterogeneous relations that come into being through the use and circulation of the artifacts that mediate almost all bureaucratic activities. As Veena Das and Deborah Poole have observed, documents "bear the double sign of the state's distance and its penetration into the life of the everyday" (2004:15). As we've seen, even the most modest documents of the South Asian bureaucratic traditions similarly aimed to create a boundary between the corporation and its servants, the government and its subjects, the public and the private. In practice, such documents often become mediators that incorporate aspects of the people, things, and processes they were designed to control from a distance.

Attention to the associations emerging through the production and circulation of documents can help us understand the relations between activities inside the offices and those outside. The concept of association and a methodological focus on graphic artifacts are thus complementary. Tracing associations allows us to capture the social range of graphic artifacts, which don't confine themselves to offices. And tracing the careers (Harper 1998) of graphic artifacts is a way of getting a handle on the boundaries of this bureaucratic association, since almost all bureaucratic activities are mediated at some point by graphic artifacts. One might say that if you want to understand bureaucratic activities, follow the paper, things like Ahmed's possession certificate and house plan. Although we should not lose sight of the ideological distinction between the state and the society it governs, the concept of the association can help gather people, things, and processes that come together across a fuzzy border between the state apparatus and its social surround and that indeed help to define that border. Ahmed's possession certificate joins him and his house to bureaucrats and offices even as it defines the boundary between them by excluding him from its authorized production.

This approach also helps us to address what is something of a paradox when viewed from the standpoint that bureaucratic writing is mainly about fixing the relation between words and things: In Islamabad, even though documents are known to be easily and frequently manipulated, they nevertheless remain an essential basis for action. How can this be? As I demonstrate, these documents often function less as instruments of documentation than as tools for building coalitions or oppositions among government functionaries, property owners, businessmen, and builders (see also Tarlo 2001). Artifacts precipitate and graphically represent (partially) the formation of shifting networks and groups of functionaries and clients. When these social organizations compete with rather than converge with formal bureaucratic divisions, such artifacts (rather than the formal organizational entities) are the effective agents of bureaucratic actions shaping the built environment. Every kind of graphic artifact has its own politics (Winner 1980). These may be large in scale, as when the maps and reports of the Master Plan of Islamabad help to constitute alliances and antagonisms among the army, bureaucracy, politicians, and business groups or Bengalis, Muhajirs, and Punjabis. Or they may be small in scale, as when Ahmed and the inspector came to terms over the issuance of an inspection certificate for his newly built house. Graphic artifacts themselves help constitute the scales at which they operate.

In addition to mediating semiosis, graphic artifacts as things are involved in nonsemiotic events and happenings. The study of writing must attend not only to communicative practices but to the social life of things (Appadurai 1986). The two are closely intertwined, but they are never identical. As I'll argue for files (chapter 3), lists (chapter 4), and maps (chapter 5), it is often precisely the disjuncture between communicative processes and the life of the artifact supporting them that shapes the significance and consequences of the graphic artifact for its producers and audience. At different points in its social career, a graphic artifact may be duplicated, bound to other artifacts, supplemented, abridged through the removal of parts, displayed, transported, locked up, defaced, destroyed, stored, misplaced, lost, forgotten, stolen, and bought. Some of these actions, such as the circulation of files within an office, may be steps of relatively regimented practices. Others, such as the theft or "mislaying" of a file on a controversial matter, may be occasional events. Through such events, artifacts move through different sociocultural categories, becoming simultaneously or successively, for example, information bearers, ritual objects, commodities, and fuel.

Actions upon artifacts may be the direct result of the discourses mediated by an artifact, such as the order to transport a file written on the file itself. Actors' projections of the discourses an artifact might mediate can also shape the career of the artifact, as in the destruction of incriminating documents in the face of imminent investigations. In other cases, such as the loss of components of a file due to poor binding, the cause of artifactual events might have virtually nothing to do with the semiotic processes they mediate, though these events too shape discursive possibilities. The material and discursive aspects of bureaucratic representations provide different handles for connections with other people and things. The agents and tactics that engage with bureaucratic discourses (such as narratives, laws, and classification schemes) can be very different from those engaged with the artifactual vehicles of those discourses. Officers of the East India Company did not challenge Mughal tax policy; rather, they undermined the policy by producing and distributing duty-free passes. Similarly, the owners of expropriated land, as I show in chapter 4, failed to reshape expropriation laws and policies, but they virtually took control of the expropriation process by intervening in the production of required documents and determining matters of fact for courts to consider.

Attention to how artifacts perdure, circulate, change, and cease to exist takes us beyond notions of information "storage" to an understanding of how material artifacts shape the discourses they mediate. Practices of consulting records, for example, are often far more important to their function than the fact that they have been generated and maintained. The quiet return of a case file to the (perhaps temporary) oblivion of the record room can settle an issue as much as the signature on a decision. We have to understand processes of recontextualization, which are at once material and semiotic. In recent years, linguistic anthropologists have emphasized the way the significance of texts is shaped by their relation to a theoretically unspecifiable variety of contextual factors. Since the significance of texts depends on contextualization, through recontexualization they are open to semiotic transformation in a number of dimensions. For orally mediated texts, Charles Briggs and Richard Bauman identify various dimensions of semiotic transformation: framing, form (from grammar to genre), function, indexical grounding, and translation (1990:75–6). All these dimensions of transformation are important for artifactually mediated discourse as well. But to this we can add that these transformations may be driven by nonsemiotic events involving the artifact itself. In this respect, the producer of graphic artifacts may have much less control over his or her text than a speaker. Accounts of writing often emphasize the greater fixity of meaning of artifactually mediated texts in relation to orally mediated ones because of the perduring character of graphic forms. Perdurance is an abstraction covering the widely varying durability of different graphic media. But more important, it is precisely this perdurance that affords more radical recontextualizations and allows them, in Latour's terms, to translate a wider array of interests than that allowed by speech.

The efficacy of graphic artifacts comes as much from how they circulate as from what they say. In a lively passage concerning writing in nineteenth-century West Africa, Jack Goody describes how peoples without writing tended to consider the written treaty "subject to exchange or capture like other material objects" (1986:100–1). When the Asante conquered a neighboring power, they took over its "books" (treaties). Such captures voided treaties for the British. By contrast, the Asante tried to assume the place of the conquered signatories to the treaty and expected the British to adhere to the original terms. Goody characterizes this as a misunderstanding of writing stemming from the equation of "the paper with its contents, the medium with the message" (1986:101). The Asante may have misunderstood the graphic genre of the treaty (or, more neutrally, may have simply been insisting on a different interpretation). But the example shows how radically circulation can recontextualize a document.

Many of the features of bureaucratic writing that have led to its characterization as decontextualized (impersonal voicing, minimal use of expressions referring to the writing context) come about precisely because the producers imagine that their writings might be radically recontextualized or drawn into a new association. As Briggs and

Bauman observe, "the decontexualization and recontextualization of texts . . . [are] two aspects of the same process" (1990:75). An artifact is decontextualized, disconnected from some of the elements it was associated with, only by being recontextualized, that is, brought into association with other elements. The perdurance of the artifact, as Silverstein and Greg Urban (1996) note, belies the transformation effected through recontextualization, so that transformations are frequently taken as the original.

Let me now turn to the second way that documents build associations, that is, through involvement in the enactment of the objects they talk about, such as authorized mosques, expropriable plots, compensatable houses, and so forth. Weber observed, "Bureaucratic administration means fundamentally domination through knowledge. This is the feature of it which makes it specifically rational" (1978:225). According to him, this knowledge takes two forms: technical knowledge and "knowledge of facts" (225). Writing here is seen as a means of materializing reference and predication to establish and communicate a stable relation between discourse and individuals, actions, objects, and environments. Writing establishes the stable relation between words and things necessary for bureaucracies to effectively implement regimes of control. In both the self-understanding of bureaucrats and classic accounts of bureaucracy, documents represent or engage with autonomous entities, realities "in the world" independent from the processes through which they are produced. Suzanne Briet, a pioneering theorist of documents, in answer to the question "What is documentation?" argued that a document must have been "preserved or recorded toward the ends of representing, of reconstituting, or of proving a physical or intellectual phenomenon" (2006:10). And yet social scientists have grown increasingly skeptical where questions of evidence are concerned, highlighting the mediations that saturate the production of facts. Recent scholarship has shown how bureaucratic documents are produced, used, and experienced through procedures, techniques, aesthetics, ideologies, cooperation, negotiation, and contestation. To what extent and in what way is the efficacy of bureaucratic texts due to their capacity to represent, to stand for something else, to be, as Brian Cantwell Smith puts it, "*about* or *oriented toward* some other entity, structure, or patch of the world" (1996:13)?

Until revived in science and technology studies, the study of how words refer to and describe the world (denotation) had fallen on hard times within the social sciences. Much of linguistic anthropology has been devoted to criticizing the folk wisdom of European language communities that see "reference or propositionality" as the "essence of language" (Woolard 1998:13). Cultural anthropologists have similarly emphasized how denotation is "overdetermined" by the sorts of "social" processes I have been describing, leaving the objects little role in their discursive definition. Anthropologists have observed that documents, like other forms of material culture, such as uniforms, cars, and official buildings, are central to the everyday representation and, thereby, the reproduction of states (Das 2004; Hansen and Stepputat 2001; Messick 1993; Poole 2004; Sharma and Gupta 2006). Aradhana Sharma and Akhil Gupta, for example, argue that "proceduralism"— routine, repetitive practices of rule following—and its violation are central to "how the state comes to be imagined, encountered, and reimagined by the population" (2006:12). Many other recent treatments of documents invoke a form-content distinction in emphasizing the greater social salience of form. Annelise Riles, for example, argues that aesthetics—"properly patterned language" (1998:387)—rather than the "meaning" of the document guided the process of negotiating an NGO document sponsored by the United Nations.

This emphasis on the aesthetics and broad significance of documents is a welcome corrective to an exclusive focus on the knowledge function of records. Using this perspective, I will show in chapter 3 that the powers of graphic artifacts depend on their place within a regime of authority and authentication. However, the focus on the normative commitment to following rules or on the aesthetics of form can lead to the view that the specificities of individual documents are secondary, even unimportant, beside their formulaic and pro forma aspects. What this emphasis obscures is the problematics of enacting objects at the center of bureaucratic practices. For Sharma and Gupta (2006:12), the importance of "observing the correct bureaucratic rule" is evidenced by the divergence of documentation from the reality it purports to represent, as in their example of a supervisor accusing a subordinate of cheating because the subordinate irregularly documented a meeting the supervisor must have known the subordinate actually attended. But, in accounting for the efficacy of documents, one does not have to choose between proceduralism and reference. Procedurally correct documents compel compliance not because the documents they generate supersede the realities they purport to represent, but because, much like scientific protocols, bureaucratic procedures normatively embed documents in those realities (Latour 1999:24–79). Particular utterances and referential processes, even when they are compromised, account for much of the efficacy of individual documents. Discursive logics, concepts, norms, and social relationships can often account for classification schemes, such as the criteria for a house to be eligible for expropriation compensation or the distinction between authorized and unauthorized mosques. Such accounts, however, break down in explaining how *this* came to be a compensatable house (chapter 4) or *this* an unauthorized mosque (chapter 5). To understand these latter processes, we need to account for how documents engage (or do not engage) with people, places, and things to make bureaucratic objects, for how bureaucratic objects are enacted in practice.

Graphic artifacts are a kind of semiotic technology. Semiotic technologies are material means for producing, interpreting, and regulating significance for particular ends. They include rituals, clay tablets, the telegraph, PowerPoint, cryptography, and email, to name just a few. The study of semiotic technologies has much to offer our broader understanding of artifacts and materiality. Semiotic technologies present us with an immediate challenge to come to terms with both their meaning and their material efficacy. Although both anthropology and science and technology studies are concerned with representation and materiality, they have had different emphases. Anthropology has tended to highlight how the material qualities of things shape what they mean to their users. In contrast, science and technology studies has stressed how the material qualities of artifacts shape what they do and what humans can do with them. This study of graphic artifacts encourages a comprehensive social theory of material artifacts by synthesizing these insights.

BACKGROUND OF THE STUDY

Like the government activities this book is about, my own ethnographic research was mediated to a great extent by paper. My visiting cards, bearing an unauthorized reproduction of my university's seal (which, the department administrator had told me with a wink, graduate students aren't allowed to use), were always an element of my initial meetings with government officials. One official preferred that I put my inquiries in written form, and in response to my signed list of numbered questions I received a detailed account of the workings of the office that handles mosque issues, generously prepared by a junior officer.

I had begun my research at the National Archives of Pakistan. I thought there would be a wealth of well-kept records on such a celebrated national urban planning project, only to find that the few records there that pertained to the early planning of Islamabad were still under seal. Not long after, I met a CDA officer with an interest in the history of the city who remembered hearing about some old records stored somewhere. He enthusiastically led me on a two-sector scavenger hunt, but we abandoned the search after hopefully opening several storage rooms filled with broken-down furniture. Later, one day while drinking tea with assistants in the record room of the Urban Planning Directorate, I looked up and spotted stacks of files snowed with years of brown dust on a high shelf set into the wall. None of the clerks knew what they were or how or when they got there. After climbing a ladder and browning myself in their retrieval (under the amused gaze of the clerks), I was elated to discover they included many files from the early 1960s for which I had been searching.[28]

As it turned out, it was much easier for me to read what are called "current files," that is, not archives, but active files and other documents that were currently in use within the two main governing bodies of Islamabad, the Capital Development Authority and the Islamabad Capital Territory Administration.[29] As in other South Asian states, these records are normally not open to researchers, the public, or individuals, which is why Ahmed couldn't see the official file on his house.[30] Active records were first made available to me by a planner whom I'd been talking with for a few weeks. One day, as his account of the development of a sector in western Islamabad grew more elaborate, he saw the confusion growing on my face. He broke off his explanation and told me I just really needed to read the files to understand what he was saying. I thought this meant the end of our discussion, but he got up and led me into the record room of his directorate and, to my surprise, asked one of the assistants to give me the files covering the matter. Before long, he invited me to look at any files that interested me. After seeing the richness of these materials, I started to pursue them in other offices.

On my first attempt to get access to other records, as I describe in chapter 2, I tried my own hand at submitting a written request for documents, which circulated through the bureaucratic hierarchy in an informal simulation of how regular petitions are handled. The mixed success of this petition led me to adopt a more informal method, trying to recreate the sort of relationship with other officers that had prompted the officer to grant me access in the first case. My efforts to get access to documents had another unexpected benefit: it gave me a clear reason to talk with busy officers who expect those who meet them to have a matter to be dealt with, something more definite than talking with them about their work. In pursuing documents, albeit not my own, I was like most of those who meet with government officials, whose business is defined in the end by the acquisition of particular documents.

Initially, like many of those who engage the bureaucracy, I was frustrated by how slowly my efforts bore fruit. I managed to see the files of the ICTA (Islamabad Capital Territory Administration) regarding mosques only after nearly eight months of almost daily hours-long visits with the officer in charge of this division. However, I soon realized that these protracted efforts allowed me to witness office doings firsthand. The way that officers often see a number of people at once, which I discuss in chapter 2, was a great boon to my research, since I was usually welcome to sit (with varying degrees of obtrusiveness) among the other visitors as they discussed their business with officers.

In many offices, I was kindly given work space and delegated the authority to request files from the record rooms, much like a junior officer, or even to fetch them myself from their cabinets, like an assistant. While reviewing files and other documents, I had the opportunity to ask the officers and staff who had produced them about their contents as well as how they shaped bureaucratic processes and outcomes. Officers and staff within both the ICTA and the CDA were usually eager to discuss their work, including the records whose production and circulation consumes so much of their time. Over the course of my research, I was given broad access to files covering a wide range of matters from the early 1960s to 2007, including public relations, private houses, government housing, mosques, slum redevelopment, land expropriation, land revenue, mosques, urban planning, and new private housing societies.

Through my many visits to a printing firm to have my wedding invitations made (I returned to the United States briefly to get married in December 1996), I developed a strong friendship with the owner's son and soon found his office to be a congenial site to drop in for tea and talk with a wide variety of clients, including government officers, journalists, lawyers, calligraphers, and businessmen of all kinds. Through conversations with him and his staff and looking over the materials the firm printed (business cards, government reports, real estate brochures, and of course wedding invitations), I learned an immense amount about the production and aesthetics of printed materials. Here, I even got involved in the work when some developers learned of my interest in their promotional brochures and recruited me to rewrite the materials I had been analyzing.

In the Islamabad bureaucratic arena, I was much more observer than participant, but my troubles with car papers gave me a firsthand, if short-lived, experience of the absurdity and power of documents that Pakistanis commonly expressed to me. I had bought a Daihatsu Charade whose original engine had been replaced by a more economical diesel engine. The mechanical work was competent, though after a few months a mechanic told me the weight of the heavier diesel engine was causing the CV joints to break down. There were problems with the car's documentation too. When I tried to sell it, a buyer more careful than I scrutinized the car's "book," as the small bound packet of registration documents is known, and discovered that the engine number and chassis number had been reversed. The buyer immediately lost interest. My friends laughed but insisted with a graveness I did not yet understand that no one would buy it at any price until the error had been corrected.

Initially, I thought it would be no problem. It was an obvious clerical error—I would simply show the registration authorities that the two numbers actually matched the ones engraved on the two different parts of the car and have a new book made. Unfortunately, it was not that simple. After repeated visits to the office that handles car registration in Rawalpindi, where I was living at the time, I finally spoke with the director. The officer was very sympathetic but stated bluntly that the paper documents took precedence over the metal engravings and, while this was obviously a matter of transposition, from a legal standpoint the book might just as well have been the documentation of another car altogether. It didn't help that the car had been registered in Dera Ismael Khan, a town in the Kyber-Pakhtunkhwa Province (formerly the Northwest Frontier Province) that was known for the rehabilitation of the appearance and documentation of stolen vehicles. He told me that the problem could only be fixed by taking the car for a physical inspection by officials there. Friends I consulted were skeptical that even officials in Dera Ismael Khan would make the change. With a substantial portion of my research grant sunk in this car, what had seemed like a joke became very alarming. In the end, I paid someone who worked for a friend of a friend to go to Dera Ismael Khan and have the numbers put in their correct location. The man didn't want to say how he'd done it.

Ironically, the kind of document that conventionally plays a central role in ethnographic research, field notes (think of the pictures of Malinowski sitting among the Trobrianders, notebook on his lap), remained in the background of most of my interactions within offices.

Ethnographic note taking is always subject to local ways of viewing writing. Matthew Engelke writes about the challenges of ethnography among African Christians who reject the Bible as a worldly material obstacle to "live and direct faith" (2007:35). They would have seen his attempts to take notes in religious meetings in the same light, as an impediment to direct experience of the divine. As I show in the pages that follow, writing in the bureaucracy is a serious and fraught business. My own note taking during the early period of my research clearly made some bureaucrats uneasy. For this reason, with the exception of formal interviews, I rarely took notes during my conversations within offices but would hastily scribble my recollections at my first opportunity and flesh them out later.

Many of the government employees I met in the office became friends and welcomed me into their homes to meet their families over tea and meals. Beyond the office, I also talked with a broad range of Islamabad residents, including house owners, residents of informal settlements, imams, bankers, politicians, shopkeepers, architects, and real estate dealers. In a large number of cases, I managed to discuss a pending matter with both the residents and the "concerned" bureaucrats and to read the documents produced and maintained by participants inside and outside the bureaucracy, as in the vignette that opens this introduction.

To become familiar with different parts of the Islamabad, I lived for several months each in three neighborhoods of the city: in the oldest sector, G-6, dominated by government housing of low and middling rank; the elite area of E-7, with its wealthy population of generals, diplomats, and businessmen; and F-10, a newer neighborhood containing a variety of well-to-do business families, from chicken farmers to oil distributors. Watchmen (*chowkidars*) who guard the gates of many houses in these sectors were a source of immense insight into neighborhood goings-on, and we would occasionally crowd into a little guardhouse for tea made over an electric heater in humble replication of domestic hospitality. To understand the specificity of Islamabad within the Pakistani urban context, I lived in a neighborhood of small lanes in northern Rawalpindi for the year of my research.

Many readers will note the contrast between the great detail of my descriptions of documents and my indistinct portrayal of most people I discuss. With the exception of public figures, the names I use for all individuals are pseudonyms and most individuals in this work are described only by their rank and directorate, by their position within social settings outside the bureaucracy such as villages, neighborhoods, and slums, or by their business. This is only partly an effect of the focus of the book on graphic artifacts. Beyond the usual concerns for the anonymity of informants, there are others particular to the Pakistani bureaucratic arena. This book will also be situated within the writing practices I describe, and so I must keep in mind the possibility that my writing will produce unforeseen results. Although most quotations are uncontroversial opinions or open secrets, such statements might expose the speaker when they take written form. The importance of maintaining such discretion was made clear to me in various ways. One condition of my access to active files in the Auqaf Directorate, which oversees mosques and shrines, was that I allow my notebook to be copied for review by the assistant director. While no pages were ever removed during this procedure, one of the office assistants meticulously whited out his own name, which I, forgetting to use a pseudonym, had scrawled above a note about some casual remarks he made concerning the administration of mosques. It is my intention to avoid reinscribing his or others' names here.

Similar concerns shape my identification of files. As I have noted, files are normatively confidential and inaccessible to anyone not part of a "concerned" division of the bureaucracy. However, I fit into the very networks of prohibited file circulation that I was studying. Like many things done by officials, passing files to me was not an official action. Additionally, the files I examined were overwhelmingly active files, written on by current officers and staff members. Identifying files too precisely would also identify both the officers who wrote on them and those who kindly gave me access to them, exposing them to potential charges of wrongdoing as their actions or writings are recontextualized in a public forum. While the lack of identification of these sources may lessen the scholarly authority of my account, such identification would in any case not serve the usual function of providing others with the possibility of evaluating my work in light of the actual sources. The active files I examined are never likely to find their way to "the archive," and many of the inactive files were, unfortunately, destroyed after I read them. The larger point, however, is that this book is less about documents as traces of what happened and more about their active role in the flow of bureaucratic process and the production of the city.

Just as paper artifacts mediated the government activities I observed and my own ethnographic research, they also organize this book. Each chapter is focused on the discussion of a particular graphic artifact or set of graphic artifacts. The book can be roughly divided into two parts. Throughout this work, I emphasize the relations among place, people, and paper, but the first three chapters thematize each of these in turn. Chapter 1 charts the role of the Master Plan in formatting the space of Islamabad according to political and bureaucratic order, and the more routine documents that address its contradictions. Chapter 2 shows how visiting cards and *parchi*s (chits) on the one hand and petitions on the other differently shape the ways people engage the bureaucracy and enact different political subjects. Chapter 3 gives an overview of paperwork through an account of how files individualize and collectivize agency and facilitate the pursuit of private projects through the mechanisms of government. These three chapters contribute to an overall picture of how sociospatial organization, relations between citizens and bureaucrats, and paperwork constitute government in Islamabad.

The second part of the book traces the relations among place, people, and paper in the government of specific projects. Chapter 4 shows how lists of villagers to be compensated for expropriated land and other documents of the expropriation process have figured in a conflict that has brought the planned westward expansion of the city to a virtual halt. Chapter 5 describes the role of maps in the failing efforts of the government to control the unauthorized construction of mosques in the context of sectarian contestation of sites and officially sanctioned Islamic opinions on how land may be appropriated for prayer.

The conclusion traces the broad story of postcolonial paper in Islamabad and suggests ways that paperwork in Pakistan can illuminate the politics of documents more generally, including newer electronic forms.

CHAPTER 1

The Master Plan
and Other Documents

Islamabad is linked to Rawalpindi, a city in the Potohar region of Pakistan in Punjab province, by several miles of the Islamabad Highway, a divided four-lane road from which autorickshaws, ubiquitous in Rawalpindi, are banned. The car-driving classes frequently quip, "Islamabad is five minutes from Pakistan," with Rawalpindi standing in for Pakistan. Poorer residents, often relegated to slower modes of intercity transport such as buses and minivans, more commonly joke, "Islamabad is ten minutes from Pakistan." The joke is a comic recognition of one of the original goals of the Master Plan: to distance the government from the society it was to govern. In its initial conception, Islamabad can be seen as giant anticorruption machine, an effort to use spatial isolation to engineer a social isolation of government servants from the wider populace. Unlike most modernist projects that aimed to make aspects of a wider society legible to the government (Scott 1998), Islamabad was designed to make the government legible to itself, partly through isolation from the wider society and partly through its own internal order.

Timothy Mitchell argues that the distinction between state and society "is a defining characteristic of the modern political order" (1999:184), even though "the edges of the state are uncertain; societal elements seem to penetrate it on all sides, and the resulting boundary between state and society is difficult to determine" (88). He argues that an "apparent boundary" (176) between state and society is produced by Foucauldian "disciplines," practices of "spatial organization, temporal arrangement, functional specification, supervision and surveillance, and representation" (185). As an effect of such practices, the line between state and society is not the perimeter of a separate entity, but "a line drawn *internally*, within the network of institutional mechanisms through which a certain social and political order is maintained" (175, emphasis added). Seen in this light, the spatial organization of Islamabad was not the project of an autonomous state actor, but an attempt to create such an actor by cutting the entanglements of the state bureaucracy with Pakistani society. It was an effort to make officials of a modern state who are, in James Scott's words, "at least one step—and often several steps removed from the society they are charged with governing" (1998:76). The city thus takes its place in the traditions of South Asian dual cities and *cordons sanitaire*.

Islamabad also drew on much older practices of separation: those effected by documents. Scholarship on colonial India has emphasized the objectifying knowledge practices of documentation: surveys and ethnography, mapping, and enumeration. However, the most fundamental function of documentation, evident in the earliest practices of the English East India Company as in all bureaucratic organizations, is to constitute the organization by distinguishing actions done for the organization from all others. In contrast to the gross social sorting of physical planning, documents differentiate among the actions of individuals, distinguishing official from unofficial, or public from private, actions. This problematic of separation was especially acute in the early Company because of its corporate character and the organization of its trade.

Although the Letters Patent (charter) specified who would be a member in the early East India Company, the Company needed to determine when its members were acting on their own and when on behalf of the Company. It was the documentary practices of accountability more than the Letters Patent that constituted the Company as an *organization* rather than simply a society of individuals with trading privileges. Company documentary practices exploded with the consolidation of trade in joint stock, constituting the "jointness" of joint stock trading by defining when a purchase, payment, or shipment was a Company action. Important in London, such documentation was even more central in India, where the so-called private trade, that is, the trading of Company servants on their own accounts, constantly threatened the integrity of the organization. These concerns about differentiating the private actions of Company servants from their Company actions were later expanded and racialized in the mature colonial state as a problem of native corruption. I'll argue that this problematic partly accounts for the pervasiveness of writing within the Company, within the British colonial governments, and within contemporary Pakistani governance.

As Akhil Gupta observes, discourses about bureaucratic corruption in India portray the actions of low-level officials as "thoroughly blurring the boundaries between 'state' and 'civil society'" (1995:384). But rather than focusing on the blurring of a boundary between two independently constituted domains, it is more productive to follow the practices that make, remake, and undermine the difference between the actions of government and all others. As we would expect, the Master Plan has been only partially successful in establishing a sociospatial order liberated from spatial practices prevailing throughout urban Pakistan. Islamabad may be five minutes from Pakistan, but banned horse carts (*tongas*) still ply the shoulder of the Islamabad highway. Neighborhood and kinship relations pulse within the bureaucratic procedures designed to ensure the correspondence of residential and bureaucratic hierarchies. "Private" work is still done through government offices. Documents, the very mechanisms for protecting the integrity of government, are often the means through which it is undermined.

SPLENDID ISOLATION

The establishment of a capital city for the new state of Pakistan was part of the turbulent politics of the state's first decade. The issues that came to the fore in the debates about a new capital were those that dominated national politics more generally, especially the fundamental question of the relation of the government to the populace. The halting failure of electoral politics in the 1950s, undermined by the maneuvering of an alliance of the civil bureaucracy and the military, eventually brought a martial-law government to power in 1958. As Ayesha Jalal argues, the new civil and military officials embraced "a policy aimed at depoliticizing Pakistani society before it slipped into the era of mass mobilization" (1995:55; see also Alavi 1983; Burki 1986; Sayeed 1980). The establishment of Islamabad was an expression of this program.

The founding of Islamabad followed years of debate on the construction of a new capital area in Karachi. Following Partition in 1947, civil servants of the government of Pakistan were housed in evacuated buildings, tents, and temporary quarters in Karachi. Two alternatives for a permanent government seat in Karachi were considered. The first plan was hastily produced by Lt. Col. G. Swayne Thomas, an Australian who was a town planning consultant to the Government of Sind.[1] The plan advocated a new administrative satellite city of sixty-five thousand inhabitants twenty to thirty miles northeast or east of Karachi. This city would have contained the offices as well as the residential areas of civil servants, creating a postcolonial version of the "civil lines," the orderly civilian settlements of British colonial government servants. Objections to the plan were raised, however, because it isolated the government from the rest of Karachi and, symbolically, the Pakistani people.

A second plan completed in 1952 by the Swedish firm Merz Rendel Vatten responded to this criticism:

> The authors of the Plan have, at an early stage, emphasized the desirability of promoting as close a contact as possible between the state administration and the economic and cultural functions. Specifically this means that the Capital and its administrative buildings should be located near the old town, with its business life and its cultural institutions. . . . The desire to isolate the Capital in a new and separate town, or section of the town, has appeared to the authors to be an echo of ideas from a past era during which the functions of the state were confined merely to the responsibility for a certain degree of order and a certain disposition of justice. In such a community the state system could be segregated and could, in magnificent surroundings, manifest its supremacy in splendid isolation. (Lindstrom and Ostnas [1952] 1967:36)

The new plan placed the federal government enclave in the middle of Karachi, on an extension of the existing central business artery. The report stated, "The new capital and the existing business section should be given the possibility of growing together into one common core, built around one axis only" (Lindstrom and Ostnas [1952] 1967:2). The large avenue, running from the central business district to the capital area, would open up onto a large open space framed by public buildings dominated on one side by the parliament building and on the other by a mosque. This space, a hexagon with sides 1,400 feet in length, would be large enough for a million people to gather for political meetings, public assemblies, and Eid prayers. Housing for government servants was to be distributed throughout the city in new finger-shaped districts extending from existing boundaries of Karachi.

Criticism was leveled at the Merz Rendel Vatten plan for its costly traffic plan and its extravagant central plaza, but this second capital plan was undone not by the expense; rather, it was soon overrun by the tumultuous political events of the 1950s.[2] In 1951, before the report had even been published, Liaquat Ali Khan, the prime minister who had initiated the project, was assassinated. He had succeeded Mohammad Ali Jinnah as head of the Muslim League, the party that had lead the movement for the creation of Pakistan. The Muslim League was the only national party at the time, but its support came mainly from Urdu-speaking immigrants from north India (so-called Muhajirs). Ironically, the Muslim League had never enjoyed strong support in the areas that came to make up Pakistan. Liaquat Ali Khan's death severely weakened the party and initiated an "institutional shift from elected to non-elected institutions" (Jalal 1995:55).

Years of deeply contentious politics followed, in which various prominent political leaders from Karachi attempted to govern at the center through opportunistic and quickly shifting alliances with political leaders from East Pakistan and the West Pakistan regions of Punjab, Northwest Frontier Province (NWFP), Sind, and Baluchistan (see map 1). A more stable alliance between the civil bureaucracy and the military shaped the political intrigues in an effort to consolidate state power itself. Simultaneously, the prominence of Muhajirs within the upper echelons of these two institutions was gradually replaced by that of ethnic Punjabis. In 1956, the Constituent Assembly ratified a constitution, but the document generated strong opposition from provincial leaders outraged by its centralizing provisions and from religious leaders decrying its tepid Islam. Infighting among National Assembly members, challenges from the provinces, monstrous inflation, and wheat shortages combined to generate massive street protests by public and private labor unions, opposition parties, Karachi businessmen, and students. The army presented itself as the only guarantor of stability and openly confirmed its dominance over elective politics. In October 1958, Field Marshal Mohammad Ayub Khan, soon after becoming chief martial law administrator, deposed President Iskander Mirza and installed himself as president as well.

Shortly after assuming office, Ayub Khan formed the Special Commission for the Location of the Federal Capital to reexamine the establishment of the capital in Karachi and, if necessary, recommend another location. While most of the commission members were technical professionals, it was headed by Major General Yahya Khan, a close associate of the new president. The Final Report of the Special Commission has never been made public and, as Frank Spaulding (2003:369–70) observes, while Ayub Khan later claimed that the commission recommended the Rawalpindi region for the new capital, there are sugges-

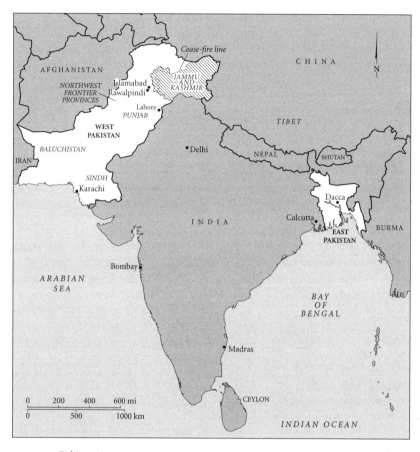

MAP I.I. Pakistan in 1959.

tions the commission called for further study. At the time, with the Final Report remaining secret, officials spoke for it through the press. Newspapers reported that the Special Commission report found Karachi unsuitable and recommended locating the capital at its present site in northern Punjab, on agricultural land north of Rawalpindi, near Ayub's native village of Haripur. Newspaper accounts, at least one of which claims to quote the report, state that the report of the commission articulated a range of reasons to move the capital to the north. The region's moderate climate and changing seasons would prevent boredom and lassitude and promote health and administrative efficiency. Lying on the Grand Trunk road, the site offered advantages as a center for the region's economic development. The availability of cheap rural land would decrease development costs. The geography of the region and the military base in nearby Rawalpindi gave the site greater strategic security than the seaside Karachi. Planning from scratch would allow greater order and beauty; the Commission reportedly observed that "although Karachi is a relatively modern city, its development has been unplanned and grotesque. It cannot be converted into a city of aesthetic beauty—an essential requirement of a capital."[3] In addition to these advantages of the northern location, Constantinos Doxiadis, the Greek planner appointed to design the new city, would soon praise the "typical, characteristic architecture of the [Rawalpindi] area, growing out of the land, the people and the climate," while finding "that of Karachi area . . . strongly influenced by Hindu principles" (Doxiadis Associates 1960b:68).

However, although most of the commission's purported justifications for shifting the capital were technical or aesthetic, the strongest reason was openly political. The commission reportedly argued that Karachi was unacceptable because commercial development rendered it "unwholesome from the point of view of administrative integrity."[4] Having just moved against the commercial groups in Karachi with the support of the military and civil bureaucracy, General Ayub was anxious to protect government servants from what he considered the corrupting influence of Karachi businessmen, most of whom were Muhajirs (Ayub Khan 1967; Jalal 1990; Sayeed 1980). A newspaper quoted the commission report declaring that:

> Close contact between the business community and personnel of the Administration at Karachi has not done any good to either. Too much of social contact between those who want things to be done to suit them and the officials cannot lead to healthy results. It is desirable both for the business community and the administration that the capital should be away from the commercial center of the country.[5]

The commission was quoted arguing that not only the location of the capital but also its layout "should be designed to restrict contact between Government servants and business circles."[6] While the report emphasized the distance from Karachi, many observers suspected that the proximity to Rawalpindi was equally important to the new bureaucratic military government. From the new site, Ayub Khan could keep a close eye on the army, which was in Rawalpindi, to prevent moves against him. In fact, Rawalpindi was immediately made the interim capital, even though most of the ministries were expected to remain in Karachi until the new capital city had been established.

Fifty years earlier, the British had similarly opted to escape the political agitation in Calcutta and the city's "foreign" associations (stemming from its origin as a British trading settlement) and located the new imperial capital outside Delhi. Following a major uprising throughout north India in 1857, the British had established a major military center southwest of Delhi and developed the city as a transportation center. Delhi had been the seat of the last major indigenous political power, the Mughals, and the British attempted to portray themselves as the successors of the Mughals in the subcontinent's grand history of imperial rule (Cohn 1987; Metcalf 1989). The British imperial capital been completed only three decades before Partition and had been home to many of the officials who left to form the new government of Pakistan. The Merz Rendel Vatten plan made indirect reference to Delhi in its criticism of the proposal for an isolated administrative satellite city. The significance of Ayub Khan's decision, therefore, was obvious. This was a move from a city founded by English traders, still strongly identified with British colonialism and dominated by in-migrants from north India, to a city in the Punjab near Taxila, seat of the Mauryan Empire, now claimed to be the forerunner of modern Pakistan. The move took the government away from a contentious political environment in a geographically peripheral coastal city and placed it alongside the country's military center in the geographic center of the dominant West Pakistan territory.

Under martial law, public opposition to the move was muted. However, many considered the move disrespectful to Jinnah, head of the Muslim League party, who had selected his new political base in Pakistan, Karachi, as the site of the new capital. Many businesspeople thought it would stunt economic growth. Opinion in East Pakistan was even more sharply opposed, suspecting that the shift would destroy the precarious balance between the two distantly separated and culturally different wings of the new country. East Pakistanis, recognizing the political impossibility of locating the capital in Dacca (now Dhaka), were satisfied with the cosmopolitan Karachi, which was dominated by migrants and accessible by a relatively inexpensive sea route. While Karachi was obviously much harder to reach from East Pakistan, it was at least geographically peripheral to West Pakistan and could therefore represent a meeting of the east and west wings of the country on something approaching equal terms. The move from Karachi to a city in northern Punjab confirmed the suspicions of East Pakistanis that West Pakistan, and in particular Punjabis, intended to dominate East

Pakistan. East Pakistanis were not mollified by the plan for two parliamentary buildings, one in each wing, in which parliament would sit in alternate sessions. However, with the bureaucratic military government dominated by Punjabis in place, opposition to the move was ineffective.

Construction on Islamabad began in short order, but the location of Pakistan's capital was not settled finally until 1970. Following a short and indecisive war with India in 1965, deteriorating economic conditions, labor militancy, student radicalism, and opposition from provincial leaders led by East Pakistan generated demands for a restoration of parliamentary government. By the end of 1968, Ayub was also facing street protests from Islamists and even from usually quiescent groups such as teachers, doctors, and low-ranking government employees. In March 1969, Ayub ceded power to general Yahya Khan. By the end of that year, a wide range of political leaders were calling for the capital to be returned to Karachi. Once again, the main issue was the relation of the government and the "people."

Both the English and Urdu press covered the issue with enthusiasm, giving extensive coverage to arguments by political leaders in East Pakistan and Karachi from the Muslim League, Awami League, and the United Front. "Both provinces have a claim on this city [Karachi]," declared the Karachi United Front president.[7] A veteran Muslim Leaguer from Karachi argued that east-wing political leaders considered it their "second home" and many owned property there; furthermore, they thought that "if Karachi became again the capital of Pakistan Quaid-i-Azam's [the Great Founder Jinnah's] wish would be fulfilled."[8] Newspaper articles argued there were no advantages to shifting government employees from Karachi to Islamabad and confidently discussed the future of Karachi as a capital.[9] Soon east-wing politicians demanded that the capital be moved to Dacca. One leading East Pakistan Muslim League officer declared that a dictator had moved the capital to Islamabad "purely in his own interests" and that the "sufferings of East Pakistanis will not come to an end until the central capital is shifted to this Wing of the country. . . . [I]f the capital is shifted here the integrity, sovereignty, existence, and ideology of Pakistan will be free from challenge."[10] While many in the civil service supported the return to Karachi, the military was set against it. President Yahya Khan, the chief martial-law administrator, argued such a transfer would be too expensive and difficult. Talking with reporters, he quipped, "you don't want us to be a mill ox [*kolhu ka bail*], do you?" likening moving the capital back to Karachi to a mill ox going round and round.

Facing a complete refusal by the central regime to consider moving from Islamabad, east-wing leaders had accepted by the fall of 1970 that the capital would not be shifted but insisted that the "Second Capital at Dacca" would not be allowed to be a "Consolation Capital."[11] The position of Islamabad was confirmed the next year when East Pakistan broke away after a brief war to become the independent state of Bangladesh. The war also brought the populist bureaucrat and landowner Zulfiqar Ali Bhutto into power. Bhutto himself was invested in Islamabad, having been involved in its design and construction as minister of works under Ayub. His populism led him not to return the capital to Karachi, but merely to add to Islamabad a grand prime minister's residence.

THE DYNAPOLIS AND THE COLONIAL CITY

Following the report of the commission, Ayub Khan put the planning of the city in the hands of Constantinos Doxiadis, a Greek modernist architect and planner.[12] Doxiadis had founded one of the largest architectural firms in Europe and was given the title of "chief consultant" on the Islamabad project. He had proved himself to the new regime by quickly completing Korangi, a housing development in Karachi for the resettlement of seventy-five thousand refugees. Even so large a project as a new capital city was hardly a match for Doxiadis's ambitions. His grand vision transcended monumentality, focusing on the universal requirements of a whole society, even a civilization: "I have an obligation to follow only that road ahead of me that is not obstructed and cluttered up with monuments, a road whose largest shadows will be cast by simple plain human buildings" (Doxiadis 1963:195). Following this road required nothing less than the foundation of a new practical science, which he called "ekistics" (from *oikos,* the ancient Greek word for "house" or "household"): the study of human settlements to discover the relations among nature, man, society, "shells" (buildings), and "networks" (communications) (Doxiadis 1968). Such a broad approach demanded an all-encompassing role for the planner: "He must become a scientist, carry out research, create a system of thought, devise a programme of action and carry out proper schemes of organization in government, in industry, in production, in design" (Doxiadis 1963:9).

For Doxiadis, egalitarian concern for the life of the common citizen required a scientific organization of cities as a solution to the contemporary "urban nightmare" of unregulated growth (1963:19). However, the political role entailed by this technical program converged with the authoritarian political program of Ayub Khan's bureaucratic military regime. James Holston has observed that modernist architects maintained affiliations across the political spectrum, aligning themselves with "whichever authority, on the Left or Right, seemed capable of implementing total planning (1989:42). Le Corbusier, the leading figure of modernist architecture, dedicated his major publication, *The Radiant City*, to "AUTHORITY" (Holston 1989:42). Doxiadis too welcomed the establishment of political power strong enough to carry through planning programs of massive scope. In his first major report on the Master Plan for Islamabad, he defined his own political role and that of his successors using the rhetoric of technical necessity: "It is imperative to create the master builders, the people who are going to be in charge of the overall city, from its conception to the implementation of every detail. There is a necessity for a conductor of the whole orchestra which is to create the symphony. He must be a strong conductor, for he will be responsible for everything within Islamabad" (Doxiadis Associates 1960b:435). This conductor was institutionally realized in the Capital Development Authority, established in 1960 and granted comprehensive planning and administrative powers, which I discuss in detail later.

While Ayub Khan saw the isolation of the bureaucracy as a means to control the country, Doxiadis saw it as means to control the city. Doxiadis declared that the city of the future must include "all social, all income groups and all types of functions" (Doxiadis Associates 1960b:108). However, he embraced the views of the Federal Capital Commission:

> The influence of the diverse in origin and cosmopolitan population of Karachi on government administration would be eliminated, if the Capital were to be a capital only without non-official civilian population located in it and pulling it in different directions. . . . The capital should be in a place where the business community does not come into contact with administration on a social level. (Doxiadis Associates 1960b:54)

The unity of the Master Plan itself was an icon of the single-mindedness of a modern administration and its insulation from the social influences of the present as well as the tenacious grip of the traditional past.

Not only the provisions of the Master Plan but also the process of its production and authorization were covered extensively in the English and Urdu press, fed liberally by government press releases. Newspapers carried articles about the preparation of various reports, Doxiadis's comings and goings, and his meetings with senior government officials, including Ayub Khan. The Master Plan itself was the object of well-publicized state rituals in the 1960s and 1970s. Foreign dignitaries received tours of a museum enshrining the plan, materialized through city maps, photos, models of buildings, and charts of statistics. Afterward, such dignitaries were taken to Shakarparian Park, where they would ceremonially plant a tree beside the concrete garden grid plan of the city. Echoing the future-oriented nationalism of the new government, Doxiadis proclaimed that Islamabad was "to be created without any commitments to the past" (1965:6). The development of the metropolitan complex in Islamabad and Rawalpindi, however, lay in the tradition of British colonial city building.[13] The political program of the bureaucratic military government and the spatial organization of the new metropolitan complex parallel the British colonial government's political objectives and the spatial orders through which it attempted to realize them. The division of the metropolitan complex in Rawalpindi and Islamabad into areas for the bureaucracy, military, and "non-official civilian population" was a perfect spatial expression of the new regime's vision of the polity. The absence of a spatialized colonial racial division is certainly significant. However, this tripartite organization can be placed in the context of colonial patterns of bureaucratic and military control and urban configuration, well exemplified by Rawalpindi itself.

Located on the roads linking the Khyber Pass and the Kashmir Valley with the cities of Lahore and Delhi, Rawalpindi was for centuries a minor trading city and district administrative center under the successive regimes of the Mughals, Sikhs, and British. The city was surrounded by hundreds of agricultural villages ranging in size from a few dozen to several thousand inhabitants. Rawalpindi became a major city after 1880 when the British selected the site as a military center for the forces defending the northern "frontier" of the empire. From a population of only 52,000 in 1880, Rawalpindi grew into the largest city of the region after Karachi and Lahore, with a population of 185,000 in 1940 (Specht 1983:37). Since the British recruited their military forces heavily from the Punjab, the ethnic composition of the city remained relatively similar despite the population growth. In the tradition of British colonial city building (King 1976), spacious areas for civilian authorities ("civil lines") and military forces ("cantonment") were added to the densely settled area of the indigenous city. The distinctness of each of these three zones is easily exaggerated, since each of them included human and nonhuman elements of the other two within them (Glover

2008; Hosagrahar 2005). This was even more the case in Rawalpindi, where the areas allocated to the civil lines and cantonment virtually surrounded the indigenous city to the south, east, and west.

The Indian areas of Rawalpindi, east of the Leh *nala* (seasonal river) and north of Murree Road, were structured by *mohalla*s (neighborhoods) generally divided from (and joined with) one another by bazaars along wide transversal roads. Bazaars were not considered part of any individual neighborhood and had only the broadest social affiliation, permitting the passage of any person for any purpose any time. Bazaars thus served as gathering places of socially diverse people for trading and small-scale manufacturing. Mohallas were usually structured by *gali*s (narrow branching lanes) usually stemming from single points of access that terminated in cul-de-sacs. The entrances to mohallas were generally from bazaars and were architecturally marked by wooden doors or gates, or simply by the narrowness of the lane. The branching and sharp turning of lanes limited physical and visual access, providing gradient degrees of seclusion to residents, shielding them from nonresidents and from residents of other parts of the mohalla. Small internal *chowk*s (squares or intersections), usually at junctions of lanes, provided collective space for weddings, holiday celebrations, and political meetings.

In the architecture and use of domestic space, there was a similar progression from common to possessed areas continuous with that of the mohalla as a whole. Most houses were made of brick, stood one or two stories, and had a central courtyard with rooms opening onto it on the first story. In multistory dwellings, upper-story rooms opened onto an internal veranda that overlooked the courtyard. Many of the structures, often grouped around small open spaces, were occupied by several families. Although most of the buildings were occupied by a single household, in many cases a single family would have exclusive use of only one room and a small storage area; all the residents of the dwelling would share the internal veranda, courtyard, roof, and toilets. These shared spaces mediated between the common space of the lane outside the dwelling and the spaces reserved for the exclusive use of the family.[14]

In Rawalpindi as elsewhere, the social and spatial organization of the older urban areas frustrated the attempts of authorities to make them legible and governable. As is often remarked, British colonials found Indian areas of cities to be disorderly and confusing, by nature inaccessible to colonial modes of surveillance and control. The streets weren't numbered and seemed innumerable, in both senses. The definition of the house was complicated by the variance in the number of physical structures and social groups found behind a single door or mohalla gate. The complexity of the ownership of structures in Indian areas made the purchase of land for reconstruction projects costly and complicated. Furthermore, government intrusions in these areas frequently provoked political unrest. For these reasons, the British usually resigned themselves to fragmentary or small-scale interventions, such as regulating building heights and setbacks and widening existing roads. Aside from the major restructurings for strategic reasons following the uprising in northern India in 1857 (Gupta 1981; Oldenburg 1989), the only large-scale government undertakings in Indian areas were utilities infrastructure projects: drainage, water supply, and later electricity (Glover 2008).

The expansion of the British presence in Rawalpindi coincided with the admission of the first generation of Indians into the civil service. In Rawalpindi, many of these civil servants moved into newly developed areas outside both the indigenous city and the developed areas of the civil lines. The settlements of these better-off Indians were often followed by those of low-ranking government employees and household servants, who gardened, cooked, and cleaned for the nearby British residents. Colonial officials sometimes surveyed the land and shaped the overall layouts of these new settlements through the construction of road networks, but often the land was sold on the open market and houses were constructed according to the owner's preference. The result, here as in many north Indian cities, was a new urban form that Mohammad Qadeer has termed the "new indigenous community" (1983:180–84). These indigenous enclaves near and in civil lines, never mastered by the colonial administration, featured many of the elements of the indigenous city.

Covering entire lots, the two- and three-story houses of these neighborhoods created a street facade of continuous high walls broken only by screened windows and balconies. These houses overlooked linear streets usually about twelve to fifteen feet wide, wide enough to permit vehicular traffic, but far narrower than the avenues of civil lines. The interiors of houses were generally built around atriums or enclosed balconies, allowing for sunlight and air circulation, but at the same time structuring the interior spaces to face inward and away from the public spaces of the street. While the blocks and streets were laid out in discernible geometric patterns, rectangular or semicircular, land uses were not segregated by function. Artisan workshops, bakeries, firewood stalls, and warehouses were interspersed with homes, and the continuous buildings accommodated shops at ground level. In new indigenous communities, as in precolonial urban cores, linearity marked market sites. The main thoroughfares of new indigenous communities quickly developed into markets.

In Qadeer's view, this new form of community combined modern conceptions of public health, ease of access, and land subdivision with the more traditional preference for spatial proximity and an interweaving of living areas and commercial sectors. The symbolism of these modern "utilitarian" aspects of the new communities was also important for the new class of educated Indians. In the 1930s, with the growing salience of communal identities, corporate groups began to develop exclusive new indigenous communities for Sikhs, Hindus, Christians, and Muslims. Following Partition in 1947, Rawalpindi grew rapidly as immigrants from eastern Punjab, now under Indian control, settled there, making up 40 percent of the population of 340,000 in 1959 (Ahmed 1960). From 1947 on, the salience of religious identities to the differentiation of neighborhoods was eliminated by the departure of Sikhs and Hindus, and more residences of civil lines itself became available to the now-Pakistani elite as the British exited. The organizational basis of new and existing indigenous communities also shifted at this time. From this period, the construction of new indigenous communities was led by extremely varied types of associations and corporations (sometimes including a range of classes), such as government departments, military divisions, private corporations, and ethnic or regional associations.

Indian enclaves in civil station—never mastered by colonial administration—had many of the elements of the indigenous city itself. These neighborhoods filled in the areas between civil lines and the indigenous city. The civil lines of Rawalpindi, like that of Lahore as described by Glover, "never attained the grid-like, tree-lined, bungalow-dotted clarity" often described for civil lines (1999:100). This blurring of the indigenous city and civil lines was greatly accelerated by the arrival of immigrants following Partition.

It was precisely this gradual intermixing that Doxiadis sought to prevent through his plan for the region. In line with his science of ekistics, Doxiadis, unlike more conventional modernists, insisted that planners needed to understand local conditions to plan effectively. He little comprehended the sociocultural dimensions of urban environments in the region; nevertheless, through careful studies of Rawalpindi and the surrounding rural areas, he came to understand at least the physical structures of dwellings and some of the environmental factors that contributed to them. One senior planner told me that, having conducted systematic studies, Doxiadis was better informed about traditional rural and urban architecture than today's planners. While Doxiadis was fond of the humble adequacy of Punjab rural houses (he did not examine villages as wholes), his understanding of local urban areas only increased his revulsion for them. Like most planners, he disliked the haphazard development of Rawalpindi, the lack of distinction among transportation arteries, the intermixing of functions, the congestion, and the lack of simple overall unity apparent from maps (Doxiadis Associates 1960a).

Doxiadis bluntly argued that "Rawalpindi should not have any role [in the capital]. It should remain the regional center . . . [and] the servicing center of the capital" (Doxiadis Associates 1960b:244). Doxiadis wrote, "a green belt is provided between Islamabad and Rawalpindi in order to form a physical barrier between them" (Doxiadis Associates 1960a:54). The Master Plan for Islamabad called for Islamabad and Rawalpindi to expand indefinitely on parallel rays out from their nuclei, forever divided by a green belt, a major transportation artery, and a linear industrial zone (see fig. o.1 in the introduction). Initial plans even provided for a wide military zone running parallel to the industrial zone (Yakas 2001:82), highway, and green belt, but this was eliminated in later plans. This division loudly echoed the one between New Delhi and Old Delhi and similar divisions in many other colonial cities, which represented the relation of the imperial government to its subject population and functioned to ensure or reinforce the social division between rulers and the ruled. There was, however, one major difference: New Delhi's hexagonal Beaux Arts plan was a complete whole—a symbol of imperial order and permanence—and no provision was made for the city's expansion or articulation with peripheral growth. By the 1950s, however, large-scale urbanization made the management of expansion a major priority of urban planning throughout South Asia (Hull 2011). Doxiadis planned for growth. His plan provided for the parallel, unidirectional expansion of Islamabad and Rawalpindi to ensure that they would never grow together and that concentric growth would not choke the "center" of Islamabad (Federal Capital Commission 1960). This program has indeed succeeded in keeping the two cities at a distance.

The monumental "national administrative" area was sited at the highest point of Islamabad, against the Margalla Hills, at the origin point of the city's ray of extension. The President's House, sometimes called the "Presidential Palace" in early newspapers, was placed on a small hill at the focal point of the city.[15] The Federal Secretariat and the National Assembly buildings were located directly in front of the President's House, at a lower level. As one senior CDA official put it to me, "The president is on the hill and the parliament is under his feet."[16]

The main axis of Islamabad, a large avenue officially named with the honorific form of reference for Jinnah, the Khayaban-i-Quaid-i-Azam (Avenue of the Great Founder), begins at this point. The land on both sides of this avenue was zoned as the central business district and early on became known as the "Blue Area" after its color designation on initial zoning maps.

The basic spatial structure of Islamabad is a grid of 1¼-mile square sectors that extends from northeast to southwest down a gentle slope, articulated by roads cutting through hillocks and spanning shallow gullies.[17] Each sector was given an alphanumeric designation for precise location within the overall plan.[18] Doxiadis called Islamabad a "dynapolis" (from "dynamic" and "metropolis") and praised the grid because it "can develop dynamically, unhindered into the future, into space and time" (1965:26).[19] In Doxiadis's vision, the nucleus of Islamabad would remain serene, secure, and static while the city expanded indefinitely, eventually to be absorbed by what he called an "ecumenopolis," an urban blur smeared from Brussels to Beijing. For this reason, the limited set of alphabetic designations was assigned to the northwest to southeast axis, while the northeast to southwest axis of expansion was given the unlimited set of numerical designations. The grid of the Federal Capital Area, approximately 3,626 square kilometers annexed from border areas of the Punjab and North West Frontier Province (now Khyber Pakhtunkhwa), surrounds Rawalpindi on three sides, much as the British cantonment surrounded the indigenous city. While publicity focused on plans for the civilian population of Islamabad, as Frank Spaulding (1994:193) points out, the army was the quiet recipient of the largest amount of land allocated to any single institution or to any single function, save that of civilian residence.

COMMUNITIES OF ALL CLASSES AND CATEGORIES

Doxiadis conceptualized Islamabad as a hierarchy of "communities," from the smallest gathering to the city as a whole. In a rationalized form of the neighborhood unit originally developed by American planners (Hull 2011), each sector was functionally differentiated and subdivided into a five-level hierarchy. The principle of subdivision was division into four parts, to preserve the geometry of the square, though irregularities of terrain often impeded the realization of this ideal order. The sector as a whole, a class V community, was to contain between 30,000 to 40,000 people. The sector was subdivided into four quadrants (subsectors), class IV communities, to house roughly 10,000 people. Four class III communities (sub-subsectors), with populations of around 2,500, were to make up each class IV community. Each class III community contained a number of class II communities, a block with a population of 100 or more. The lowest level, class I, was to consist of a family or any gathering of two or more people (Doxiadis 1964:332). Subsectors and sub-subsectors were numbered from one to four in a clockwise direction beginning with the southernmost division. So a particular area might be designated with a letter and up to three numbers, for example, G-6/4–1. Doxiadis observed that geometrical orders, in particular that of the square, were prevalent in the architecture of the region from Mohenjo Daro to the Lahore Fort (Doxiadis Associates 1961c:139)—leaving aside the aberrant "old cities" like Lahore and Rawalpindi. His real source, however, was the rationalism of European modernist planning, so striking in its simplicity.

> Good architecture demands rationalism in the city plan, and this rationalism in turn requires consistency in the conception of all spaces forming the city. The room, the smallest nucleus of a house, must have straight walls, and these must be at right angles to each other so that they can be connected with the other rooms; otherwise there is no house. The house and its plots should have straight walls at right angles to each other so that they can be connected with other houses and other plots. The plots as a whole form a block, and the blocks, too, should have straight walls at right angles to each other so that they can be connected in a rational way to the other blocks. More blocks form a neighborhood, more neighborhoods form a city (Doxiadis Associates 1961c:12).

Schools, markets, mosques, medical institutions, and recreational facilities commensurate with their populations are focal at every level of community (fig. 1.1). In contrast to the mohallas, these functions are located in the center of each community. Thus, at the center of a class V community is a post office, a fire and a police station, a large mosque, clothing and food markets, and so forth. A class III center includes a primary school, a teahouse, a few shops, and sometimes a small mosque.[20] Internal streets are numbered but not named. Doxiadis intended that each level of community be laid out so that its boundary could be seen from its center and the whole of its area easily imaged. Each community

ISLAMABAD - THE COMMUNITY CLASS Ⅳ · G6-1

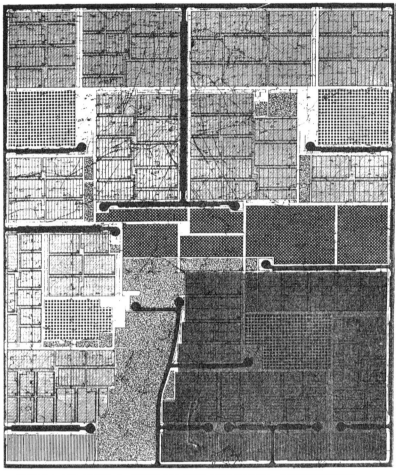

COMMUNITY CENTRE Ⅳ HANDICRAFT - LIGHT INDUSTRY RESIDENTIAL
COMMUNITY CENTRE Ⅲ OPEN SPACES - PLAYGROUNDS
FIRST COMMUNITY Ⅲ UNDER DEVELOPMENT   D-PA 3293

DOXIADIS ASSOCIATES — CONSULTING ENGINEERS

FIGURE 1.1. Community Class IV, subsector G-6–1 (Doxiadis Associates 1961d).

was to be iconic of the whole. The size, location, and quality of materials of every structure and street were planned so that it would be possible to see their replication of and incorporation into a higher order (Doxiadis Associates 1961c:18).[21]

This ordering of space was consistent with a totalizing and external perspective on the city (de Certeau 1984), which could not grasp the mohallas of Rawalpindi. William Hanks (1990:296) contrasts two kinds of spatial systems: "centered" systems, in which spaces are defined relative to activities and speech events; and "co-ordinate" or "grid" systems, in which relations among objects are computed relative to fixed axes and dimensions. Hanks discusses these systems in relation to the social actors' spatiotemporal orientations and representations. Such orientations and representations may, in addition, provide bases for the material organization of a built environment. Islamabad is literally organized by a grid down to a small scale, making any location in the city theoretically specifiable in coordinate terms. By contrast, the mohalla, originally organized to control visual access and movement, is a centered system. While structurally the area of a mohalla is precisely (if irregularly) defined perimetrically, the perimetric definition is not directly perceptible.[22] In contrast to Islamabad, it would seem that a location within a mohalla is almost unspecifiable in coordinate terms.

This spatial and functional order was to be the foundation of the social order as well: "The structure of a residential community is that its physical pattern should be in complete accord with the social organization of the human group which is to settle there" (Doxiadis Associates 1961a:6). The future inhabitants of residential sectors were conceptualized as a population organized by the national bureaucratic hierarchy, rather than as groups formed around family, religion, tribe or ethnicity, regional affiliation, or wealth, all of which are significant bases of social order in Pakistani society. These forms of sociality largely shaped the settlement patterns of Rawalpindi's mohallas. The social homogeneity of squatter settlements testifies to the continuing salience of such regional and religious affiliations even in urban Islamabad. As Spaulding (1994) has shown in his study of ethnic Gujars in Islamabad, the bureaucratic process through which government housing and plots are distributed makes it impossible for any group to establish itself in a particular area.

Continuing a British colonial practice, planners prescribed a hierarchy of lot sizes and house designs corresponding to residents' salary level and position in the government bureaucracy (King 1976; Nilsson

TABLE 1.1 1960S HOUSE TYPES BY BASIC PAY SCALE.

House type	Scale (BPS) ("grade")	Area (sq. ft.)
A	1-4	350-550
B	5-6	550-800
C	7-10	800-1,000
D	11-15	1,000-1,150
E	16-17	1,150-1,800
F	18	1,800-2,000
G	19	2,000-2,100
H	20	2,100-2,800
I	21-22	2,800-3,200

1973). The initial Master Plan provided for the construction of nine types of government houses (see table 1.1).

The correlation of house types with income, however, is misleading. The *Socio-Economic Survey of Rawalpindi,* while hastily completed in 1960, gave the planners an impressive range of information on housing and income in urban Punjab. However, the income divisions employed in the plan were not derived from this study but from the salary scale corresponding to the rank hierarchy of Pakistan's National Civil Service. Furthermore, government houses were to be allocated on the basis of the occupant's government rank, not income derived from any source. Doxiadis's criticism of variety within house types makes clear the status basis of the housing policy.

> Civil servants who have more or less the same income and belong to the same class of civil service should be allocated to similar units. They should all be treated in a similar manner and on an equal basis as far as possible. Houses given, for example, to peons should all be of the same nature, of the same design, and the same accommodation capacity. Otherwise, bad feelings would be created among civil servants belonging to one and the same class (Doxiadis Associates 1961b:24).

Even by the mid-1960s, on Doxiadis's recommendation, the direct reference to income found in early reports had been replaced by correlations with civil service rank, as in table 1.1.[23] The rank hierarchy of the civil service is officially called the "Basic Pay Scale" (BPS), a finan-

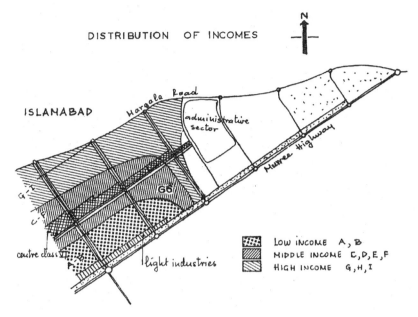

FIGURE 1.2. Doxiadis drawing showing the spatial distribution of house types based on income (Doxiadis Associates 1961d).

cial designation that is somewhat misleading, since the more important role of the scale is status rather than income differentiation. "Grade," the term for the rank of a government employee used in common conversation, better captures its social significance.

In general, higher-rank houses and larger plots for private houses were distributed within the northern sectors, with particularly high-status plots found in the easternmost areas near the administrative area (fig 1.2). The F-series of sectors, on the whole, contains government and private houses that are much larger than those of G-series sectors. However, Doxiadis's "neighborhood unit" plans did provide for a degree of integration of income groups.

The neighborhood unit was a notion developed in the United States in the early twentieth century as a means to generate and represent the egalitarian and democratic community.[24] In laying out the basic objectives of Islamabad, the Federal Capital Commission had proposed "to create neighborhoods that will foster a sense of belonging to a community and promote social cohesion" (1960:19). Drawing an implicit contrast between the modern, nationalist social divisions of government rank and the socially retrograde hierarchy of traditional Hindu India, the Federal Capital Commission feared what it called a "caste system" based on income groups (19). This goal limited slightly the commission's emphasis on the isolation of the bureaucracy. The plan for the new city, declared the commission, would not "segregate *completely* for the distribution of incomes government servants from other groups" (19, emphasis added).

In the Master Plan, however, the egalitarian planning notion of the neighborhood unit was given a hierarchical and paternalist cast. It was feared that an attempt to integrate too broad a spectrum of residents would lead to social conflict.[25] Rather, a principle of a "gradual integration" of a narrow range of income groups was adopted "to help lower income people mature and assure comfort to the higher income classes" (Doxiadis 1964:333). Accordingly, the range of house types in any given area was limited to two or three steps on the schedule. In a review of the Master Plan, a newspaper article enthusiastically praised this aspect of the plan, echoing the Federal Capital Commission's invocation of caste:

> Another notable aspect of the Capital's "personality" would be the absence of a "caste system" among its inhabitants. Efforts will be made to secure an integration of the various strata of society. The higher classes will jostle with their fellow citizens in the lower income brackets. It is fully realised that this cohesion is possible only up to a point if embarrassments are not to mar the atmosphere. Anyhow, the planners appear keen that Islamabad should come as near to the ideal of a "casteless" city as humanly possible.[26]

Over the last four decades, housing for lower-income classes has continued to be built, but Doxiadis's original plan for a gradually integrated city stretched no further than his designs for F-6 and G-6. Even F-7 contains few smaller plots and no government housing. As a senior CDA planner, observed, "Over the last twenty years there has been a complete separation of income groups." According to him, mixed-income projects simply cannot be pushed through nowadays. Why could it be done before? "Because," he said puckishly, "the *gora* [white] *sahib* had the clout" to push it through. While the disappearance of this objective is clear, accounting for it is more difficult. His explanation points to how much planning, conceived as the realization of rational intention, is shaped by wider sociocultural trends: "I can't point to a specific place in the record that the decision was made. It was not a conscious decision. It was a matter of a change in the culture."

As many have observed (King 1976), government grades constituted a kind of social template through which all members of British colonial society, not only government servants, could be placed in a social hierarchy. The Pakistan scale of government grades performs a similar function in contemporary Islamabad, where even positions for private teaching and business jobs are given a BPS equivalence in advertisements. The tendency to use the government scale as a representation of the general order of social status, while a national phenomenon to some extent, is especially strong in Islamabad. In its early years, the macrosocial order of the city was roughly co-extensive with the organization of the government, leaving aside the limited population of traders and workers. An article from the early 1970s describes Islamabad as "still a government city predominantly populated by government employees neatly divided into so many classes inherited from the good old colonial days."[27] Today, class or status (rarely distinguished with Weberian precision) is still commonly identified with government rank. In discussions with me in Urdu about the social order of the city, residents moved fluidly among the terms *haisiyat* (roughly, "status" with an emphasis on capacities and resources), *category*, and *scale*.

FROM SEPARATION TO PARTICIPATION

In October 1963, the CDA terminated its contract with Doxiadis Associates, two years before the end of the scheduled five years. The reasons for the early termination are unclear, though it appears that two of the central factors were disputes over the pace of Doxiadis's work and the desire of Pakistani officials to play a greater role in the development of the city (Yakas 2001:147–51). Several important CDA officials had been influenced by Doxiadis's approach through training in the School of Ekistics in Athens and through their work on the Master Plan itself. Eminent international architects such as Gio Ponti, Edward Stone, and Derek Lovejoy continued to design major buildings and landscapes for Islamabad. Lesser-known architects, mostly English, labored on designs for houses, mosques, and markets. Nevertheless, after the charismatic Doxiadis departed and the senior political and military officers withdrew from direct involvement in the planning, long-standing South Asian bureaucratic practices began to assert themselves in the development of the city.

One CDA planner told me, "The Master Plan is our constitution, the constitution for the city, for the country." Doxiadis's Report No. 32 has continued to be the basic reference for the Master Plan, though slightly revised in 1985 and again in 2006. However, few CDA officers

I talked with have a copy. When I asked about Report No. 32, I was referred to the CDA library in a building away from the main CDA compound. As with legal practice, the day-to-day tasks of the CDA are not constitutional matters. Although the basic provisions of the report are rarely violated, the planning and regulation of the city are carried out through millions of more humble documents such as files, house plans, and forms.

As with the spatial plan of the city itself, the politics of reports produced by technocratic planners and high-level committees effectively isolated broad public participation in plans for the new city. As we've seen, even the most modest documents of the British South Asian bureaucratic tradition similarly aimed to make a boundary between the government and its subjects, a division between public and private. In practice, such documents are often mediators that incorporate aspects of the people, things, and processes they are designed to control from a distance. This was brought home to me one day when I saw a CDA draftsman storm down a hallway and explode into a heated argument with a building control officer who had rejected a house plan on a technicality. The clerk I was with explained that the draftsman himself had made the drawings for a private client, which his superior knew. The plan had transformed them from superior and subordinate into bureaucrat and client. According to the norms of this latter relationship, the superior was reportedly hitting up the subordinate for Rs. 3000 to pass his plan. The house plan articulated conflicting market and bureaucratic relations. The two men simultaneously argued about the technical application of rules as subordinate and superior and the just price for approval as bureaucrat and client.

It is not so much that documents like this house plan move through distinct "regimes of value" (Appadurai 1986), in and out of commodity phases, but that they can be at once a thing paid for and an object of bureaucratic practice, mediators of practices that are at once bureaucratic work and a paid service. The paradigmatic case of corruption understood as the marketization of government is when a functionary profits purely from his control over a government resource, such as when an officer accepts a bribe in exchange for a signature approving an application, or when a clerk demands a hundred rupees to find a file or to register receipt of a letter. In many other cases, however, the functionary does a substantial amount of work for the client in *producing* required documents.

One town planner who worked in the government overseeing the projects of housing societies, for example, ran what he called "private work" from his office with the help of another town planner who was not a government servant. The government planner described himself as a "silent partner." According to this planner, housing societies must in any case "go to the market to find a planner, so I tell them, 'I am a planner, and it is better that I do your work.'" With his partner, he drew up plans and advised the societies on regulation issues. He saw the money these societies pay him—which always went to his partner—as fees rather than bribes, just compensation for the integrated services of town planning and help in satisfying regulatory demands. He admitted the conflict of interest, since he was the one who scrutinized the plans and made the recommendations for approval, but stressed that he could do nothing illegal since his superiors reviewed all the proposals. His signature of approval was the essential attraction for clients ("If I leave the seat, they will leave me," he admitted to me), but it is not the only service sold. His services included a considerable amount of work beyond the "resource" he can deliver as an officer in the review process. Even what seems to be the clearest expression of the marketization of government, the sale of official approval, almost always involves more than a signature. Officials accepting bribes for a contract or for the approval of a project usually serve the functions of lawyer and lobbyist for those who have paid them, shepherding documents through bureaucratic processes over which they, like their clients, have limited control.

As in the case of the architect, the product or—in the language of management consulting—the "deliverable" of private work is a document. When accompanying this planner on some of his private work, I observed one of his clients when she suddenly realized how a plan of her plot of land was to figure in his service. The planner had met the woman when she had come to the CDA on some unrelated business several years earlier. She had contacted him again regarding the subdivision of her plot in the elite E-7 sector, inherited from her father, on which she planned to build a second house. After the three of us enjoyed a pleasant lunch at her house, the planner unfolded the site plan he had brought, and we went upstairs to a little balcony to inspect the plot lines. She noted immediately that the subdivision map did not show the portion of the existing house that sat on the second lot. She was very concerned about this. She said that there was a legal case proceeding on the property, and that such an irregularity might cause some problem if it fell into the adversary's hands and was subsequently presented in court. The planner acknowledged her concern, but without elaborating he said that since the CDA had done it this way it was best just to leave it the way it was. When she insisted, the planner told her that he had had quite a difficult time getting the CDA draftsmen to make the site map without showing the projecting structure, precisely what she was objecting to. He explained that if the projecting part of the house had been shown, the land covered by it could not be included in the new plot under subdivision rules, so the plot would not reach the minimum area required for subdivision. If the map were "corrected," the subdivision could be revoked. She readily agreed to leave the issue but complained about regulations regarding subdivision, saying, "Why isn't a father's daughter able to do this?" (*Bap ki beti aise kyon nahi ker sakti?*). The planner smiled and replied in English, "I'm am sorry, but CDA doesn't care who you are; whether you are a brother, a son, a mother or a daughter, the rules are the same."

The way that documents draw together bureaucratic and other kinds of relations can be seen in how people morally evaluate actions like the planner's production of an inaccurate site map. Since the postcolonial Pakistan state is often not regarded as a moral actor, standards of public service do not play as great a role in evaluations of bureaucratic activities as prevailing Pakistani public discourses on corruption might lead us to expect. Most people consider actions corrupt when they transform administrative relations into another sort, as in marketization or "personalization." The transformation itself, however, is often not the crux of moral condemnation. Often more important is how the action is evaluated in light of the moral norms invoked by the transformation. That is, actions within the bureaucracy are translated into analogous contexts of social life outside the bureaucracy and evaluated in light of the moral norms reigning there. If a bribe was taken, did the service provided make it a fair exchange? If merit was disregarded in hiring, was it for money or to help a needy relative? Actions are strongly condemned as corrupt only when they violate *both* the norms of public service and the morality governing the analogous social domain. Many violations of norms of public service are excused on account of their conformity to other moral norms. Thus, the moral category of corruption, while only applied to activities within the politico-bureaucratic realm, nevertheless converges with conceptions such as greed (*lalach*), selfishness (*matlabi*), dishonor (*beizzati*), dishonesty (*beimandari*), injustice (*beinsafi*), oppression (*zulum*), and impiety (*fisq*), which are grounded in moralities prevailing in other social domains.

This was the sort of thinking that a major client of this same planner used to evaluate the planner's activities. The client distinguished him from other bureaucrats who demand bribes, telling me, "It is not like he is charging for just a signature." By contrast, the planner's partner, who in his own opinion did most of the planning work, was much more ambivalent in his evaluation of the town planner's practice.

When others evaluated the town planner's activities, they translated his actions into the market realm, and the question of corruption became one of a just price for services. Similarly, the woman for whom the planner had made the inaccurate map, while seeming uncomfortable with the matter, was willing to go along with it since she considered it her right to modify her own father's house as she saw fit.

CDA record-keeping practices can also facilitate the involvement of those outside the bureaucracy, promoting precisely the practices that the records were intended to curtail. Blueprints for private houses provide an enlightening example of this phenomenon. Until the 1960s, most urban houses in the region were built by contractors who worked from rough sketches and the regular input of owners. In contrast, the Islamabad building codes required that plans drawn up by a licensed architect be submitted to the CDA. One goal of this code was to compel compliance with regulations; another objective was to ensure the uniqueness of each house. Ironically, the CDA architecture record storeroom has provided a supply of ready-made plans for reproduction. At the prompting of clients who have admired a particular house, architects would buy these blueprints from CDA staff in control of the record room for Rs. 500–1000, change the names on them, and sell them to clients for Rs. 7000–10,000. In other cases, CDA architects, like the planner discussed earlier, offer the same service. One private architect I spoke with sees himself as a competitor of the CDA architects and draftsmen, who try to "steal" his clients when they file their application forms. There are now at least nine reproductions of one large, white, pillared house placed on a prominent road that was featured in a popular television serial drama as the residence of a very rich family. (Architects told me people would often come in and tell them they want to live in a "White House.") The trade in blueprints is such a common practice that, in a conversation with me, one architect marked it as a point of pride that his firm usually designs houses from scratch. One rough measure of the scale of traffic in house plans is provided by statistics compiled by an officer in the architecture directorate showing that an architectural firm with just one architect produced 396 plans in 1997.

In the cases I've discussed so far, the nonsanctioned production and use of documents draw other sorts of relationships into bureaucratic practices. In other practices, formal bureaucratic procedures themselves blur the boundary between the bureaucracy and the wider society of the city. Such is the case with the allotment of housing to government employees.

In principle, the original plan to make government house type correspond to service rank could not have been simpler. In practice, it has been more difficult to realize. There are no statistics that I know of, but it is common for government employees to live in houses of types far below or above that to which the allocation rules entitle them. For example, one resident of the oldest sector of Islamabad, G-6, whom I'll call Ahmed, has lived in a type A house for nineteen years, though in this time he has moved from grade 4 to grade 15 and is now entitled to a type D house. While many of the original allottees of these houses have retired and are entitled to retain their quarters only for six months after their retirement, few quarters have ever left the family. Statistics on house transfers are not available, but good estimates suggest that in G-6/1, for example, since the departure of Bengali government servants during the war in 1971 that resulted in the creation of Bangladesh, less than 10 percent of the houses have left the families of their original occupants.[28]

Although some residents like Ahmed have been trying for years to obtain the housing to which he is entitled, others have been pressing the government to award them ownership of their current unit. Residents of this area refer to themselves as "owners" (*maliks*) of their houses rather than "allotees" or "renters" (*karaedars*). Most occupants have invested substantial resources into the modification of their government dwellings, modifying the front *purdah* (seclusion) wall and interior layouts and adding typically two more rooms at the back of the large rear courtyard.[29] Ahmed told me he waited five or six years before realizing that he might remain in the house another fifteen years, at which point he began modifying and adding to it. While he vows that he will not try to retain the house for his children after his retirement—"They should go out and get something better"—he recognizes that they may have no alternative. Residents of G-6 have organized and agitated for decades to have what they see as their customary rights to their quarters confirmed through the grant of legal ownership. During the 1980s and 1990s, Pakistan presidents and the heads of both leading political parties have promised to grant ownership rights to occupants of those houses, but the awards have never come. While electoral politics has continued to fail these residents, they have been better served by bureaucratic practice.

Though legal ownership has not been granted, individual and family rights to their quarters, irrespective of government service, are recognized in both the legally sanctioned and informal aspects of the allocation process. The "Out of Turn Allotment" (OOTA), an ad hoc rationalization in both the Weberian and moral senses of the term, has been codified in the allocation rules in order to regularize the ad hoc allocation of quarters to those who are not entitled to them according to service qualifications.

If a son enters government service before his father's retirement, for instance, the allotment of the family quarter may be transferred to the son, as long as the son is entitled to it by service rank, a qualification that is rarely enforced. In practice, if the father occupies a house commensurate with his service rank, the son, rarely having a rank equal to his father, is allocated his father's house, one of a higher classification than that to which he is entitled. Ironically, in cases of a retiring father living below his entitlement who irregularly transfers his house to his son, these two factors combine to realize something approximating the planned relation between the rank of occupant and the house classification.

OOTA forms (fig. 1.3) also figure in the cases in which houses have been transferred outside the family. The way records on government quarters are maintained plays an important role in such transfers. At least through the late 1990s, the CDA office that allocates housing, the Administration Directorate, did not have synoptic documentation of the units under its authority, that is, a single register of all of its housing units. Information on each unit was contained in a file of its own, stacked one upon another on the shelves of a large number of cabinets. As I will discuss in the next chapter, files are network documents that move along narrow paths, greatly restricting the range of people who have access to their contents. The file-based organization of government housing records, by limiting the knowledge of housing units and their occupants, enabled the allocation of housing units to run almost entirely on the local knowledge of those with access to the records, coworkers, and neighbors who come to know of a retirement, transfer, or illegal sublet.

Generally, when a government servant with no children eligible to take over the unit is retiring, he (and occasionally she) is approached by new prospective occupants, before official procedures of reallotment have even begun. We might call such transfers friendly takeovers. In recognition of the occupant's right to the house, the prospective occu-

APPLICATION FOR OUT OF TURN
ALLOTMENT OF ACCOMMODATION

1. Full name (in block letters) ....

2. Designation with BPS No. and department ....
    ....

3. Class/category of accommodation to which entitled ....

4. Date of first entry in Government service.....................................

5. Date of arrival/posting at the present station ....

6. Does the applicant or his wife possess own house or rented accommodation,
    etc. anywhere in Pakistan? If so, give particulars (If the accommodation is not
    available for his family full reasons should be stated) ....
    ....
    ....

7. Details of present accommodation ....
    arrangements...

8. Is the applicant still retaining the house where he or his family were living
    before his transfer to the present station (Please give full particulars of the
    house)..
    ....

9. Number of dependent family members of the applicant residing with him with
    details of major and minors one...
    ....

10. Special consideration of health, if any..
    supported by the certificate from a ....
    Civil Surgeon of F.G. Hospital/dispensary ....
    in case of BPS-16 and above and from ....
    Medical attendant in case of officials in BPS 1 to 15 ....

11. Any other fact which the applicant wishes to put forward.........................

                                             Signature of applicant

       No................................   Date..................................

       Forwarded to the Estate Office, ... I am satisfied that
the facts stated in this application form are substantially correct.

                                             **Signature of the Head of
                                             the Department/Office**
Decision by OOTAC

FIGURE 1.3. Out of Turn Allotment of Accommodation form (Ministry of Housing and Works 1993).

pants pay him or her (Rs. 2000–10,000 in the late 1990s) to move out and let them take possession (*qabza*). Only after settling in do the new occupants submit a letter to the government stating that they have taken possession of the quarter and are petitioning to have it officially allotted to them through the OOTA process. Possession is nine-tenths of the allocation, so such petitions are usually accepted.

Hostile takeovers take place when an individual comes to know that the allottee of a quarter either has illegally sublet it or, when the allottee is retiring, is unwilling to accept a financial offer and vacate. In yet another example of the explicit codification of a practice originating outside the organization, the allocation rules stipulate that the "first informer" to bring a violation to the notice of the authorities may claim the quarter through an OOTA application. Retiring officers, whose ineligibility is easily verified, often accept the offer of the "informer" as an alternative to official action.

In contrast to retirement, the case of subletting is difficult to prove. The CDA officer in charge of investigating such charges told me that if his investigators ask about the clothes and other furnishing in the quarter, the allottee will simply claim they are his. If the renters are present, the allottee will say they are his good friends and they are staying free. Inquiries from neighbors are no more help; they usually lie to protect their neighbor, especially since they themselves are often subletting a portion of their quarter. Moreover, in most cases, the officer told me, the allottee learns well in advance that an investigation is imminent and will be expecting the arrival of inspectors. This observation was borne out by the experience of a friend of mine who was occupying a quarter allocated to his uncle. He and his family were summarily hustled out of the quarter when the uncle got wind of someone filing a claim against him. Even when such claims against illegal occupation are successful, though, the claimant will usually end up paying a substantial sum to the occupant to dissuade him from tying up the case in court for years.

Clearly, the file organization of housing documents is an important factor in the divergence of the occupancy of government housing from the planned (and legally stipulated) correspondence between house type and the service rank. The allocation office acts more like a registrar of market transfers than an agent of those transfers in accordance with the allocation rules. The records of CDA government quarters are another example of how a documentary infrastructure facilitates practices it was produced to prevent. The documentary infrastructure has enabled other practices to overwhelm house allocation rules.

CHAPTER 2

Parchis, Petitions, and Offices

The entire plan of Islamabad was a grand project to distance the government from the society it was to govern, an effort to use spatial isolation to engineer a social isolation of government servants from the wider populace. Similarly, the documentary regime through which the plan was administered was designed to institute a separation between the workings of government and those of the broader social world. But the spatial order of the city has been shaped by the social processes the plan sought to curtail, partly because documents such as the files of government apartments, house plans, and site maps work not only as instruments of bureaucratic control but also as media of dissent and negotiation between the government and populace.

Official documents can be the mediators of a shadowy engagement between government servants and others. But there are other channels through which government is directly approachable: face-to-face meetings and petitions. Face-to-face meetings, the paragon within social science of the unmediated encounter, are shaped by the layouts of offices, chairs, desks, buzzers, and teacups, the things that form the material infrastructure of the social relationships in the bureaucratic arena.[1] Like the city as a whole, offices are designed to enact a division between the official and the private, but office practices fuse the two in different ways. Office meetings are also often mediated by *parchi*s or "chits" (slips of paper or visiting cards), the material elements of connection with powerful supporters that people present to officers. Condemned by liberal discourse in Pakistan, the parchi contrasts with the petition, which is normatively the document of a citizen's direct and open approach to government. The material infrastructure of offices is central to how parchis and petitions work in the Capital Development Authority (CDA) and the Islamabad Capital Territory Administration (ICTA). The chapter begins here, moves on to the use of parchis and petitions, and ends by showing how, despite their ideological opposition, these two forms of document often work together.

AT HOME IN THE OFFICE

The grand division between government and populace that the original Master Plan was intended to impose is reproduced at the scale of smaller spatial divisions of office compounds and individual offices. As Weber observed, "the modern organization of the civil service apparatus separates the bureau from the private domicile of the official and, in general, segregates official activity from the sphere of private life" (1978:957). Akhil Gupta (1995:384) observes that low-level rural Indian officials "blur" the boundary between "state and civil society" by doing business in tea stalls and in their homes rather than in their offices. By contrast, official work in Islamabad takes place almost exclusively in offices sociomaterially distinguished from areas of general social traffic. A large steel fence surrounds the compound of CDA offices on the southern edge of G-7. CDA police, in dark gray *shalwar-kameez* (baggy pants and a long shirt), with rifles slung on their backs, guard the two gates, suspiciously questioning drivers and pedestrians. However, the separation of these islands of office compounds from the surrounding city obscures the mixing of official business with the other activities of CDA officers and staff.

Officers often leave during the day to pick up their children from school or to do other errands. Government cars are routinely used for personal business. Drivers and cars serve officers in both personal and official business. Menial office staff often function much like domestic servants, frequently being sent on a variety of personal errands for officers, such as buying groceries and paying utility bills. Many government servants break up their workday once or twice (depending on the time of year) to say prayers (*namaz*).[2] In principle, such prayer presents no great interruption of the affairs of the bureaucracy. The disjunctive relationship it has with bureaucratic activity is materially produced by the lack of provision for mosques or prayer spaces within office complexes. Under pressure from employees, a mosque was eventually added to the national ministry office complex. However, no such facility has been constructed within CDA or ICTA areas. CDA employees spread reed mats out in the little-used lobby of one of the office buildings, and ICTA employees gather in an office emptied for prayers. But such practices are only the most obvious ways that official spaces, resources, and authority are blended with other concerns. Even the activities that take place around the chairs and desks of offices are shaped by practices more closely associated with the home.

Like drawing rooms—the more public areas of houses which are predominantly gendered male (though women use them too)—CDA and ICTA offices are male spaces.[3] Most of the officers and staff are male.[4] During the period of my initial research in the late 1990s, in CDA Urban Planning, Architecture, and Lands Directorates, for example, there was only one junior female officer; there were no women among the most senior officers of the CDA. In the ICTA, there was one woman holding the post of assistant commissioner and one woman leading the women's division of the police. In the opinion of many men and women, single women who work harm their marriage prospects, and most husbands are willing to forgo a second income to avoid exposure to rumors of their wife's impropriety. Many women do not consider government service a desirable pursuit in light of the imputations of sexual immorality such service may bring, particularly at the staff level. As we talked casually in the office of one of her colleagues, a woman at the clerical level in the CDA complained that her every interaction with a man generated looks and gossip: "Imagine it, if I am speaking to some man, then other people will keep looking our way and asking, 'So what is this? What are they talking about?'" Then, she abruptly broke off her speech to point around the room, exclaiming, "See, they are doing it now!" The presence of women in offices does more to highlight their male character than to transform them into more gender-neutral spaces. One day when I visited the CDA Public Relations Directorate, there was a fracas over where an attractive young woman taking up the post of a lower division clerk would sit. A junior assistant, opposing the rest of the staff of the directorate, had temporarily gained the upper hand and settled her at a vacant desk in his room. A bitter staff member with a desk in a different room complained to me, "He just wants to have her there to look at all day," then admitted he wanted to do the same thing. Traffic through the assistant's office dramatically increased and whenever she talked with anyone others gossiped jealously.

Although relations of all sorts find a place within offices, the CDA office complex is first a durable enactment of the CDA's *Rules for the Conduct of Business,* the document that lays out the division of labor within the organization. The eight "wings" containing roughly fifty "directorates" are distributed among four closely grouped, two-story, unfaced brick office buildings. The three older buildings were built in the early 1960s, while the executive building occupied by the chairman and the most senior officers was constructed in the late 1970s. Unlike the open floor plans of the sleek, newer banks in the Blue Area (the central business district), these buildings are structured by a long, single hallway or veranda from which all the office rooms are entered. Dark-brown wood plaques with painted gold writing affixed outside office doors announce the name of the organizational unit or the name and title of the officer who occupies the rooms. The offices of each wing and directorate are grouped and assigned to a post or unit.

The CDA is staffed by government servants in grades 1 through 21 of the 22 grades organizing government servants since 1973. At the bottom of the scale are various menials in grade 1. At the top are the member (Administration) and chairman, usually grade 20 or 21 officers who entered service via success on the Central Superior Services examination and training at the Civil Services Academy. These high-flying, generalist officers are transferred among various federal bureaucracies and rarely remain at the CDA for more than a few years.

Beneath these senior officers are grade 17, 18, and 19 officers, who are either directly recruited to the CDA in grade 17 or transferred on deputation from a provincial government. These officers may spend their entire careers in different posts within the CDA. With great experience in the organization, they sometimes resent their subordination to higher-status, generalist superiors, who often move on before they have understood the institution. One director complained to me on this score: "We are not government servants, we are servants of government servants." Officers involved in general management may rise relatively quickly within the CDA, moving among different posts in different directorates, for example, from Deputy Director (Lands) to Director (Administration). In contrast, technical officers, such as planners and architects, generally remain within the same directorate, rising (if at all) on the strength of good confidential annual reports and connections when a superior retires or transfers. Such officers make slow progress down the hall from office to office as they are promoted, occupying the same post for as long as eight to ten years. Similarly, staff in nontechnical posts may move among directorates and climb gradually, though they rarely cross the line dividing staff from officers. Technical staff members move up slowly as posts open above them in the same directorate. One day several junior officers discussed the unhappy pace of this gradual progression between offices. When their director popped into the room and caught the drift of their conversation, he quipped, "So you are all waiting for me to die!"

Clerical and technical staff, that is, CDA employees below grade 17, work at desks or drawing boards irregularly arranged in large office rooms with concrete or terrazzo floors. Their desks are usually piled with different kinds of registers and files moving to or from their immediate superior officers. Metal cabinets (*almirah*s) and shelves, containing files not in immediate use, line the walls. The doors of staff offices are usually open and, since they don't have locks, are left unlocked even when no one is present.

The lowest-ranking officers, such as town planners and engineers, usually share with one or two others an office crammed with a couple desks and four or five worn chairs (fig. 2.1). The white walls are usually bare, though a city or regional map hangs on some of them. Officers at the deputy-director level and above enjoy their own offices. The size is proportional to rank, ranging from the tight spaces of deputy directors to the spacious rooms of members of the CDA board. The terrazzo floors are usually covered by carpet, and pictures of gardens or Quranic calligraphy often decorate the walls. Large wooden or particle-board laminate desks face away or at a ninety-degree angle from the door, so that entrants to the office do not face the officer when they cross the threshold. Four or five modernist chairs usually surround the desk, though there are sometimes more. One officer wryly remarked to me that "the number of chairs symbolizes the importance of the officer." Stuffed vinyl or fabric couches and chairs are placed flush against the walls, usually in a corner, as in domestic drawing rooms. In the offices of the most senior officers, a coffee table focuses these peripheral chairs and couches (fig. 2.2).

Staff directly serving an officer, consisting of at least a personal assistant (PA), occupies an office adjacent to the officer's. The main instruments of bureaucracy, including a phone, a copy machine (for executive-level officers), typewriters, stamps, registers, and files are located here. The distinctive status of computers, for those very senior officials who have them, is indexed by their placement within the officer's room itself, though not on the desks of officers, who rarely operate them. The rooms

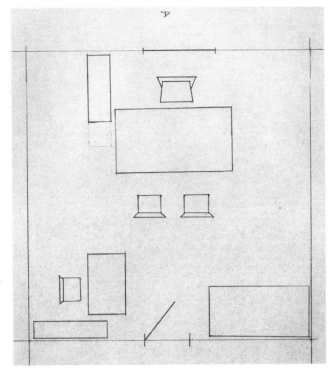

FIGURE 2.1. Office of a CDA town planner, 1998. (Illustration by Krisztina Fehérváry.)

of support staff are accessed from the hallway or veranda and may also have another door opening directly into the officer's office. Such internal doors do little to facilitate communication between the officer and staff; with or without such doors, officers summon staff by pressing the buzzer fixed to their desk. Such "reception" rooms are used more to prevent the entrance of clients and other officers seeking an audience. The name and title of the officers are placed on the hallway wall next to the door opening directly into the officer's room, and the officers enter and exit via this door (which often keeps PAs and clients guessing about their presence). However, a paper sign on this door often directs clients to the reception room; the locked door will stop any would-be entrant not redirected by the sign.

Status distinctions among employees are also materialized in bathroom facilities. Junior officers and staff use common bathrooms, but senior officers usually have one to themselves, accessed from the interi-

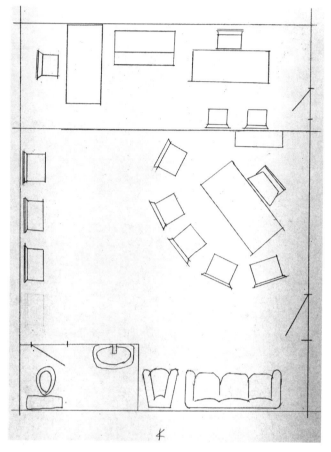

FIGURE 2.2. Office of a CDA director, 1998. (Illustration by Krisztina Fehérváry.)

ors of their offices. The kind of toilet in each marks a presumed difference in the bodily habitus of officers and staff related to rank, styles of dress, and Islamic norms of piety. The common bathrooms have a line of what are called "Asian WCs," which are meant for use in a squatting position and include an ablution area. As one of the more minor measures of his Islamization program, President Zia-ul-Haq prohibited urinals in public places because the Prophet Mohammad advised against urinating while standing (Haqqani 2005:139). In contrast, officers' bathrooms have the kind of toilets common in Europe and the United States, often called an "Angrezi WC" (English WC), designed of course for sitting, though sometimes used awkwardly like an Asian WC.

Toilet paper makes an occasional appearance, but *lota*s (small water vessels, usually plastic and with a shape somewhere between a tea pot and a watering can) are more common.[5] According to a Quranic injunction, men's clothes must be free of urine to say prayers (*namaz*). As one dealer in bathroom fixtures told me, "Those who say prayers [*namazi log*] can't use Angrezi WCs because the splatters make their clothes impure [*napak*]." With this problem in mind, he called the Asian WC an "Islamic WC." Although Western toilets are always oriented so that one neither faces nor turns one's back to Mecca while sitting (urinating while standing is uncommon even for men), they have for many a mild association with impiety, or at least with a reproachable lack of concern for regular prayer.[6] A regretful wave at one's lower body to indicate impure clothes and a quiet "napak" (impure) is a common reply to an exhortation to pray by those who are disinclined. The namazi in a billowing shalwar may have a difficult time piously negotiating a Western toilet, but the Asian WC is no friend of the panted merely trying to stay clean. As the bathroom fixtures dealer in shalwar-kameez told me with delight, "Bureaucrats wearing pants have a lot of trouble with Asian WCs."

Perhaps the starkest material division between officers is the temperature of their office air during the hot summer months. Window-unit air conditioners cool the office lives of officers at the level of director and above. As the fictional Professor Superb of the novel *Moth Smoke* observes with comic exaggeration:

> There are two social classes in Pakistan. . . . The first group, large and sweaty, contains those referred to as the masses. The second group is much smaller, but its members exercise vastly greater control over their immediate environment and are collectively termed the elite. The distinction between members of these two groups is made on the basis of their control of an important resource: air-conditioning. (Mohsin 2000:102)

The benefits of air conditioning units also trickle down to the staff of the environmentally distinguished officers. On not a few summer days, I walked into the office of an absent officer and surprised an assistant or menial dozing coolly on a couch. In the summer months, staff work to the constant snapping sound of paper blown by ceiling fans. On busy summer days, they appear to be playing a bureaucratic shell game as they dexterously move documents between piles anchored by paperweights as if they are about to look up and ask, "Ok, where is your document now?"

Then there is the arrangement of chairs, desks, and couches within offices, which is essential to the form that interactions between officers and visitors take. Officers admit any number of visitors at once, seat them, and give audience to all of them simultaneously. Requiring visitors to wait while the officer sees them serially would imply an invidious status distinction between those waiting and those being seen by the officer. As one private architect who regularly visited the CDA told me, "It is a matter of pride to be admitted, and no one wants to wait." In this milieu, the priority of arrival is not a principle strong enough to overcome the sense that visitors should be seen in accordance with their status. The annoying but egalitarian message used by American service industries to mollify callers placed on hold, "All our service representatives are currently assisting other callers," wouldn't be acceptable. An officer engaging with a number of visitors seated before him appears to be an egalitarian form of interaction, but it results from the hierarchical demands for status.

This mode of conducting office business is comparable to the way that small grocery store shopkeepers interact with their customers. Shopkeepers don't service customers serially and customers rarely form clear lines: it's much more like the rush for a drink at a crowded American bar. As customers approach the counter dividing them from the shopkeeper and the products, the shopkeepers ask each what they want. They don't wait for a complete list but set off to retrieve the first item or two the customer has requested, before turning their attention to another customer, moving roughly in rounds from customer to customer. One customer is given butter, another salt and sugar, a third toothpaste, and so on, until each has gotten all that was wanted, pays, and leaves. Similarly, in offices, officers control the discussion, giving each visitor in turn his attention and having brief exchanges about the matter in question. The dialogue between an officer and a visitor is often completed only after three or more rounds of exchanges between the officer and the other visitors. Most matters are discussed openly before the other clients, which promotes the rapid spread of gossip. If a particularly sensitive matter comes up, rather than clearing the room, the officer and the client usually retreat to a corner of the office or duck into the hallway for a quick confidential conference. As at the counter of a grocery shop, the time it takes to deal with a visitor depends on the complexity of the issue, though of course status is also a factor.

Interactions with women clients are an exception to this mode of dealing with visitors. Out of concern for propriety, women rarely come to the CDA offices. One officer told me how his wife was having some trouble with the owners of some land she was involved in developing for a college. Not wanting to deal with it himself, he told her she should go file a complaint, to which (he said) she had replied, "We [women] are in purdah, so how can we come to the office?" He said he told her they should go in *burqa*, but she still refused to go. Usually a male family member or other representative will deal with government business on behalf of a woman. Nevertheless, when women themselves go to offices, officers usually treat them with great respect, whatever their status. Officers take up their matters immediately and discuss them fully, rather than in the intermittent manner they typically use with men.

Concern for status, however, is not the only motivation accounting for this mode of doing business. Many of the visitors to offices are merely dropping in to chat, though the line between chat and business is, of course, often blurry. One officer commented to me that "here official and social life overlaps . . . while you are in your office you are in your club. There is no other place for social life to take place in Pakistan, so it goes on all day in the offices. Offices are our clubs." The division between client and friend is not sharp, and all visitors are referred to as "*mehman*" (guest) in Urdu or "guest" in English. "Guests" of senior officers are usually served tea, sometimes several rounds. Unlike domestic hospitality, office hospitality blends practices of rights with those of generosity (Shryock 2008).

I often heard the quip that the only indispensable person in an office is the one who serves the tea. Tea is an important mediator of relations not only between officers and "guests," but between officers and their staff, especially the lowest man in the hierarchy, called the "peon," a term that is not pejorative. The numerous menials who serve officers are essential actors in these office interactions and in office activities more generally. One peon told me, complaining resignedly about the habits of senior officers, "They won't even get a glass of water for themselves but are entirely dependent on us for every little thing." Such mediation of action by subordinates is obviously a matter of status deployed through an elaborate formal and informal division of labor based partly on the comparatively low economic value of human labor in Pakistan. Moreover, such interactions reflect the habitus of individuals and the basic texture of sociality in Pakistan, which are manifest in actions ranging from simple physical acts to more complex social projects, such as those involving files, which I describe in the next chapter. This is not a collective mode of action, but one in which individuals act through (not with) others. In domestic spaces, servants, women, and children often act as immediate extensions of the body of more senior women and men. One woman I knew would yell irritably for her servant for quite some time before she would so much as lean forward to pick up her tea cup. The daughter of a wealthy merchant, she grew up with several servants at her command and seemed almost physically disabled by having only one servant after a decline in her economic circumstances. But this form of sociality is limited neither to physical actions nor to actions directly expressing status. In search of a phone number, for example, individuals are much more likely to open a series of contacts than obtain it from telephone directory assistance. The formal division of labor in the bureaucratic arena intensifies the fine-grained mediation of individual actions in Pakistani social life.

The mediation of actions is enacted in the frequent use of causative verbs in Urdu, formed through the addition of the suffix -a or -wa to the verb stem, which yields the meaning of "to cause to have done" the action designated by the verb. For example, the causative form of *karna* (to do) is *karana* or *karwana* (to have done). This form represents the subject as the agent of actions done by another. The do-it-yourself manual genre is entirely absent in Pakistan. The only analogous genre, though itself rare, is what might be described as the "have-it-done-yourself" manual. One such manual, entitled *Makan Khud Banwaen* (Have Your House Built Yourself), extols the advantages, satisfactions, and virtues of personally directing the contractor who oversees the building of your house and provides the technical knowledge necessary for such oversight (Qureshi 1995).[7] An extraordinary example of this grammatically represented mediation of action is the use of the verb *mangwana* (to have something asked for). Officers, for example, occasionally direct their PAs with the imperative "*Chai mangwao*" (Have tea asked for), which projects the bringing of tea as involving four persons: the officer, the PA, the addressee of the PA, and the menial who actually brings the tea.

The relations of officers and low-level staff within the office often parallel or even merge with those of master and servant in domestic spaces. Although many officers are much younger than the menials who serve them, officers often address them, not as subordinates, but with kin terms commonly used with domestic servants, such as *beta* (son). Newspapers occasionally report that officers have taken this personalization and "domestication" of servants beyond the limits of the law, installing them in their houses as domestic servants, cooks, or gardeners, while they remain on government salary. Judging by similar articles from the early 1960s, this is a long-standing practice. A newspaper article from 1965, for example, reported that an officer was charged with having a salaried government servant work privately (*naji kam*) at his home as a cook for over six months.[8] Since many officers live in government housing, these low-level employees cross a faint boundary between office and home to become servants.

A senior officer of the ICTA, whom I'll call Zaffar Khan, was a virtuoso of office practice. Already a grade 20 officer when I first met him in the late 1990s, Zaffar Khan is the second son of a native prince of the British empire who ruled a small territory in what was called the Northwest Frontier Province, recently renamed Khyber Pakhtunkhwa. It is a point of pride for Zaffar Khan that his family was never defeated by the British, but the family was less successful against the Pakistan state, which expropriated most of the family lands under Zulfiqar Ali Bhutto's so-called land reforms in the mid-1970s. However, he and his brother still maintain substantial land holdings and remain the leading notables of the area. He is related by marriage to one of the most powerful political families in Pakistan. After attending the elite Aitcheson College in Lahore, Zaffar Khan entered government service as an elite officer.[9] Although proud of being a government servant, he maintains equal pride in being a landed elite (or a "feudal," as detractors call them). Zaffar Khan's lordly manner gave his office more the atmosphere of a *durbar* (a princely court) than a drawing room. While his office practice was exceptional, it is illustrative in its exaggeration. His office was typical of senior officers, with a desk, chairs, a couch, and a couple of stuffed chairs arranged around a coffee table in the corner. But Zaffar Khan put this arrangement to unusual use. As Raby (1985) has pointed out in her study of a Sri Lankan bureaucracy, the "seat" is a central artifact in South Asian bureaucracies. The difference between a "seat" and a "chair" is important. In Islamabad offices, as in Euro-American organizations, the "chair" in "chairman" is a conventional symbol of formal position, a conceptual bundle of powers only weakly associated with an actual chair. In contrast, the "seat" is a much more material entity, something actively occupied in the act of wielding power and authority. An officer who, in American terms, is "away from his desk," in Islamabad, is "not on his seat." Zaffar Khan proudly identified as a "government servant," which meant for him that he was an elite member of the Civil Service of Pakistan cadre. But he enacted his distance from the workaday bureaucratic role by never sitting in the chair behind his desk, always occupying instead the stuffed chair in the corner, a perfect structural reversal of the bureaucratic organization of the office space (fig. 2.3). He had his two phones moved to the little table beside this chair and the button for his buzzer installed, oddly, on the seat cushion, toward the back. All official written work was done among the tea mugs and ashtrays on the coffee table.

Since he was an officer with many friends, influential connections, and authority over a wide range of government activities in the city (including police, land revenue, mosques, and commerce), traffic through his office was heavy. It was not uncommon for him to hold court for as many as nine or ten "guests," who were distributed on the chairs and couch roughly according to status. During the first period of my research, a government doctor with a rural post who was working his connections to secure a transfer to Islamabad spent most of the working day in Zaffar Khan's office. A large, portly fellow with a hearty laugh, he played Ed McMahon to Zaffar Khan's Johnny Carson. He often arrived with Zaffar Khan and would sit on the couch on the end nearest him. As guests would arrive, he would move down the couch, giving the guests pride of place nearest Zaffar Khan. He provided a kind of verbal MSG for Zaffar Khan's discourse, amplifying its humor, disgust, disbelief, triumph, and regret with additive commentary. When a new guest arrived, those already present would size him up, yield a seat commensurate with his apparent status, then all shift their seats. If there was no more space on the couch, one of the chairs near the desk would be pulled toward the coffee table and turned to face Zaffar Khan's direction. (These chairs were used only in this manner, but every evening Zaffar Khan's peon would reposition them in their normal place facing the desk, as if hopeful that his officer would one day reform and assume his proper seat.) If this process did not position the new entrant in his appropriate place, Zaffar Khan himself would often direct a rearrangement, as when a former minister of the North West Frontier Province ended up relegated to the far end of the couch. He would invite close friends and very important guests to sit on the seat to his left, a chair most people avoided since it meant that Zaffar Khan had to twist uncomfortably to talk to the occupant. Zaffar Khan smoked constantly and liberally provided tea for his guests (in generous mugs rather than the typical little cups), reaching behind himself to press the buzzer to summon his peon, then barely interrupting the flow of his speech to fling a cursory "*Chai*" (Tea) in his direction.

Much of the conversation in Zaffar Khan's office concerned national

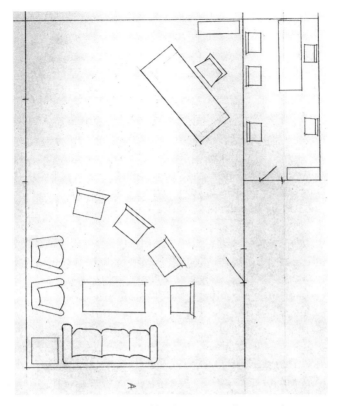

FIGURE 2.3. Zaffar Khan's office, late 1990s. (Illustration by Krisztina Fehérváry.)

politics or events within the bureaucracy. In the lulls of such conversation, Zaffar Khan, like other officers, would shift his attention between his guests, deftly speaking, in turn, English, Urdu, Punjabi, or Pashto, each time moving a little bit forward in his discussion of the matters that concerned them. He chose his languages tactically. Shifting into the "mother tongue" of his addressee, he would make him feel directly engaged. Sometimes he would pick his language to create the discursive space of a private colloquy in the middle of the group by choosing a language known to his addressee but poorly controlled by or completely incomprehensible to others in the room. These subtle and infrequent movements forward often continued for hours—to the manifest frustration of many guests—not ending until Zaffar Khan himself tired of their company or had to leave. At such points, if he did not request that they return the next day, he would suddenly call for the required letters or files to sign, phone the necessary official, or send the guest off to the appropriate contact.

This method of doing of business is not high on the list of common complaints about the bureaucracy, but it does occasionally come in for criticism. Once, I was sitting with a CDA officer when a man was admitted to the office. When the officer offered him tea, he turned to me and quipped, "If you sit down and he doesn't offer you anything, you know you get your work. He is offering me tea, so I will not get my work!" In the early days of Zia-ul-Haq's martial law, the Martial Law Administrator of Punjab Zone A issued Instruction No. 5. This stated that "it has been noticed that visitors normally disturb the Administrators in efficiently performing their duties during working hours" and directed that "no visitor will be allowed to visit any official office before 12 noon except those on official duty/purpose."[10] A number of officers and others familiar with American office practices considered Pakistani office practice yet another index of Pakistan's backwardness. In reply to a question from me about this office practice, one such officer lamented, "Norms and systems have not been developed here." A private architect and planner with experience working in Nigeria told me that this practice showed Pakistan was behind even Nigeria: "The people here are not cultured." For such critics, good norms, systems, and even culture require that nothing enter into bureaucratic interactions but the formal equality of individuals before the law.

PARCHIS, CONNECTIONS, AND RECOGNITION

Although forms of interaction in offices converge with those of drawing rooms, office interactions are complexly mediated by paper, particularly parchis or "chits" and, as I'll show later, petitions. Unlike domestic hosts who typically greet guests at the gates of their properties or at least the door of their houses, officers almost never emerge from their offices to receive visitors. A friend of mine illustrated the rarity of such a greeting by recounting a recent meeting he'd had with the director of the Directorate of Worker's Education, a grade 20 officer. After he sent in his card, a man wearing shalwar-kamiz, rather than a shirt and pants, came out of the office to meet him. From his dress and greeting, my friend assumed he was the director's peon and asked again to meet the director. The man, who in fact was the director, accepting the mistake in good fun, went back into his office, pressed his foot buzzer, and instructed his peon to admit the man sitting outside. For my friend, the officer's emergence from his office was enough to mark him as a subordinate, though he later understood the director's manner as an expression of his populist convictions and humble social origins. Visitors to offices often avoid confusions of identity by negotiating access to offices and their occupants with paper in one of two forms: a chit or parchi; or a business or visiting card. These forms of paper mediate encounters between visitors and officers by materially testifying to and helping to constitute the relations individuals have with institutions and powerful supporters.

The words "chit" and "parchi" are similarly used to refer to slips of paper that visitors present to the personal assistants of officers before they are admitted. However, of the two the English term "chit" (derived from the Hindi/Urdu word *chitthi*) is morally much more neutral, because it is associated with formal, if obstructionist, bureaucracy. The chit is typically a small scrap of paper with the visitor's name, position, and perhaps a word or two regarding the matter the visitor wishes to discuss. Alternatively, it may be a note from a powerful individual recommending aid to the bearer. Older officers told me that twenty to thirty years ago, one was required to send a chit in to the officer before being admitted. Officers don't demand them routinely nowadays but do in some cases. A village leader from western Islamabad involved in disputes with the CDA over land expropriation complained to me that the CDA chairman wouldn't admit him to his office without a chit from the wafaqi mohtasib (the federal ombudsman). This sort of referral is entirely proper, without the taint of undue influence.

In contrast, the defining feature of a parchi is the name of a powerful person who requests that a favor be granted to the bearer. In common discourse, *parchi* is virtually synonymous with *sifarish*, a connection or "approach." Critics of government corruption decry Pakistan's "parchi system" and "parchi culture." A person holding a position through connections rather than merit can be called a "*parchiwala*" or simply a "parchi." A popular Pakistan television comedy in the 1980s called *Parchi* featured the exploits of a character always on the hunt for opportunities to be gained through use of parchis. A movie released in 2003, *Baba Parchi,* similarly centers on a character who strives to obtain a parchi without which he will not be able secure a job.

In 2008, an extraordinary contemporary example of a parchi, purportedly from the sister of Prime Minister Yousuf Raza Gilani, was posted on the web for ridicule and condemnation (fig. 2.4). It was a "form" parchi created on printed letterhead, with the common Arabic

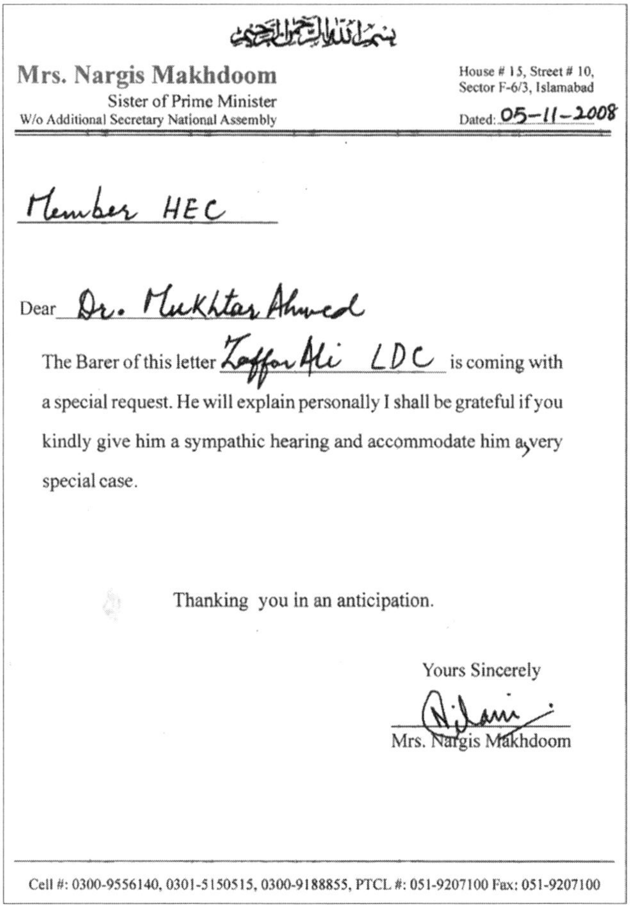

بسم الله الرحمن الرحيم

Mrs. Nargis Makhdoom
Sister of Prime Minister
W/o Additional Secretary National Assembly

House # 15, Street # 10,
Sector F-6/3, Islamabad
Dated: 05-11-2008

Member HEC

Dear Dr. Mukhtar Ahmed

The Barer of this letter Zaffar Ali LDC is coming with a special request. He will explain personally I shall be grateful if you kindly give him a sympathic hearing and accommodate him a very special case.

Thanking you in an anticipation.

Yours Sincerely

Mrs. Nargis Makhdoom

Cell #: 0300-9556140, 0301-5150515, 0300-9188855, PTCL #: 051-9207100 Fax: 051-9207100

FIGURE 2.4. "Parchi letter" allegedly from the desk of the prime minister's sister (www.flikr.com posted 2008).

Islamic injunction "In the name of Allah, the Gracious, the Merciful" (Bismillah al-Rahman al-Rahim) at the top. "Mrs. Nargis Makhdoom" is identified as both the "Sister of the Prime Minister" and wife of ("W/o") Additional Secretary National Assembly. The parchi form has a generic message, indicating that the "Barer of this letter [sic] . . . is coming with a special request. He will explain personally. I shall be grateful if you kindly give him a sympathetic hearing and accommodate him a very special case." Spaces were left open so the names of the recipient and client with the special request could simply be filled in—in this case that of a member of the Higher Education Commission

("HEC") and a humble lower-division clerk ("LDC"). Many participants in online forums doubted the authenticity of the parchi, but more assumed its authenticity and went on to comment on its significance.[11] Many expressed shock and outrage at the blatant use of a form ("probably printed by a government office!" exclaimed one post), but few were surprised that papers invoking the support of powerful patrons were being used to gain access to officers. If it is a forgery, then, like all forgeries that are taken seriously, it is close enough to what a good many Pakistanis imagine to be the paper forms of connection among elites, subalterns, and the bureaucracy. It was clearly in the realm of the possible even for the prime minister's press secretary, who was reported to have claimed, "if Nargis Makhdoom had printed such a letterhead, then she had not sought prior permission of the PM for this."[12] The press secretary added that the "Prime Minister Yousuf Raza Gilani has issued strict instructions to his family members not to use his name to influence anyone in any way."[13]

Today, printed visiting cards are more commonly used in bureaucratic encounters than are handwritten pieces of paper. Pakistani visiting cards are just like business cards used elsewhere in the world, including a name, title, logo or institutional symbol, and contact information. The only difference is that these elements are sometimes printed on both sides, on the front (as defined by the side most commonly presented up) in English and on the back in Urdu. And, much like elsewhere in the world, visitors present a card to PAs and officers to identify themselves and provide contact information. In Islamabad, however, visitors sometimes present not their *own* card, but that of *another,* usually a powerful politician or government officer, situating the visiting card within the long-standing and morally fraught practices of the parchi. The card of a powerful person serves as his emblem and implies a material and therefore social relation of support between him and the bearer. Often the influential person will pen a brief, signed note on the back vaguely directing that the bearer (usually identified by name) should be assisted in any way possible. If such notes are not addressed to a specific individual (implicitly, a kind of "to whom it may concern"), they are returned to the bearer, making them reusable instruments of access. Early in my research, while perplexed by the frequent requests for my own visiting card bearing the seal of my graduate institution, I distributed them liberally (sometimes two or three to a person), though I don't know if they were a help to anyone. Low-ranking staff, policemen, and guards (*chowkidar*s) would sometimes ask me to pen and sign an English testimonial on the back that the person (identified by name) is a good man ("*accha admi*") and my friend ("*dost*"). While cards with a signed request are the most influential, even unsigned cards without a message serve the bearer as political currency, because of the assumption that the source of the card must be the hand of the powerful person himself. A printer in Islamabad who prints visiting cards for a large number of powerful officers makes good use of this assumption. He always keeps for himself a few of the cards he prints and files them carefully. With a well-chosen card, he can facilitate his business in any office he deals with. Although he was on good terms with most of the officers whose cards he printed, it is unclear if many would have given him carte blanche to use their cards as he did.

The role of chits and visiting cards is made clearest on those occasions when they are not used, when visitors turn up empty handed, undocumented, and unendorsed and simply ask to see the officer. Personal assistants are acute judges of who should be immediately admitted with a quick introduction and who should wait outside the door pending approval of the officer. PAs, assuming the status and interests of the officers they serve, receive would-be entrants with something of the warmth, indifference, or arrogance they judge the entrant might expect from the officer himself. Thus, junior officers seeking access to the offices of senior officers are often treated rather disrespectfully by PAs, who would never respond to an officer in this fashion if they were not elevated by their relation to their officer. PAs permit the close friends of officers and visitors of obviously high status or known influence to walk in immediately.

PAs do, however, sometimes misjudge entrants. These misjudgments highlight a practical problem of ethics organized around individual status in social life at larger, urban scales: Encounters often occur in which the status of an individual is not known to interlocutors and cannot be certainly discerned. My questions to Islamabad residents about how accurately they could judge the status (*haisiyat*) of individuals they encounter from their appearance always provoked lively discussion. Most bureaucratic staff would measure status by "grade," that is, their bureaucratic rank according to the numbered Basic Pay Scale. Noting this tendency, one junior officer laughingly told me, "People in Islamabad especially are concerned about the grade of the person," contrasting the city with Lahore and Karachi. Some claimed to be able to determine with some precision a person's exact scale and to discern not only how much wealth he or she possesses, but the legality or illegality of its source. Most, however, commonly admitted that from appearance and manner of speaking they can only make a guess. In urban Pakistan, this fact makes the performance of status (normatively anchored in land, monetary wealth, family, and government position) as important as it is in places like the United States, where the presentation of self is itself seen to be a major constituent of status or social identity more generally (Goffman 1959, 1974). A senior official of the Islamabad administration recalled to me that he ran into his immediate subordinate one night in Jinnah Supermarket, the premier shopping center in the city. As they were chatting, a car came down one of the streets of the market and an attractive young woman threw a beer bottle out the window of her SUV. As officials with authority over the police, it was incumbent upon them to do something. However, the official told me he just looked at his subordinate and said, "Run for your life!" and they both bolted. The official explained, "She was trouble. If she was behaving like that, she was someone's daughter or someone's mistress and either way best left alone." The normative requirement to respond to individuals according to their status is commonly complicated by an ignorance of that status, a difficulty often faced in unstructured interactions within urban spaces of general circulation (public spaces) such as markets and the counters of public services.

The performative dimension of status in such settings is illustrated by a joke in Pakistan about an unsophisticated village man trying to go through a palace gate guarded by a Sikh. The setup is strikingly similar to Kafka's short parable in *The Trial* in which a country man begs a doorkeeper to be admitted through a gate to The Law, growing old and finally dying in futile longing for admission. The theme of the Pakistani joke, however, is not the transcendent inaccessibility of order, but rather its accessibility through the successful performance of status.

> A villager comes to the gate of the palace and is uncertain whether he will be allowed to enter. He holds back and watches as several men in succession walk through the gate, past the Sikh guard who doesn't even look at them. Seeing no difference between the men and himself, he gains confidence. He walks up to the Sikh and asks, "May I enter?" The Sikh replies curtly, "No." After pondering the refusal for a moment, the man objects, "But you let those other men through." The Sikh answers, "Well, you didn't see them ask for permission, did you?"

While bureaucratic functionaries are obviously much more likely than interlocutors in markets to know one another's identity or at least recognize one another's status, misfires also occur in bureaucratic settings. One senior officer of the Islamabad Administration recalled to me how he had once gone to see an officer under his authority who had never met him. The junior officer was probably confused by the senior officer's shalwar-kamiz, uncommon dress for a man of his position, which he had adopted after joining the Tablighi Jamaat, an Islamic pietist movement. According to the senior officer, after the junior officer treated him badly, saying he didn't have time to talk with him, he told him, "Well then, I will just order you to come to my office and you will have to come!" The junior officer immediately changed his manner and began to apologize profusely, saying, "I didn't know who you were." Another senior officer told me a similar story about how he had gone to the Ministry of Culture to meet a junior officer. The junior officer's PA perfunctorily told him he would have to wait. After three-quarters of an hour waiting in his car, he returned and began to menace the PA. In response to his assertiveness, the PA anxiously asked, "Who are you?" (*Aap kaun hen?*). As these examples suggest, dress is an important indicator of status but is often not adequate to place an individual socially. Proud demeanor is, if not a more certain index, one doubted with greater risk.

PETITIONS: CITIZENS, BUREAUCRATS, AND SUPPLICANTS

In the graphic ideology of liberal Pakistanis, parchis and petitions ideally are opposites in form and in the relationships they constitute and represent. Parchis are sized for the pockets that carry them unofficially; petitions are sized for the files that convey them officially. (Thus the A4-size paper of the alleged parchi of the prime minister's sister was another violation of parchi norms.) If parchis stitch together an opaque world of private, discreet connections and call for special treatment, petitions are an open engagement with government, publicly invoking their citizen signatories' rights to or needs for just treatment under policies and laws. Parchis are drafted for the use of others, explicitly invoking their bearers' dependence on the more powerful; they are representations by others. Petitions are the documents of formally autonomous citizens, self-representations submitted under the names and signatures of their principals. The meanings and effects of parchis are deeply dependent on the contexts in which they are deployed: they are trafficked in undocumented face-to-face encounters of bureaucrats and clients, read, and then secreted in the pockets of their bearers or addressees. Parchis mark the absence of their writers but require the presence of their beneficiaries, animated if not by the voice then at least by the hands of their bearers. Petitions, in contrast, are written to stand on their own, their signatures a graphic proxy for the presence of their writers. They straightaway take their place within the open, robust, artifactual documentary order of the bureaucracy through formal procedures of registration and other practices of written response. Parchis represent the proximity of their bearers to wealth and power and can only be used by those able to establish such proximity. Petitions provide a substitute for this proximity. Although the capacity to produce institutionally acceptable petitions is differentially distributed, petitioning is a basic political right, and petitions are artifacts that may be submitted by the humblest people.

In practice, however, petitions are often drawn into the parchi politics to which they are ideally opposed. One day, I was sitting in Zaffar Khan's usual gathering when a lower-division clerk in service to the ICTA administration was admitted. He couldn't think of sitting down. He walked straight over to Zaffar Khan, greeted him solemnly and respectfully, and handed him a single sheet of paper. When Zaffar Khan asked what it was, the man began to tear up as he told him that he has been at the same grade for fifteen years and has no hope for promotion. He said that the paper was a petition for a promotion. He had personally presented it to no less a person than then Prime Minister Nawaz Sharif in a public meeting. Sharif had promised to help, but nothing had come of it. By the time he finished telling his story, he was sobbing. He suddenly went to his knees and leaned into Zaffar Khan who held him firmly as he wept on his shoulder. Zaffar Khan told the man reassuringly that he would try to do something. After the clerk had been comforted and left, Zaffar Khan told me bluntly that, in view of the law banning the creation of new posts in force at the time, he was powerless to help the man. Nevertheless, Zaffar Khan, with more care than usual, initialed the petition and directed his assistant to register it and introduce it into the procedures of bureaucratic consideration. The man's petition was a political act of self-representation, but his dramatic abasement before Zaffar Khan showed it would need a patron to be effective. As we'll see, this ambivalence concerning the character and efficacy of petitions also shapes their discourse.

Broadly conceptualized as documents directed to an established authority requesting a favor or redress of a grievance, petitions have received much scholarly attention (van Voss 2001) because they expressly articulate political relationships: Identifiable groups and individuals explicitly address particular authorities with a clear request or grievance. I argue in this book that, like petitions, documents such as Out of Turn Allotment forms, lists, files, and sector maps are also instruments of dissent and negotiation between the populace and government. But unlike such documents, petitions tell us much about how government is normatively perceived and engaged by those outside it. Commonly used throughout South Asia (Cody 2009), petitions are particularly important as representations and enactments of normative political subjectivity in Islamabad, a city with no representative municipal institutions to channel the expression of popular political will. Petitions also offer bureaucrats a very different sort of engagement with the populace than the one provided by bureaucratic techniques of documentation (Scott 1998), giving bureaucrats a view of how the populace sees the state.

Petitions are central artifacts constituting political subjects in Islamabad, but they do not converge on a singular normative subject. Furthermore, practices of submitting petitions reveal the doubts of petitioners about the adequacy of any of these forms of political subjectivity and the efficacy of the artifacts that constitute them. In practice, petitioners recognize the inability of petitions to stand for them in their absence by complementing them with the presence of parchis.

As van Voss points out, if we define the genre broadly, "petitions seem to be a global phenomenon, stretching back in time almost as far as writing" (2001:2). Although modern petitions are commonly associated with constitutions and democratic bodies, petitions have been an integral part of political orders of all kinds. Contemporary Pakistani petitions are not only instances of a global phenomenon; they have a global history. Many of their contemporary features and uses took their form in the colonial period as English and South Asian practices of petitioning combined in the practices of early East India Company rule. South Asian petitions emerged from colonial rule as a multivalent genre, employing the idioms of modern democratic citizenship, bureaucratic process, and subordination within a kingly or modern authoritarian order. The present Pakistan state, as a combination of democratic and authoritarian governmental processes, has maintained the political vitality of all these idioms, provoking petitioners to constitute themselves as supplicants, citizens, bureaucrats, or some ambiguous combination of the three.

Petitioning had been a part of English political practice since at least the medieval period. As David Zaret argues, quoting a seventeenth-century commentator, petitioning was "the indisputable right of the meanest subject" (1999:86). But as late as the Renaissance period, petitions had little to do with individual rights. They were rather deferential requests or expressions of grievances that emphasized the prerogative of authority in a society whose politics were structured by deference and patronage. Petitions constituted "a privileged communicative space" that offered petitioners "limited immunity to norms that otherwise restricted public commentary on political matters" (Zaret 1999:88). Part of a political culture oriented to central authority, petitions had to express "deference, humility, and supplication" (81). Yet, despite their comfortable place in a hierarchical world, petitions played an important role in the rise of democratic concepts and institutions. By the middle of the seventeenth century, petitions increasingly found their way into print and began to address an anonymous audience of readers rather than specific authorities and to assume the voice of public opinion. While retaining some of the rhetoric of deference, petitions increasingly included demands for the recognition of rights rather than pleas for the favor of authorities.

Petitions were even more central to political practice of the Mughal empire and the kingdoms that succeeded it. Although the importance of broad administrative policies within the empire should not be underplayed (Richards 1993), much of the imperial political process consisted of the acceptance or rejection of petitions to officials at all levels expressing requests or grievances. S.I.A. Zaidi (2005) catalogs the variety of issues of the day that were settled by petitioners. Petitions presented to emperors included requests to return to court, to celebrate the emperor's birthday, to retire from military service, and to be appointed to administrative office. Lower officials received petitions from workmen who had not been paid, clerks whose immediate superiors unjustly refused to sign the salary voucher, and landowners tangled in controversies over mortgages.

As Zaidi observes, "there was a well established and sophisticated mechanism to file petitions to superior authorities" (2005:14). Higher-ranking Mughal officers were served by an *arz-begi,* an officer whose job was to receive petitions, prepare a summary of their contents (*yaddashti*), present them to the officer with authority in the matter, and record his decision. As in all communications within the imperial arena, the status relation of the petitioner and the receiver of the petition was central. This status relation was the criterion for Mughal categorization of petitions: *arzdasht* was the term for a petition from anyone to the emperor; *ariza* and *arzi* designated petitions from employees to patrons or nobles; *vajib al-arz* denoted an administrative epistle from a subordinate to a superior official; finally, *iltimas* was a general term covering a petition submitted to an authority by any person (Mohiuddin 1971:151–52).

The material form, the manner of presentation, and the language of petitions worked in concert to enact a strong hierarchical bond between petitioner and addressee. Petitions to royals and others of high status were sometimes gold flecked or gold sprinkled (Zaidi 2005:13). The petitioner or some worthy intermediary would ceremonially present the petition to the officer during occasions reserved for such approaches. The petition was a genre within the comprehensive art of letter writing (*insha*), which was revered by the nobility "as a form of regulating proper social relations" (Bayly 1996:76). A large number of practitioners of this art, *munshi*s, produced petitions of exquisite graciousness using a flowery Persian that was "not mere verbosity" but a device "for painting pictures in words and illuminating rank" and for establishing a strong affective bond between petitioner and addressee (77). Addressees of petitions were not addressed by proper name but by third-person plural pronouns qualified by adjectives of praise, words such as, in the case of the emperor and princes, *hazrat* (excellent, eminent, holy) and *alampanah* (asylum of the world). They were dense with terms of devotion such as *murid* (disciple, follower), *fidvi* (devoted servant), *ghulam* (slave) or of abjectness such as *kamtareen* (lowly one) or *faqir* (beggar) (Mohiuddin 1971:155–6). Petitions concluded with a prayer for the addressee that varied with his rank, fusing the language of prayer, praise, and petitioning.[14]

As the Company operations expanded in India in the late seventeenth century, Company servants added another strain of bureaucratic rhetoric to the mix of monarchial deference and the assertion of rights found in petitions addressed to governmental authorities. Company servants taking issue with the decisions of their superiors often went outside the normal hierarchical chains of communication to appeal to higher authorities. Such appeals were respectful and deferential but appealed matter-of-factly neither to general political rights or norms nor to patrimonial favor, but to the bureaucratic discretion of senior officials in applying rules or extending precedents. During the colonial period, petitions from Indian subjects combined these various practices of petitioning in highly variable mixes. As Laura Bear has observed about petitions from railway employees in the colonial era, "we do not have a simple recurrence of older forms of address; instead we have a palimpsest of experiments" in how to address authorities (2007:116).

The linguistic register of Mughal petitions translated into the grandiloquent "Babu English," which combined profuse praise for the power and virtue of the Company and, later, imperial officials, extravagant accounts of hardship and grievance, and demands for benevolence (Bear 2007:114; Raman 2007:319–21). Colonial officials viewed such petitions as the product of a "native propensity" for exaggeration and misrepresentation (Raman 2007:321), and British translators of Persian and vernacular-language petitions tended to omit florid passages altogether (Bayly 1996:78). Bhavani Raman sees in early colonial petitioners the emergence of a new Company subject deploying older idioms in vastly changed political circumstances. Petitioning was a gesture that was simultaneously "compliant and defiant," a form of both "dissent and negotiation" (Raman 2007:301), a central means through which "questions of the sovereignty of Company rule and the self-fashioning of subject petitioner were constantly renegotiated" (299).

Indians from across the social spectrum eagerly seized on what they recognized as a Company obsession with mediating its activities with documents, in particular, signed self-representations. Adapting English political traditions to Company practice, an early-nineteenth-century governor of Madras called petitioning a "natural right" (Brimnes 1998:146). Although many Indian scribes of the precolonial clerical establishment were recruited into the Company and, later, imperial government of India (Bayly 1996:73–78), others established a vibrant business preparing petitions. According to one late-nineteenth-century observer,

> The production of petitions is quite an industry in India. Every town of any importance had its petition writer as it has its solicitor or its doctor and the larger towns have scores. The lower class Indian whether he be a government servant or a domestic in the household of a European, has a great faith in the efficacy of written appeals. It may be a rise of pay, a spell of holiday, or an appointment for some relative that he wants—whatever it is, he avails himself of the epistolary talents of a letter writer, who for a modest sum of money, speedily furnishes him with a moving appeal to his employer or official superior. There is no attempt made to conceal the source of origin of these productions. In the market places and street corners, the ingenious scribe may be seen with his legs tucked under him—a rude writing pad on his knee laboriously writing out, with the aid of a native reed about the thickness of a walking stick, the communication, which his humble patron

who squats placidly by his side, pours into his ear. Naturally in the process of translation the sentiments of the customer are curiously presented and as often as not the petition furnishes material for the merriment in the family circle of its recipient (Wright 1891; cited in Raman 2007:300).

Today the issues of petitions submitted to the CDA and the ICTA are as varied as the kinds of activities these organizations are involved in. Petitions request the construction of drains; the repair of roads; the installation of lights; the approval of government posts, transfers, and promotions; better compensation for expropriated land; the allocation of plots for private houses or mosques; and the sectarian allocation of planned mosque sites. What I am calling "petitions" are written communications that their writers call, in English, an "application," "petition," "appeal," or "request," and, in Urdu, an "*arz*" or "*darkhwast*." In internal government writings, they are most frequently referred to with the depoliticizing bureaucratic terms "application" and "letter," but references to "requests" and "appeals" are also common. Accounts of such communications within newspapers usually call them by more overtly political terms: "darkhwast" (application, entreaty, petition, appeal), "petitions," and sometimes even "*multalbat*" (demands).

The petitions that I examined were submitted to the CDA from the early 1960s through 2005; they vary considerably, but their layouts and discourse genres are very stable through this period. They are written in both English and Urdu, but even petitioners in Urdu display a good familiarity with English-language bureaucratic terms. Like spoken Urdu in Islamabad, Urdu petitions usually include a large number of English-language bureaucratic acronyms (for example, "CDA," "NOC" [No Objection Certificate], "BUP" [built-up property]) and words ("surrender certificate," "award," "family unit," "bulldoze") rendered in either Roman or Perso-Arabic script.

English-language petitions are occasionally handwritten, but most often they are produced on typewriters or, increasingly since the mid-1990s, computers. Petitions on major issues were sometimes printed, though the computer has taken over this role in the last couple of decades. Many English-language petitions are produced in government offices: officers often have their staff type up petitions as they would a final copy of any official letter; staff also produce them for themselves on office typewriters. Urdu petitions are sometimes penned by the untrained hand of the petitioner, but they are more commonly written by a trained scribe who helps the petitioner shape the language as well.

The role of a scribe in Islamabad, however, is rather more calligraphic than elsewhere in Pakistan and India (Cody 2009), since an understanding of bureaucratic language processes is widely distributed in a city of so many government servants. People connected with government departments overseeing Islamic matters, where Urdu typewriters are commonly used, often submit petitions in typewritten Urdu.

The material production of petitions is part of the enactment of political subjectivity. The handwriting of parchis is valued for its material connection to the writer and his or her unique investment in the bearer—hence, the mocking of the alleged parchi form of the prime minister's sister. By contrast, petitions are valued for their public connections to education and wealth, which are indexed by the quality of their production. Better-produced ones, especially those in English, receive greater regard.[15] For this reason, when petitioners repeatedly submit petitions, each is usually "better" produced than the last. For example, the first submission in Urdu might be in an untrained hand and subsequent ones by a calligrapher; Urdu petitions are sometimes followed by English-language ones.

We can distinguish three different political subjects enacted through petitions: the citizen, the bureaucrat, and the supplicant. It should be clear from what I have written so far that petitions are mixed, in language (English and Urdu), script, discourse, signatures, and graphic layout.[16] Likewise, some petitioners deploy the language of all three kinds of subjects to persuade the government to act in their favor, at turns demanding their rights, abjectly praising an officer, and requesting some particular document. However, petitioners enact these forms of political personhood in particular discursive and graphic genres of petitions, and we turn to these now.

From the early 1960s, during both martial-law and civilian governments, residents of the area have submitted petitions as citizens appealing for their rights in the liberal tradition. Although the language of these petitions is deferential and patriotic, demands for the recognition of rights are forthright. Consider a petition written in 1964 from an association of villagers whose land had been expropriated. Chapter 4 will discuss the substance of this conflict, but here I would like to draw attention to how the petition enacts the rights-bearing citizen. The petition begins with an extensive testimony to the patriotism of the petitioners:

We the affected and displaced persons welcome the shifting of the Capital from Karachi to the Site named Islamabad. We assure you, sir, that our patriotism is none the less than our other countrymen, and we grudge no sacrifice to be too high if made for National Interests and for the solidarity of our country. We realise and sincerely take pride in the fact that our hearths and homes and all other things appurtenant thereto, have been and are being taken over for the higher interests of the Nation.

Having declared that they are patriotic citizens, the petitioners bluntly assert that the government has trampled on their rights as property owners:

Notwithstanding the above considerations, we believe that when lands and houses are being acquired on compensatory basis, it shall not be inconsistent to demand that the considerations of Natural justice and fairplay shall not have been ignored. Basically, it was unjust that a special law should have been formulated for acquisition of Capital site with provisions stricter and water-tight than the General Law of acquisition prevalent in the land.[17]

The petitioners argue that by taking their lands to give to others the government is creating a "disparity" among citizens, violating egalitarian norms of citizenship. The petition goes on to articulate six "genuine grievances and demands for their redress and relief" using an active voice: "we submit with full force at our command." Although the petition is deferential to the overarching authority of "our benign Govt.," it never acknowledges the bureaucratic authority of officials in setting expropriation policy. It repeatedly portrays the actions of specific officers involved in expropriation in relation to a general standard of justice embodied by the government as a whole. One officer's actions are "unwarranted and unjustified in law"; another's are a "travesty of justice and fairplay." Petitioners enact the same political subject in Urdu as well; a petition written in 1991, also about land expropriations, declares that the "rights [haquq] of law-abiding affectees are being trampled" and makes demands (multalbat) for justice (insaf).

The form of such petitions embodies this relationship of citizen and government. It begins with the heading that identifies the petitioners and the general matter:

MEMO OF REPRESENTATION OF GRIEVANCES OF THE AFFECTED AND DISPLACED PERSONS FROM THE ISLAMABAD SITE

Its primary addressee was the President of Pakistan, whom they addressed with the respectful but unelaborated "Sir." Urdu petitions also take this discursive and graphic form, with the addressee addressed in a similarly honorifically neutral register with "janab ali!" (Sir). One important difference between Urdu and English petitions is that Urdu petitions often set the engagement between citizen and government within an Islamic context by beginning with the Quranic invocation "In the name of God, Most Gracious, Most Merciful" (Bismillah al-Rahman al-Rahim) (fig. 2.5).

The significance of this graphic form is clear when we contrast it to the form that petitions in both English and Urdu have increasingly taken over the last few decades: the bureaucratic letter (figs. 2.6 and 2.7). Although petitions taking the form of the bureaucratic letter often speak the language of rights, they are dense with bureaucratic signs. They begin not with a title but with "To:" followed by a title that precisely locates the addressee within a bureaucratic order. The heading of the traditional petition, which gives the petitioner and issue, is analyzed into discrete conceptual and graphic units in the bureaucratic petition: the name of the petitioner follows a "From:" and the issue of the petition is written in underlined text next to "Subject:" or, in Urdu, "*unwan.*" This is followed by the date, which articulates the petition with bureaucratic temporality, unlike petitions taking the more traditional form, which are usually not dated. Petitions from established groups even include a "letter number" or, in Urdu, "*hualeh* number." Often, no number actually follows this heading, which suggests that the letter number is more a means of presenting the petitioner as a bureaucratic entity (a bureaucrat or an organization) than a designation with a functional significance for the petitioner. As in bureaucratic prose of all kinds, every paragraph is numbered. The growing adoption of the bureaucratic form of petition can be seen over the series of petitions submitted by individuals and groups. In the mid-1980s, petitions from the representatives of the mosque Mogheera bin Shobah, for example, were in Urdu and took the traditional form, but by the mid-1990s their petitions are paragons of the English-language bureaucratic petition, even though these latter petitions are typed on Urdu letterhead. In such bureaucratic form petitions, the citizen-government relation is often still central, but the very form of the petition implies a bureaucratic addressee, an effort to articulate the political demands on paramount government with the processes and discretion of bureaucratic activity.

Such hybrid petitions enact the citizen through discourse but the bureaucratic subject through graphic form; the discourse addresses a guardian of the rights of citizens, while the form addresses officials who process paperwork in their sphere of authority. Many other petitions, especially in English, reproduce not only the form but the discourse of

بسم الله الرحمن الرحيم

خدمت جناب ڈائریکٹر لینڈ کیپٹل ڈیولپمنٹ اتھارٹی اسلام آباد

جناب عالی! اہم الہیان بادیہ قادربخش سیکٹر جی-11

متاثرین ہونیکی حیثیت سے حسب ذیل

مستدعی ہیں ۔ ۔ ۔ ۔ ۔ ۔ ۔

حضور والا! نہایت ہی ادب سے گذارش ہے کہ ہم الہیان بادیہ قادربخش سیکٹر جی اسلام آباد کے متاثرین میں ہیں اور اس حیثیت سے چند مطالبات بذریعہ درخواست ہذا جناب کے گوش گذار کرتے ہیں اور واثق امید ہے کہ جناب ہماری درخواست ہذا پر ہمدردانہ غور فرمائیں گے اور درج بالا مطالبات پورے کرنے کے سلسلے میں حکم صادر فرما کر ہماری حوصلہ افزائی فرمائیں گے۔ ہم متاثرین کی گذارشات/مطالبات درج ذیل ہیں۔

دو، یکے س سیکٹر جی-11 میں سی ڈی اے نے 341 پلاٹوں کے آفر لیٹر متاثرین کو جاری جبکہ چند افراد کو اصل الاٹمنٹ لیٹر بھی مل گئے ۔ مگر اکثریتی متاثرین کو اصل لیٹر نہیں وصول ہوئے جنکے جاری کئے جانیکا حکم صادر فرمایا جانا منظوری ہے۔

دو، یکے س سیکٹر آئی-11 اسلام آباد میں ہم نے 273 پلاٹوں کی منظوری دی تھی لیکن ابھی انکو یا اصل الاٹمنٹ متاثرین کو نہ دیئے گئے ہیں۔ اصل الاٹمنٹ کا اجراء کردینے کے سلسلہ میں حکم فرمایا جانا قرین الانصاف ہوگا۔

دو، یکے مورخہ 6 اپریل 1994 کو ہم نے ہمارے مکانات بلڈوز کئے تھے جن میں سے چند معاوضہ پیمنٹ ہوئی ہے۔ لیکن اکثر کو پیمنٹ ہونی باقی ہے۔ جنکی لسٹ میں 188 مکانات بلڈوز ہوچکے ہیں۔

ان ذیل حالات استدعا ہے کہ درخواست ہذا پر غور فرماتے ہوئے مطالبات بالا پورے کئے جانیکا حکم صادر فرمایا جاوے ۔ لہذا از ال ہم ثنا جی-11 عنیفہ جواب دہ کرنے کونیار ہیں۔ مورخہ

الہیان متاثرین سیکٹر جی-11 بادیہ قادربخش

بذریعہ محبوب الٰہی نمبردار بادیہ قادربخش اس

FIGURE 2.5. A petition from residents of the village Badia Qadir Bakhsh in
G-11, 1994.

bureaucratic communication. A petition written in 1994 from an untitled "Management Committee" of residents (including both a chairman and members) from F-10/2 addressed the ICTA in the respectful but nondeferential language that officers use with other government divisions. There are no references to the petitioners' rights or testaments to their good citizenship. In contrast to the active voice of petitioners who make demands, these petitioners laid out a factual case for another mosque in the area, then wrote in the bureaucratic passive voice, "It is, therefore, requested that the permission to allot a plot of land by the CDA may kindly be accorded." Many Urdu petitions are written in a similarly respectful but honorifically neutral language and are equally at ease with bureaucratic procedures, referring to particular letters by CDA number and dating every action mentioned. One villager petitioning the CDA regarding land expropriation did not demand a restoration of his rights but requested that his name be included on a list of residents of a particular village. Such petitioners enact a bureaucratic subject through the use of the discourse that one officer uses to recommend a course of action falling under the authority of another.

Despite the increasingly bureaucratic quality of petitions, older forms of supplication remain vibrant, especially when petitioners can make no strong arguments on the basis of rights or bureaucratic rationality. Consider the petition of an imam written in 1985 to request a plot of land to build a house, written in an elevated, emotionally intense Urdu register dense with honorific language. He opens his petition by describing himself as a pious and dutiful family man deserving of help from the CDA.

> With great courtesy and reverence, I present the submission that I am a humble family man. For around twelve years, in different mosques I have continued to fulfill the duties of pesh imam. And at this time, I am fulfilling the duties of pesh imam at Allah Wali in sector G-7/2.

He explicitly frames his petition as a substitute for the oral pleading he was not able to do.

> For around two years, I had remained present in your esteemed house [*daulat khana*] in the state of a petitioner and at your office many times, but was not permitted to meet you. Two times, a meeting with you took place in your office and you told me to meet with the Director of the C.D.A., Waris sahib. And even after I have already gone round and round the office many times, I have not obtained a hearing.

As Francis Cody has observed with respect to petitioning by uneducated villagers in south India, the imam's petition uses "an interactional

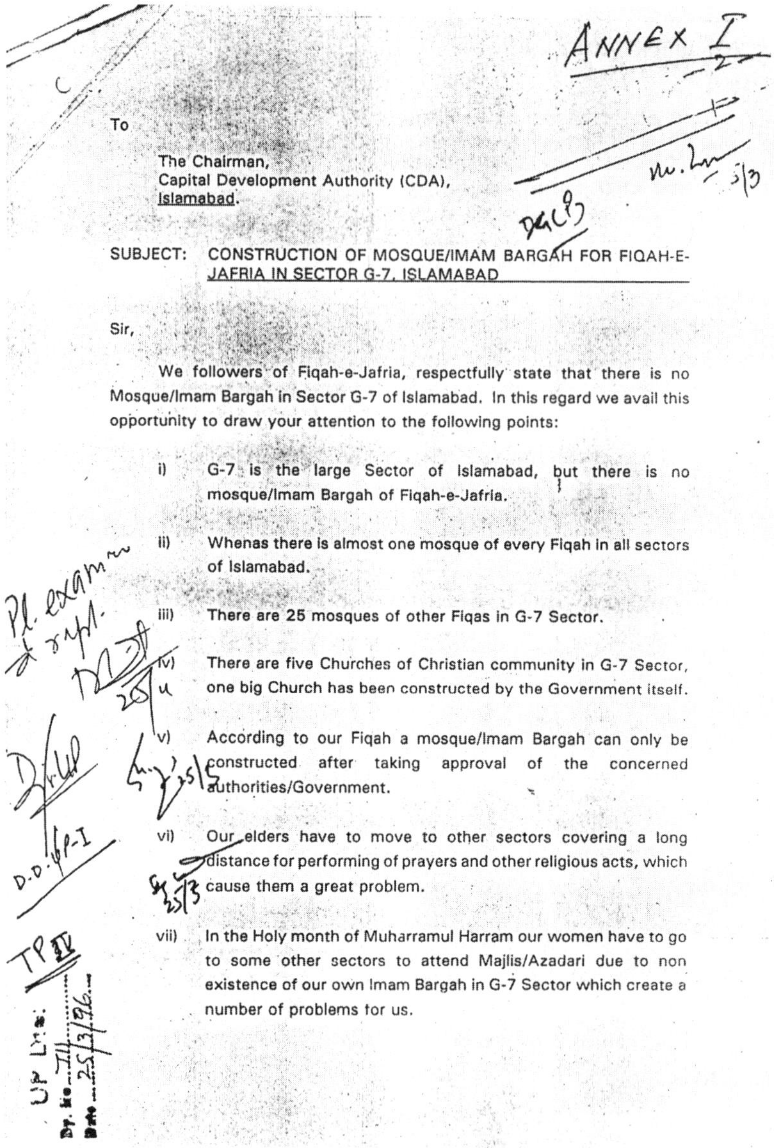

To

The Chairman,
Capital Development Authority (CDA),
Islamabad.

SUBJECT: CONSTRUCTION OF MOSQUE/IMAM BARGAH FOR FIQAH-E-
JAFRIA IN SECTOR G-7, ISLAMABAD

Sir,

We followers of Fiqah-e-Jafria, respectfully state that there is no Mosque/Imam Bargah in Sector G-7 of Islamabad. In this regard we avail this opportunity to draw your attention to the following points:

i)   G-7 is the large Sector of Islamabad, but there is no mosque/Imam Bargah of Fiqah-e-Jafria.

ii)   Whenas there is almost one mosque of every Fiqah in all sectors of Islamabad.

iii)   There are 25 mosques of other Fiqas in G-7 Sector.

iv)   There are five Churches of Christian community in G-7 Sector, one big Church has been constructed by the Government itself.

v)   According to our Fiqah a mosque/Imam Bargah can only be constructed after taking approval of the concerned authorities/Government.

vi)   Our elders have to move to other sectors covering a long distance for performing of prayers and other religious acts, which cause them a great problem.

vii)   In the Holy month of Muharramul Harram our women have to go to some other sectors to attend Majlis/Azadari due to non existence of our own Imam Bargah in G-7 Sector which create a number of problems for us.

FIGURE 2.6. First page of a petition for a Shia mosque in G-7, 1995.

2. Keeping in view the above facts and problems of Shias living in Sector G-7, our grievances may be redressed constructing a mosque/Imam Bargah in G-7 Sector. It may also be mentioned here that there are two plots in this sector where CDA has planned to construct Public Parks, one plot is located near F.G. Girls School No.9 and second near WAPDA Office/ADBP Colony. Construction of mosque/Imam Bargah for Fiqah e Jafria on one of the above plots may be approved and oblige us.

Yours faithfully,

Followers of Fiqah-e-Jafria
residing in Sector G-7, Islamabad

1. Syed Zahoorul Hassan

2. Syed Sibtain Hussain

3. Syed Wazir Ali

4. Syed Al-Murtaza

Strongly Recomended & Forwarded for furendall consideration

FIGURE 2.7. Second page of a petition for a Shia mosque in G-7, 1995.

model of pleading" to elicit an affective relationship (2009:364). This oral mode is evidenced by the way the imam begins most of his sentences by addressing the recipient as "Sir . . ." (*janab-e ali . . .*), unlike petitioners in the rights-claiming and bureaucratic modes who typically address the reader only once at the beginning.

> Sir, by God and his beloved friend and by your soul would you give me a ten *marla* [302 square yard] plot in the empty place on street no. 9 G-7/2 so that I can take out a loan and so forth and build a small house so that I can provide a place for my children to hide their heads. Sir, my family numbers 11 people. I am the only support for children and elder parents.

Rather than simply articulating his request, the imam adopts a hortatory tone, repeating his request for a plot several times, then characterizes the allotment in an idiom of Islamic praise.

> I am helpless . . . . With courtesy I submit that a ten marla plot on the empty place on street no. 9 G-7/2 should be allotted to me. This will be your small kindness and your offering of charity will endure until the resurrection. Sir, this world will pass away. But this benevolence will, like the names of God and his Messenger, endure until the Resurrection Day. If you by your hand you show mercy and allot a plot, I and my children will keep praying for you and your children.

Raman (2007:307) and Cody (2009:357) have analyzed such petition praise using Appadurai's concept of "coercive subordination," a discursive strategy by which a person obligates a superior precisely by enacting subordination and dependence within an Islamic "community of sentiment" (Appadurai 1990:94).

Petitioners writing in Urdu more often enact supplication because they are usually lower in status relative to those able to petition in English, and because formal Urdu remains closer to the flowery Persian literary tradition. However, this form of political personhood is also enacted in many petitions written in the so-called Babu English so often ridiculed by British colonial officials. A petition written in 1995 for a Shia mosque in G-7 emotionally describes the hardships faced by "our elders, weak, sick persons, and ladies" in going to another sector to pray in congregation. The petitioners phrase their request in a manner that emphasizes their dependence on the power and grace of the officers: "We beseech your kind honor that keeping in view our difficulties as explained above, a plot may kindly be allotted." As supplicant petitioners usually do, the petitioners end with a prayer for both the officer and the CDA: "We pray to Almighty Allah to bestow all his blessings on your good self and for the better development of the Capital Development Authority in Islamabad." Similarly, a petition written in 1994 for a mosque in I-10 addresses not a bureaucrat impersonally carrying out policy, but an officer who will be personally moved to grant a favor: "Keeping in view, the position to take personal interest favouring us with permission to construct a *masjid* [mosque] as this is a dire need of the residents of this area."

In his examination of petitioning by poor rural residents of contemporary Tamil Nadu, Cody links supplication in petitions to longstanding conceptions of government in terms of godly and human patron-client relations. But these Tamil villagers are also relegated to enact supplication because they do not control the "embodied, material means to satisfy the requirements of political self-representation" in the modern bureaucratic arena (Cody 2009:355). Villagers in rural Pakistan and some in Islamabad are likely to face similar problems. However, the use of supplication cannot be cast within a modernization account. The majority of Islamabad petitioners are ignorant of neither democratic ideals nor bureaucratic discourse and procedure. Both of the English-language petitions emotionally pleading for mosques are models of bureaucratic graphic layout. And finally, we see petitioners moving among these different political subjects as they tangle with the bureaucracy over a series of petitions. After unsuccessfully "beseeching" the officer for a Shia mosque in 1995, these same petitioners turned around and wrote several unemotional, perfectly formed bureaucratic petitions from 1996 on. In Islamabad, petitioners cast themselves as supplicants because it remains a vibrant form of political relationship within the most modern arena of government.

INFLUENCE

The discourse and material form of petitions enact proper relations between political subjects and government. Ideally, petitions are written to stand on their own, making just claims that the bureaucracy must address on their merits. But the ways that petitions circulate show that few petitioners have confidence in this ideal efficacy. Petitioners try to help their petitions in one of two ways. By submitting petitions to newspapers (as well as the bureaucracy), they attempt to construct around their petitions a broad public opinion. Alternatively, they present their petitions in person or through the mediation of an influential person to place it in a narrow network of moral or political relationships. Although mustering public opinion for a petition is a sanctioned pressure tactic, the fabrication of focused social relationships around petitions puts them in an ambiguous relation with government policy and procedures.

Petitioners sometimes present their petition to newspapers by simply delivering it to the editorial offices. Petitions representing larger constituencies might be launched with a press conference where an organization leader or a leading signatory will describe the contents of the petition. Minor petitions, such as demands for the approval of the construction of a carport, might end up in the Letters to the Editor section. More controversial or broadly supported petitions can end up with a front-page headline. The CDA takes such press submissions very seriously. From early 1960s, before the city was built, the CDA Public Relations Directorate has reviewed all the English- and Urdu-language newspapers published throughout the country. Articles or letters that feature the city even tangentially are cut out, grouped by story, pasted onto A4 sheets, and later bound into blue books that now fill a large number of cabinets. Before they are archived, the Public Relations Directorate circulates them to the relevant departments for written comments on the issue raised. Drawing on these responses, the director of Public Relations then submits vigorous written rebuttals to all the newspapers that publicized the petition.

Petitioners rarely send their petitions to the CDA by mail or even deliver them by hand to the central registry of an office to be logged. Rather, they usually attempt to present the petition in person to the official to whom it is addressed. Such meetings have varying significance depending on the status of the petitioner and the nature of the petition. But for all petitioners the general aim is the same: to try to overcome the very distance from influence that required their resort to a petition in the first place, to generate as best they can the sort of favor with influence created by parchis.

As in the case of the clerk who begged Zaffar Khan for a promotion, low-status petitioners attempt to gain the sympathy of officers and to perform a subordination that makes a moral claim on the superior. But for a better-placed petitioner, a face-to-face meeting around a petition is not an occasion to perform subordination, but to communicate circumstances relevant to the petition that the petitioner prefers not to articulate in the petition itself, including who might be supporting him and his petition. If the ideals of parchi (personally presented writing testifying to a personal connection) and petition (autonomous writing articulating a just cause) conflict, in practice they are complementary. Face-to-face meetings provide the opportunity to use a parchi to support a petition, to insert the petition into the networks traced by parchis.

Many petitions from nonofficial people come to the CDA forwarded from officials in the senior ranks of the federal government and, occasionally, the army. While openly sent through the usual channels, the cover letter that accompanies such a forwarded petition functions much like a parchi, materializing the influential person's interest in the case. Sometimes the person forwarding a petition has no official authority whatsoever over the matter. For example, the then–minister of education in 1995 forwarded a petition for a Shia mosque in G-7/2, a fact mentioned in subsequent petitions on the same matter. But more often, petitioners submit their petitions to politicians and bureaucrats who have formal authority over the CDA, though authority far removed from concrete decision making. It is not uncommon to find a petition for a minor matter, such as the extension of a mosque or the adjustment of a financial compensation award, forwarded from the office of a federal secretary, a member of parliament, a minister, or even the president or the prime minister. For example, a petition in 1995 for a mosque on Jinnah Avenue was submitted to the president of Pakistan before being forwarded to the CDA. During Zia-ul-Haq's rule, petitions were addressed to him. A letter written in 1978 from the "People's Welfare Committee G-6/1–2" appealed directly to the chief martial-law administrator, Zia-ul-Haq, to order the CDA to repair the leaking roofs of their government quarters. Submitting petitions through an influential person is so common that petitions sent, according to prescribed procedure, directly to the officer with authority over the matter sometimes call attention to their good behavior by including an underlined "Through proper channel" on the top right corner of the first page. Those submitting petitions to high officials hope that the officials will forward the petition with a favorable recommendation, though letters accompanying the copies of petitions are usually neutral, requesting that the CDA "take appropriate action" or resolve the matter "on its merits," according to policy and the facts of the matter. This written directive, however, is sometimes preceded by a phone call in which the sender implies or states what he or she would really like done.

Although petitioning was part of both metropolitan English political practice as well as Company business, the contemporary Pakistani practice of submitting petitions to the highest political authority has its roots in precolonial South Asian political traditions. Brimnes argues that "direct access to relevant and responsible authorities was ... the central feature of the old political order" (1998:145). In the Mughal period, the term *arz-dasht,* from which *arz,* one of the contemporary Urdu words for petition, derives, meant any letter private or official submitted to the emperor (Mohiuddin 1971:151). As the Company established its rule in India, "its administrators found it extremely difficult to force supplicants to desist addressing their letters to the highest authority, i.e., the Governor of Madras, and later, after the formal takeover by the Crown, to Queen Victoria herself" (Brimnes 1998:145). In 1814, as Company frustration with this practice grew, the Madras government even refused to receive petitions directly and established a "petition department" to channel worthy appeals to departments with authority over the issue (145). Such measures appear to have had little effect. By Siddiqi's (2005:22) count, from 1857 to 1885, petitions presented to the highest level of offices of Governor-General, the Secretary of State, and the Queen (from 1877, the Queen Empress) numbered between three hundred at the very least to over a thousand.

The practice of submitting petitions to the highest authorities is the material enactment of the widely held views that influence is strongly concentrated at the apex of government and that petitions will only be successful if senior politicians and officials put their weight behind them. The role of influence within the bureaucracy is much debated within Pakistan, but no one puts much credence in a classic Weberian picture. A critique of reified structural order is commonsense in Pakistan. Despite the mass of statutes and rules governing the formal organization of the federal bureaucracy, it is a popular conception that even the smallest actions of government are done at the behest of senior politicians and officials. The highest offices of the state are seen as sites for the exercise of influence over all the activities falling within a sphere of authority rather than for the execution of statutes and rules. This conception combines, with some tension, the concepts of centralization and individual discretion. A dispirited former CDA chairman succinctly summarized this view for me:

> The institution does not matter, only the man. And it doesn't matter to anyone whether a genius or a buffoon is sitting there. No one tries to build institutions and if they exist, we just try to rip them apart. Developing countries are developing countries because they are developing—they don't have any institutions. We had some institutions in the beginning here, but they have now all been overpowered by Pakistani culture—now only the person matters.

Especially since the collapse of the Soviet Union, this conception not only integrates the most minor activities of the government into the hierarchy of the Pakistan state, but it positions them within a world political order understood as a hierarchy with the United States president at its apex, European leaders below him, followed by the heads of less powerful states such as Pakistan. This conceptualization of the flow of influence downward from the apex of the political order to its lower levels is illustrated by a story several people told me, giving it varying credence, about a member of an official Pakistan delegation to the United States asking President George H. W. Bush to appoint a relative of one of the delegates to the plum post of deputy commissioner of Lahore.

While this conception oversimplifies the routine operation of the bureaucracy, it is encouraged by the frequent interventions of senior bureaucrats and politicians in even the most minor affairs of the bureaucracy, particularly in Islamabad, with its concentration of powerful people. Neil Brimnes's characterization of kingly rule in South Asia suggests the continuity of such interventions with precolonial modes of kingly rule. The king "was supposed to hold the capacity to regulate all political relations by personal intervention" (1998:146; see also Richards 1993). This type of intervention can be more proximately traced to the patronage populism cultivated by Prime Minister Zulfiqar Ali Bhutto in the 1970s and continued by his successors. Examples of the intervention of powerful political and bureaucratic figures in minor issues are common. To cite one from the early years of Zia's regime, in a letter to an Urdu newspaper, a man claimed that no less a personage than the Pakistan president had directed the federal minister of Housing and Works to recommend his case to the CDA chairman for appointment as a humble watchman.[18] None of the many comments on the parchi alleged to be from the prime minister's sister suggested it was implausible that the sister of a prime minister would involve herself in the minor affairs of a low-level clerk. Unlike the officials of the Madras government, senior government servants and politicians of the Pakistan government have an interest in promoting rather than curbing the submissions of petitions to high authorities, because the practice can subvert the administrative hierarchy and rules of business by giving them influence on matters outside their direct authority.

The conception of concentrated power is publicly enacted in the meetings known as "open *katcheris*" (open courts), meetings in which common people can approach government officials and political leaders to voice complaints or present petitions. A newspaper account of a recent open katcheri held by a police official offers a succinct narrative: the officer "gave a sympathetic hearing to every visiting citizen, individually, and issued on-the-spot instructions to a number of applications."[19] This forum was especially popular with Prime Minister Nawaz Sharif during his second term, or "rule" as the English press routinely and unironically calls the tenure of the governments of prime ministers and generals alike. Sharif was widely reputed to be modeling himself on Mughal emperors, and these open katcheris, like those of the British colonial government, were modeled on imperial *durbars* (courts). In different cities, Sharif, along with a full consort of assistants and senior bureaucrats representing most government divisions, would meet a large gathering of common people (*aam log*). While the form resembled the "town meeting" of recent American presidential elections, the statements of individuals rarely touched on principle, policy, or personality. Rather, they were requests for the prime minister's intervention in minor government affairs such as the award of a pension, the transfer of a family member, the improvement of local trash collection, or the award of a bank loan. Nawaz Sharif would listen patiently to the petition of the speaker, express his sympathy or indignation, and solemnly vow that something would be done immediately. Then he would call an assistant or the concerned official and publicly give him instructions to resolve the matter in favor of the petitioner.

Egregious violations of regulations are the staple of Islamabad gossip, yet it is difficult to judge the overall extent and effects of the intervention of the influential. One measure of such influence, of course, is the frequency of permitted violations of CDA regulations. In the area of building regulations, officers and staff members estimated that 70 to 80 percent of the structures in the city are compliant with regulations, while 20 to 30 percent of them violate them with the impunity obtained through a varying mix of bribes (*rishvat*) and influence (*sifarish*). But the effect of interventions by powerful individuals is complex, sometimes stimulating outright illegality, but in other cases merely eliciting shortcuts to approved results. One CDA director told me that such pressure didn't usually make functionaries move in directions they didn't want to go and often supplied much-needed initiative. Pressure from above, he said, "is good for us. It gets us moving and sometimes we need that. Often it's just a matter of circumventing procedures. Someone calls up and says 'Just get it done.'"

Influence may in fact be less pervasive than prevailing discourses about bureaucratic corruption suggest. At different moments, officers and politicians may exaggerate either their influence or their subordination to the influence of others. As the open katcheris demonstrate, politicians and bureaucrats have a strong interest in convincing others of their ability to influence the course of bureaucratic events. A reputation for influence is, of course, one constituent of being influential. In many cases, to protect this reputation, they disguise their inability or unwillingness to get things done for others. Nawaz Sharif's exhibitions of influence were occasionally shown to be instances of this tactic. Several times an individual allowed to address the prime minister claimed that a petition granted by the prime minister in a previous open katcheri had not been accepted by the concerned office. Sharif usually responded to the embarrassing evidence that his grandiloquent public orders were not carried out with frothy fulmination against his staff and a renewed command that the matter be handled forthwith.

Additionally, officers sometimes portray themselves as acting according to the wishes of others even as they adhere to regulations. This unacknowledged conformity to regulations is generated by the fear of repercussions from irregular actions and the collision of the ethics of public service with those of the market, of patronage, of friendship, of kin, and of Islam. Propriety, like impropriety, sometimes requires deceit. Paradoxically, officers disguise not only their violations of regulations but also their adherence to them. The latter form of dissimulation is generated by the political risks of openly opposing an influential individual. Such lying is often more a matter of respect than truth (Bailey 1991). One CDA director claimed that

> Here one has to lie to get by. Someone calls and says, "So and so told me to call you and I need this done." I know it can't be done, but I can't tell him that straightaway. I will ask him to come down, discuss his problem, and tell him I will try to do something—it will come out at some point; he will come to know that either it can't be done, or I am not trying to do it, but only later. And I can't just tell him "no" right off, because that would indicate I don't respect the person who told him to call me. Out of respect for this other man I have to be very indirect, smooth things over, waste my time and his time.

As the director observed, such indirectness may be a waste of time in getting some particular task done, but not for maintaining valued relationships. Sometimes an official will represent his adherence to rules not as a principled stand, but as subordination to some other influential individual or group. If he claims that he openly stands for the rules, the responsibility will rest with him. By claiming he himself is under pressure, he deflects this responsibility elsewhere while not making himself an enemy.

Rumors among subordinate officers and staff concerning the origin of orders they receive on file also exaggerate the role of high-level, irregular influence. One assistant in the ICTA described how orders frequently come from "high-ups," but his evidence was nothing more than the verbal testimony of his immediate superior accompanying written orders. "When someone high up wants something done irregularly or quickly, we must do it because we are told that the orders come from high up. But we never know who or why—we just do it." There is plenty of evidence that senior politicians and bureaucrats do intervene in this fashion, but probably less frequently than they are rumored to. At every level, an officer takes the word of his immediate superior that someone important above this superior is behind an issue, when this is often not the case. At least in some cases, officers falsely report high-level involvement to push matters along with their subordinates.

The frequent invocation of the names of particular influential individuals, while more verifiable, also contributes to an exaggeration of the role of influence. As we've seen, visiting cards often circulate without the consent of those they name, but names in oral form are even harder to control. When opposed by approving officers or confronted by the CDA staff who enforce building codes, individuals sometimes claim that an influential officer has agreed to the proposal or allowed the violation. Influential officers aggressively police such uses of their names to maintain the integrity and market value of their name. However, the whiff of impropriety usually discourages subordinate would-be fact checkers from confirming whether the influential officer has in fact lent his support. This opens up the possibility for individuals to claim the support of influentials with whom they have no such relationship. Although the prevalence is hard to judge, names are likely invoked more often than support is actually lent. This helps explain the power of parchis, which, however covertly and ambiguously, document the backing of the influential figures.

Such "unauthorized" use of names usually goes undetected, though not always, as the owner of a prominent Blue Area restaurant unhappily discovered. According to one officer involved in the case, the owner had begun to construct a large fountain in the public space in front of his restaurant. When cited for the violation by a CDA enforcement officer, the owner claimed a connection with the CDA chairman and threatened to have the officer sacked. According to my interlocutor, when word of this got back to the chairman, "he was angry at the use of his name and said to us, 'If anyone comes to them saying his name, officials should check with him.'" In response to this outrage against his name and concerns about the precedent of granting a variance to "all those millionaires in the Blue Area," the chairman engineered a clever scheme to work around a stay order and demolish the fountain. He waited until the owner had completed the construction with expensive imported Italian tile. The owner, meanwhile, obtained a stay order against the demolition. On the last day of this stay order, which ended at midnight, one of the members of the CDA board entertained the owner in his office with cookies and tea. According to my interlocutor, the member gamely chatted with the owner saying things like, "Oh, you are so well connected, we cannot touch you." Lulled by the officer's false declarations of impotence, the owner delayed his request for a renewal of the stay order until the next morning. He never got the chance. At 12:15 that night, CDA bulldozers arrived in front of his restaurant and plowed over the gorgeous, illegal fountain.

The concealment of illegal activities from outside actors can make these activities opaque even to those involved. A young entrepreneur who worked the Islamabad bureaucratic arena exploited this opacity. One day, while I was sitting in Zaffar Khan's office, a slender man with a clubfoot, well dressed in an immaculate white shalwar-kamiz and custom black leather sandals, walked in unannounced. He sat down nonchalantly and lit a cigarette, though most men of his age as a sign of deference would not smoke before Zaffar Khan. While the man sat there mischievously smiling, Zaffar Khan fondly and grandiloquently introduced him to me as "a fraud, a cheat, a liar, and a rogue of the highest order." He explained that the man is "a brilliant conman, with unmatched abilities." His main con was fashioned for the Pakistan bureaucratic arena, playing upon the office interactional form, the social organization of bribing, and the contending moral frameworks of relationships between bureaucrats and clients. Well educated and very sharp, he would tutor the children of bureaucrats to gain entree into their offices. He would sit among clients who had come on business and wait for one of them to pose a definite problem or to make a request. When the bureaucrat, as is common, would tell the client to come back after some days or weeks (either to put the client off or because the matter would take that long to deal with), the conman would go to work. He would wait until the client left the office then quickly excuse himself and catch up to the client before he had departed. He would tell the client that the bureaucrat was demanding a bribe of a certain amount and that he would act as the bureaucrat's agent in the transaction. Mistaking the conman for the bureaucrat's *chamcha* (flunky; literally, a spoon), the client would make the payment, sometimes as much as several hundred thousand rupees. According to Zaffar Khan, only people's irresistible pity for his physical infirmity used to save him from being severely beaten or killed by some of the people he defrauded when they found the bureaucrat no more agreeable on their next visit.

Zaffar Khan later claimed that the he himself had had the man beaten for persuading his nephew to cheat on an exam, which resulted in the nephew's expulsion from national exams for three years. On the other hand, Zaffar Khan saw the conman as meting out justice in an unorthodox form and had become his protector, if not his benefactor. As on the day I was introduced, the conman used to come to Zaffar Khan and admit to him what he had done, and Zaffar Khan, with no sympathy for those bilked while bribing, would save his neck. The success of this conman's scheme highlights how difficult it is for those engaged with bureaucracy to understand the patterns of influence that a formal organizational structure aims to make transparent.

As I've described, senior officials often represent themselves as possessing influence commensurate with their status. They are, however, often unable to overcome the combined forces of regulations and their subordinate staff, whose interests, recalcitrance, or sheer lethargy constrain the actions of their superiors. One day, when I was sitting in an office, a former minister from North West Frontier Province came with an older man to the office of a senior ICTA officer to persuade him to appoint the older man's son as a grade 7 clerk. The officer, who respected the character as much as the status of the minister, explained that such an appointment was impossible since the government had ordered a freeze on new appointments to control the budget. After some thought, however, the officer hit upon the possibility of a temporary appointment to the "surplus pool" of government employees, a loophole in the freeze order, perhaps intended for just such cases. Later, I expressed to the officer my surprise at the difficulty even a minister seemed to have with such a minor matter. The officer replied, "It is just a grade 7 appointment, but not even an MNA [Member of the National Assembly] can get such a thing done" in violation of the rules.

One afternoon, Zaffar Khan was holding court, telling stories of how he had boldly bested various bureaucrats and politicians. A pause between stories allowed me to inquire about the documents I was seeking from a department under Zaffar Khan's authority. Zaffar Khan replied resignedly, "You may remember I told you the current director of Auqaf [Directorate] is retiring next month. Now he will not do anything I tell him." Then, recovering his bravado, he continued, "But I have not forgotten you. I promise that on the morning of October 8th [the day following the director's retirement], I will go into Auqaf and scream at them until they shake, and you will have your information by the end of the day on October 9th." Zaffar Khan's declaration that he would intervene through bodily presence and voice was not incidental, for he saw his power lying in his formal rank and personal strength. By contrast, in his view, the source of the recalcitrant subordinate's ability to oppose him was writing: "You know, when you have a big post, it doesn't mean you can get anything done. It just means that you and your friends don't have any personal problems. *Badshah* [Emperor] Clerk runs this country." But just how does writing constrain the actions of officers? The next chapter takes up this question through an account of the most pervasive artifact of writing within the Pakistan bureaucracy: the file.

CHAPTER 3

Files and the Political Economy of Paper

Typically, between 3:45 and 4:15 p.m., toward the end of the office day, when his visitors—or at least the ones deserving his full attention—had left, Zaffar Khan would sigh and reluctantly reach for the buzzer to call his peon. He would mark his transition to a different mode of work by waving his hand in the direction of the coffee table and ordering his peon tersely, "Take it away" (*Le jao*), referring to the milk, sugar, soggy teabags, and numerous half-drunk mugs of tea left by the last of his visitors. Then he would say, "Call him," referring to his personal assistant. The assistant would appear a few minutes later bearing a pile of twenty or thirty files, the blue-green note sheets folded over to the pages where Zaffar Khan's notes and signatures were required, and place them on the coffee table in front of the stuffed chair in which the official spent all his office time. He would light a cigarette, adjust his glasses, and bend wearily toward the files on the coffee table. He would move his cigarette to his left hand and hold up his right hand. His assistant would put a ballpoint pen in it, then stand at attention on his left. Picking up each file without reading it, the officer would settle his gaze irritably somewhere between the assistant and the file and ask his assistant peremptorily, "What is this?" (*Yeh kya hai?*). The assistant would give him the gist of the matter: someone was being transferred to another department; a corruption investigation of someone would be suspended; an NOC (No Objection Certificate) for petrol distribution would be issued to someone. Zaffar Khan would respond to each with a nod, a raised eyebrow, a word of affirmation, "Yes" (*han*) or "Ok" (*thik hai*) or, occasionally, "Nonsense!" (*bakwas*). Whatever his opinion, he would almost invariably pen only a word or two simply affirming the trail of his subordinates' notes or just sign it and toss it with disdain onto the couch next to the coffee table. This would continue until the files were gone, the call to prayer was heard, or he decided the rest of the files could wait until tomorrow. Then, rising abruptly, he was usually out the door before the assistant had finished collecting the files from the couch.

Although Zaffar Khan performed this duty in his own unique style, similar scenes played out in the offices of senior officers throughout the Capital Development Authority (CDA) and the Islamabad Capital Territory Administration (ICTA). As we saw in the last chapter, much of the work of the bureaucracy takes place in reception-like encounters between officers and clients. But the requests, complaints, decisions, understandings, permissions, evasions, and refusals of these conversations eventually must find their way onto the paper of files to have a life beyond talk.

The file is the workhorse of the Pakistan bureaucracy. The vast scope of planning and administrative activities of the CDA and the ICTA is reflected in the variety of file subjects. Land acquisitions, the sectarian allocation of mosques, squatter eviction proceedings, private houses, the demolition of illegal structures, personnel transfers, prosecution of food adulterers, control of the wild boars that nightly descend from the hills behind the city—all of these and more are consecrated in paper shrines of varying age, thickness, and consequence. The uses of files in Islamabad challenge the classic Weberian account of bureaucracy as well as those of its critics.

Weber's account of bureaucracy has been subjected to a range of theoretical and empirical criticisms. However, writing, as in the Weberian model, has remained the very image of a formal organizational practice ensuring control. In his classic account, Michel Crozier, who stressed the interdependence of "rationality and dysfunction" in actually existing bureaucracy (1967:183), saw writing in the pure service of organizational control. He observed that apathetic dependence on documented facts and adherence to written directives and rules could stymie the efficiency of an organization by intensifying superiors' control over subordinates. Thus, he concluded that writing may be dysfunctional by the criteria of efficiency, but it nevertheless promotes formal organizational control. Jack Goody's (1986) account of the "communicative systems" of bureaucracies emphasizes the use of writing as an instrument of organizational control through the storage and transmission of information. Following in this vein, JoAnne Yates's (1989) pathbreaking study describes the large late-nineteenth- and early-twentieth-century American business enterprise as both the impetus for and result of the development of systems of control enabled by new inscriptional communication technologies. Foucault (1977) complicates this picture by highlighting the ways in which documents cannot be seen simply as tools, since they help produce the very individual and collective subjects who use them; inscription is one Foucault's main terms for characterizing the relation of discourses and individuals.

Despite their diverse approaches to bureaucratic writing, these accounts similarly portray writing in the service of hierarchical structures of authority and control.[1] The organization and circulation of written materials is conceptualized as isomorphic with formally structured social organization and interaction. Files in Islamabad are generated in relation to established hierarchies of authority. With respect to a particular case, however, files can virtually reconstitute the roles of functionaries in decisions, remaking formal organizational relations of hierarchy in unpredictable ways. As the head of his division of the ICTA, Zaffar Khan signed off on dozens of files every day. His usual practice was not to read files himself, not to try to follow the episodic accretion of decisiveness through the serial notes of his subordinates. In an extravagant expression of contempt for the writing of his subordinates, he once told me, "No one can understand what *Badshah* [Emperor] Clerk writes. . . . I have read through thousands of files in my career and I have never gotten a straight story out of any of them." In fact, he was an experienced and savvy operator who could penetrate to the heart of the bureaucratic politics shaping the proposals that came to him for approval in the form of files. But the files constructed a material infrastructure of decision making that often considerably constrained or sometimes eliminated his capacity to intervene in matters under his formal supervision.

The inscription and circulation practices of files in Islamabad offices constitute a complex political economy of paper. The discourses and movements of files shape and are shaped by the efforts of functionaries at every level to avoid responsibility, influence cases, and sometimes to raise money. This political economy of paper is not a market economy but neither is it a command economy. Zaffar Khan could not control files with the absoluteness with which he ordered about his office staff.

As I described in the introduction, this political economy of paper has deep historical roots, beginning with republican constitution of the East

India Company and the earliest efforts of Company directors in London to control their unruly agents in the subcontinent. Furthermore, from a nearer historical perspective, we can see an expansion of this political economy over the last half century in Islamabad bureaucracies. That is, in comparison to the early 1960s, today files move through a greater number of functionaries, and through each one more often, and these movements are more intensively documented. This historical process is not driven by some kind of intrinsic "'autonomous' logic" of modern rationalization (Weber 1978:1002), but by the effectiveness of using particular kinds of graphic artifacts to diffuse the responsibility of individuals. Functionaries have increasingly endeavored to produce this diffusion of responsibility as the autonomy of the bureaucracy—its insulation from military and partisan political accountability—has declined since the first two decades of the Pakistan state. Contrary to the predictions of prevailing views of government documentation, the elaboration of file circulation and inscriptional practices does not produce a greater concentration of institutional capacities of control. I argue, rather, that the intensification of file-mediated decision making undermines the ability of superiors to isolate individual functionaries and hold them responsible for particular actions. In short, these practices make it hard to understand who does anything. This diffusion of agency as officially interpreted provides some functionaries with job security and others with cover for questionable or outright illegal activities.

The larger politics of files is embedded in their material qualities and in procedures, so I turn to these first, before moving on to how file practices constitute a collective agent, and then to how this collective agent may be harnessed for particular projects.

THE MATERIALITY OF CASES

A case is an irreducibly material entity, and the file is one its essential elements. The file is the most complex graphic genre in use within the Pakistan bureaucracy, physically and discursively incorporating most other graphic genres, sometimes including portions of other files. Pakistan government files are made up of three sections: first, a "notes" portion, comprising official serial entries of different functionaries including commentary on the matter at issue, directives, responses, documentation of actions, accounts of conversations, reports of petitions, and so forth; second, a collection of copies or the originals of all the internal and external correspondence (including drafts) issued or received that pertain to the subject of the file; and third, a section containing maps, plans, lists, schedules, reports, newspaper clippings, and any other kind of relevant document. Papers are secured within folders by a single string with a metal catch on both ends that is fed through the papers and the holes punched in the upper corner of the front and back of the folder, enabling items to be added and removed easily. The folders and plans of a single file are tied together with a string attached to a strip of thick, cloth-reinforced, off-white paper, a less colorful descendant of the infamous "red tape" that became the symbol of bureaucratic inefficiency under the British (fig. 3.1).

Files materially and discursively recontextualize the other graphic artifacts they contain, transforming letters into cases. Just as a strip of dialogue changes its significance as it is repeated in different circumstances or quoted in writing (Bakhtin 1986:62), the meanings of memos, petitions, and plans are transformed when they are placed in or "on" (as Pakistani bureaucrats put it) a file and, as we'll see, literally overwritten and commented upon by functionaries.[2] A petition from the imam of a mosque requesting a water hookup for ablutions, for example, becomes a request for regularization as it is put in a CDA planning file that carries it into a bureaucratic discourse about the illegality of its location. Placed within an ICTA file and commented upon by officials concerned with sectarian mosque allocation, the petition becomes a threat to sectarian harmony. Through incorporation into a file, other graphic genres become part of different sociomaterial practices, the circulation processes through which official decisions and actions are taken. The imam's petition cannot become a case and begin to move through the bureaucracy until it finds its way into a file. Until it is put on file, the imam's petition would have a liminal existence, recognized in registry books, but not yet in the material disposition to be acted upon. In the "disposal" of an already established case, materials not referenced by or placed on a file do not exist as far as officials are concerned.

As Mauss was among the first to observe, the significance of many artifacts, from Persian carpets (Spooner 1986) to Massim *kula* shells (Munn 1983), are deeply embedded in their histories: how they were made, who has acquired them and how, how they have been used, and so forth (Appadurai 1986; Kopytoff 1986). A Pakistani government file, however, is an unusual sort of artifact because signs of its history are continuously and deliberately inscribed upon the artifact itself, a peculiarity that gives it an event-like quality. A file is a chronicle of its own

FIGURE 3.1. CDA file opened in 1961.

production, a sedimentation of its own history. Specifically, a large portion of a file consists of explicit—if selective—documentation of its role in the social world: graphic representations of the relations between the file (or certain of its components) and people, spaces, times, other graphic artifacts, actions, and speech events. Unlike published books or even memos distributed in identical form to several recipients, files are unique, singular artifacts, a quality that is central to their capacity to shape how cases are handled. Portions may be copied (usually for insertion in other files), but only the original maintains its status as an official record of deliberations, decisions, and actions. Although officially sanctioned access to files varies depending on the issue, even files concerned with the most uncontroversial and public issues are officially confidential and are not to be seen by people outside government or functionaries not concerned with the case. As I describe later in this chapter, this is often not the case in practice, but it is a rule officials may invoke at will.

To understand what bureaucrats do with files and why, one needs to know some of the specificities of the procedures they involve. In the rest of this section, I describe these procedures, highlighting a trend toward greater procedural rationalization of activities since the early 1960s. I describe practices in the present, noting where they have changed from the early 1960s. The following account is based upon the examination of hundreds of active and inactive ICTA and CDA files of several directorates that were created and added to from the early 1960s until 2007.

Despite the myriad changes in recruitment rules and the organization of the state bureaucracy, the normative formal procedure for handling communications and files has changed little over the last hundred years. Indeed, a Calcutta clerk in the mid-nineteenth-century Public Works Department of the colonial government would need little formal retraining for service in the contemporary CDA.[3] Since the 1970s, however, these procedures have been extended to a wider range of routine interactions; furthermore, the extension of these procedures has led to a greater range of routine interactions among functionaries at all levels of the bureaucratic hierarchy. I should note here an imbalance between my accounts of earlier and later practices involving files, owing to the difference in the sources upon which they are based. For the contemporary period, I was able to examine files, talk with functionaries about their use, and observe the role of files in ongoing bureaucratic processes. In contrast, my account of the earlier period relies almost exclusively on files themselves, supplemented by general observations of CDA staff who have worked there since the 1960s. As my own observations on the contemporary use of files will suggest, we should be cautious about relying on the files themselves as evidence of the practices that involve them. Much of what is important about the use of files is not documented within them. They are artifacts that are often partial in both senses. Nevertheless, what is written on the older files, I will argue, testifies to growing proceduralization in the discourse and circulation of files.

In the chapters to follow, I focus more directly on the role of files and other graphic genres in social processes beyond the office. But my interest here is mainly in how files shape relationships within the bureaucracy itself. Such an account does not begin to exhaust the significance that any single file, deeply entangled in specific social processes, has for the full range of social actors they involve in and out of the bureaucracy. An account of the processes I am trying to elucidate might be better constructed around a social process involving a file or set of files. My approach is close to this in the next two chapters, oriented around particular events and arenas of activities. However, the method of following the full careers of files is unworkable owing to the difference between the duration of my ethnographic study and the duration of the processes precipitated in and by files. Although the speedy disposal of a case may take less than a month, many files were opened decades ago and may be expected to be "current" (active) for decades to come. In this respect, my perspective is coincident with that of functionaries, who find themselves in the midst of events involving files. Functionaries are often familiar with the interactions that produced and were produced by a relatively recent portion of the file, but they are dependent on their own memories, hearsay, and the testimony of the file itself to reconstruct earlier events.

The process that generates a file begins with the receipt of a written communication on a subject for which no file in the directorate exists already, in the judgment of an officer or assistant. As I described in the last chapter, the process by which a letter is written and eventually delivered to the CDA is very complex, often involving conversations with CDA officials and the mediation of officials and politicians in the senior ranks of the federal government, who are often the original recipients of letters forwarded to the CDA. The authors of communications are as varied as the work of the CDA, including, for example, other government officers; representatives of business, civic, and religious groups; and individual merchants, houseowners, and imams of mosques. Many communications are addressed to the chairman of the CDA, and few are addressed to an official lower than a director, the head of a directorate.

Petitioners often present their letters to officials in a personal meeting because they recognize that a letter on its own is vulnerable to the indifference, the misinterpretation, the happenstance, and the intentional misdirection that threaten all physical artifacts. A letter requesting the allotment of particular government quarters that are to be vacated soon might get mired at a low level of the hierarchy through the negligence of an officer's personal assistant. Or another government worker might learn of the opening through the letter and substitute his own request for the quarters in its place. A meeting with an official not only ensures he receives the petition, but it provides an opportunity to preclude misinterpretation of the petition through framing oral discourse and to discuss aspects of the situation the petitioner was unwilling to commit to paper but would like the officer to consider. For example, the petitioner for government quarters might like to make known to the officer that they share an influential friend, that both went to the same school or come from a particular region, or that he might provide monetary inducements.

Whether a letter has been presented in person or received by mail, it is first registered in the central registry of the CDA, a series of large log-books of all the "receipts" or communications received by the CDA. A receipt clerk stamps it with a large oval stamp bearing the full name of the authority, over which the diary number of the letter and the date it was received are written in hand. Until a communication has been registered, it has not been officially received. Receipt clerks can make a solid living from the small gratuities of clients ensuring the registration of their letters. (One unusually successful former receipt clerk was widely rumored to drive an expensive SUV and to own a commercial plaza in his hometown.) Following central registration, the letter is distributed to the "concerned" office.

The "diary clerk" places all the mail on a "*dak* pad" (mail pad) and several times a day presents it to the most senior officer of the organizational division. The officer reviews the mail and handwrites brief notes on the first page of each. Since the note of an officer on receipts is always followed by the notes of others, we could call it a turn at writing (De Rycker 1987), a conventional graphic genre with several components arranged in three compartmentalized spatial units. First, there is a brief question, comment, or directive regarding the issue (for example, "*Pl. obtain the ref at A from M/S Dox.*"). Second, below his note and to the right, the official initials it, writes a slash, and dates it below and to the right of his initials.[4] Third, below his initials and to the left, as far as the blank space of the letter allows, the official "marks" the letter, that is, writes and underlines the title of the functionary to which the letter should be presented next. While the title of very senior officers is written in full (for example, "Secretary," "Chairman"), the rest of the officers' titles are designated by initials: "DDG(W)," Deputy Director General, Works; "D(P)," Director, Planning; "DD(P)," Deputy Director, Planning; "TP(I)," Town Planner (I); and so on. Clerks are marked by "Mr." followed by their "formal" name, for example, "Mr. Zahir." Before noting on a letter, every officer, to indicate that he has received the letter, strikes out with a single pen stroke the mark designating him.

Before passing on the receipt, the diary clerk first enters each letter into the office diary, a large book containing columns for the serial number, the receipt date, the letter number, the name and position of the author, the subject of the letter, and the designation of the person to whom the official marked the letter. All government and many unofficial letters are numbered. All government correspondence and many English and Urdu letters from even unofficial parties adopt the form of the bureaucratic letter, which includes a characterization of the letter in the form of a subject entry above the body of the letter. English-language letters without such a subject entry are often considerably delayed because the English of many of the diarists is so poor that they have difficulty in determining the subject. They often resort, correctly or incorrectly, to reviews of previously diarized letters with similar verbal formulations to make this determination. After registration, the letter itself is then stamped with a round or oval image including references to the section, the directorate, and the CDA, over which the clerk handwrites the receipt date and the diary number. Through the taciturn medium of stamps, clerks create a metatext that emplots the official career of the artifact in time, space, organizational order, and the order of other graphic artifacts. With respect to individual communications, the most important function of stamps is to document the purported flow of documents under people's eyes. More generally, much as passport controls define state borders, stamp practices help to define the office as an organizational entity, since they are applied only when communications move across "borders" between offices.

In the 1960s, communications were usually marked first to either the person who had direct knowledge and responsibility for the issue or someone who had to be consulted regarding it. The next and subsequent recipients would similarly note on the letter and mark it on similar grounds. Marking was flexible with respect to the organizational chain of command. While letters were more often marked down the organizational hierarchy, they were often marked up as well; in either case, they often skipped a level or two of the hierarchical organization. The chairman, for example, marked communications to his entire staff of officers, from the secretary down to deputy directors. Deputy directors marked letters to their assistants and clerks as well as directors and deputy directors general. Files were more a record of activities than an instrument of decision making, and much of the intraorganization communication regarding issues took place through notes on the letters themselves rather than on the note sheets of files. This practice made the functional and graphic distinction between the notes and correspondence sections of these early files rather fluid.

Typically, a single letter accumulated no more than three or four notes as it circulated among two or three officers at different hierarchical levels. The last officer to note on a letter usually took action on it and marked it to his clerk to be filed. Only if it was necessary for an officer to review related documents or plans before taking action would he order his assistant to "place the letter on file" and resubmit it with the required materials. Receipts were circulated in a manner that, as we'll see, is reserved for files nowadays. Often, the matter had been completely dealt with before the officer marked the letter to his clerk for filing.

Although the formal procedures haven't changed since the early 1960s, the handling of receipts in the contemporary CDA is a much more elaborate process. Few decisions are made before the receipt has become a properly established component of a file. Officers quickly skim letters and make brief notes in the margins of the first page. The basic components of the genre of the note have not changed, but the comments and directives have become briefer and less specific. In contrast to the notes of the 1960s, contemporary notes on receipts rarely touch on the substance of the issue and are usually formulaic procedural directives (such as "Pl examine" or "Please check for previous references") or a characterization of the urgency of the matter (such as "Immediate" or "Priority"). In many cases, the note consists entirely of the initials, date, and mark. Receipts are almost always marked to the officer's immediate subordinate, neither moving up nor skipping levels of the organizational hierarchy. The letter continues downward as each officer perhaps adds a word or two echoing that of the most senior officer of the organizational hierarchy, initials and dates the letter, and marks it to his immediate subordinate. The downward movement of the letter continues along the organizational hierarchy until it reaches the lowest officer—for example, a town planner, engineer, or architect. The grade 17 officer writes a note to return the letter to him in a file (for example, "Put up on the file") and marks it to his assistant. By placing the letter in an existing file or opening a new one, the assistant materially frames the letter as a new episode in an ongoing story or the start of a new narrative.

Note sheets and correspondence are contained in separate legal-size folders of thick, brown, gray, green, or blue paper, often with "CAPITAL DEVELOPMENT AUTHORITY" printed in black across the top. Some folders also have "VIP" printed in even larger letters above. A large percentage of the files dealing with commercial structures in the Blue Area and private houses in the elite areas of F-6, F-7, E-7, F-10, and F-11 bear this descriptor. When I asked the record clerk in charge of these records why all such files weren't marked "VIP," he replied, "There is no need because these are all big people, all are VIP people [VIP *log*]." Below these broad headings, the "file number," a unique alphanumeric designation, is written by hand (for example, "CDA/PLD-9(1)/62").[5] When a receipt is placed on file, it is inserted at the end of papers in the correspondence folder. These papers are all serially numbered, and a "flag" (a small slip of paper) with "PUC" written on it is pinned to it to designate the letter as the "paper under consideration." The receipt is then "docketed" on the notes pages, legal size off-white or light green papers with a thin line at a margin of 1¾ inches (fig. 3.2). Docketing is the process through which the official writings on the letter are transcribed from the letter to the notes sheet. The docketing procedure has not changed since the early 1960s, though nowadays a much greater percentage of receipts—virtually all of them—are docketed and accompanied by fuller documentation.

In the docketing process, the dialogue of officials with the letter writer and with each other is reconstituted on the note sheet as dialogue only among officials. Below the receipt date, the name of the letter's sender, and the page of the original in the correspondence section, the clerk transcribes on the note sheet—in type or handwriting—all the notes on the receipt. The spatially compartmentalized segments of each officer's note on the receipt are transcribed as paragraphs that are numbered as a series continuing through all the notes, a practice that dates from the 1670s (Ogborn 2007). Through their placement and non-linguistic marks, the original notes on the letter are in direct dialogue with contents of the letter. When these spatial and graphic indexes are replaced on the file by a simple linguistic signs, the voice of the letter writer is eliminated.

The linguistic transcription of initials is impossible since there is no speech act representable in language that corresponds to the signature.[6] In the 1960s, when a signature was moved into the reporting frame of the note sheet, in place of the actual signature or initials of officials the clerk would write the abbreviation "Sd./-" for "signed" followed by the name of the signing officer. In contrast, today signatures are transcribed as "Sd x" followed by the title of the signatory with no reference to the actual individual, obscuring the individual identity expressed by a signature.

The serial order established by the numbering of paragraphs is reinforced by the spatial ordering of the turns. The haphazard placements of the turns of different officials on the letter is translated into the spatial order of the note sheet, where the direction from top to bottom represents prior to later temporal relations. On the letter, the interspersal of official notes with the text of the letter is a visual iconic representation of an unequal dialogue among officials and the author of the letter. The

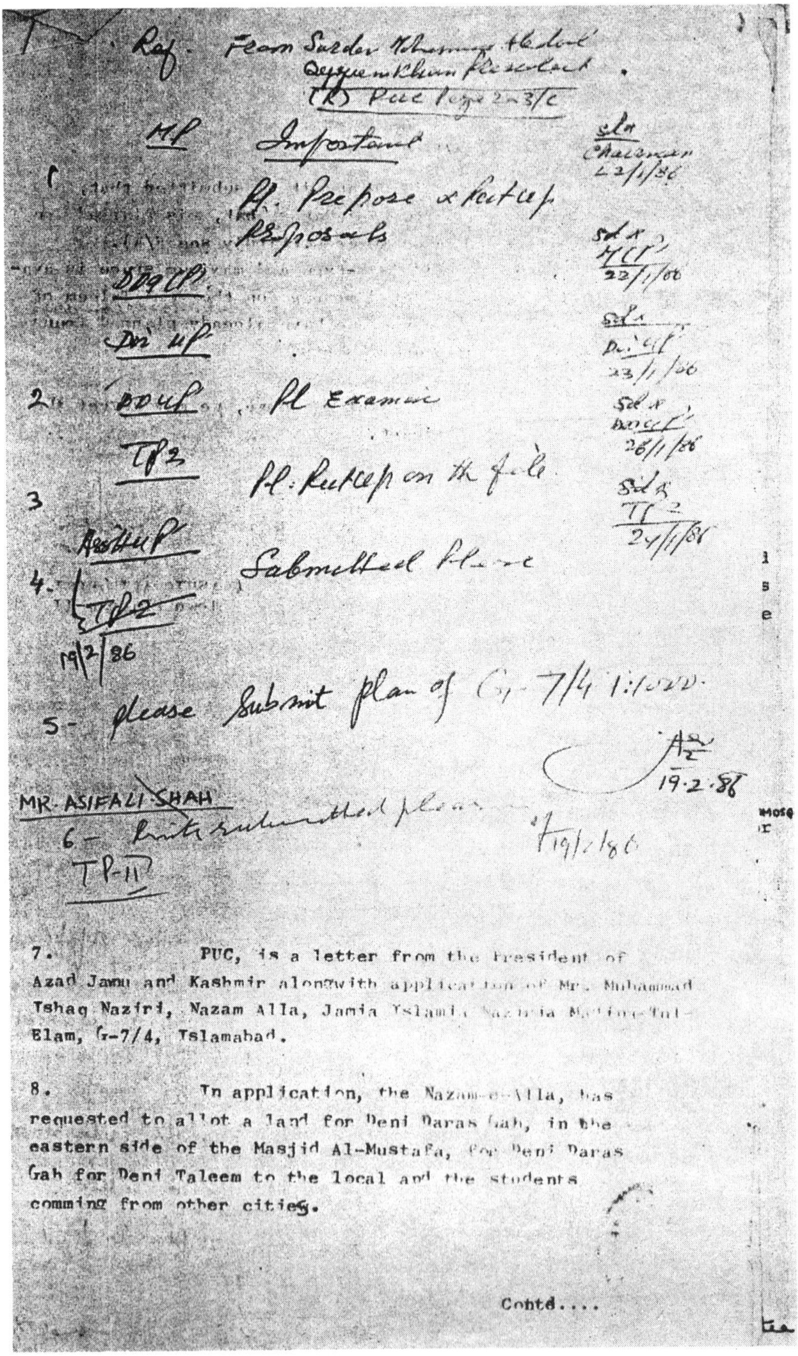

Ref. From Sardar Mohammad Abdul Qayyum Khan President (AK) PUC Page 2 & 3/C

Important

Pl. Prepose & Put up Proposals

DDG(P)

Dir UP

2. DDUP Pl Examine

TP2

3. Pl: Put up on the file

Asstt UP

4. Submitted please

TP2

19/2/86

5- please Submit plan of G-7/4 1:1000.

19.2.86

MR. ASIFALI SHAH

6- Kindly submitted please

TP-11

19/2/86

7. PUC, is a letter from the President of Azad Jamu and Kashmir alongwith application of Mr. Muhammad Ishaq Naziri, Nazam Alla, Jamia Islamia Nazimia Madina-tul-Elam, G-7/4, Islamabad.

8. In application, the Nazam-e-Alla, has requested to allot a land for Deni Daras Gah, in the eastern side of the Masjid Al-Mustafa, for Deni Daras Gah for Deni Taleem to the local and the students comming from other cities.

Contd....

FIGURE 3.2. The first page of a note sheet in response to a letter, 1986.

visual separation between official notes and the letter requires the substitution of a discursive and more mediate relation between the writing of officials and the letter to which they were responding. The official notes are extracted from their immediate dialogic relation with the letter and recontextualized in a wholly official graphic space.

Notes written directly on files have the same components as those on letters, but they are more elaborate, as will be described in detail in the next section. Here, I will just sketch the normal (in both the senses of being normative and the most commonly occurring) path of a file from this point to its "filing," its return to the record room until another letter or petition calls it forth.

Following docketing, the assistant gathers relevant facts and precedents in the form of documents and submits them with the file to his superior, a town planner, an engineer, or an architect, or another junior officer depending on the directorate. Sometimes, the assistant also produces a background note, a common source of amusement and frustration for officers, one of whom complained to me, "Staff copies what was done in the past and most of the time reproduce old notes if they even remotely touch the subject!" It is the task of this officer to summarize the "relevant facts and precedents" and suggest a course of action. Files usually spend a considerable amount of time here. In contrast to the offices of higher officials, these offices are heaped high with languishing files. From here, the file is passed up the chain of the organization or laterally to other departments until an official passes orders on it, usually in the form of an approval of the original suggestion of the grade 17 officer, supported by the notes of the officials through whom it has passed. When a file goes out of a major office or directorate, it receives a rectangular "despatch" stamp, including a date and diary entry number; when it comes in, it receives a round or oval "receipt" stamp with the same information. When an official approves a proposal, the file changes direction and moves downward again to the grade 17 officer, beneath the pens (and, perhaps, by the eyes or ears) of all the officials in between. The grade 17 officer will then direct staff to carry out the action and draft a reply to the petitioner. Usually, he dictates the draft to a typist and edits the draft before sending the file back up the chain to the officer who approved the proposal. If approved, the file descends to this officer to order a "fair copy" or "fair" (a retyped letter) for signing and issuance. Sometimes this officer will sign and issue the letter himself and sometimes it will be passed up the chain to the most senior officer involved in the decision. From wherever it is signed, it descends again to the grade 17 officer who orders the assistant to issue the letter and "files the case" by returning the file to the record room of the directorate, where it remains until another receipt on that subject is received. While every file makes a minimum of three trips through the organizational hierarchy, a controversial case, which no senior official wants to decide on, may make several more cycles. Files tend to bounce back and forth between the posts of the highest and lowest officer levels in an organization. For reasons I'll analyze in the next section, files have what we might call a social momentum that keeps them traveling in the same direction. Other than the initiative of an intermediary officer, only the boundaries of the organization force a reversal of direction.

At any particular time, the bulk of the files of a directorate are not being worked on. Files for the Auqaf Directorate of the ICTA, which administrates the government mosques and shrines of Islamabad, has perhaps several hundred files and keeps them piled in several metal cabinets within the office of the subordinate staff. Most directorates, however, manage a much larger number of files and maintain at least one record room for the storage of "current" files, that is, files that are still in use. The physical organization of files is part of the constitution of the relations of the people and things they talk about. Record storage is sometimes zoned like city space. The Estate Management Directorate, for example, keeps the ownership records of all Islamabad properties in three record rooms. In this arrangement, the files of the expensive residential properties of the E-7 and F sectors keep their distance from the poorer ones of the G and I sectors, and the files of residential properties are protected from commercial ones. Each record room is under the direct control of a single clerk, the record keeper, who is the only person to record the movement of files in or out of the room, which he does in a register. He keeps the cabinets and the door to his room locked to ensure files aren't removed without his authorization.

INDIVIDUAL WRITERS AND CORPORATE AUTHORITY

Files are not simply replacements for oral communicative acts, as they are treated within an oral-written paradigm (Vismann 2008:8–13). Yet, much of the capacity of files to do more than communicate depends on the discourse they support. Just as hypertext can only exist in an electronic medium, files are the material supports of particular forms of discourse that can be mediated by no other form. A file is both the occasion and the means of a particular form of dialogue. Much of the authority of bureaucratic documents and modern government more generally comes from the use of a particular register of language (Bakhtin 1981), the uniformity and regularity of documentary forms (Feldman 2008:31–61), and the symbolism of employing a whole apparatus of records (Messick 1993; Sharma and Gupta 2006; Vismann 2008; Weber 1978). Yet, language, uniformity, and symbolism are rarely enough to confer authority on a particular document. Authority is made in particular sociomaterial processes of document production that generate corporate authorship and agency. The file is a technology for materially enacting an authoritative decision, for making a decision out of various utterances and actions.

Written bureaucratic discourse is often characterized as impersonal and anonymous on the basis of lexical and semantic features: the prevalence of passive verbs, abstract nouns, and the like. As one observer puts it, "The effect is to create an impersonal tone, and to eliminate information about who is responsible for what" (Charrow 1982:183). This view of bureaucratic discourse corresponds to the common image of bureaucracy as the epitome of collective social organization, the authority of which depends in part on its representation of itself as a collective agent. Although there is some validity to the characterization, it is at best only half the story, an outsider's perspective based on analysis of published or publicly distributed documents. Things look different from the inside. Written materials circulated within the Pakistan bureaucracy share these lexical and semantic features. But many pragmatic features of this discourse and its material medium precisely index the individuals who write every word and make every mark. While analysts of bureaucratic discourse, taking the outsider's perspective of the client, complain of authorless bureaucratic discourse, for functionaries of the Pakistan bureaucracy, the authorship of written discourse is all too precisely specified.

The precise specification of authorship is a source of considerable anxiety in the uncertain political arena of the Pakistan bureaucracy. This anxiety is linked to long-term processes affecting the position of the bureaucracy in the political order of the Pakistan state. Prime Minister Zulfiqar Ali Bhutto's reforms in the 1970s, designed to clip the wings of the bureaucratic establishment, were the first attacks on an institution that had carried the power and autonomy of the colonial government into the postcolonial era. From the late 1970s, President Zia-ul-Haq allied himself with the bureaucracy and undid some of Bhutto's reform measures, but he made no attempt to restore the bureaucracy to its former power (Kennedy 1987). During the last twenty years, the bureaucracy has been buffeted by less institutionalized political and military interventions. Successive governments have sought to purge the bureaucracy through the transfer, early retirement, or dismissal of officers and staff tied to political opponents, particularly those of the former ruling party. Similarly, on a more local scale, personnel changes within the senior ranks of government divisions threaten functionaries with transfer to unfavorable posts or outright dismissal. Investigations of official activities, such as those of the Federal Investigative Agency (FIA), the *Ehtesab* (Accountability) Commission in 1997 and 1998, and most recently the National Accountability Bureau (known by its frank acronym, NAB), are always underway. Important or controversial issues bring official activities under the scrutiny of contending individuals and coalitions, who often try to shape outcomes by undermining the functionaries who oppose them. Such events sometimes generate a kind of paranoia about writing in some functionaries, but even the most uncontroversial writings are accompanied by routine concern.

Although official sanctions and criminal punishments are linked to politics (inside or outside the bureaucracy) and usually motivated by more than a concern for official propriety, written records of actions provide the main evidence for them. Through routine acts of writing, functionaries submit themselves as individuals to the opacity of the present and the vagaries of the future. They well understand the potential for their writings to be radically recontextualized. In the bureaucratic arena, dissimulation is common and interested actors often rely on several links of intermediaries to pursue their projects. What might be called conspiracy theories from a democratic and empiricist view of sociopolitical process are common explanations of ordinary events, explanations that frequently prove accurate. Bureaucrats are often troubled by the question of who is really "behind" a proposal. Written materials are notoriously peripatetic and might encounter an unrecognized interested party, opportunist, or malefactor who will turn them against their author. Even when the present is clear, the future is cloudy. With the perdurance of the open file, file discourse is never finalized in Bakhtin's (1986:76) sense, that is, brought to a point at which its significance is relatively fixed and not subject to revision. Files may be maintained for decades and functionaries never know when the propriety of their actions will be called into question by later unforeseen events. Instability is a fact of Pakistani social life that all sorts of people, including government officials, used to explain their actions to me. "Who knows what will happen tomorrow?" is a refrain I often heard. The perdurance of files beyond the circumstances of their creation situates them within a horizon of uncertainty. As one town planner explained it to me, "Files are always ready to talk, if not now while you are in your seat then later. The file is there, perhaps someone will read it later." As she put it, "Files are time bombs."

Bureaucratic organization is a social form designed for collective action, a social technology for aligning the efforts of a large number of people so that they act as one. And yet, the mechanism by which this is done is the precise individuation of action—defining appropriate actions for individuals and identifying them with particular acts—to a degree not known in any other kind of social organization. The historical development of bureaucratic organizations and theoretical reflections upon them are part of the larger history of individualism in modern political institutions and thought (Foucault 1977; Giddens 1984). Bentham, to cite one of the earliest proponents of an organization of government (and many other institutions) that we would call bureaucratic, based his proposals for efficient collective action on a thoroughgoing individualism and nominalism that denied the reality of all but individual persons, acts, events, and experiences (Bentham 1932; Hume 1981). Bureaucracies are among the most consciously materialized of social collectives—painstakingly fabricated in the layouts of offices, the writings of functionaries, the stampings of clerks, the movement of files—because they are designed to unify and control individuals conceived as either naturally independent and refractory or entangled in other collectivities.

The construction of collective agency from the agency of individuals (no less than the individuation of action) is a central task of bureaucratic activities. Sherry Ortner (1984) observed that a much earlier anthropology privileged the individual as the presumed locus of agency. Such an approach to bureaucratic agency would lead us to a reductionism, to debunk the bureaucratic myth (the belief in reified structural order) by showing that bureaucratic discourse and action are in fact the result of the actions of individuals. However, from the point of view of both the organization and the individual, successful bureaucratic processes result in action that is not dissolvable into the agency of distinct individuals. My objective is not to debunk the legitimating actions of individual bureaucrats, but rather to describe how and why in bureaucratic processes corporate agency is realized in any sense in which we can talk about collective action being real. The challenge is to understand collectivization and individualization as simultaneous functions of the same bureaucratic processes, taking neither the agency of the individual nor the organization as given.

In Islamabad bureaucracies, written administrative materials are the main semiotic technology for, paradoxically, both the individualizing and the collectivizing of agency. As in the historical development of bureaucracy in European institutions, the functional end of precise specification of authorship is to fix individual responsibility for actions. And yet, bureaucratic writings in Islamabad whose authorship is so precisely specified are often *not* attributed to the agency of its authors; or, to put it more simply, functionaries are often *not* judged responsible for what they write. This empirical fact cannot be explained only through an analysis of the linguistic features of an isolated piece of writing. The collective voice of a newspaper editorial, for example, is achieved mainly through the use of an anonymous first person plural, "we." In contrast, in Islamabad bureaucratic writings, this collective voice is built progressively through the documented participation of different actors; correlatively, attributions of responsibility for authorship of a piece of writing are based upon the dialogic process through which it was generated. As I will show, bureaucratic agency is at once individualized through autographic writings and collectivized through the dialogic discursive and circulatory construction of those writings.

A key concept of official bureaucratic ideology in Islamabad, as indeed elsewhere, is the identification of autographic authorship with agency. Autographic writing is supposed to accompany, produce, or be action. Many actions, such as commanding subordinates, approval of proposals, and communication of information and opinions, are normatively accomplished through writing. This contrasts, for example, with early late-medieval European and "premodern" Islamic conceptions of writing, which was seen as a means of recording acts accomplished in speech (Clanchy 1979; Messick 1993). When actions are not performed through writing, they are supposed to be autographically documented. From the official bureaucratic point of view, a person who is an agent but not an author, who causes things to happen without writing or being written about, is improper at best, corrupt at worst. Official procedures of file production are designed to determine agency (and therefore responsibility) absolutely by comprehensive documentation of authorship. Through autographic writing, the actions of individuals within an organization are made visible.

The requirement that official writing have an autographic component is part of the practical attack on the problem of words and things. This approach to the problem is based on the notion that certain kinds of graphic signs anchor written discourse in the world because they are the causal result of physical events involving the file. Official recognition of graphic forms such as signatures and stamps as the visible, perduring, physical result of unique events (and types of events) makes them officially sanctioned indexes of one or more elements of those events, such as the person, place, or time. Only discourse anchored through the use of such signs has the status that authorizes its use in official proceedings. Of course, not all graphic forms that might be judged to be the physical result of particular kinds of events are routinely sanctioned as official indexes. For example, the qualities of a particular handwriting are not official signs in routine business, though they become so in the hands of criminal investigators.

The main such sign, of course, is the signature or initials. The graphic ideology of the signature establishes a semiotic relation between a specific individual and a specific graphic form, produced, crucially, by an ostensibly inimitable biomechanical act, signing.[7] A signature is, to use Grice's term, a "natural" sign (causally produced by a physical event) and a conventional sign (a token of a type of graphic form socially recognized as the representation of an individual). The thumbprint one sometimes sees on petitions can function as a signature because it has the essential feature of a signature: its graphic qualities have a biomechanical connection with the person. Other graphic forms of identification, such as the *tughra* of the Mughal emperor (a calligraphic image) or the seals of Chinese imperial officials, index an individual, but this relation is based primarily on the political control of the image (unauthorized production of the imperial *tughra* was a capital offence) and, as in the Chinese case, on the physical control of the artifact capable of producing the image. Ideologically, the signature is unique not in indexing an individual but in establishing this relationship solely through bodily action.[8] The images produced by office stamps, which trace the movement of graphic artifacts among offices, also normatively function through a mechanism of physical causation: the image is produced by a stamp physically controlled by a group of functionaries in a particular physical location. In recognition that the stamps can be reproduced or removed from their rightful place in an office, stamp images are supplemented by autographic writing, which establishes an intertextual and interartifactual relation between the stamped graphic artifact and a diary book where movements are registered.

Graphic artifacts like files are so central to bureaucratic practices because they mediate the actions of individuals and larger groups, including that of the organization as a whole. The usefulness and authority of files arise in part from their mediating position between the corporate order of authority and responsibility and the specific event of writing. Translating Webb Keane's (1997:96) observations on the mediating role of ritual speech, we can say that this mediation of files is dialectical insofar as it does not simply attempt to fit specific events into a preexisting template but also works to construct in concrete forms the very corporate order that it appears to reproduce. Through graphic artifacts, functionaries locate their actions within a presupposable social context and create a social context around their actions. The circulation of files and the use of linguistic and nonlinguistic forms that weakly or obscurely index individual authorship are strategies functionaries use to escape the consequences of the precise pragmatic specification of individual authorship. The objective of the circulatory and discursive strategies of functionaries is to pragmatically and metapragmatically construct their writings as corporately authored.

The effort to achieve corporate authorship and agency may be compared to ritual in its use of hypertrophied semiotic means to create self-grounding discourse.[9] John Kelly and Martha Kaplan, following Valerio Valeri, observe that "rituals displace authority and authorship." They argue that the "special power in ritual acts, including their unique ability to encompass contestation, lies in the *lack* of independence asserted by a ritual participant, even while he or she makes assertions about authority" (Kelly and Kaplan 1990:140). The authority of ritual flows from the ability of the speaker to divorce speech from the immediate context of its production, to transform particular utterances made by an individual in particular circumstances into discourse that is autonomous, grounded in some order beyond the speaker's intentions. Correlatively, as Keane puts it, ritual speech constitutes "the participants, speaking and nonspeaking, as representatives of social entities that exist beyond the time and space of the momentary context. *Semiotic* representation here functions as *socio-political* representation" (1997:135).

I think we can see an analogous process at work in files in the Pakistan bureaucracy. When compelled to act on an issue, functionaries employ various circulatory and discursive strategies to divorce their writings from themselves by merging them with the broadest context of their production, so that autographic writings become grounded in the corporate order of the bureaucratic organization beyond the individual agency of their authors. In the use of CDA files, the individualizing and collectivizing procedures extend themselves together. As practices are rationalized from the point of view of organizational control (by subjecting actions to a regime of written documentation), these practices are elaborately deployed to generate a collective agent. The irony is that the more you try to pin responsibility to individuals, the more responsibility is collectivized. These procedures are elaborated not because of some immanent logic of rationalization, but because functionaries protect themselves by deploying them vigorously and widely.

Authoritative, collective discourse results from the cooperative and competitive efforts of individuals to escape the responsibility that rationalizing procedures link to authorship. While a functionalist sociology would see the operational needs of a bureaucratic organization generating collective discourse, such discourse is better understood as an important byproduct of individual efforts to avoid individual responsibility. The contemporary emphasis on bureaucracy as an institution of domination has occluded the degree to which subsumption into the corporate organization protects the individual even as it controls him or her (Sennett 1998). As I will discuss later in the chapter, in addition to protecting individuals, the strategic use of graphic artifacts can enable individuals to collectivize their individual projects, both legal and illegal.

In his treatment of bureaucratic writing, Goody (1986) focuses on the role of records as an instrument of stable reference and predication about states of affairs behind and beyond the office doors. Certainly, this is a function of many official graphic genres in different settings, but in the Pakistan bureaucracy it is often not the main function of files. In the fertile discursive soil of the Pakistan bureaucracy, great flowering jungles of file-mediated discourse grow from the seeds of a few facts. Much of the denotational discourse mediated by files refers not to the matter under consideration but to the actions and statements of functionaries. Furthermore, denotational discourse on the matter under consideration always functions tropically as a representation of agency or, what is the same thing, the relations among functionaries in various official interactions.

The authority of bureaucratic discourse—that is, why it compels agreement and obedience—is not simply a function of referential correctness, official position, and the use of a certain linguistic register (for example, Bakhtin's [1981] "authoritative speech"). Rather, this authority is a pragmatic discursive achievement that fabricates an artifactualized representation of a political alliance of functionaries (cf. Latour 1987). This explains the paradox (from a referentialist functional perspective) that in Islamabad documents are widely seen as manipulable while at the same time they are an essential media of bureaucratic action. The authoritative agency of the organization is out of the hands of any single individual. Documents are powerful when constructed jointly (and usually in an unequal way) by a number of individuals through their writings. Through compelled or voluntary alliances with graphic artifacts, functionaries are brought into willing or unwilling alliances with other functionaries. Documents can be more like other material elements of bureaucracy such as chairs and desks than we typically think. For many genres of documents, it is often less important what they stand for than, like tables and desks, how they arrange people around themselves.

The effectiveness of the alliance-making process is an achievement, a semiotic process that can fail, rather than simply a mechanistic procedure or construction. Many factors may condition the success of bureaucratic collectivization, such as competition of interests and the uncontrollability of the artifacts. Furthermore, the achievement of corporate authorship is never secure. Functionaries never know when it will be called into question for some reason and dissolve into the specific written statements of individuals. A disciplinary investigation proceeds in the opposite direction as the collectivizing practices by attempting to dissolve corporate authorship and identify particular writings with individuals. So, how do bureaucrats deflect the individualizing effects of signatures, stamps, and diary logs?

TACTICS OF IRRESPONSIBILITY AND THE BYPRODUCT OF THE COLLECTIVE

The simplest and most obvious response to the predicament of authorship is not to write at all. The Llewlyn-Smith Report reviewing the office practices of the British Government of India, published in 1920, observed disapprovingly that government departments "have developed a type of organization more suited for criticism than for direct initiative" (Government of India [1920] 1963:35). The report attributed the reactive character of departments to the artifactual foundation of official work. Work was rarely initiated from within because casework proceeded as a response to an initiating petition or written representation from another department. The recommendations of the Llewelyn-Smith Report to resolve this problem of initiative implicitly recognized that inscriptional practices rather than organizational role definitions were more fundamental determinants of bureaucratic action. Rather than trying to change the inscription practices within a particular organizational structure, the reforms recommended changing the organizational structures to fit the inscriptional practices. Both of the report's proposed solutions amounted to an organizational doubling that formally redefined a part of the department as external so that correspondence from this division would be treated as external and therefore would require a response. The first solution was to appoint an officer to the department as an "advisor" or as an "attached officer." The attached officer was able to initiate projects within the department because "the proposals of the Attached Office come to the Secretariat as a receipt from the outside" (Government of India [1920] 1963:36). Similarly, the report called for the establishment of special committees or commissions to advise departments, the recommendations of which would be received and examined "in the same way as any other 'receipt' from without" ([1920] 1963).

Internal initiative is no less rare today. In the hundreds of files I examined, not a single one had been opened on the initiative of an officer in the same directorate. Officials are often informed of issues through oral discussions with other officials or nonofficials, but they will not begin official procedures on the basis of this knowledge, preferring to wait until some written representation is received. A recent manual on office procedure even defined noting as "the written remarks recorded on a note sheet in regard to a communication under consideration in order to facilitate its disposal" (Malik 1999:28). Even when they do receive a communication, they may look for ways not to respond to it. In several cases I examined, officials recommended that the CDA ignore letters from representatives of civic and religious organizations because they were not officially registered with the government. In addition to the desire to avoid involvement in matters, the status implications of initiating communication with someone over whom one has no direct authority, which would position one as a subordinate petitioner, also shape the disposition of officials for inaction.[10]

Complete inaction, however, is usually not an option. Moreover, as one official quipped playfully, "The ideal is always to appear to be busy while actually doing nothing." With respect to writing, this means writing a lot and saying nothing—or at least nothing that was not said by someone else. Practices of corporate authorship are a means of approaching this ideal.

The most basic practice in the construction of corporate authority is the circulation of the file. Circulatory practices are central to the construction of corporate authority because a file is the sole embodiment of a case. That is, a single file contains all the material representations that reference a particular case, at least during the period when a matter is under consideration. The identification of file and case is codified in the official definition of "case" given in the CDA *Rules for the Conduct of Business* in 1985: "'Case' means [a] particular matter under consideration and includes all papers relating to it and required to enable the matter to be disposed of, viz. correspondence and notes and also any previous papers on the subject or subject covered by it or connected with it."

This identification is also commonly evidenced in discourse that figures the case itself as physically and socially located and mobile, for example, the statement of one officer that "cases just get passed up and around when no one wants to make a decision." This aspect of files contrasts with CDA reports, for instance, which are printed and distributed in a diffusely defined field of both internal and external readers, something like a limited public (Warner 2002). In fact, artifacts with more general circulations are often channeled into social networks by being placed on file. I sometimes found whole reports inserted in a file, becoming the captured writing of the case file. Similarly, memos, distributed by what we might call a narrowcast system, cannot provide the basis for an artifactualized representation of an alliance among officials. Graphic evidence of who has read the memos and how they responded to them is dispersed in different artifacts. To reconstruct the authorship of a decision developed through memos is a complex task that would demand gathering separate artifacts dispersed in different locations. The continuance of file circulation practices is perhaps evidence of the greater salience of the complementary functions of surveillance and the collectivization of authority in the bureaucracies of the Indian subcontinent compared to those in Britain. As early as 1920, Llewellyn Smith observed that "this practice [of file circulation] is in sharp contrast to that which prevails in the United Kingdom where (as a general rule) files are not sent from one Department to another, but formal references take place by the transmission of written letters of memoranda" ([1920] 1963:71).

Files are kept moving up and down the chain of command, through the cooperation or competition of functionaries. As described earlier, the file is normally moved on the established vertical paths of the organizational hierarchy. The file is even marked to officers on leave, even if they are known to be absent. The assistant to the absent officer or the next recipient does not strike the mark of the absent officer, but notes next to his name, "On leave." One file on a sensitive issue I read had been moved up and down the organizational hierarchy through an absent officer's office several times. The objective is to demonstrate that the attempt was made to consult the absent officer and no irregularities of procedure occurred. Files on minor matters routinely reach the office of the chairman, as officers pass files up the chain to avoid having to make a decision. One former CDA chairman told me that his efforts to stem the exasperating flow of files to him had failed completely, though he had authorized his subordinate officers—in writing, he emphasized—to handle various classes of cases. Officials also extend the scope of those involved by circulating files to other departments that might be affected by the matter. And almost every file can be "referred for comments" to the departments of administration, law, finance, and personnel, which are always concerned (*mutaliqah*). In explaining this practice, one officer of the Lands Directorate cited the example of a file he had recently encountered regarding the straightforward transfer of land by someone having power of attorney. The file should have been handled immediately by the Law Directorate but was passed around for three months, to Lands, to Finance, then back to Lands, where the officer found his staff had diligently generated a several-page report of the property detailing its history from the late nineteenth century to the present.

Even when an issue is dealt with in speech rather than writing, the movement of the file may structure and document oral discussion, as when the file is used to issue instructions to "discuss." Consider the following exchange among a town planner (TP-1), an assistant town planner (ATP), and a surveyor, which lasted nearly two months:

> *TP-I:* 14. Pl discuss.
> *[signature] TP-I*
> *16–3–82*

> *ATP:* 15. Please discuss with TP-I.
> *[signature] ATP*
> *18–3–82*

> *Surveyor:* 16. After discussion the file is submitted on 28–3–82.
> *[signature] Surveyor*
> *28–3–82*

> *TP-I:* 17. Please discuss.
> *[signature] TP-I*
> *6–5–82*

ATP: 18. Discussed.
[signature] ATP
7–5–82

The circulation of the file precipitates a multiparty interaction through which authorship and therefore agency, as constructed in official ideology, is distributed over a larger and larger network of functionaries. The achievement of movement up and down the chain of command and laterally to other departments produces on the note sheet a representation of collective agency. In cases where circulatory and discursive events are successful, individually authored notings are procedurally transmuted into corporate discourse. The last of the material accretions through which a decision is enacted (made) is the initials of the most senior functionary, like Zaffar Khan at the start of this chapter. The transmutation from a collection of utterances to an authoritative collective decision is then finalized through its repeated circulation to all the functionaries who had commented on it before, and they merely initial it (fig. 3.3).

The most subtle ways that responsibility is distributed, while usually depending on circulation, are fundamentally discursive and inscriptional. We can roughly distinguish two broad sets of language practices that represent the writer as a constrained, passive, or uninvolved agent: first, those that accomplish this through representation of *people, states of affairs,* and *nonverbal actions* and, second, those that do it through representation of *writing* and *speech.* In particular written utterances, of course, these devices are often used in concert.

Note sheet discourse exhibits the formal linguistic features commonly found in ritual speech. Kuipers argues that ritual speech attempts to avoid or deemphasize personal reference in contrast to nonauthoritative but contextualized speech, which is personal and individuated (1990:64–65). The first person pronoun *I* was commonly used in files from the 1960s but is rarely found in contemporary files. I have no comprehensive statistical evidence, but one measure of the almost complete absence of *I* in contemporary files is that, in one series of notes with over 180 paragraphs, *I* was used only once, in the note of an official informing his superior that he should discuss the case with others in the future since he will be on leave. In this case, responsibility is avoided rather than embraced through the individually distinguishing use of *I. We,* the collective inclusive first person, is the most commonly used personal pronoun. Writers rarely refer to themselves as individuals using the deictic *I,* which directly indexes the writing situation. More commonly, they refer

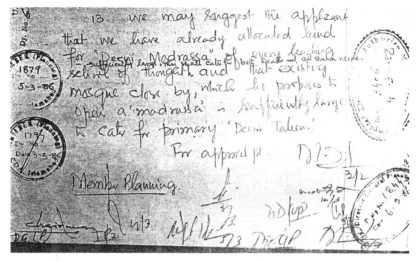

FIGURE 3.3. Initials on a note sheet that produce a decision, 1986.

to themselves via references to their signature, which references them as a node in the chain producing a file, as in the following example.

> 78. However, the Member Planning, Director (UP) and undersigned visited the site in detail.

The numbering of paragraphs places notes in series undifferentiated by author, time, and so forth. The employment of a numbered paragraph scheme makes it possible to refer to the writings of others without referring to them as individuals, as would be the case in speech: for example, "123. Vide para 119/N . . . " The "metricality" index of numbering paragraphs paces each turn in a poetic contextualization structure that substitutes for reference to the world beyond the file.

References to other officials are, however, necessary when the discourse referenced is oral rather than written. In such cases, officials are generally referred to or addressed in the third person by title, as in the following example of a deputy director general addressing a member of the board, his immediate superior: "7. The Member Planning may kindly recall his visit to the site when it was agreed to permit plot size of 40' × 32' for the Madrasa close to the existing water tank." Such references to officeholders may actually refer to different individuals in narratives that cover a period in which one occupant of an office has succeeded another. In such cases, the former occupant may be referred to as the "then" official, for example, the "then chairman." In the rare occurrences of the second person pronoun *you*, it is used by superiors forcefully conveying their disapproval or annoyance at a subordinates performance, as in the following example of a superior upbraiding a subordinate for delaying a site visit: "You may use my Suzuki on 12/9/88 for site visit."[11]

The signature is the one unavoidable reference to self. However, an informal ideology (elaborated from a simpler official ideology) of the signature blunts the force of self-reference. According to this graphic ideology, which several functionaries described to me, there is a hierarchy of signatures that differentially indexes the degree of involvement indicated. From most involved to least, they are: (1) full typed name and title, with full signature and stamp; (2) full typed name and title without stamp; (3) full signature; (4) initials; (5) small initials. The graphic area occupied by this self-reference is an icon of involvement. Small initials, the weakest index of commitment, no more than a graphic nod of the head, are the most common.

The prevalence of passive verbs, which obscure or minimize the agency of officials by allowing the omission of agentive subject specification, is a commonly identified feature of written bureaucratic discourse (Charrow 1982; Sarangi and Slembrouck 1996; Shuy 1998). The specificity of the functionary-client interaction, however, is not taken into account when the use of passive verb forms is described as a general feature of bureaucratic writing. Most studies of oral discourse in formal institutions have focused on the interactions between representatives of the institutions and clients. This is also the emphasis of the work on written bureaucratic discourse, which is based upon analysis of genres through which organizations represent themselves to clients or the public at large: letters from institutions to individuals, forms for gathering client information, and published documents and reports.

In CDA letters to petitioners, functionaries almost always use passive forms to represent the decisions or actions of the CDA. For example, a CDA official wrote in a favorable reply to a petition for a mosque site, "You are requested to nominate the management committee and intimate the CDA so that possession of the site may be handed over." However, in internal written discourse, that is, in discourse addressed to other functionaries, the use of passive forms is more complex. The passive is, in fact, the most common verb form for the representation of action in internal writings as well, but it would be wrong to conclude that the passive is simply the generic verb form for the representation of bureaucratic action. The passive voice is prevalent because functionaries are so often describing their *own* actions or actions that involve them. Functionaries tactically use passive forms to represent their own actions, but they use active forms to represent the actions of other officials and nonofficial actors. Consider the following example.

> 161. PUC at page 62/c is a letter from Director Co-ordination in which he asked the information regarding the mosques in Islamabad. A detailed mosque survey was carried out and requisite information were collected. Accordingly the plan showing the above-informations was prepared which was shown to D.D.G. Plg.

Note first the typical narrative structure of this example. The action of the writer or a group including the writer is explicitly represented as a response to an initiating action of a superior officer. This portrayal of self as reactive is buttressed by the shift from active to passive voice. The functionary represents the action of the Director Co-ordination in the active voice: "he asked the information." In contrast, he represents his own actions and the actions of his subordinates in the passive: "was carried out," "were collected," "was prepared," "was shown."

Rather than the simple English contrast between active and passive, Urdu has a more elaborate grammatical system for the expression of the relationship between an actor and an action. In the files of the Auqaf Department of the ICTA, where noting of the lowest functionaries is often in Urdu, I found the same contrast between the use of relatively more active and relatively more passive verb forms. Also prevalent were the use of nominal forms that do not grammatically express an agent, which are quite natural in Urdu, for example, *"Fair tayar ho gaya"* (The fair [letter] became prepared) and *"Masjid committee se bat hui thi"* ([There] had been a meeting with the mosque committee). Braj B. Kachru (1992:539) has even suggested that passive and impersonal grammatical constructions in Hindi and Dravidian languages developed under the influence of English, especially, we might add, English experienced predominantly in bureaucratic settings.

In reporting the facts of cases, what linguists call "evidentials," linguistic forms that express the writer's subjective orientation to a proposition or its evidentiary grounds are almost never used. Here, the ideals of transparent, objective language and self-effacement converge. Propositional discourse is always in the simple declarative (for example, "no unauthorised Abadi [settlement] sprung up in the city has been recognized as katchi Abadi [informal settlement] by the CDA"), the "epistemically unmarked" form with which a speaker "presents [a proposition] without actually signaling commitment" (Palmer 1986:86–87). Lexical evidentials such as "maybe," "probably," and "certainly" are almost completely absent.

Given that the CDA is a planning agency, concerned with determining future developments of the city, we might expect to find the future tense used in reference to proposals. But the future is never used, because it invokes the will of the writing subject and commits him to action, which he might be held accountable for executing. This bureaucratic ethic converges with an Islamic evaluation of the use of the future tense. In ordinary conversation, it is rarely used without *inshallah* (God willing). For example, in arranging to visit a friend's house, someone might say, "Inshallah, I will come tomorrow." Without such an invocation, the use of the future is seen as a hubristic or even impious assertion of oneself over the will of God. The virtual absence of the future tense in reference to official plans was pointed out to me by a town planner when I asked him about the relation of planning to Islamic notions of God's omnipotence and therefore ultimate control of the future. "In planning," he replied, "we are not talking about the future." This surprising observation is grammatically accurate at least. Plans for the future are represented through the performative approval of a proposal.[12] Sometimes, the head officer will write something like "89. We may approve the proposal at Para 87" and sign it. More often, the head officer just pens his signature or initials following a subordinate's note such as "157. Submitted for approval."

In deliberations on applications, functionaries use a variety of words and phrases that portray themselves as subject to external control. Such locutions deny the agency of writers by representing them as willing but unable in view of official compulsion. The best example of this is the use of "regret" to mean "reject," which is a contracted characterization of denial ("regret to reject").

> 20. Another of those cases which have to be re-considered as applicants are never satisfied with a "NO".

> 21. Yes, we may regret, once again.

> 23. The Board has already regretted his case vide para 13/N. If agreed we may again regret the case.

In the following example, we find an innovative descriptor, "regretion," characterizing the total event of deliberation resulting in the communication of a "regret": "24. We may maintain our earlier decision for regretion vide para 13/N." "Accede" is also commonly used, as in "34. We may not accede to the request," in which functionaries portray themselves as willing but unfortunately unable to go along with the desires of the petitioner.

File discourse is saturated with indexes of hierarchical relations between functionaries that express the relative status of writer and addressee and lay discourse into the frame of the bureaucratic order as a whole. These indexes of hierarchy frame the material transfer of a thing, the file, as an act of subordination or superordination. One of the more interesting examples is a ubiquitous exchange (a pragmatic pair part structure) in which the syntactic placement of "please" indexes the relative status of writer and addressee. Superior-to-subordinate utterances begin with "please" and subordinate-to-superior ones close with "please," as in this exchange between a deputy director of urban planning and his subordinate town planner:

Deputy Director: 35. Pl put up draft.

Town Planner: 36. DFA is submitted please.

It is significant that the only official whose noting I read who did not employ this structure in addressing subordinates was an official with significant foreign experience who was well known for treating subordinates with greater respect. He often ends his notes to subordinates with "please." His notes to superiors, however, were structured according to the norm.

This order serves subordinates better than superiors when it comes to responsibility. It is easier for subordinates to shift responsibility up than for superiors to shift responsibility down, because superiors are giving the orders. In her discussion of Wolof discourse, Judith Irvine (1996) observes that the utterances of a low-status Wolof bard in Senegal can never bear the same responsibility as those of a noble, because the nature of their ranks presupposes different participations in decision making and dialogue. Similarly, an official ideology of organizational hierarchy shapes varying conceptions of agency, as well as different levels of responsibility among CDA and ICTA functionaries. We can see in verb forms of written directives the way superiors try to minimize the representation of their control of subordinates. The way officers direct their subordinates in speech and in writing is quite different. In speech, when directing subordinates in English, officials almost always use direct imperatives. Similarly in Urdu and Punjabi speech, they employ imperatives or other various constructions indicating compulsion (for example, "You must make a plan" ["*Aap ko naqsha banana hai*"]). In writing, however, the strong English form "must" is never used, and imperatives are used only where some purely procedural action is commanded. Most common is the weak form "may" in the passive, particularly if a substantive action is enjoined:

32. Dft may be issued & copy of letter may be sent to all concerned.

In purely denotational terms, the superior is simply giving permission to someone to take such action, licensing agency downward. We could gloss the typical formulation "we may regret the request," for example, as "in the range of possible responses, an expression of regret is one, of which you will be the author." Such a locution directs the subordinate even as it indexes his or her relative independence. Pragmatically, however, it is clearly a directive aimed at the addressee. In reply, subordinates usually make this pragmatic implication explicit, reporting their superiors' "permissions" as directives. An account of action (which is usually addressed to a superior) almost always includes a characterization that casts the action as done at the behest of a superior. Consider this exchange between a town planner and his assistant:

Town Planner: 78. Case may be put up.

    Assistant: 79. The subject case file is submitted as desired in pre para 78/N please.

In reporting actions, even simple things like making copies, there is a major amount of explicit reference to the directives of superiors. In most cases, as in this example, these directives are contained in the previous note, so the reference is not simply a device to expedite reference to a directive buried somewhere in the note file.

The material of inscription is also significant: inscriptions are always made in ink. Use of other media is so rare that I might have overlooked the significance of ink, if not for my own incompetent attempt to use what, after learning a little (but not enough), I thought to be the usual means of obtaining documents: a petition. The very senior deputy director general (Planning) received my petition with enthusiasm and said he would happily instruct his staff to give me the documents. After a pleasant chat about my project and a second cup of green tea, he took out a pencil, put a sidebar next to one set of documents and an aster-

isk next to the other, marked it to his immediate subordinate, the director (Planning), and gave it to his menial to transport. Pleased with my
command of local bureaucratic practice, I followed my petition to the
director's office and told the officer that his superior had approved the
request. After he scanned the petition, he looked puzzled and a bit concerned. He marked the petition to his deputy director in pencil and sent
it and me off with the menial. The deputy director also received the petition and me with confusion, but quickly marked the petition (and, by
extension, me) in ink to the town planner and personally escorted both
of us to the town planner. After a few words to the town planner, which
I didn't follow, he left. I was on good terms with this planner and I sat
down and told him with some self-satisfaction that indeed my request
had been granted. He looked at the petition, frowned, and began to
laugh. He explained the meaning of the inscriptions my petition had
gathered along its path. The asterisk, he said, meant "stay away from
this [set of documents]" and the sidebar highlighted the second set of
documents. According to the planner, however, the key to the inscriptions of the two most senior officers was that they were in pencil, signaling the officers' lack of commitment, since they could be erased if
need be. The use of pencil was a material index that these marks were
(or could be made to be) off the record. The planner summarized the
meaning of the inscriptions as "I am not taking responsibility for this.
Do the second part if you want and don't do the first part." This, the
planner told me, was precisely what the deputy director had told him
before leaving. The planner nevertheless generously had both sets of
documents given to me the next week.

Another set of tactics bureaucrats use to deflect responsibility
depends on the ways they position their own inscriptions and discourse
in relation to those of others. As Bakhtin observed,

> The topic of a speaking person has enormous importance in everyday life.
> In real life we hear speech about speakers and their discourse at every step.
> We can go so far as to say that in real life people talk most of all about what
> others talk about—they transmit, recall, weigh and pass judgment on others
> people's words, opinions, assertions, information; people are upset by oth-
> ers' words, or agree with them, contest them, refer to them and so forth."
> (1981:338)

If we substitute writing for speech, this observation is especially true of
file-mediated discourse. Much of what bureaucrats write is about the
writing of others. Bakhtin was characterizing speech as an aspect of

social life in general, but in the Pakistan bureaucracy functionaries write about the writing of others—using the writing of others—for a specific purpose: to diffuse responsibility for their own writing.

Goody argued that in written form, commands and therefore responsibility are more precise: "personalized commitment 'in writing' also means that responsibility for giving and receiving orders is more highly individualized" (1986:124). He contrasted this with a chain of oral messages where the identity of the originator gets lost. This might be the case for some governmental genres, for example, the "executive order" of the United States president, issued solely under the authority and signature of the president, directing an agency to execute a law in a particular way.[13] However, in the complexity of roles embedded in orders executed through the circulation of Pakistan files, responsibility is a much murkier issue.

Erving Goffman (1974) observed that what we commonly designate with the term "speaker" is actually composed of a several distinct kinds of participants. Among other possible realizations of a "speaker," he distinguished an *animator* who utters the talk, an *author* who has chosen the words that are uttered, and a *principal* "whose position is established by the words that are spoken . . . someone who is committed to what the words say" (Goffman 1981:144). Thus, a politician delivering a speech written by others is the animator and the principal, but not the author, of the speech. The United States president is the principal of an executive order, but is usually neither its author nor its animator, since they are usually released in writing. Others have expanded Goffman's scheme, analytically distinguishing as many as seventeen different participant roles in speaking (Levinson 1988). However, as Irvine (1996) has argued, the analytic decomposition of speaker roles misses how discourse itself fragments speaker roles in unpredictable ways, how complex participant roles are generated in the structure of ongoing speech itself. She shows this process in Wolof insult poetry directed at the bride and her kin, which is performed at weddings by low-status poets but composed somewhat secretively with the help of women of the groom's lineage. The practices of composition and performance disperse responsibility for the insult among a number of participants in a historical chain of speech events "because the insult utterance can be presumed to be part of a sequence of utterance events" (Irvine 1996:139). The poet can claim to be merely transmitting the insult while the sponsoring women deny responsibility for "the special nastiness of a particular poem" (136).

The written utterance sequences of files have the same pragmatic effect, though the tactics of dispersing responsibility are of necessity much more complex, since the whole discursive process is visibly documented (rather than only presumed) and is designed, as in Goody's ideal, to resist just such dispersal. In practice, although the formal organizational hierarchy lays down role categories for all participants (a hierarchy of offices), the roles linked to responsibility for a particular "disposal" of a case emerge through that disposal, that is, in writing. Goody, following Weber's classic treatment of bureaucracy, underestimates the importance of these emergent roles or merely assumes they are congruent with formal positions.

One of the main ways that bureaucrats position their inscriptions and discourse in relation to those of others is through "reported speech" and what we might call "exhibited writing." Bakhtin and V.N. Volosinov defined "reported speech" as simultaneously "speech within speech . . . and speech about speech" (Volosinov 1986:115). In Volosinov's account, direct or verbatim quotation and indirect quotation or description of speech are the extremes of a continuum of the ways reported utterances relate to the utterances that report them (reporting discourse), a continuum from relative separation to relative fusion. In direct quotation (for example, "'I forge banknotes?' Chichikov exclaimed" [Gogol 1985:231]), the reported utterance maintains its autonomy from the reporting discourse. Bakhtin described how the novelist, in order to represent the intentions of others within the novel, uses direct quotation to maintain a maximal distance from the discourse of his or her characters: "those words that are completely denied any authorial intention: the author does not express himself in them . . . rather he exhibits them. . . . [T]he author ventriloquates" (1981:299). In indirect quotation (for example, "To this Chichikov assented readily enough—merely adding that he should like first of all to be furnished with a list of the dead souls" [Gogol 1985:131]), the reported utterances are transformed in accordance with the interests and style of the reporting discourse. The author of indirect quotation is intimately involved with it, commenting on or evaluating it in the very act of reporting it.

Volosinov intended the term "reported speech" to refer broadly to all forms of representing "outside" discourse. However, we need to distinguish between oral and written reporting discourse because, in addition to the linguistic means for representing discourse as Volosinov described, the material qualities of files enable kinds of reported discourse not possible in an oral channel.

A common example of this is what we might call "exhibited writing," a portion of another person's writing that the noter exhibits by underlining it or by placing a sidebar and sometimes a letter next to it in order to refer to it in his or her note, for example, "12. We may not accede to the request on grounds |x|." References to paragraph numbers on note sheets function similarly. Like footnotes or endnotes, paragraph numbers point to inscriptions that are easily accessed if not present in the same visual field as the reference to them. The material structure of files and the visual channel of writing render the referenced writings as much a part of the discourse as they would be if they were linguistically represented through direct quotation. Both these forms of reference render other writing even more autonomous from the author than direct quotation. On a cline from the least to the greatest involvement of the author, the order of these different types of reports is the following: visual index, paragraph reference, direct quotation, and indirect quotation. This order corresponds to the frequency of their occurrence within files. If reported text is on the same page as the reporting note, a sidebar is almost always used. If the reported text is not on the same page, a paragraph reference is used.

When a paragraph reference can't be used because the writing quoted is not on current file but on some other file or in a policy document, direct quotation is used. Usually the document quoted will also be put on the file. The author of a note proposing the rejection of the request to use green space for a mosque site, for example, quoted the order written in 1986 from then Prime Minister Junejo prohibiting the conversion of green areas and also put a copy of his order on the file. Indirect quotation is used sometimes for reporting speech (where it is unavoidable because direct quotation is not certifiable) but never for writing, for it most directly implicates the author in the reportive frame and thus identifies him to a greater degree than the previous three methods with the reported words.

Given the volume of files that surge to the senior officers of a division, they usually write very little on files beyond their signature. Even reading may be similarly minimized. Like Zaffar Khan at his coffee table, superior officers sometimes consciously and conspicuously use the tactic of making their assistants tell them what is in files rather than reading files themselves, so they are protected by yet another mediation. In Zaffar Khan's case, this practice obviously expressed his contempt for paperwork and, he admitted to me, his superior frowned on it. However, as he explained to me, his reputation for disposing of files in such a fashion served him well in the event that a proposal he approved generated adverse results or was subject to an audit or disciplinary review. Everyone knew he never read the files he signed. He could always be accused of negligence, but could never be held responsible for making a wrong or irregular decision. He was not informed of the particulars and literally took his subordinate's word for it.

If circumstances demand a more substantial contribution from senior officers, they usually do not introduce new facts or change the evaluative stance of their subordinates' writings. They can also have their notes typed and sign them without reading them, so liability can be attributed to their assistant or the typist. By signing their own typed note without reading it, they attempt to turn the note they sign into the typist's graphic report of their speech, rather than the animation of it.

Most of the substantive writing on files is found at the lowest level of officers—for example, town planners at grade 17. Unfortunately for them, they have no one to whom to delegate writing. As one Indian bureaucrat working in a similar system put it wittily, "Remember the mathematical formulation that responsibility is directly proportional to the size of one's written contribution to a file" (Kaw 1993:96), a principle we saw at work in the evaluation of signatures as well.

Not only must they write more, but such lower-ranking officers also have almost no writing of other officers from which to compose their own. In addition to citing precedents, policies, and maps, they assemble much of their notes by translating the discourse of communications received into a note. However angry, false, desperate, indirect, humble, pious, or condescending the written communication, these officials almost always characterize its discourse using the dry, neutral verbs of report, "write" and "request," to avoid the evaluative responsibility of verbs such as "claim," "argue," "imply," "plead," "demand," and so forth. For example, a letter written in 1996 from Shias in G-7 very assertively articulated the injustice and hardships of not having a Shia mosque in the sector ("our grievances"). Translated into the file, this demanding petition became "an application . . . wherein they have requested allocation of site for Shia Mosque in Sector G-7." However, officials will sometimes report the petitioner's own characterization of their discourse to present an evaluative position without implicating themselves. Thus, one official who was sympathetic to petitions for the regularization of illegal mosques—a very controversial issue—added moral support to a letter by presenting it in the following way: "The petitioners write that they plead that the said mosque be regularized."

Similarly, facts relevant to an issue are usually presented as reports of others' writing, rather than as the writer's own statements about actual states of affairs.

In addition to presenting the matter, these officials are also supposed to make a recommendation regarding it. This puts them in a difficult position, for they become the authors of definite proposals. Fortunately, they have recourse to "putting up" the file to a superior, who must reject the note or assume partial authorship of it through approval. The final numbered paragraph on a subordinate officer's note is usually a characterization of the note as a "submission": "25. Submitted please" and "37. Submitted for approval pl." Often, beyond deferentially characterizing his or her note, the subordinate will emphasize that it was done at the superior's behest, for example, "102. Submitted as desired for necessary further action please."

Like Bakhtin's ventriloquating novelist, bureaucrats use reported inscriptions and discourse to distance their discourse from themselves. But they try to adopt the role of the dummy, not the ventriloquist. The novelist uses reported speech to differentiate, particularize, and dialogize a text wholly authored by him- or herself. In contrast, by submerging their discourse in that of others, by writing through the writing of others, bureaucrats transform a multiply authored and dialogic text into a monologic one, dispersing authorial responsibility for even the notes he or she has signed.

Through all these circulatory, discursive, and inscriptional practices, functionaries try to maximize the mediations of their actions and writings, transforming the procedures designed to specify responsibility into the means to disperse it. When they are successful, autographs are the only inscriptions that can be wholly identified with individuals.

PARTICULAR PROJECTS AND COLLECTIVE AGENCY

The powerful process through which corporate authority is generated allows particular projects to be collectivized and executed by the organization. Some bureaucrats identify with the passive, constrained, and scrupulous characters they create for themselves in their writings on files. However, in conversation, many bureaucrats portray themselves and others as different sorts of vigorous actors: powerful heroes battling other bureaucrats, politicians, and the system as a whole; venal and corrupt villains undermining the integrity of government; or clever operators outwitting other bureaucrats and artfully playing the game.

Beneath the cover of corporate authority and using the corporate agency it enables, such bureaucrats, as individuals or in combinations, attempt to get things done. Bureaucrats increase their influence by diligently cultivating relationships beyond the circulation of paper, with subordinates, superiors, and colleagues well placed elsewhere in the bureaucracy, and patrons in senior political, bureaucratic, and military positions. To be successful in a particular case, however, such work must come to be grounded in files. Influence over the movement and content of files is the most direct way officials exercise power over people and things. Influence over files is itself a sign of power.

When, as in many American offices, emails and memos mediate deliberations and directives, cases are distributed over a dispersed set of artifacts—common servers and individual hard drives, folders, and desks. Such a loose connection between a case and any one of its material elements makes it easy to think of a case as a set of circumstances or facts. But this view of a case is an abstraction from the material practices that sustain it as a particular kind of bureaucratic object. Material documentation is an essential component of the case; we might even say, adapting the quip that "a language is a dialect with an army and a navy," that a case is a set of circumstances with some material documentation.[14] Cases in Pakistan are not unique in being materially enacted. Rather, it is the form of that materiality that interests us: the Pakistan case is enacted through a *single* file. Though this is a routine fact of bureaucratic process little remarked upon in Islamabad, the consequences of this ontology of the case are far-reaching and perhaps the aspect of cases with the most significance for the functioning of the bureaucracy.

The misrouting or loss of a file shows how much the sociomaterial dispositions of files shape the disposal of cases. When the file is neglected, so is the case, because the file is the only means to grasp the case (in both senses), to distribute work on the case, and even to have work count as being on the case. A languishing case concerning the construction of a church in 1992, for example, shows how the file is both a prompt to and an instrument for dealing with the case. The CDA received a reference on the church from the *wafaqi mohtasib* (the federal ombudsman), an office established with an Islamic title as part of Zia-ul-Haq's Islamization program. By statute, communications from this office must be replied to within a matter of days, but the case was delayed. The account of these events produced by the officers involved is a story of the file. The deputy director reprimanded the town planner on the file at issue as follows:

Action was required to be completed on immediate basis as it was desired at P148/N and file was got delivered personally on 02/01/92. Instead of completing action TP preferred to go on leave and marked the file to ATP and thereafter it remained unattended at TP's table up to 08/01/92.

In his defense, the town planner similarly defended himself through a report of the assistant town planner's (ATP) mismanagement of the file:

I had clearly instructed to return the file to DD(UP-II) immediately after doing the needful but ATP returned the file to TP5 [a different town planner]. . . . ATP should explain the reasons why he returned file to TP5 marking wrong date, inspite of clearest instructions given at para 149/N.

In acknowledging his responsibility, the assistant town planner wrote, "It is admitted that the file was wrongly marked to TP-5 instead DDUP II by me contrary to contents of para 149/N."[15] The question of whether someone else who was aware of the case should have known to deal with it even without possession of the file never arose.

Happily, this file was merely mismarked. A lost file poses greater problems, showing the total dependence of a case on its file. Officers are often vexed by the loss of a file and sometimes take up the issue in writing. One file was inauspiciously opened in 1967 to discuss a file that had gone missing:

1. The file No. CDA/PLD-11(24)67 relating to construction of State Bank of Pakistan in Islamabad is not traceable in this section. Efforts have been made to locate the file within the office but of no use. If agreed to, we may issue a general circular to all the Directorates, offices of CDA to execute a thorough search within their limit + let us have our file back if found with them?

The missing file was needed to respond to an inquiry from the State Bank. The lower officers wanted to obtain copies of earlier correspondence from State Bank itself, but the director was concerned that "it will look very peculiar" and directed his staff to keep looking for the file. They sent a "circular," a memo, around to all the CDA directorates, but no one else had it. The estate office, which had some of the required information, wasn't cooperative and did not reply to either oral or written requests. By the fifteenth note on the investigation file, responsibility became the issue: "We will have to fix the responsibility," wrote the director. Unfortunately, only the file itself could help. Looking hopefully toward the recovery of the file, the office assistant wrote, "The responsibility can easily be fixed, when the file is found as its last note will indicate as to who lost it." After a month of searching, the "possibility of reconstituting the lost file" was considered, but the officers who would do it were new to the office and didn't remember what was in it. Eventually, they depended on the recollections of typists to bluff their way through a meeting with State Bank representatives. The results of this meeting were recorded at paragraph 30, and from there the investigation file became a substitute for the file it was opened to discuss.

The disruption of casework from the loss of files is often inadvertent, the effect of the constant movement of files among offices and desks. But functionaries sometimes intentionally stop consideration of a case by simply interrupting the normal movement of a file and returning it to the record room before a decision is reached. In my survey of housing files in the record room, I found many files in which the final entry on the note sheet was a description of a violation of CDA building or zoning regulations. No further entries followed, and yet the files had been returned to the record room without the requisite written orders concerning the violation and the return of the file to the record room. When no one marks these files back to the record room, no one, not even the last officer to note on it, can be held directly responsible for the irregularity of a violation not pursued. Once lying quietly in locked cabinets, the file's documentation of violations ceases to matter, at least until the file is called by someone to deal with a new matter.

But this tactic only works for minor violations that can easily escape broader attention and will likely be allowed if discovered at a much later date. For authorized decisions, the route among officers becomes central to the outcome. The routing of files can reconstitute the relations of influence normatively established by the organizational hierarchy. One senior officer with a reputation for extreme rectitude complained that files with irregularities were routed around him until everyone else had signed them. While his position in the formal hierarchy granted him authority over such matters, the paths of files constituted the effective lines of control. If he opposed the decisions of earlier signatories, he would be alone against a graphically manifest alliance of functionaries who had nearly achieved corporate authorship. Ironically, he would stand out visibly, vulnerable to charges of impropriety.

While this officer decried the irregular routing that boxed him in, regular routing can have a similar effect. Zaffar Khan talked with me one day about a file he was about to sign. The case concerned an employee of the ICTA who was being investigated by the Federal Investigation Agency (FIA), the agency that deals with crimes committed by government employees. The Interior Ministry, the government division that included Zaffar Khan's ICTA, was concurrently conducting its own investigation. An officer several levels down from Zaffar Khan had recommended stopping the Interior Ministry investigation on the grounds that conflicting findings between the Interior Ministry and FIA investigations could cost them the conviction. Zaffar Khan was convinced that the note was really meant to quash the Interior Ministry investigation in order to protect the official under scrutiny. Though no supporter of corruption, he signed off on the proposal. While he admitted that his view of the situation was softened by his paternalist desire to protect one of his own (the accused), he said his decision to sign had more to do with his support for several officers who had signed the note on its way to him. Furthermore, did he alone want to look like he would scuttle a conviction? The desire not to appear to have one's own particular interest is not confined to files with irregularities but rather routinely prods senior officers, like Zaffar Khan in his signing sessions, to sign off on graphically well-supported proposals.

Functionaries also sometimes simply keep files circulating up and down the organization to keep some case from being resolved or a project from going forward. The town planner in charge of a project to redevelop slums into a planned neighborhood in G-7 was frustrated by the slow pace of the project. In his view, for reasons he didn't understand, the chairman of the CDA was against the project but wouldn't directly oppose it. Rather, the chairman just kept sending the files back down the chain of command with very minor objections and requests for points of clarification.

Files may also circulate outside official circles and become the media that enable collusive networks of functionaries and interested parties. Files dealing with the interests of nonofficial individuals, such as compensation claims or houses, as we will see in the next chapter, are especially likely to spend some of their time outside the office. A notice issued in 1987, posted prominently in several record rooms of the Estate Management Directorate at least through the late 1990s, explicitly prohibited giving files to "unauthorized people," copying files, and even showing files. A directive posted above the earlier one, issued in 1990, ordered that "no one should let outsiders sit in their sections/rooms" and warns that staff members will be held responsible if any files disappear. Yet, despite the backing of official rules, the lowly record keeper is often unable to refuse well-placed clients in search of information.

Record rooms are the bureaucratic equivalent of the village well, frequented by the large number of clerks and peons who are charged with transporting files among various functionaries in different locations. At most times of the day, a spontaneous gathering of peons and clerks can be found in a record room, sitting in metal chairs with tattered wicker seats, chatting over tea and cigarettes while they wait for the record keeper to retrieve files for them or issue receipts for files they are returning. An officer with some urgent need or an absent staff occasionally appears and demands a file, scattering the gathering. But during my time reviewing files in the residential record room, I more commonly saw private architects, contractors, house owners, and prospective buyers coming in to look at and copy parts of files. Minor gratuities from clients seeking access to files is an important source of revenue for poorly paid clerks. Clients may often come seeking more than visual access to files. Opportunities for unauthorized parties to see and copy the contents of files are found all along their path of circulation. But record rooms are among the easiest (and therefore cheapest) place for clients to gain possession of the original file, since it is only here that a file, heaped among hundreds like it, is not in the direct documented possession of a specific functionary. Most of the files that are "lost" disappear from here.

In some cases, the goals of a house owner or a businessman can be realized by simply getting their files out of the CDA. But simply keeping the file is not an effective tactic when a positive action of the government is needed. As we'll see in the next chapter, brokers and villagers have shaped the compensation process for expropriated land not merely by getting physical possession of their case files, but by altering and tactically returning them to the CDA when they had prepared the bureaucratic ground for favorable decisions.

Functionaries also influence the outcome of cases by slowing down or stopping files. One officer explained to me that issuing a written instruction to subordinates to "please discuss" is simply a way to slow down the file: "if he really wants to discuss it, he'll call him on the telephone and say, 'Come over and let's discuss this.'" The file is put into the possession of a subordinate officer, but he or she can't work on it or mark it on before having a conversation with the superior, and the occasion for this discussion is entirely at the discretion of the superior officer.

Often, controlling the timing of file movements merely delays a case or shapes its outcome in minor ways, but in some cases this control is absolutely decisive. For example, the management of an unauthorized mosque on public property wrote to the Water Meter division of the CDA requesting a water connection in 1987. The Water Meter division could have decided the issue on its own, but it sent the file over to the Urban Planning Directorate for advice. The Water Meter division had written that this would only be a "temporary water connection . . . only for the time being and to honour the MNA [Member of the National Assembly] Md Nawaz Khokhar Sahib, who has recommended this case till the approval is obtained by them." Urban Planning was very concerned because, as one officer noted on the file, "water connection to the mosque would mean regularisation." The Urban Planning Directorate decided that the mosque should be demolished but was concerned that, with such strong political pressure, the Water Meter division would approve the connection, effectively regularizing the mosque despite the objection of Urban Planning. To prevent this outcome, the Urban Planning director ordered that the "request for water connection is to be considered *after* demolition!" (emphasis in original). To make sure of this, he instructed his staff to return the file to the Water Meter division only after they had managed to demolish the mosque. In the meantime, without the file, the Water Meter division had no way to take action on the request for a water connection. By delaying the return of the file, Urban Planning took control of the case from the Water Meter division.

Most government officers have more files to deal with than they can manage, so explanations for delays usually need not be given, aside from exceptional cases like that described earlier concerning a reference from the federal ombudsman. This opens a space of unofficial discretion for officers, who can hold up a file in order to come to terms with the private parties concerned in the matter. A powerful person can use connections (*sifarish*) to move a "stopped" or "stuck up" file, a file languishing in negligence or intentionally withheld from circulation. Those without influence have to "put wheels on it" (*us ko pahiye lagana*), as an Urdu idiom for bribing puts it. A person unwilling or unable to use connections or provide gratuities often experiences exasperating waits. Some clients face the opposite problem of not being able to stop their file from moving because no official has an interest in deciding the case. As a senior official put it to me, "If you don't pay someone, they just send you up the chain."

This was the experience of the developer of a now-defunct $4 million project for a theme park in F-9 Park as he pursued the file addressing his license through the CDA. This wealthy developer was trying to avoid using either connections or money to get his project approved, for fear that the slightest of improprieties could be used as grounds to revoke his approval if political winds shifted within the CDA or in the national government. After several months of what he considered unnecessary delays in the review of his project, he tracked down the officer with the file. The developer recounted to me how this "obstructionist" officer, who it seemed to him had been expecting his visit, spoke pessimistically of the approval prospect of the project, vaguely referring to "what was on the file" and teasing him by smiling and tapping his finger on the closed cover of the file on the desk in front of him.

On rare occasions, some personal interest of an officer—other than gratuities from a concerned party—will motivate him or her to stop a file. One day in 1997, an officer was recounting to me and another officer her trouble with a house she had rented. Because of the difficulty of evicting tenants in Pakistan, owners typically require tenants to pay in advance at least one year of full rent, if not two. She had put down half of the full year of rent and the CDA was going to pay the second half but hadn't yet. The owner was pressuring her to give him the CDA portion of the rent rather than waiting. She complained that he was stalling on finishing the house so he could keep her out while he showed the house to someone else who would pay the full year of rent. Her sympathetic colleague replied with relish, "He doesn't have a completion certificate, does he? Well, we have the file, let's see what we can do. It will be no problem." His suggestion was to threaten to hold the file so that the completion certificate, a document certifying that the construction is complete, would not be issued by the required deadline and the owner would be charged surcharges for the extension of the construction time. They agreed this would change the owner's perspective, but she decided to that situation hadn't yet become dire enough to risk such a solution.

In other cases, officers pass files on very quickly to escape the pressure that interested parties bring to bear on them. A former subengineer in the Lands Directorate recounted to me how he had evaded the pressure of a large landowner in western Islamabad whose land would soon be notified for expropriation. In 1995, the subengineer was working on a report analyzing the costs to the CDA of different formulas used to calculate compensation for land to be expropriated in D-12 and E-12. According to the subengineer, the landowner made inquiries through his CDA contacts to find out where the subengineer came from, who he was related to, what sort of person he was, and so forth. He eventually contacted a relative of the subengineer, who told the subengineer that the landowner wanted to meet him. After sending a car for him and settling him down in his drawing room with tea and biscuits, they "just chatted about nothing in particular," though the landowner insisted the subengineer visit a few days later. At this meeting, the landowner got right to business: he knew about the various formulas under consideration and wanted the subengineer to push for the one that would give the greatest compensation award. The subengineer said he replied, "The high formula is not right, but I'll see what I can do." Young and poor, he was very concerned that the landowner's efforts to influence the process had come to focus on him. The subengineer returned to the office the next day and began to rush through a note recommending the middle formula. His superior followed his lead and also passed the file quickly on. By the time the landowner contacted him by phone in the afternoon, the file was already on the desk of the CDA chairman. With a mix of triumph and relief, the subengineer recounted how he had said to the landowner, "You have to talk to the chairman now. I have already put up the file." In fact, the landowner did just that. He met with the chairman, and soon the director of the Lands Directorate had become an "officer on special duty," that is, he was prematurely transferred out of his office without a new assignment. For the landowner, this was both a retaliation against the director and the removal of an obstacle to a favorable reconsideration of his case.

As this example suggests, the ultimate aim of controlling the movement of files is of course to get certain people at a certain time to write a certain thing. Government actions can be forestalled without engaging paper. Action on a building code violation discovered by CDA inspectors, for example, can be stopped before it is written down. But to induce some positive government action, eventually one must make mediated contact with paper. Even Asif Ali Zardari, the husband of former Prime Minister Benazir Bhutto, who was perhaps more influential during her tenures than now during his own presidency, appears to have had to follow this law. Nicknamed "Mr. Ten Percent" during Bhutto's second term in office, Zardari was usually seen as entrepreneurially corrupt, more Schumpeter's creative capitalist than Weber's calculative one, aggressively demanding kickbacks, proposing new ventures, and taking over enterprises through political influence.[16] But according to press reports on a government investigation following Bhutto's second term, even Zardari depended on the bureaucratic modality of written documentation. Despite his vast and unconventional power as "first husband," he allegedly ran his corruption empire through files. In a shady facsimile of bureaucratic procedures, he would allegedly issue directives ("notes" we might call them) on Post-It notes stuck on files and return them to the concerned department, where his notes would be removed and followed (Burns 1998). The detachability of Post-Its, an extraordinary artifact in Pakistani government offices, supported an extraordinary bureaucratic practice.

The most junior officer in Auqaf described to me how he thought such very high-level political and bureaucratic figures influence his work through a chain of oral instructions running through the state hierarchy: "The PM contacts the minister, the minister the secretary, the secretary the DC [district commissioner], the DC the deputy, and he tells me to do it." Although orders represented to him from what he called "high-ups" are not uncommon, they remain mysterious and he never knows from how far beyond his own superior they actually originated. Such mediated oral instructions are never referenced in the file but must be translated into some particular aspect of the case to support a course of action.

The need to frame cases in a particular light from their initial commitment to paper gives the lowest-ranking officers far greater influence than we might expect from their subordinate position. In a discussion with a planner about political intervention by well-connected people, she told me that most cases are handled according to the rules and estimated that only 5 percent of cases involve irregularities. She said in these latter cases, at the outset the CDA chairman directly contacts the low-ranking officer who will put up the first note. She did an impression of the CDA chairman requesting her colleague, whom I'll call Iqbal, to approve a violation. Adopting a pleading tone, she said, "Oh Iqbal, *kuch* accommodate *karo, kuch* adjust *karo*" (Oh Iqbal, make some accommodation, make some adjustment). Then, she said, Iqbal will think for a while about how he can put the violation in a positive light. He will write "only positive things on file," suggesting spurious reasons for why it should be allowed, such as "it will not bother anyone," she said laughing at the ridiculousness of the claim.

Even staff below the rank of bureaucrats authorized to note on files under their own signatures can sometimes determine the notes of their superiors through their control over the typing process. One day, I was in the office of the director of the Lands Directorate. When his personal assistant came into the room, he began to berate him for tricking him into signing a file two days before. (Recall here that assistants often type up the draft notes of their superiors and present them to their superiors for signing.) In this case, the assistant had taken advantage of the material form of the note sheet. On the front side of the note sheet, the assistant had typed a note that was directly contrary to the director's decision; on the back side was a final paragraph consistent with what the director asked for in his draft note. He presented the back side to the director for signing. Unlike Zaffar Khan, the director usually read everything he signed, but from the writing visible to him on the back page, the note looked in order. Without turning the page, he had just gone ahead and signed it. The director had discovered the deceit when the CDA chairman reprimanded him. The director was convinced that his assistant had been paid for this trickery and the assistant might have even claimed the "Director Sahib" himself was demanding a bribe. The director was kicking himself for not being more careful, since this was not the first such incident with the assistant. "The man is highly incompetent and corrupt . . . though competent in his corruption," he quipped. "There is nothing I can do about it. If I transfer him they won't give me anyone else. So I just have to endure it."

A CONTEST OF GRAPHIC GENRES

The vitality of the file in Islamabad comes from its ability to support the formation of an authoritative voice of government, to allow individuals to escape responsibility, and to facilitate individual and small group enterprise within the larger organization.

The semiotic and material forms of files and their circulation supports a bureaucratic political economy far more complex than one in which superiors control subordinates or one in which all are subject to a single irresistible discursive formation. This system is not only one of "control through communication," to use JoAnne Yates's incisive phrase, but evasion of control, as well as enterprise aimed at promoting the goals of the organization or others. Although files are the basic artifacts of Islamabad government organizations, they are nevertheless social network artifacts, generating, as they circulate, the networks of people and other artifacts that will settle cases. Files are the basic artifacts of bureaucratic organizations in Islamabad, which are formally arranged by principles of strict hierarchy. But as used in Islamabad, files support a social network politics that is consonant with the prevailing ways of getting things done in Pakistani society more generally.

Graphic artifacts that do not circulate through social networks—and are therefore less vulnerable to capture by a small number of individuals—have had dismal careers in the CDA. Through the early 1970s, the CDA and its consultants produced hundreds of reports on every aspect of the city. It is significant that the only reports produced from the early

1970s to the early 2000s have been the work of foreign consultants engaged by the highest levels of the CDA and its superior body, the Cabinet Division. This kind of synoptic documentation, which is often taken to be a fundamental element of state practice, is mostly absent in Islamabad. An often-neglected requirement for synoptic documentation is some degree of material unity: the unity of perspective depends on a material unity. That is, synoptic documentation must be embedded in some single or relatively limited set of artifacts, even if these artifacts are widely reproduced and distributed.

Recall how we saw in the last chapter that the thousands of dispersed files on government housing units provide the material infrastructure for a politics of allocation that runs through bureaucratic and neighborhood networks. A more materially restricted and therefore synoptic documentation of housing units would open the allocation process to the application of policy rules of eligibility and priority, limiting the power of officers who oversee allocation and hampering the network politics familiar to and—with more or less enthusiasm—embraced by much of the population of Islamabad, across all classes.

A powerful and expensive computer system the CDA acquired in 1996 to run a database on land holdings and compensation records ran into the same problem. The dispirited manager of this idle system complained to me at the time that no one would give him any information to put in the system. It is telling that successive chairmen of the CDA, at the pinnacle of the hierarchy, have been the main supporters of efforts to establish electronic databases to replace files and other more localized genres of information storage. These efforts have been thwarted by all the functionaries beneath the chairmen, from the members of the CDA board to the peons who carry files. Since a database, like a published report, would be accessible to a wide range of CDA officials and staff, this artifact would mediate organization-wide social processes that transcend bureaucratic divisions and networks. It would therefore undermine relations of influence organized through files.

The predominance of the file, the rarity of reports, and the (at least temporary) defeat of the database show the strength of the political economy organized by files. Although this chapter has concentrated on the files as they figure in bureaucratic activities in the office, they are enmeshed in a range of other genres of graphic artifacts that are more directly involved with events beyond the office. In the next chapter, we will see how files engage with other sorts of graphic artifacts in Islamabad's political economy of paper.

CHAPTER 4

The Expropriation of Land
and the Misappropriation of Lists

Even at this writing, the boundless westward expansion envisioned by Doxiadis is stalled in the 11-series of sectors, just six miles from the president's house. "Now there is no chance to go onward," one town planner told me in 1997, waving his hand toward the western part of the city map on his wall, which showed the development status of each sector in a different color magic marker ink. "D-12, E-12, F-12, and G-12 were acquired, surveyed, planning prepared, and sold to others. But in the last seven years, nothing. Zero development. The locals didn't allow us to enter the sector for development purposes. . . . There are so many legal complications, so we cannot use police, even army. We cannot even enter the premises without [the residents'] clearance. . . . More than half of Islamabad is waiting for us." To confirm his observation, he again looked at the map and began counting the orange boxes, "32 boxes, yes, 32 sectors still to develop." The left of the map had gotten wet, and north-south streaks of ink blurred the divisions between western sectors.

Divisions were clearer on the ground. Through the late 1990s, between sectors G-11 and G-12, an uneven muddy path ran where a four-lane avenue had been planned for decades. This path marked the battle line between the Pakistan federal government and villagers who rejected the compensation the government offered for their expropriated land and houses. On one side, a picket of large, marble-faced houses guarded the western front of the city. Across the path, water buffalos lumbered among the low, sprawling house compounds and little patches of wheat of the village of Badia Qadir Bakhsh (or, as it is bureaucratically designated, BQB).

In the English-language press and official writings of the early 1960s, inhabitants of villages like this were referred to as "displaced persons," "oustees," and "evictees," premature labels that confidently invoked their future dispossession. Today, the official designation for these people is still "displaced persons." However, in most official writings, in the English-language press, and in conversation, they are more commonly called "affectees," reflecting the fact that they are affected by development planning but rarely displaced anymore.[1] The Urdu press, more in touch with the perspective, plight, and tactics of the villagers from the beginning, has always called them what they call themselves, *mutassareen* (the affected).[2] The term "affectee," like the many other designations generated with the productive, patient -*ee* suffix in Pakistani English, captures a whole vision of the relation between government and populace. It is applied to a broad range of people whose interests are negatively affected by the government: shopkeepers who have to pay a general sales tax; government servants whose state housing tenure is limited by eligibility policies; worshippers who pray beneath the hot summer sun because the government has not completed a mosque. The term is also applied to the victims of droughts and floods. Government action, like a natural force, is figured as an overwhelming power wholly external to the people it controls.[3] As a term for the villagers tangling with the Capital Development Authority (CDA), however, "affectee" is less accurate than "effectee," the misspelled version one occasionally finds in official writings and poorly edited English-language newspaper articles. This oxymoronic term captures the peculiar mix of agency and subjection that has characterized the owners of expropriated land in the last two decades. For these disaffected "effectees" came to effectively control what the CDA did to them.

Whatever the utility of the dominance-resistance frame of reference elsewhere, it is not productive here. Ortner (1995) has criticized anthropological studies of "resistance" for ignoring the ambiguity of political activity characterized as resistance. Such studies have also concentrated on situations in which the sociological constitution of agents and their relations of domination and subordination are rather straightforward and stable. As we will see, while the expropriation conflict is often portrayed as a simple struggle between villagers and the CDA, the agents of this conflict are much more numerous, heterogeneous, intermingled, and unsteady. Only in the episodes of the legal drama, in the characters of petitioner and respondent, do village groups and the CDA encounter each other as separate, unified agents with transparent interests. Furthermore, state actors cannot be clearly characterized as dominant.

The CDA has expropriated "undeveloped" land in several sectors of western Islamabad and paid villagers like those of BQB the equivalent of millions of dollars in compensation. Meanwhile, the villagers continue to occupy the land and houses for which they have been paid. How do we account for this stalemate in the midst of one of the most highly planned and bureaucratically unified cities of the subcontinent? One day in 1998, I asked the special magistrate of the CDA, an elite officer who dealt with building and commercial regulation. Like others, he told me the key was to control "the list," that is, the list of property holders entitled to compensation for expropriated land and structures. "Why the CDA is begging for land?" he asked. "If I were doing this job, I would make a final list and keep it in the custody of the CDA chairman under lock and key. . . . Every day the list is tampered with. No one should be allowed to see or tamper with the list." But why should a list be so important? And why did the magistrate emphasize controlling it physically rather than discursively?

Addressing these questions requires following the lead of the magistrate and treating the expropriation process as material as well as discursive. The focus on materiality foregrounds the issue of reference and predication, often underemphasized by discursive approaches to government, which focus on classification schemes, statistics, and policy. Although affectees managed to change no laws or policies, they have established a strong basis from which to increase their compensation profit from expropriation: a mass of fraudulent documents referring to property and people. Affectees gained control over the production and circulation of the documents through which regulations and laws are exercised. The fraud illustrates the paradoxical relationship between government documentation and corruption. It has become a commonplace of science studies that the workings of a machine are often ignored and poorly understood until it breaks down (see, for example, Latour 1987). Similarly, while, from the perspective of the state, this is a story of government breakdown, it has much to tell us about its everyday functioning.

This chapter, like the next one on maps, concentrates on the ways that bureaucratic processes engage with people and things outside the office. Attempts to redirect the expropriation process by changing laws failed because no groups in a position to make such changes saw them as unjust or stood to gain from amendment; the coalitions opposing the law included only villagers. More effective collectives of villagers, brokers, politicians, and CDA officials have formed around artifacts—buildings as well as graphic artifacts. Following Latour, I argue that these collectives are not reducible to sociologically defined coalitions that put artifacts to use; rather, these collectives are formed in encounters precipitated by artifacts.

The first part of this chapter discusses how we can understand state representations—particularly the sort of abstract classificatory schemes that have come to epitomize state discourse—as material processes. The rest of the chapter is a historical account of the changing role of artifacts within the Islamabad land expropriation process from 1960 to the present, which highlights how actors negotiate different relationships with these artifacts over time. I begin with the early phases of the expropriation process and the field of action opened up by the two systems of land measurement in use by the CDA. I follow this with an account of the use and disavowal of a variety of other graphic genres involved in expropriation proceedings. These include powers of attorney, demolition certificates, schedules of houses, petitions, communal agreements, files, and most important, lists. Networks of villagers, officials, and politicians formed around the production and circulation of these documents in order to fraudulently increase compensation. In an effort to break these networks, some officials began to refuse to employ these artifacts.

PROBLEMATICS OF REFERENCE AND MATERIALITY

The intervention of Islamabad villagers in the expropriation process suggests the need to adjust the accounts of governmental technologies that have followed from Michel Foucault's treatment of the modern European state. In standard accounts, cartographic, statistical, and other documentary techniques plunge into domains that were previously crudely known. James Scott argues that through these forms of representation "an overall, aggregate, synoptic view of a selective reality is achieved, making possible a high degree of schematic knowledge, control, and manipulation" (1998:11). As Scott (1998:2) puts it, modern administrative technologies attempt to "make a society legible" to the government. The history of Islamabad land expropriation challenges these accounts by presenting a case in which illegibility and opacity have been produced by the very instruments of legibility.

Backed by authoritarian power and facing little organized opposition, the modernist schemes Scott describes are carried out mostly according to plan and run into problems mainly because of informal processes they ignore. But, more commonly, the effort to use categories and measuring techniques to enact bureaucratic objects—like actual houses and land to be expropriated, displaced persons to be compensated—is a much more complicated task than planners envision, one mediated by elaborate documentary practices. Complications arise not only from the infiltration of the formal by the informal but also, as Harold Garfinkel (1967) emphasizes, from the formal procedures themselves, especially from the translations of official categories into the operational realm of documentary artifacts. These translations shape the work done by state categories. As work on passports has shown, for example, the functioning of categories of nation-state membership depends on how they are translated into documents identifying individuals as members of a particular category (Bowker and Star 1999; Caplan and Torpey 2001; Torpey 2000).

This insight about bureaucratic objects suggests two limitations of Scott's powerful visual metaphor. First, figuring the state as an observer looking from a singular perspective can lead one to assume the unity of state representations rather than demonstrate how such unity is achieved (or not) through coordination in practice (Abrams 1988; Li 2005; Mol 2002). I return to this point later in the chapter. Second, Scott's account insightfully demonstrates the importance of classificatory schemes and conceptual logics employed by state actors. But the visual metaphor can suggest that these conceptual schemes and logics are rather flat filters that color the viewer's image of the object. The metaphor of sight underplays the numerous mediations necessary to achieve links between state representations and the objects they represent. As Scott (1998:76, 83) points out, seeing like a state means looking at records more often than the things they represent. Categories, statistics, logics of abstraction, and so forth are generated from and applied to their domains of reference through extended and complicated chains of documents and other representational artifacts (Harper 1998). This is especially true for simplified, abstract, synoptic state representations because the more abstract the scheme is, the more mediators are required to link it to empirical objects.

Mediating processes of abstraction have been better studied in scientific than in governmental practices. Latour shows, for example, how scientific classifications of soil on the border between a forest and a savannah in the Amazon are at the end of a long series of mediating artifacts, including boxes for organizing soil, color charts, and graphs (1999:24–79). Latour's term "circulating reference" highlights that, for these classifications to refer to the soil, the series of mediations must remain unbroken and stable, like electricity flowing through a circuit.[4]

This approach to abstract representation moves us from the logics of particularity and generality to the actual processes through which abstractions are generated and used to enact objects. Abstractions depend at every point on mediating particularities. Drawing on the work of Witold Kula (1986), Scott characterizes customary measures as concrete and local, embedded in a "logic of local practice," in contrast with modern state measures, which are abstract and relatively context-free. However, if we emphasize the mediators required to make a measurement, we see that the modern state systems are everywhere equally dependent on the articulation of local practices; they appear to be context-free because they depend on the alignment of a large number of local contexts. From this perspective, customary measures can be defined in relation to the artifacts used with the object or process being measured. The change from customary forms of land measurement to modern state forms would be less a move from the concrete to the abstract, and more one from the employment of an ensemble of particular artifacts (plows, seed, a human body, the soil itself) to the employment of an ensemble of standardized artifacts (transits, compasses, satellites, files, registers, maps, computers). The locality or generality of a measuring system is not dependent on abstraction so much as on the distribution and articulation of the mediators through which it is deployed. While measuring systems seem to float in the realm of abstraction, any actual measurement is dependent on the deployment of a particular series of mediating artifacts. As we'll see, the vulnerability of abstraction to materiality is central to the articulation of two land measurement systems used today in Islamabad—the *khasra* (holding) system and the modern transit–stadia survey system.

As I argued with respect to the discourse of files, we have to understand how governmental classificatory logics, statistics, and cartographic techniques are generated from and work through material artifacts, particularly graphic artifacts. The material and discursive dimensions are commonly conflated, for example, in the following observation of Scott: "The functionary of any large organization 'sees' the human activity that is of interest to him largely through the simplified approximations of documents and statistics: tax proceeds, lists of taxpayers, land records, average incomes, unemployment numbers, mortality rates, trade and productivity figures, the total number of cases of cholera in a certain district" (1998:76–77). It might seem irrelevant to distinguish between the ideational and material dimensions of bureaucratic semiotic technologies, since they are always fused. However, my objective in this chapter is to demonstrate that it is a distinction that we had better attend to if we are to understand the varieties of interventions possible in bureaucratic arenas. The sociopolitical significance of what we abstract as representations (law, policy, categories, and so forth) comes largely from their use in generating artifacts and from the careers of these artifacts. This point becomes clearer when we consider the role of law in the expropriation disputes. Sally Engle Merry observes that "law maintains power relations by defining categories and systems of meaning" (1992:362). In the expropriation process I describe, the law was equally influential by defining what artifacts were required to put those categories and meanings to work. The agents who engage with bureaucratic representations (such as narratives, laws, classification schemes, statistics, and cartographic images) and the strategies they employ are very different from those engaged with the artifactual vehicles of those representations.

This raises the general question of the circumstances in which the difference between ideational techniques and artifacts matters relatively more or less. Under what circumstances do graphic artifacts withdraw behind the modes of representation they embody and the discourses they support? Johns (1998:3) has addressed a similar question regarding the development of the book and print culture more generally. He argues that the attributes of the book today—veracity, authorship, publication, general addressivity, fair use, and so forth—are not the determinate result of printing as a material technology. He claims that the very identity of print had to be *made*. It came to be as we now experience it only by virtue of hard work, exercised over generations and across nations. That labor has long been overlooked and is not now evident. But its very obscurity is revealing. It was dedicated to effacing its own traces, and necessarily so: only if such efforts disappeared could printing gain the air of intrinsic reliability on which its cultural and commercial success could be built.

Clanchy's (1979) treatment of the use of documents in England following the Norman invasion similarly suggests that a great amount of effort over centuries has been necessary to create the reliable modern document. While such longer historical narratives are not the focus of this study, they converge in many places with the argument I develop through the details of the Islamabad land expropriation process. Here, it is worth pointing out some general features of Euro-American governmental artifactual regimes—the reference for most scholarly work on bureaucracy—that contrast with those of Islamabad and account in part for the differences in the way documents are used. First, in most contemporary Euro-American bureaucracies, graphic artifacts are not the unique vehicles of the discourse they carry because of norms and technologies of reproduction and distribution. Second, state bureaucracies have established stable regimes of artifactual authentication. Third, norms for the storage, access, preservation, and organization of graphic artifacts are well established. Latour frequently argues that the character of techniques and artifacts are best studied in their early formation, before they have been stabilized. For this reason, I have found studies of the use of documents in medieval and early-modern Europe to be more revealing than those about the late-nineteenth and twentieth centuries (Bryan 1999; Heidecker 2000; Mostert 1999; Petrucci 1995; Stock 1983). I hope, nevertheless, that this chapter shows there is as much to be learned about techniques and artifacts from their dissolution as from their formation.

An ambiguously authored eighteenth-century Yemeni commentary, produced within a Muslim metaphysical tradition that placed more stock in spirit than matter, saw the problem clearly.

> As for the falseness of the position of him who holds for the valuation of documents without restraint, this is obvious. Because if the door of unlimited acceptance of them were opened, the wealth of the community would be lost and people's possessions would be removed from the permanence and security of their hands. In this position there is immoderation and a disdain for principles, because any claimant can make for himself what he wants in the way of documents, proceeding with craft and skill in reproducing the papers he thinks will advance his circumstances. (cited in Messick 1993:212)

The commentary points to the bureaucratic irony that dependence on written artifacts to secure fixity can result in its opposite. As Armando Petrucci put it, "maximum . . . authenticity" tempts "maximum nontruthfulness" (1995:247). Crucially, the basis for the insecurity the Yemeni commentary identified is not referentially incorrect representation or the semantic slippage highlighted by Derrida and Garfinkel (and any good lawyer), but the manipulation of artifacts. Following this insight, I will describe the fraud endemic to the Islamabad expropriation process as an illicit production and circulation of things, showing that this fraud is less like lying and more like the theft or forgery and sale of a painting, a material intervention in discourse.

The paper regime the British intended to hermetically seal the bureaucracy has become extremely porous in the CDA. Far from remaining in desks and file cabinets, graphic artifacts are now crucial mediators of the engagement of the government and populace, shaping settlement patterns, social networks, political cleavages within villages, and financial compensation. I now turn to the history of expropriation in Islamabad, which shows this mediation clearly.

EARLY PLANNING AND FAILED OPPOSITION

On the original planning maps for Islamabad (for example, fig. o.1 in the introduction), the squares of sectors are empty white spaces, and early documents describe the site for the new city as "open land." But officials were well aware that over fifty-four thousand villagers inhabited the area of the future capital (Federal Capital Commission 1960:12). Early plans envisioned preserving some of the villages, such as Saidpur and Nurpur Shahan, located on the periphery of the area to be developed, as "tokens of traditional village life."[5] Most of the villages, however, lay within the grid of sectors and were to be removed. One official wrote regretfully, "While it is not a pleasant job to throw people from their houses or land, we have to do it in the larger public interest of establishing Islamabad." In a modern administrative city, there was no place for villagers. "Displaced persons" were to be resettled in agricultural land elsewhere in the Punjab or in nearby model villages. As one early newspaper article put it, "The people, who may have to leave their ancient abodes, will be rehabilitated as far as possible in similar environments."[6]

Under the Capital Development Authority Ordinance, executed under Martial Law Regulation 82 of 1960 (MLR 82), owners of expropriated land were paid the average market price in 1954 to 1958 for their land, plus 15 percent for compulsory acquisition. Compensation for what is called "built-up property" (or "BUP"), documented built structures, was similarly based on average market sales in 1954 to 1958 using a formula that included the area of the structure and the quality of construction. Later, these rates were augmented to offset monetary inflation, but the base rate was frozen at levels from 1958. Under this regulation, compensation for land and houses was effectively fixed at the amount a farmer or sheepherder might have paid in the 1950s, although eventually it would be not farmers but wealthy military officers, government officials, and investors buying the land from the government at high rates for large houses and commercial plazas. This was all according to plan. The fixed rate of compensation was to prevent a speculation market from developing, which would slow construction and drive up development costs for the CDA. More importantly, as the government saw it, the benefits of government actions should accrue to government. If land prices went up as a result of the development of the capital, then the government rather than "individuals" should earn the profit (Federal Capital Commission 1960). For the CDA, this was not only just but financially necessary, since the funds raised from the sale of developed plots would finance future developments.

Under the same expropriation law, new construction on land notified for expropriation was banned. The CDA relaxed the enforcement of this law for the growing number of cases in which only part of the land was acquired, leaving a substantial portion to be looked after by owners. But the ban was rigidly enforced on wholly acquired lands. In 1965, five men were sentenced to a year in prison for the construction of new houses on land acquired by the CDA.

Officials recognized that, under the CDA Ordinance, the CDA had "no legal obligation, but could help these evictees on moral and humanitarian grounds only, if possible." Efforts were made to find alternative sites within Rawalpindi District, but officials considered this, as one wrote, "an act of grace on our part as we have no obligation to provide such sites." Aside from the shortage of land outside the area to be developed, the main problem with this effort was that any land awarded in Islamabad would first have to be acquired from others. Officials considered it logistically difficult as well as unjust to displace some people in order to rehabilitate others, "robbing Peter to pay Paul," as the chairman characterized it. But the CDA could not avoid this well-meaning sin altogether. In 1962, nearly fourteen hundred plots in I-9 and I-10, an area originally reserved for light-industry laborers, were made available to owners of expropriated land for purchase at discounted rates. Most of those who bought the plots sold them immediately because they were considered a poor investment.[7] The CDA granted agricultural plots in other areas, exchanging as much as 12.5 fertile acres in southern Punjab for as little as half an acre in Islamabad.

Many villagers were unwilling to part with ancestral land. In conversations with me in 1997, Raja Zahoor Ahmed, *numberdar* (official headman; literally, "keeper of numbers") of Sheikhpur, a village yet to be possessed by the CDA that spreads over sectors I-14, I-15, and I-16, said that residents, especially elders (*buzurg log*), were devastated by the news that they would have to move. Retelling a story that has entered the folklore of the expropriation process, he claimed that four of five old people died from shock immediately upon hearing the news. "They loved the land. Their ancestors had cultivated the land with such effort—now there are tractors, but in those days it was all done by hand and with plows and bullocks. And this land was the source of their honor [*izzat*]." A long-standing rural vision of the city as a place of strange and immoral ways fueled villagers' anxieties that they would be duped out of their money and perhaps corrupted as well. Other reasons for opposition to surrendering their land were more economic. The CDA rates of compensation were often below market rates prevailing in the late 1950s, since the sales upon which the average market values were calculated included a large number of transfers within families at low, nonmarket rates. Moreover, if they declined to farm agricultural plots granted elsewhere, most villagers would have trouble finding another source of income.[8] As uneducated farmers, they would have difficulty making a livelihood from the new business of the area, government. Nevertheless, villagers inhabiting areas of the early phases of development left their houses and lands peacefully in the face of bulldozers. Eight widows of Ratta Hottar village were unusual in their steadfast refusal, prompting one official to write grimly in 1967, "unless we take a firm stand, these widows would not vacate the acquired area." These widows too were eventually persuaded to leave when construction activities began.

While associations of affectees proudly professed their willingness to sacrifice for the new national capital, they often criticized the process as a grand scheme to take land at low rates from the poor for the benefit of well-placed government officials and the wealthy. In 1970, a spokesman for affectees demanded that "acquisition should not be made for allotments later to capitalists."[9] At a meeting of the Association for Islamabad Displaced Persons in 1977, the head of the organization demanded that "land should not be acquired for forests, clubs, race courses, golf courses and for favoring the rich and bureaucracy."[10] In public discourse and conversation, villagers characterized the whole process as *zulum,* a word meaning injustice with the taint of cruelty.[11]

However, some villagers eagerly took the cash the government offered and quit their land. Although the Punjab is known for some of the richest agricultural soil in South Asia, much of the land in the Islamabad area is rocky and yields a poor crop. In the early 1960s, few thought that the government would make a go of the new capital and that their land would someday be worth millions. Through the mid-1960s, the name "Islamabad" was embraced by doubtful quotation marks even in Rawalpindi newspapers. According to one official I spoke with who was involved in early acquisitions, some residents even approached the CDA and requested that their land be expropriated. When they were told that the government had not yet allocated funds to acquire their land, they insisted that the CDA take their land now and pay them whenever the financing came through. After giving up their land, many former male residents could be seen stepping out in Rawalpindi dressed in fancy clothes and gold-embroidered Kohati sandals, driving cars or new horse carts. Some gambled away their financial awards. Others who were more thrifty bought land, a long-standing use for surplus funds in rural Punjab.

Those opposed to expropriation or to the specific compensation awarded, however, had little recourse. Under martial law, the CDA could not be challenged politically. There were also no legal options. MLR 82 declared that regulations made under its broad provisions overrode any other existing law or contract. MLR 82 explicitly banned recourse to any court (including the Supreme Court) in disputes with the government over land and building in the so-called Specified Areas slated for the development of the capital. Paragraph 49E of the CDA Ordinance, buttressed by MLR 82, also explicitly denied court jurisdiction in disputes with the CDA over any matter, including expropriation and compensation. Under the populist government of Zulfiqar Ali Bhutto of the early 1970s, however, courts began to accept petitions from villagers. In numerous legal cases against the CDA expropriation laws in the 1970s and early 1980s, affectees invoked the rights of the sons of the soil, the just-price ethics of the market, and the Quranic injunction never to compel a sale. But except for a few cases that turned on technical aspects of the expropriation process, courts found against these petitions in every case.[12] While the legal basis for courts to hear these cases was shaky, the CDA law was clear regarding the CDA's powers of expropriation and requirements for compensation.

In the disputes over land in Brazil described by Holston (1991),most of the conflict centered on the role of law in defining categories and systems of meaning. In those cases, categories defined by different laws conflicted; different laws were embedded in different historical narratives of the individual holdings and the polity. In contrast, Katherine Verdery (1994, 2003) describes how a simple postsocialist law restoring the property of collective farms to their original owners ran into the complications of changed kin relations, shifting rivers, different measuring authorities, lost records, new records, effaced land marks, and fading memories. The contention over compensation in Islamabad is more like the Romanian situation. Martial-law and CDA regulations of Islamabad are paragons of clarity and simplicity; no court rulings have involved significant reinterpretation of these laws. However, contention over the evidentiary artifacts required to implement these laws has produced as much conflict and irresolution as in Brazil and Romania. In this case, the law was not "converted into a contested site of meaning" (Sieder 2001:204), but into a site of material struggle.

SHIFTING HOUSES AND DUMMY HOUSES

In this section and the next, I will describe how, through the 1980s and 1990s, affectees were able to intervene in increasingly sophisticated ways at later and later stages of the process in which compensatable built-up properties (BUPs) were enacted. My narrative begins, as affectees began, with the initial material referents in the chains of reference leading to compensation checks: houses. Money for fancy clothes, gambling, and the purchase of more were not the only reasons some villagers were eager for expropriation. Early on, there were indications that "oustees" were, as one official wrote, "shifting to adjoining areas unauthorisedly." By the mid-1960s, officials were already concerned that the expropriation process itself had changed the dynamics of settlement in the area. Officials noted that mud huts were springing up at night like mushrooms north and west of the city. In 1971, a CDA representative, in response to complaints about CDA efforts to evict residents of one village without compensation, claimed that half the population "consisted of itinerant villagers who had flocked to the area in hope of getting compensation money and other privileges intended for bonofide [sic] displaced persons."[13] The official contended that there was a thriving rental market in the village, all of which had been CDA property for nearly a decade.

According to a CDA working paper written in 1967, "Ejectment of unauthorised occupants," the CDA policy of allowing displaced persons to remain in their houses and to continue to farm acquired agricultural land, if they paid rent, until the CDA provided land or houses for them had contributed to this problem: "So our kindness and concession have been taken undue advantage of by some of the evictees." The minutes of the meeting to discuss this paper pointed obliquely to another major factor: the tacit acceptance or collusion of CDA officials themselves. According to the minutes, it is the responsibility of the Lands Directorate to check unauthorized occupation and construction, and "any unauthorized construction or occupation will now be considered to have taken place with the connivance of the Lands Directorate."

The CDA itself inadvertently promoted this process by allowing oustees to buy the building materials (*malba*) of their demolished houses for 15 percent of the house value. The original objective of this policy was to help displaced persons build houses elsewhere at no financial cost to the CDA. In explaining why this policy of selling the building materials was reversed in 1989, the director of the Lands Directorate wrote that the "selling of malba invariably resulted in the issuance of a fresh lease for exploiting the Authority as the malba was conveniently transported a little distance away and the new houses used to be built with old material which was sufficient evidence to support false claims."

Badia Qadir Bakhsh illustrates many dimensions of the expropriation process over the last four decades. According to the residents, most of them are descendants of Mughal soldiers who fled Delhi following the failure of the rebellion against British rule in 1857. Continuing north to this sparsely settled area, they established a village and hid their true identity by taking up an agricultural life. Whatever the accuracy of this account, later British settlements confirmed their holdings and established the head of the leading family as *numberdar,* a low-level though locally powerful official of indirect rule. When the expropriation of BQB began in the late 1960s, the village, according to records, occupied around 294 acres spread across what was slated to become sectors G-11 and G-12 (fig. 4.1).

When I first visited BQB in 1997, the hodgepodge of brick houses faced with concrete gave the look of an old village renovated by the affluence that has come to the area in the wake of the capital. In fact, most of the structures at that time were less than twenty years old. According to CDA records, 263 acres of BQB land lying in G-11/1 and G-11/2 were acquired in 1969 with compensation following two years later. The built-up property on this land, 97 houses, was acquired more than six years later in 1975; the compensation award for this property

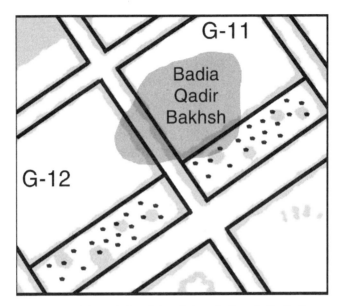

FIGURE 4.1. My rendering of the relation of village Badia Qadir Baksh to sectors G-11 and G-12.

came nearly a decade later in 1984 in the form of money and 109 plots in I-10/1. Through the mid-1970s, the 31 acres of BQB lying in G-12 was mostly occupied by *baithaks*, structures for entertaining guests and travelers on their way from Rawalpindi to the popular shrine of Golra Sharif to the north. Before the CDA took possession of the G-11 land, residents began to move across the planning border and to convert these baithaks into their primary residences, ironically becoming guests of themselves on their own land. Others who did not have baithaks in this area built new houses there in violation of the fraying CDA ban on construction in notified areas. After building their houses anew, they simply waited to profit from another expropriation. One CDA official I talked with likened the expropriation process to rolling up a carpet: no one was removed from the planning region, but just rolled into the next sector.

This resettlement tactic of villagers was inadvertently promoted by the disjuncture between two kinds of land-reckoning systems used by different organizational divisions of the CDA. Although it is generally known that all the land of the region will eventually be expropriated, land acquisitions, by law, have to be made for some definite development scheme. The determination of which land is to be acquired in any particular proceeding is therefore made by the Planning Wing of the CDA, which plans by sector. The officials of the Planning Wing submit requests to the Lands Directorate, which then determines who owns the land falling in a particular sector and what structures ("BUP") exist on it. Through the chairman of the CDA, the district commissioner of the CDA (DC-CDA)—a CDA official with special judicial powers within the larger administrative structure of the Pakistan state—is directed to acquire these lands and structures and to award compensation. The acquisition of land and built-up property are often executed through different awards, often many years apart.

A complication is that the Planning Wing and the Lands Directorate use different systems of reckoning land area. Planners, engaging the city through area and topography, rely on maps produced by modern transit–stadia measurements using metric system units and organized by the areal division of the sector. Although the field notes of surveyors are usually jotted down in Urdu, the notations on these maps as well as the accompanying documentation are in English. In contrast, the Lands Directorate uses the *revenue record,* the complex land holding system developed by the British from a Mughal system (Baden-Powell 1892; R. S. Smith 1996). This record is written in Urdu (one summary version that the CDA uses to record residential structures is officially called the "Urdu List" or "Urdu Fehrist"). The revenue records and the CDA records derived from them use the areal divisions of village or revenue estate (*mauzah*) and holding (*khasra*) measured in units of acres, one-eighth acres (*kanal*), and 30.25 square yards (*marla*) (fig. 4.2). *Patwari*s, the lowest-level officials of the revenue administration, measure holdings using chains (and sometimes pacing) and landmarks. Ledgers (collectively known as the *jamabandi,* literally, "settled revenue") record the ownership, tenure, size, and other characteristics of the holding. Since these records are organized around individual land holdings for taxation purposes, they do not readily or accurately offer the synoptic spatial perspective of the planning maps. The property maps of villages are on large irregular pieces of paper or cloth scrolls (*latha*s) showing individual holdings in blue, black, and red ink (fig. 4.3) and are made by assembling sketches of individual holdings like a jig-saw puzzle, making the revenue map a haphazard assemblage of the shapes on the scroll.

Survey maps and revenue maps are not incommensurable but uncommensurated, because the practices that generate them include no common elements. To overcome this problem, CDA surveyors add something to the landscape that can be shared by the two practices: a concrete pil-

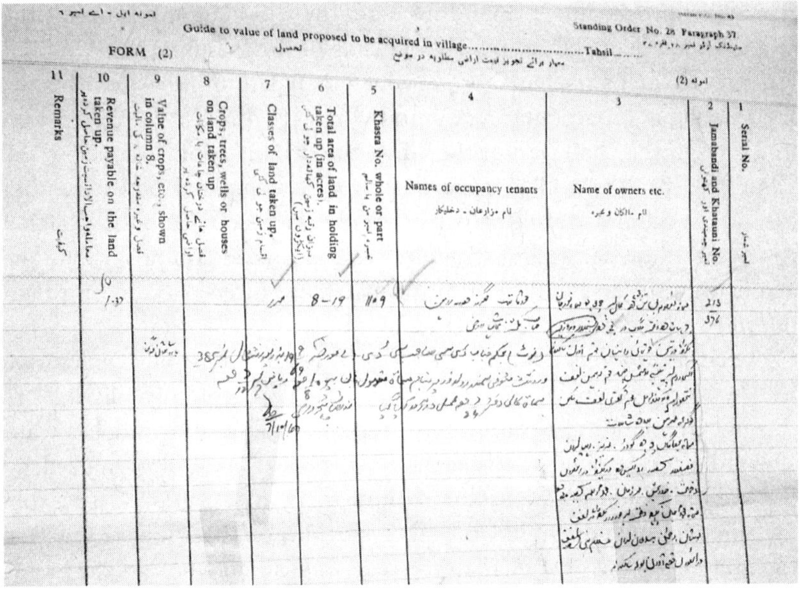

FIGURE 4.2. A 1967 CDA record of a village holding to be acquired. (Photo by Faiza Moatasim.)

lar that is sunk into the ground so that it can be located on both maps. This pillar translates between the maps to determine which land and built-up property have to be acquired under a given acquisition directive. Although erecting a pillar is not usually a problem, in Sheikhpur, a village that spans sectors I-14, I-15, and I-16, villagers physically threatened surveyors, refusing to allow pillars to be established, and the police would not come to force the issue.[14] After making their measurements, the CDA surveyors could have ostensively referenced—that is, pointed to—which lands and built-up property in the village were to be acquired under acquisition directives for I-14. Without sinking markers, however, they could not legally determine which holdings these were on the basis of the revenue map. Similarly, CDA officials could not prohibit new construction in the village because the location of the structures could not be legally established. The villagers affected the legal discourse about their houses by controlling the artifacts necessary for its production.

Functionaries in both the planning and acquisitions divisions of the CDA know something about both land-reckoning systems, but expertise is not evenly distributed. The Planning Wing employs its own revenue-record specialists to deal with problems blending planning and owner-

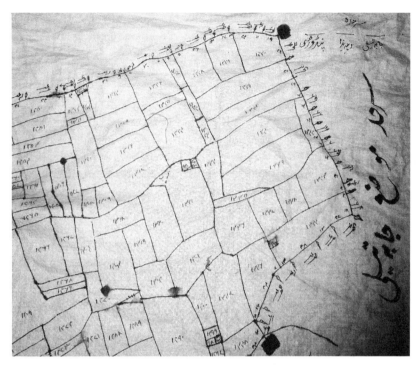

FIGURE 4.3. Cloth map (latha) showing property holdings of a revenue estate in western Islamabad. (Photo by Faiza Moatasim.)

ship of undeveloped land. Frustrated in my early attempts to understand the technicalities of the revenue records, I acquired a copy of an Urdu-language manual for training revenue staff (Ali 1997). When I mentioned this to officials in the Planning Wing, several asked me to make them copies, eager to be free of dependence on their subordinates' command of this system. This dependence is illustrated by the case of a civil engineer in a major Pakistani construction company who bought land from the CDA in an industrial section of I-9. When he went to "take possession" of it by building a wall around it, he was met by residents of a nearby village who said it was not his land. The man returned with a CDA surveyor, Enforcement and Security staff (a CDA police force), a lower officer of the Lands Directorate, and a CDA patwari. The village residents met them with their village patwari. While the engineer and the rest of the CDA staff stood by looking on uncomprehendingly, the two patwaris squatted over the unfurled latha. After examining the scroll, the patwaris paced off the boundaries in long, loping strides. The

CDA patwari then declared that in fact one-third of the man's plot, a corner of the rectangular plot, had never been acquired by the CDA. Since none of the other CDA staff, including the surveyor, understood the latha, they accepted the patwaris' judgment of the matter and began proceedings to acquire this extra property.

This event, however, was unusual. In the normal operations, each land-reckoning system is used by different CDA organizational divisions, so discrepancies are never even noted. The kinds of conflicting claims that Verdery (1994:1095) describes when different measuring authorities in Romania surveyed the same land do not arise. In fact, the problem of reconciling the two systems was pointed out to me not by a CDA planner or acquisition official, but by a private town planner who worked for housing societies, organizations that must both acquire and plan their developments and therefore must square revenue and survey records. "The physical survey never coordinates with the patwari records," he explained. "You cannot fit khasras [holdings] in the master plan survey. When you superimpose the khasra map with the survey, they never coincide. For example, the patwari says a khasra is 500 kanals, the survey shows it is 450 kanals. . . . [I]t is almost always a decrease because the patwari measures by walking on undulating land. . . . [S]ometimes they even walk over little piles of dirt." Like the length of the British coast (Mandelbrot 1967), the size of a land holding varies with the size of the unit of measure—the smaller the unit, the larger the holding. Furthermore, since holdings are drawn freehand, the area in graphic representations of plots diverges from the area in numerical representations. For example, a 20-kanal plot may be represented on the khasra map as larger than a 25-kanal plot. With this insight, I coordinated acquisition records and planning records for several sectors and concluded that the CDA also usually acquires more land than it receives. The officials in the Lands Directorate and the Planning Wing whom I questioned about this discrepancy were not concerned—nor did they need to be. Land is what Star and Griesemer called a "boundary object" that inhabits intersecting social worlds, "plastic enough to adapt to local needs and constraints of the several parties employing them, yet robust enough to maintain a common identity across sites" (1989:393). The Lands Directorate and the Planning Wing do not cooperate by standardizing their measurement methods but by working on an object recognizable to each, despite how land becomes an element of different bureaucratic objects, revenue estates and sectors, holdings and plots.

If one is tempted by Foucault's image of the modern state as a panopticon, this disjuncture between two land-reckoning systems within the same bureaucratic organization should give pause. If we adapt Foucault's metaphor, here there are not one but two observers in the tower and the prisoners know that these observers are not looking at them the same way. Furthermore, as Latour (2005; Latour and Hermant 1998) argues, many mediations are necessary to construct a representation with credible claims to command a wide field. Latour's counter-image of the "oligopticon" is much more appropriate here: an organization employing multiple techniques with limited and particular visions. Latour points out what most bureaucrats understand: Administrative techniques do not all converge in a unified set of representations. They generate ensembles of artifacts of limited and differing perspectives that are often very difficult to commensurate. But this perspectivalist formulation assumes an underlying something—land—that is the real target of bureaucratic intervention, a something that is merely represented two different ways. If we follow Mol (2002) instead, we can say that these two different sets of practices *enact* two different sorts of objects—revenue estates and sectors—that must be "coordinated." The residents of expropriated land understand this quite well. Those in Sheikhpur defied the CDA by preventing the use of pillars to coordinate revenue estates and sectors, which is legally required for expropriation proceedings. They exploited the disjuncture between the two systems: while the CDA acquired land by sector, residents in BQB resettled by revenue estate.[15]

But there is more than simply resettlement going on in villages such as BQB. For reasons I'll describe in more detail later, population and house figures for BQB are hard to come by and highly contested. The Census of BQB conducted in 1972 counted 68 households holding a population of 425. A federal government survey conducted in 1985 put the population of BQB at 183, suggesting that a substantial portion of residents had left after the CDA took possession of their land in G-11 (Capital Development Authority 1985b). This was the last government survey conducted before such information gathering became a highly contentious activity. In 1986, however, Shehla Parveen Shamil and Roohi Sadiq gained broad access to the village for their anthropology master's research at Quaid-i-Azam University. According to their survey, there were 387 residents, in 50 "families" or households (Shamil 1987:29), a striking increase in just one year. Shamil and Sadiq wrote that of these 50 households, only 19 were "joint families," in which adult brothers maintain common ownership of residential property. Residents told them that separate houses for nuclear families began to be built in the early 1980s under the pressure of daughters-in-law, a conventional figure of subjection in South Asian kinship arrangements. It is likely that the CDA policy of compensating on the basis of built-up property occupied by a "family unit" (a word that has entered the common vocabulary of Urdu- and Punjabi-speaking villagers) also played a significant role in this change of residential arrangements.

According to Sadiq (1987), the residents of BQB upheld the status and propriety of the village by refusing to allow members of lower castes to settle there. They seem to have been much more welcoming of fictitious residents. Natural increase and even the most thorough division of joint family holdings cannot account for the fact that by 1993, 663 *more* affectees of BQB had established the right to compensation for built-up property.

In the 1980s, the number of claims increased as exponentially as the land values of Islamabad. Doubts that the new capital might not fly disappeared with the break-off of East Pakistan and the formation of Bangladesh. Nevertheless, through the 1970s, Islamabad remained a rather small, empty city, populated almost exclusively by government functionaries unlucky enough to have been moved up from Karachi. In the early 1980s, several factors made the city more popular and sent land values spiraling upward. The Afghan war brought the prosperity of a profitable export market and the lucre of United States civil and military aid. The drug trade flourished as Pakistan and the United States looked the other way in the interest of financing the mujahideen campaign against the Soviets. The Iran-Iraq war brought Iranian businessmen looking for a secure base of operations. Finally, Islamabad offered a secure, if dull, haven to wealthy Pakistanis escaping the growing violence in Karachi. As market values increased, so did villagers' unwillingness to part with their land, which accelerated the inflation created by growing demand.

The sense of injustice that affectees feel has increased as exponentially as the land values. Affectees such as Tariq Ahmed, a village leader from BQB, measure injustice in rupees: "The CDA offers to pay Rs. 350 per kanal on land they will sell for Rs. 20 lakh [2 million] per kanal." Villagers began to reject offers providing only enough cash for a new car and a little land; they demanded major financial awards and developed urban plots on the former sites of their villages. The government rejected these demands. Meeting them would entail using most of its development budget paying affectees and, with what is left over, developing the new areas solely for the accommodation of the very people it was trying to evict in order to develop the city. But affectees and their partners in the CDA have been changing their tactics as much as their demands. One affectee said to me, referring to land appropriated in the mid-1970s, "At that time we didn't know what to do. Since then we have learned."

Many of the claims for built-up property have been made on the basis of what CDA officials call "dummy houses," houses built not to be lived in but to be counted. As one CDA official testified, many of these houses "came up suddenly overnight" when the process of marking houses began. Although some of these houses are brick, they are more commonly short structures with walls of clay or a mix of stones and clay, no floors, and no roofs or, at most, "roofs" consisting of a few iron bars supporting some bricks. If they exist, doors and windows are usually broken and made of narrow strips of rotten wood.

For these cheaply built houses, "owners" received hundreds of thousands of rupees in compensation, which was sometimes regretted as bitterly as it was struggled for. One village resident involved in such schemes lamented to me that the CDA made a thief of him: "The CDA did not give us our rights so we were helpless, we had to do this dishonest work. . . . [I]f the CDA had given us our rights, then outsiders could not have come in and gotten involved."

The prospect of such a high return on investment attracted many people from outside the village to join affectees as investors or brokers in these schemes. In the early 1990s, a property dealer operating in E-12 offered a friend of mine a chance to build a house there. The dealer took him out to the area of his prospective house accompanied by the contractor who would build it. Although compensation for the structure's expropriation would depend on CDA policies, which change frequently, the dealer offered to have a one-room house built for Rs. 4,000–5,000, with an eventual estimated return of Rs. 300,000 (then about $7,200), or a three-room house for Rs. 10,000–12,000, with a return of as much as Rs. 800,000 (about $20,000). Unlike routine systems of illegal payments (see, for example, Parry 2000; Wade 1982), these kinds of deals were entrepreneurial ventures promising large gross returns, over 60 times the investment, from which the dealer, CDA functionaries, and villagers who would vouch for an individual's residence could be easily paid. One CDA official even made his own son the owner of a dummy house. An assistant in the Lands Directorate who had extensive knowledge of BQB claimed that many of the owners of such structures there used the compensation they received to purchase houses in the developed sector of G-11. They installed their servants in their dummy houses and planned to eject them when the full compensation is awarded.

The routine flagrance of this practice was brought home to me one day while I sat in the office of the Lands director, the official charged with checking illegal construction. A respectable-looking elderly man came in. The director sized up the man quickly and kept looking at files and noting while he asked him what he wanted using familiar Urdu address. Standing in front of the director's desk, the man explained that he had come representing a widow, a CDA employee, who had built some rooms on acquired land in the expectation of fraudulently receiving compensation. Afterward, a policeman in the area had come and unofficially taken possession of the structure, with a view toward collecting the compensation himself. She had filed a case in court but was doubtful of the result and pleaded for the director to intervene on her behalf to restore to her the house and, thus, eventually the compensation. The director, only slightly surprised, replied curtly that this was a "prohibited house" (*najaez makan*) and there was nothing he could do. After the man had withdrawn, the director wondered on what ground she could have filed the court case and exclaimed with a mix of exasperation and amusement, "What do you do with a case like that?!" While everyone involved understands the magnitude of the stakes of the conflict, the absurdity of the situation is often recognized. Another day, a well-to-do acquaintance of the director came to see him about some land he owned that the CDA was acquiring for a road east of Islamabad. Although the market value of the land was about Rs. 700,000, the CDA had awarded him just Rs. 5,000. The director assured him that the award was correct under the law and that his hands were tied. Then, laughing, he suggested the man just build a little brick room, marry an Afghani girl, put her in there, and claim his "four walls" (*char divari*: a metaphor for domestic space protected by Islamic norms of *purdah*)—he would even have her brothers to fight for him if it came to it! Becoming serious again, the director shook his head and said, "The problem is that while dishonest people make a fortune, honest people get nothing."

Dummy-house schemes have been helped by the difficulty of applying any definition of a house to actual houses in rural Punjab. Residential structures in rural Punjab usually consist of at least two rooms opening onto a courtyard with a stove or cooking area to one side. If grown male relatives with families occupy the same residence, each family will tend to use one or more rooms predominantly. One of the rooms in the houses of poorer villagers will be used as a sitting room for receiving guests. Wealthier villagers more concerned about observing purdah, like many inhabitants of BQB, may also have a one- or two-room structure (baithak) entirely independent of their residential compound for this purpose. This combination of physical structure and kinship patterns has created problems for CDA compensation policies. CDA compensation for built-up property is awarded to a "family unit," defined in 1984 as a bureaucratic entity combining kinship and a material structure: "husband/wife and dependent children or single person owning a separate independent house" (Capital Development Authority 1984). Given the ambiguous relationship between physical structures and settlement of kin units, the CDA, like its British colonial predecessors (Glover 2008:38), has never been able to work out a formal definition of the house for compensation purposes, in terms of either kinship or physical structure.[16] In the early period of acquisitions, this was less of a problem, because what is now called a "joint family" (father, mother, and brothers with or without wives and children) occupying a single compound was the norm, and compensation was made on this basis. In the mid-1980s, as nuclear families occupying independent compounds became more common—partly as a way to increase compensation— heads of nuclear families living together in one compound began to claim that one house is actually many, because each room has a "family unit" living in it. This drove the CDA to recognize even single rooms as "houses," which promoted vigorous building. In light of these problems, in 1996, the CDA ejected the house as an element of the "family unit," which was redefined in purely kinship terms: "the affectee, his or her spouse and unmarried children at the time of acquisition" (Capital Development Authority 1996).

DEMOLITION CERTIFICATES

Although the dummy-house schemes had been successful, affectees and their partners in the bureaucracy soon realized that all the shoddy building was unnecessary. Although walls and doors are the main elements of a house, documents are the main constituents of built-up property. They did not have to be concerned with the referents of records but could go straight to the records themselves to secure compensation. Furthermore, the direct engagement of village leaders with records gave them even greater influence as essential points on the path of various graphic artifacts necessary to the business of profiting from compensation.

Village leaders, the heads of families that have dominated villages for a century and a half or more, recognize that their political authority is embedded in their current settlements. As one leader from BQB told me, "The CDA can give us land, houses, and money, but who will make us the leader [*khan*]? Who will put the turban [*pagari*] on our heads?" This same concern was articulated by Mahboob Ilahi, the headman of BQB before the capital was established: "As long as I have the land, I will be numberdar." However, it is not the land but the process of expropriating land that has given these local leaders a new lease on power. Documents make village leaders as much as they make bureaucrats. It is one of the many ironies of Islamabad that this modernization project has strengthened the so-called traditional leaders it aimed to supersede.[17] In contrast to Lesotho, as described by James Ferguson (1994), state practices are extended but not state power. According to Sadiq, even in 1986, fewer than half of the men in BQB still farmed as a primary occupation; more than half of the men (46 of 83) were employed outside the village in government or construction, giving them independence from village society even as they were brought under the influence of different authorities beyond the village. Such a trend would likely have continued even if the village had remained undisturbed by expropriation measures. Now, however, the village leaders represent important local interests of residents to the bureaucracy. Village leaders themselves eagerly reproduce the paternalistic modernization discourse on the ignorance and childishness of villagers. In contrast, to defend their efforts to bypass leaders and deal directly with individual villagers, government bureaucrats highlight the knowledge and savvy of these same villagers.

The expropriation process has not only reinvigorated the influence of such leaders over their covillagers, but extended it, at least temporarily, into the developed sector of G-11. In 1992, when the chronic dispute with the CDA was at a boil, leaders of BQB prevented owners of plots in G-11 from beginning construction on their houses with threats of "dire consequences," as one official described it. The ICTA (Islamabad Capital Territory Administration) established a picket of thirty policemen, but they did not help a single allottee and merely referred the complaints of allottees to the CDA security force. The son of the numberdar of BQB recounted to me another encounter with one allottee in G-11.

> The land [of the allottee's plot] was open so we were growing corn. One day I discovered this guy had just cut it all down. I went to him and asked him why he just cut it down like that without finding out whose it was and so forth. It is no big deal, just around Rs. 500, I wouldn't even care if it were

a *lakh* [100,000], he could take it. But he should have talked to me first. Anyway, this guy reaches into his pants pocket and pulls out his mobile phone and says to me in a rude way, "I am going to call the DSP [Deputy Superintendent of Police, a powerful figure] and complain that the locals are threatening me and keeping me from taking possession of my land. I laughed and told him to call anyone he wants, even the IG [Inspector General, the top police official in the region], they won't come. And of course there was nothing he could do. I wouldn't let him build his house for a year, a whole year. Then he came to me and apologized and offered me money. You go ask him, I didn't take a rupee. I just said, "OK, a year is enough. Build your house." He thought we are just villagers and we don't know how things work.

He also told me gleefully of how they repulsed a group of police who came in 1996 to demolish some stores along the G-12 service road. They just fired off a couple shots in the air and the policemen fled. "What policeman is going to risk his life and children's future for his salary?" he asked.

Beyond the nearby developed sector, documents have enabled local leaders to gain influence over real estate dealers, shady brokers, and CDA functionaries involved in the schemes. Like bureaucrats, whose power is based partly on their capacity to produce and move documents, village leaders are essential nodes of the path made by various graphic artifacts (title documents, powers of attorney, compensation lists, and so forth) essential to the business of profiting from compensation. While guns helped affectees keep documents on their side, to extract the compensation they had to work on documents themselves.

In one dramatic incident in 1988, affectees gathered at the CDA offices to protest the slow processing of their claims. One official's file narrative of the event goes as follows:[18] A "procession of affectees" came to see the chairman. He was not "on his seat," so they went to see Reza Sajjad, the member of the CDA board who oversees land acquisitions.[19] The affectees demanded that he withdraw the appeals the CDA had filed against a particular compensation award. Sajjad said he could do nothing himself. Then, according to the file, the

> Mob got furious and inflicted injuries on the person of Member (P) [Member, Planning, that is, Sajjad] by every thing whatever they got in the room i.e. Flower Pot, Stainless Steel Trays, Table Glass, Chairs, and tools like sicle. Member (P) was badly hurt and ran out of his room to save his life. Member (P) came out of CDA Sectt. Building by cutting open the wire gauze of the window of the room of Member (F) and thus saved him from inflictions of further injuries of the Mob.

Subsequently, "the Mob wrecked office of Dir. Rehab [the head of the Rehabilitation Directorate]," who had already fled, and tried to steal office files. The mob then attacked the deputy director of Rehabilitation, after smashing in his locked office door. The "free-for-all" at Rehabilitation lasted an hour, and then the angry affectees were off to the Lands Directorate offices, where they used "rude unparliamentary language." Officials there had fled, but the offices were destroyed. The account concludes that the mob also made off with records. Sajjad was in intensive care for a week, but as I discuss later, there is more to this story, and the victim was not Sajjad's only role.

The rioters were not adherents of Weber's naïve Bakuninism trying to end CDA expropriations by destroying its documents. Their goal was to use them. After that violent episode, affectees and their colleagues established more routine methods of obtaining and even fabricating records. Some affectee leaders and their assistants—"approach-wallas," as one of their group called them—would spend the entire day at the CDA offices or in the courts.[20] Zahoor, the headman of Sheikhpur, joked that he arrives before government employees and leaves after they do, even though no one makes him sign a daily attendance log. The approach-wallas sit in the offices of any officers who would receive them and cultivate relationships with clerks and peons, who are informed about meetings among officers and, especially, about the movement of files. The efforts of approach-wallas and brokers to develop networks within the CDA were aided by a CDA recruitment policy aimed at the "rehabilitation" of displaced persons. Despite federal rules requiring that posts within the CDA be filled from a "surplus pool" (a group of people with the status but not the work position of employees of the federal government), the CDA gave preference to affectees when hiring lower staff from the 1960s through the end of the 1970s. This was an early concession to a demand of affectees that could be satisfied at little cost. From the list of displaced persons maintained by the Establishment Section of the Federal Secretariat, the CDA hired hundreds, perhaps thousands, of clerks, drivers, peons, guards, and sweepers. Over the years, many of these people have risen from driver or peon to lower-division clerk or from lower-division clerk to upper-division clerk or even assistant. Even those who remain at the bottom are well informed of daily goings-on within the CDA.[21] For many such CDA staff employees, the pecuniary motives that make them open to traffic in information and artifacts are augmented by empathy for other affectees.

Brokers and approach-wallas generally have easier access to the lower ranks of the CDA because they are of similar status, and the spaces occupied by staff are relatively more open. While they can often be seen chatting with clerks and assistants and occasionally a deputy director, they are rarely admitted to what they derisively call the "*durbars*" (princely courts) of more senior officers. One leader of affectees of Siri Saral, a village in D-12, complained that senior officers wouldn't admit him unless he came with a chit from the ombudsman of the federal government (*wafaqi mohtasib*) or some member of the National Assembly.

The head of the department in charge of land acquisitions estimated to me in 1998 that an astonishing 95 percent of the original files dealing with expropriation cases were in the possession of people outside the bureaucracy, who brought them in to CDA offices whenever any work was to be done on them, sometimes at the request of CDA staff whose superior called for them. Such people thus became virtual extensions of the office bureaucracy. The possessors of files removed papers that recorded denials of or objections to compensation claims and added documents supporting claims, with signatures forged or paid for. Several officials alleged that a forgery racket operated through at least the early 1990s that specialized in the signatures of all the CDA officials involved in the compensation proceedings. Brokers were often better informed of the movement of files and the progress of cases than the officers responsible for them. One senior official in the Lands Directorate complained to me that, sometimes, affectees and brokers would come into his office to push their cases and inform him that their file was sitting on his desk, before he had even had a chance to review it.

The fraud in BQB illustrates the power of this control over the modest artifacts of the compensation process. Once liberated from their houses, affectees and their bureaucratic partners began to work on artifacts with a more and more mediated relationship to the houses they were supposed to represent, a movement not from the real to representation or from word to thing, but from one thing to another.

The paper artifacts were more easily manipulated than houses and enabled the fraud schemes to vastly increase in scale during what one official described to me as a period of "lust and plunder" from 1987 to 1993. This should not surprise us. Classical liberal views of property oppose the security of law with the insecurity of force. However, we should recognize that law may often not be a source of property security. Reliance on written artifacts as a basis of controlling land and objects constitutes a new domain of struggle in which relations between people and things may be fluid because they are based upon an order of artifacts that is differently and often more easily manipulated than sociologically extensive recognition and articulation of rights to immovable objects. Examples of this can be found in different places and historical periods. In many areas of the subcontinent in the 1800s, the introduction of written records as a basis of land rights by the British led to the massive legal dispossession of village proprietors and resident cultivators by unscrupulous revenue and court officials (Misra 1977:85). Clanchy (1979) describes how long-standing land rights of the established nobility of eleventh-century England were quickly upset by the conquering Normans, who began to demand written documentation that they then controlled.

At the heart of the new schemes were "proformae," also called "demolition certificates" and "surrender certificates," that documented that houses of a certain size owned by certain persons had been surrendered and demolished. The central government figure in the fraud was none other than Sajjad, at that time the CDA board member in charge of the Planning Wing, the official who was attacked by the mob.[22] He had formed an alliance with the DC-CDA, who had judicial powers to review and amend the compensation awards submitted by the Lands Directorate. Sajjad also brought in a group of fellow officials from the province of Sindh to staff the middle ranks of the Lands Directorate: a technical assistant director (ADT) and several subengineers, whose job it was to gather information and produce documentation on built-up property.

In 1987, 1988, and 1990, the DC-CDA claimed to have heard 1,071 compensation review petitions and to have directed the technical staff to go out to the sites to verify the veracity of the claims. Whether the technical staff looked at any house sites is unclear, but they certainly did the paperwork: hundreds of demolition certificates were produced. Several CDA functionaries I spoke with alleged that the "owners" of the demolished houses paid the ADT Rs. 10,000 for each certificate. In chapter 3, we saw how a case could be controlled by creating the right path for a file. Sajjad used just this technique. He ensured that these certificates would not be challenged by diverting files from their normal paths through the organization hierarchy, effectively altering the control of the expropriation process. He "marked" files (that is, gave written orders for their transfer) directly to the DC-CDA and ADT, and they sent their files to him, bypassing the senior officers of the Lands Directorate, who would normally have signed these files but who were outside the collusive circle.

On the basis of the demolition certificates, the ADT then produced compensation lists and submitted them to the DC-CDA. Many of the petitioners were not owners of land in BQB. No petitions from the supposed petitioners were submitted to the CDA, and no separate files for individual cases were opened. Most houses acquired before 1988 had been documented to be less than 1,000 square feet in area, and nearly all were less than 2,000 square feet; in sharp contrast, the new certificates showed the demolished houses to have been between 2,000 and 5,000 square feet. According to the dates on the certificates, a single bulldozer on two busy days demolished over 700 houses. The ADT's list alone would have been sufficient grounds for the DC-CDA to make the awards. It seems likely that the only reason the demolition certificates were fabricated is that they had to be presented to the officials disbursing the compensation funds. The demolition certificates themselves had a convenient autonomy, because they testified that the owners of demolished structures had bought and removed the building materials, leaving no traces of the dwellings. Thus, these certified records were, by their own testimony, factually unverifiable, their referents no longer existing!

On the basis of these demolition certificates, the DC-CDA accepted 747 of the 1,071 claims. Most of the claims were probably bogus, so the reason he rejected some of them is unclear. Perhaps he was trying to make the review process appear authentic, or perhaps some of the house "owners" did not meet his price. The scheme was clearly in the financial interest of all parties, but the alliance showed strains at times, most evidently in the attack on Sajjad by his partners. The specific reasons for the attack are unclear. Sajjad might have been forced to support a review of the lists suggested by a subordinate or superior. Alternatively, he might have been slow to deliver on his promises of compensation (for which the affectees had already paid), or he might have made further demands on the affectees before disbursing the compensation funds. Funds equivalent to millions of dollars were disbursed, although affectees remained on their land to demand more.

PACKAGE DEALS AND INDIVIDUAL SIGNATURES

The attack on the CDA offices was a manifestation of the failure of affectees and their partners in the CDA to extract compensation with the demolition certificate scheme, which had hovered rather close to actual physical structures. However, the CDA was also not able to clear the land. The stalemate prompted the CDA to put aside official policy and procedures and to negotiate a political settlement in the form of collective agreements with whole villages, known as "package deals." As we'll see, however, this innovative solution foundered on the difficulty of articulating, on the one hand, the artifacts of collective agreement generated in encounters between CDA officers and village representatives and, on the other hand, the artifacts for disbursing money and plots to particular individuals.

Village leaders had been pushing the CDA to recognize them as official representatives of their villages for years. However, compensation policy covered individual landholders. Many CDA officers would not allow anyone to represent even individual affectees much less whole villages, insisting on dealing only with the individual residents themselves. This was undoubtedly a political strategy much like the refusal of corporations to deal with union officials representing workers, preferring to strike deals with individual employees. The numberdar of Sheikhpur frankly asserted that the CDA was trying to break the power of leaders like him. According to him, when he appears before senior CDA officers in the name of a villager concerning compensation issues, the officers say, "Who is he [the person represented] to you? I have no numberdar in my list." Such officers even reject his use of the title *numberdar*, recognized by villagers of Sheikhpur, since the office of numberdar, official representative of the village to the local council, was abolished with the acquisition order and the bringing of the area under the ICT administration in 1981.

Village leaders, however, insist that village residents can't face the CDA as individuals. As Mohammad Rehman, the father of Tariq Ahmed and a leader from BQB, said, "I don't like this individualism [*shakhsiati*] and people really can't go to the CDA, they can't talk with officers, but they can talk with us." Tariq Ahmed put the issue more bluntly, telling me that the "country man" is uneducated and can't speak with officers, he doesn't understand the rules and regulations and the ways offices run: "The villagers don't understand, when a director says he has a meeting and come back in two days, they will just pound the desk with their stick [*dandha*] and say do it now. I know how to go and come back."[23] Even so, he complained, the CDA officers refuse to meet people like him. "They are allergic to us," he told me chuckling. Zahoor pointed out that language too has been a problem, calling the officials "*angreziwalle*" (roughly, "English-speakers") who can't understand the Punjabi of villagers. While this has not been the case for most of the last four decades, during the contentious period from the mid-1980s through 1991, all the expropriations staff and officers were Sindhi, brought in by the Sindhi member of the CDA board for the Planning Wing, Reza Sajjad.

Against the position of many CDA officers that individuals and registered corporations are the only legally recognized actors in the bureaucratic order of Islamabad, village leaders and property dealers have tried to force the CDA to accept their representation by obtaining powers of attorney from owners of land and built-up property. But officials sometimes refuse to accept them, insisting that such powers of attorney are bought from owners, not for purposes of representation, but to make the purchaser the virtual owner of the property in order to receive the compensation. One Lands director refused to accept powers of attorney unless the owner himself or herself was brought into his office, at which time he explained to them what the document entails. This practice brought the criticism of his superiors, who told him they are legal documents and he has to honor them. His response: "Let them bring cases; I will not. If I am called by the court, I will explain that I think they are fraudulent."

However, the difficulty of articulating collective village representation and bureaucratic operations stems not only from legal requirements and the political strategies of CDA officers, for the CDA failed even when it cast both aside in its attempts to resolve disputes in the early 1990s. The effort to deal with villagers on communal terms was mainly the work of one official who was at home with paternalist authority, Zaffar Khan, the son of a prince of the British Empire, whom we met in chapter 2. A former member of the now-disbanded elite Civil Service of Pakistan (CSP) cadre with a high reputation for integrity and effectiveness, he was made Lands director in 1992 when the expropriation process had reached an impasse as the scale of fraud began to be more widely acknowledged in official circles. In early 1991, the CDA chairman and the member (Planning) had even proposed just leaving villages like BQB there and developing around them, but this course was not considered viable on financial, legal, or technical grounds. The CDA was also facing growing pressure to resolve the dispute from individuals and organizations such as the Federal Government Housing Foundation, which had been paying for plots on the site allotted years before. In this context, Zaffar Khan signed so-called package deals with the representatives of nine villages under dispute, including BQB, in the early 1990s.[24] Previous CDA attempts to resolve the conflict had been based on procedure, law, and force. Zaffar Khan sought a negotiated political solution. While Zaffar Khan's immensely wealthy father spent more time in London society than on his lands, Zaffar Khan had seen him play the role of dispute settler among villagers of his area.[25] In fact, when I met Zaffar Khan in 1996, he himself was using this form of dispute resolution in an effort to reclaim large tracts of his family land on which squatters had settled and who refused to recognize his family's legal title.

In contrast to previous awards, which were made to individuals without their consent on the basis of CDA policies regarding compensation, the package deals were agreements between the CDA and village representatives. These village representatives were usually the informally constituted village councils (*jirgas*), who appeared in the quasi-bureaucratic guise of what CDA documents call "committees of notables," sometimes with official titles such as The Action Committee of the Revenue Estate Sheikhpur of Islamabad. The package deals stipulated that a certain number of plots in particular subsectors would be awarded to claimants in exchange for the prompt surrender of land and built-up property and an end to the obstruction of development. Accompanying these agreements were "schedules" or lists of individuals who would receive compensation. In some of these cases, such as that of BQB, this list was provided by the village committee. As one file noted, the CDA considered "the legality or illegality of these houses" for which compensation was claimed to be "immaterial." Less frankly acknowledged, the very materiality of these houses was also immaterial: far from being illegal, many of these houses did not seem even to exist. In the package deals, many affectees received monetary compensation and plots who would not have been eligible under CDA policies. In the deal with BQB, grown sons were given plots, though they had neither land nor built-up property to surrender. Unconcerned by the bureaucratic constraint of the list, Zaffar Khan told me years later that he had simply tacked on an extra twenty plots to the package deal with BQB as incentive to get the villagers off the land. In 1992, one junior officer pointed out that the divergence of the agreements from established policy threatened to open up old settled cases. In reply, Zaffar Khan wrote that, "This is a special case. . . . [N]o decision should be quoted or made applicable with retrospective affect [sic]," unintentionally invoking the strong injustice felt by affectees whose land had earlier been compensated at official rates.

The actual agreements were among the few official CDA documents typed or handwritten in Urdu, in order to make them accessible to village residents who did not read English (fig. 4.4). The English term "package deal" was transliterated into the Urdu script in the titles, and

پیکج ڈیل مابین متاثرین شیخ پور و سی ڈی اے ۔
_____

معاہدہ ہذا آج مورخہ ۷ اکتوبر ۱۹۹۲ء کو بمقام دفتر سی ڈی اے مابین کیپیٹل ڈیولپمنٹ اتھارٹی اور جملہ متاثرین موضع شیخ پور بذریعہ منتخبہ کمیٹی قرار پایا ۔ با اتفاق رائے درج ذیل نکات معاہدہ طے پائے ۔=

اول = یہ کہ ایوارڈ مورخہ ۲ جولائی ۱۹۸۹ء و دیگر جزوی ایوارڈ ہائے کے مطابق ۲۱۲ بعد از معاہدہ ریکارڈ اگر اس تعداد سے کم پائے گئے افراد جن کو قبل ازیں پلاٹ با الاٹمنٹ با آفر لیٹر نہیں ملی ان تمام افراد کو ۳۰×۶۰ سائز کے پلاٹ بطور پیکج ڈیل آئی ۱۳/۲ با آئی ۱۳/۳ میں الاٹ کئے جائیں گے ۔

دوم = یہ کہ موجودہ سروے میں درج ۲۸۶ (دو سو چھیاسی) افراد کو بھی بطور پیکج ڈیل ۳۰×۶۰ سائز کے پلاٹ آئی ۱۳/۲ اور آئی ۱۳/۳ میں الاٹ کئے جائینگے (فہرست لف ہذا) پلاٹس کی الاٹمنٹ ایوارڈ سنانے کے بعد کی جائی گی ۔

سوم = شق اول و دوم کے مطابق الاٹ کئے گئے پلاٹ قابل انتقال ہونگے ۔

چہارم = متاثرین درج شدہ شق اول و دوم کو الاٹمنٹ لیٹر جاری کرنے کے فوراً بعد سی ڈی اے سیکٹر آئی ۱۲، آئی ۱۵ اور آئی ۱۶ میں ترقیاتی کام شروع کر سکے گا اور متاثرین کی طرف سے سلسلے میں مکمل تعاون کیا جائے گا اور کسی قسم کی رکاوٹ نہیں ڈالی جائے گی ۔

پنجم = یہ کہ سڑکوں کی دہائندہی کرنے کے فوراً بعد شق اول اور دوم کے تحت الاٹ شدہ پلاٹوں کا قبضہ حوالہ الاٹیاں کر دیا جائے گا ۔

ششم = متاثرین مذکورہ شق اول و دوم الاٹ شدہ پلاٹوں کا قبضہ حاصل کرنے اور معاوضہ مکانات وصول کرنے کے ایک ماہ کے اندر حصول شدہ مکانات کا قبضہ سی ڈی اے کے حوالہ کرنے کے پابند ہوں گے ۔

ہفتم = یہ کہ کسی متاثر کو ڈبل پلاٹ الاٹ نہیں کیا جائے گا ۔

ہشتم = سی ڈی اے متاثرین / الاٹیاں کو الاٹ شدہ پلاٹوں کا قبضہ دینے دینے سے پہلے سے پہلی پانی اور سڑک کی سہولت مہیا کریگا ۔

نہم = معاہدہ ہذا پر منتخبہ کمیٹی کے ۲۲ (بائیس) ارکان کے علاوہ دیگر تمام متاثرین بھی دستخط کرینگے ۔

دہم = یہ کہ متاثرین مذکورہ معاہدہ ہذا کے علاوہ آئندہ کوئی نیا مطالبہ یا ترمیم پیش نہیں کرینگے اور معاہدہ ہذا کی کسی بھی شق کی خلاف ورزی کی صورت میں الاٹمنٹ منسوخ سمجھ کی ۔

یازدہم = پلاٹ کی قیمت چھ اقساط میں وصول کی جائے گی ۔ پہلی قسط کی ادائیگی معاوضہ مکانات وصول کرنے کے پندرہ روز کے اندر کی جائے گی ۔

دوازدہم = معاہدہ ہذا بطور پیکج ڈیل عملیں لایا جارہا ہے اور متاثرین و سی ڈی اے معاہدہ ہذا کے مکمل طور پر پابند ہونگے ۔

سیزدہم = متاثرین اس امر کی بابت بیان حلفی داخل کرینگے کہ قبل ازیں انہیں سی ڈی اے کی طرف سے کوئی رہائشی پلاٹ الاٹ دیں کیا گیا ۔

(NAZ A BAT)

۸۸

FIGURE 4.4. Sheikhpur Package Deal, 1992.

the body of the agreement took the form of an English-language legal document, with numbered paragraphs. The package deals were signed by the senior CDA officials and members of the committees, and sometimes Haji Mohammad Nawaz Khokar, the Member of the National Assembly from the area (fig. 4.5). The status hierarchy of signatories was displayed in the placement of signatures: the MNA signed at the top right, the CDA officers to the left of him, and the committee members below them. CDA officers signed next to their typed names and titles. In contrast, each representative signed at the line of a table including his name, his father's name, his national identity card number, and his official position on the committee. The twenty-two-member committee from Sheikhpur included a president, a vice president, a general secretary, an additional secretary, a member of the executive committee, and an office secretary, as well as regular members. The officers of this committee, like the CDA officers, signed with stylized Roman-script signatures, while most of the rest handwrote their names in Urdu without stylization. Several of the members of this committee attested their consent by pressing an inky thumb to the page.

The interactional genre in which these agreements were forged was as novel in CDA proceedings as the form of the agreements themselves. While I did not witness meetings between CDA officers and village representatives before 1996, a gross sense of the differences between meetings can be gleaned from newspapers accounts and their accompanying photographs. Gardezi, the flamboyant CDA chairman in the late 1970s and early 1980s, fond of public appearances, frequently met with large groups of affectees. As at the scores of school openings, cricket matches, and concerts he attended, in meetings with affectees he figured himself as the "chief guest," sitting behind a low head table (like a coffee table) in a line of wooden chairs facing the assembly beneath a large, festive, multicolored tent erected in "affected" villages. Brigadier Jan, the exmilitary officer who chaired the CDA, adopted the formal hearing, meeting with affectees in a large event room in a CDA building, sitting behind a work table facing the assembled. More recent meetings with larger groups of affectees, though quite rare, have followed this pattern, though more often meetings take place with just a few representatives of affectees. In contrast, Zaffar Khan went out to villages and discussed terms while sitting on a cot strung with jute (*palang*) or a low wooden platform (*takht*) placed in the village mosque or the open meeting area of the villages, with villagers gathered all around him. Zaffar Khan's approach was well understood, and English-language newspapers

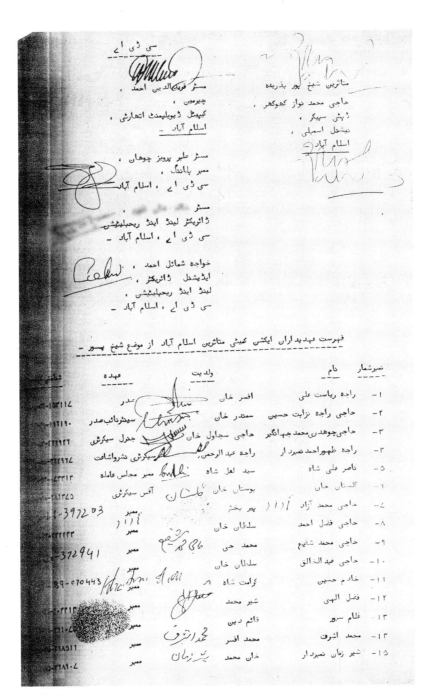

FIGURE 4.5. Signatures on Sheikhpur Package Deal, 1992.

roundly mocked it as a "jirga-style" solution. Following these meetings in the village, the representatives would meet with Zaffar Khan and other senior officials in the conference room of the CDA office to determine the specifics of the deal.

All these deals, however, collapsed in the bureaucratic process of transforming the communal agreement into the compensation packages of individuals. Village meetings and cots could constitute a collective, but documents dissolved it. When individual affectees petitioned the CDA during the negotiation of these package deals, they were told to take their claims to the committee that represented them. The real problems began after the deals were signed. Zaffar Khan wrote that after a deal had been reached between the CDA and BQB "notables" in 1991, a "number of groups of affectees came up with either fresh demands or did not agree to the terms and conditions of the said agreement stating that they are the affectees who are not party to this agreement which has taken place between a few influential affectees and the CDA." After these and other complications I'll describe later made a second package deal with BQB necessary in 1995, affectees again came forward claiming they were not represented by the committee that had signed the agreement. The director of Lands in the late 1990s told me that this had become a typical pattern: "When a deal is struck, someone always comes out and says 'I never authorized you to deal with him,' though such people remain quiet up until then. They come and want to add names, when the representatives have finalized the list." It was difficult for the CDA to refuse these claims, since under its own rules no one is authorized to make deals concerning another person's property unless specifically authorized in writing . This director claimed that this is the reason he does not deal with "representatives" or "so-called leaders." It is unclear whether the committees were themselves complicit in this tactic, but it is certain that some affectees and brokers acting in their names were exploiting the disjuncture between the artifactual basis of collective negotiations and that of individual petitioning. The most basic documentary infrastructure of the CDA would not allow a collective political solution.

LOOSE LISTS

However, as the Special Magistrate I talked with observed, the main problems of the package deals, like those of previous awards, gathered

around the lists of those to be compensated. As lists were being finalized, the CDA often received letters alleging that many of the names on
the compensation lists were fraudulent. While the CDA could not verify
these claims, it was difficult for the CDA to go forward with compensation proceedings after receiving allegations of fraud.

These letters were usually submitted by one faction of the village
against the fraudulent (and even genuine) claims made by other factions.
Illustrative in this regard, BQB had been riven by a dispute between two
loosely formed factions, the Khan and the Pir, whom people referred to
with the English words "group" or "party," or sometimes with the Urdu
"*biraderi.*" These village divisions are embedded in the history of the
wider region.[26] Around 1860, Mehar Ali Shah settled in Golra Sharif, a
village north of BQB (now mostly in E-11), after purchasing land from
the leading family of the region, the Khans. Mehar Ali Shah gained a
reputation for piety and saintly power and was soon known as a *pir.*
As the pir's following in the region grew, political tensions between the
Khan and Pir families emerged. In 1920, a Khan family member allied
with the Pirs raided a Khan house to abduct his cousin, which resulted
in the death of another prominent Khan. The Khans accused the Pirs of
sheltering the murderer. This event kicked off a series of reprisals that
has maintained enmity between the two families and their followers to
the present. This factional division was provoked in BQB by a land dispute that split the Mughals into two biraderis, who drew support from
the larger regional factions. Factional alliances usually run along family lines, and the majority is aligned with the numberdar's Pir faction.
In 1987, Sadiq found that forty families identified with the Pir faction,
seven with the Khan, and three claimed neutrality. My impression was
that the contemporary residents of the village—real and fictitious—are
aligned with the two factions in roughly the same proportion.

This factional conflict has extended into the new terrain of the expropriation process. The two factions made common cause for the package deals, since the CDA was not interested in a partial solution that
would not guarantee clearance of the land. Once the deals were signed,
however, each faction tried to expose the fake claims made by the other.
Just two weeks after the CDA had signed a second package deal with
BQB, Mehboob Ilahi, the numberdar, wrote a letter to the CDA alleging that the list accompanying the package deal included fraudulent
names inserted by CDA officials. This was not the first such letter. An
award given in 1988 to 1,612 owners of built-up property in the village

of Siri Saral in D-11 and D-12, announced in a review by the DC-CDA, provoked a series of anonymous letters. During the process of releasing funds, the CDA chairman received an anonymous letter listing the names of 348 people from the list of the award, claiming they are "outsiders and do not deserve payment." Subsequently the chairman received another such anonymous letter with 480 names, then another with 134 names. It is likely that these letters were from different factions within Siri Saral. The chairman immediately tried to the remove names from the compensation lists as "fictitious affectees," but the matter is still not resolved. While the anonymity of these letters was unusual, representatives of villages usually do try to conceal their factional affiliation in dealings with the CDA in order to maintain their credibility. As one official in the Lands Directorate put it, they come as "well-wishers of the CDA," which he considered a preposterous self-representation.

To understand why lists remained at the core of the dispute, we have to examine their specific characteristics as a graphic genre. As Pertucci has observed with respect to medieval Italian forgeries, the greater the "complexity of authenticated documentation," the greater the "capacity to produce false documents" (1995:247). But these lists are open for manipulation for a reason beyond the complexity of their supporting documentation. Here, with some adjustment, we can make use of Goody's observations on the list as a genre. Emphasizing the visuality of written lists as opposed to oral ones, Goody argued that in written lists isolated linguistic units are ordered outside the frame of a sentence, "where they appear in a very different and highly 'abstract' context," a process he called "decontextualization"(1977:78). Goody was interested in what he considered the cognitive consequences of this decontextualization. However, we can recast his observation in sociological and linguistic terms to understand how the place of lists in discursive and artifactual contexts shapes their role.

Lists of compensation for built-up property include the name of the claimant, the location of the property, the house number, the area of the structure, the quality classification of the structure, and the rupee cost (fig. 4.6). As discrete artifacts, these lists are linguistically divorced from the oral and written propositional discourse that asserts their factuality. As I described in the previous chapter, most CDA genres are anchored in the human, spatiotemporal, and artifactual orders of the CDA by the elaborate use of signatures, dates, stamps, and interartifactual references. In contrast, the lists submitted by the Lands Directorate for execution by the DC-CDA were inscribed with almost none of these

265.	Muhammad Akram S/O Mohammad Aslam Abadi Deh	265	290	"	1195/-	C
266.	Zakia Begum W/O Mohammad Aslam	-do-	266	240	"	720/-	D
267.	Said Akbar S/O Raja Kamal Khan	-do-	267	270	"	1332/-	B-C
268.	Farooq Bi D/O Said Akbar	-do-	268	144	"	432/-	D
269.	Shazia Begum D?O Said Akbar	-do-	269	264	"	396/-	D/2
270.	Sabz Sultan W/O Mohammad Anwar	-do-	270	233	"	350/-	D-D/2
271.	Zahida W/O Zamurd Khan	-do-	271	172	"	516/-	D
272.	Mukhtar Begum W/O Raja Muhamad Jehangir.	-do-	272	58	"	176/-	D
273.	Ghulam Fizan D/O Karamat Hussain Shah	-do-	273	195	"	293/-	D/2
274.	Niaz Hussain Shah S/O Mehboob Hussain Shah.	-do-	274	253	"	380/-	D/2
275.	Ashiq Hussain Shah S/O Mehboob Hussain Shah	-do-	275	217	"	326/-	D/2
276.	Rukhsar Bibi D/O Mehboob Hussain Shah	-do-	276	253	"	380/-	D/2
277.	Raja Saeed Akhtar S/O Muhammad Ayub	-do-	277	151	"	227/-	D/2
278.	Nasreen Bibi D/o Mehboob Shah	-do-	278	202	"	303/-	D/2
279.	Zulfiqar Shah S/O Gharib Shah	-do-	279	202	"	303/-	D/2
280.	Sardar Saghir S/O Javed Iqbal	-do-	280	203	"	609/-	D
281.	Javed Ahmed S/O Feroz Khan	-do-	281	195	"	585/-	D
282.	Azram Bibi D/O Raja Feroz Khan	-do-	282	175	"	525/-	D
283.	Rukhsar Bibi W/O Mazloom Khan D/O Raja Nawab.	-do-	283	175	"	525/-	D
284.	Raja Tanveer S/O Muhammad Aslam	-do-	284	120	"	360/-	D
285.	Munir Ahmed S/O Muhammad Aslam	-do-	285	150	"	450/-	D
286.	Naheeda Akhtar D/O Muhammad Aslam	-do-	286	305	"	915/-	D

13.   The properties of the above mentioned persons are being acquired on the condition that all the acquired land including built up property of village Sheikhpur falling in Sectors I-14, I-15 and I-16 shall be vacated as per agreement. In case the conditions of the agreement are not fulfilled by the expropriated owners, this award shall stand recalled and the above mentioned persons shall not be entitled to any compensation or other benefit arising from this award.

14.   I have made this award on this 25th Day of November, 1992 and announced it in the presence of the representatives.

FIGURE 4.6. Page of a compensation award list after official certification, 1992.

indexes of context. The space of the paper was no match for the great volume of activity and artifacts that was supposed to attest to the validity of every entry on the list. According to official procedures, the lists are to be compiled by junior officers after consulting the supporting documents, including petitions, verification certificates, and the revenue record.

There simply was not enough space on the list to document who had added a particular entry on what documentary grounds. Official procedures called for review and approval of the lists by the more senior officials, but this was impractical given the volume of documents that would have had to be seen for verification of the hundreds of entries on even a single list. Furthermore, in many cases, such documents were hard to locate because they had been mislaid or removed from the office altogether. Using Latour's (1999:24) concept of "circulating reference," the list lies at the end of a chain of transformations, transmutations, and translations that links a representation to its purported referent. Tracing entries on the list back along this chain to their supposed referents was difficult, if not impossible. The compensation lists, therefore, were relatively autonomous (decontextualized, in Goody's terms), weakly linked to the process that was supposed to generate them.[27]

Beyond the limitations of paper size and disconnection from other supporting documents, the semiotic nature of lists also made them objects that attracted fraud. Like items in graphic tables, the written items of a list gain their significance from their placement on a certain page and through their spatial relations with other items. Although deciding what items to include on a list can involve vast amounts of effort, making the list itself is a mostly material process of assemblage, requiring no knowledge of English, only the ability to type the Latin alphabet.

These characteristics of lists opened them up to rather easy manipulation. When a list was being prepared, an entry could simply be added, without the difficult (and expensive) effort of fabricating supporting documents, which would have involved other functionaries. As a material act—inserting characters to place a name where it didn't belong— adding an entry to a draft list was something almost anyone with access to the lists and a typewriter could do. Because signs of the process by which the list was actually produced were not inscribed on the list itself, functionaries could evade prescribed procedures and open the list preparation process to "outside" parties.[28] In practice, the award lists were produced by a variety of irregular activities in the murky transactional arenas of money, favors, friendship, and kinship. They gradually came to resemble Chichikov's registers of dead souls (Gogol 1985), except these souls were living—elsewhere.

When a list was approved by senior officials, fraudulent entries were secured. Common recognition of the practical difficulty of thoroughly verifying the lists relieved the approving officials of much of their responsibility. Senior officials, some of whom had also added fraudulent entries, could approve the lists with the certainty that false entries, if discovered, would be evidence of managerial incapacity rather than criminality. But the lists sometimes betrayed affectees and their partners as well.

Such complications have driven the disputes into the courts. The CDA has fought the BQB case and others like it to the Supreme Court of Pakistan, but with no success. In court too, the CDA has been betrayed by its own records. In postcolonial Pakistan, as in the British Indian colonial state, government records have a powerful official presumption of truth, despite the widespread knowledge that they are routinely manipulated. In official ideology, the validity of records (or, more precisely, their referential correctness) is ensured by following the procedures established for their production. Courts have been unsympathetic to factual claims by the CDA that the house counts simply did not square with earlier census data on the area or with the possibilities of biological reproduction. For the courts, even physical evidence from later CDA site inspections showing that the houses never existed was insignificant compared to the mass of previous documentation testifying to their existence.

The courts required the CDA to show convincingly that the impugned documents were not produced according to correct procedures, which, for reasons described in my account of files, the CDA could not do. The CDA has even lost in court when it has impugned its own records with the testimony of the DC-CDA, the ADT, and the subengineers, all of whom declared in depositions that they signed none of the hundreds of CDA documents that appear to bear their stamps and signatures. These claims were likely false, but they were made defensible by the rumored existence of a forgery ring specializing in Land Directorate signatures. But the CDA investigations that attempted to trace documents through the actual process by which they were produced—to identify documents with individuals—were not enough to disqualify the documents, for they had risen to the level of corporate or collective authorship. In their circulation, the documents had received numerous signatures of many

CDA functionaries other than those accused of perpetrating the fraud. These others became unwitting or unwilling supporters of the fraud. The courts have consistently refused to recognize the CDA as anything but a corporate body, and often judgments remark on the contradictory testimony of the CDA, viewing the allegedly fraudulent documents and the documents alleging that fraud as the utterances of the same voice. The documents were the contemporary equivalent of what diplomatic historians call "chancery forgeries," that is, forgeries produced by the same social process as genuine documents, with the exception of correct reference; they are authentic but false (Petrucci 1995:247).

MEDIATING LIKE A STATE

The National Accountability Bureau (NAB) brought this fraud to public view in 2000 and, with the summary authority of the new military government, stopped the remaining payments. But the BQB settlement continues to grow as officials and the courts try to sort genuine from "fake" awardees.[29] Today, some officials, like the special magistrate I quoted at the beginning of this chapter, see the solution to this predicament in the more effective deployment of the bureaucratic techniques that have failed the organization so thoroughly. Veterans of the dispute, however, are more pessimistic about the prospect of resolving the issue through more secure and more accurate documentation. They recognize the strength of the collective of artifacts, affectees, corrupt functionaries, and now courts. In 1993, a committee headed by a CDA official with an unassailable reputation for honesty and long experience in the Lands Directorate was formed to investigate fraudulent compensation claims in the area of G-11 and G-12, including BQB. After reviewing the documentary evidence, the committee attempted to conduct site inspections to measure land holdings and enumerate and measure houses. As on other similar occasions, the residents of the settlement met the CDA inspectors with guns and barred them from the site. Because the ostensible referents of the records were inaccessible, the committee, like the affectees, focused on the records themselves.

One finding of the committee's confidential English-language report was that the fraudulent award had itself become a genre of sorts. The report noted that the fraudulent awards were almost identical in their prose, down to the vague and idiosyncratically ungrammatical justification given for awarding compensation: "The houses of the petitioners were missed from the relevant award due to some mistake/overlook." The report concluded, "the current chaotic situation is a direct result of the lists of residents prepared from time to time. In each successive list, the number of affectees increased in a manner which defied the laws of mathematical progressions." Recognizing that the CDA had lost control of the bureaucratic process through which records are generated, the committee warned that the "preparation of fresh survey lists will compound the current complicated situation." In a startling finding, the committee strongly advised that there be no more investigations and, especially, "no fresh lists." The committee recommended that current claims, although largely fraudulent, be paid as soon as possible, because continued efforts to dispute them would only result in more legally incontestable claims. The committee recognized that written materials, lists, were the artifacts around which collusive networks of staff, officials, and brokers formed. To break these networks, the artifacts would have to be dispensed with.

Bureaucratic semiotic technologies are usually described as the means by which government dominates the populace. In this case, these technologies have been turned against the government. CDA officials pursuing the interests of the CDA have been forced to renounce them. Many officials no longer consider lists, maps, or property records useful for the resolution of expropriation disputes. For a brief period, one financial officer even refused to sign his department's checks to disburse court-ordered compensation.

In his excellent study of the consequences of colonial practices of land registration in India, Richard Saumarez Smith writes, "Reduction of field patterns to paper lay at the heart of the new idiom of the records, the new works of reference which could only be consulted individually, serially, and according to the procedures laid down by the Government: the venue for settling points of information, and of dispute, was transferred from the open fields to the closed courtroom" (1996:252). In contemporary Islamabad, the venue for settling points of information and of dispute remains the courtroom rather than the open fields, but the government does not control the records carried out of the fields and into the courtroom. If, as Saumarez Smith writes, the British "ruled by records," today the CDA *is* ruled by records.

Although the CDA continues to hope to gain possession of the land it has already paid so much to acquire, in 1993 it rezoned nearly a third of the Islamabad territory slated for government development under the original Master Plan. This land has now been left to private corpo-

FIGURE 4.7. Urbanizing area of former village of Badia Qadir Bakhsh in 2007. (Photo by the author.)

rations and housing societies to develop, and they are faring no better than government planners in wresting land from villagers.

When I first visited BQB in 1996, I was struck by how much house construction was going on, beyond the dummy houses meant for counting. One son of the BQB numberdar had just converted a large bait-hak compound—separate from the numberdar's house—into a well-appointed house for his family. Whenever I met the numberdar of BQB, there were stacks of bricks outside his gate, a sign of ongoing construction within his compound. At the time, I took this as a measure of how long they thought it would take before the dispute would be resolved and they would finally leave the land. The time pressure was on the side of the CDA rather than the villagers, who can demand more compensation as the market value of their land continues to rise. But I did not imagine, and none of the village residents ever suggested to me the possibility, that they would just stay on. Today, the village of BQB has disappeared, replaced by a dense, unplanned, urban neighborhood that has grown up around and within it (fig. 4.7). Real estate maps of the city now include the name of Badia Qadir Bakhsh and other similar villages. Prospects for the CDA taking this land seem remote, to say the least. It is likely that much of western Islamabad, like the area where the village of BQB was located, will develop from existing villages and resemble the "organic growth" of Rawalpindi so vilified by Doxiadis (fig. 4.8). The future lanes and streets of this urban area will almost certainly follow the banks, footpaths, and property lines that have long divided the agricultural fields of the region.

Classifications and measurements of family, populations, land, physical structures, soil, and the numerical formulas for compensation have remained remarkably stable throughout the history of this dispute. However, the stability of the more general classificatory and enumerative representations was no guarantee that they would function as intended. What does this extraordinary history of the object-making practices through which the CDA compensates affectees have to tell us about the usual functioning of government and, in particular, the kinds of schematic knowledges that fascinate Scott?

First, the beguiling simplicity and great scope of abstract state schemes can lead us to reify their influence. But as this case makes plain, the execution of these schemes depends on a host of human and artifactual mediators, even in a relatively unified governmental agency of an authoritarian state. Their very abstractness, their remove from particulars, requires the cooperation of even the most humble members of the bureaucratic collective, including runners and pieces of paper. State schemes may sit atop bureaucratic processes like powerless potentates commanding unruly masses of subjects who refuse to do their bidding. The Islamabad expropriation process shows us that actors can appropriate (or misappropriate) what Weber called the "means of administration," the sine qua non of bureaucracy as a social form. To explain the ordinary success of bureaucratic schemes, we must always discover how obstreperous mediators have been made allies.

Second, the expropriation process dramatically demonstrates that the politics of representation has a material component. Accounts of the politics of representation typically describe discursive interventions—literature, position papers, newspaper opinion pieces, videos, protest placards—that dialogically engage dominant representations in an attempt to reframe, transform, refute, or silence them. Affectees made such interventions to convince political leaders and CDA officials of the injustice and political costs of the expropriation policies. On a

FIGURE 4.8. Badia Qadir Baksh and G-11 in 2011 (© 2011 GeoEye).

smaller scale, various village leaders and brokers petitioned CDA officials to have their, or their clients', names included in compensation roles legally. They failed in these efforts. Success came through material intervention with records, changing marks on paper, the effectiveness of which depended on the complete effacement of their actual discursive engagement with CDA officials.

CHAPTER 5

Maps, Mosques, and *Maslak*s

One day in 1997, I was talking with Raja Zahoor Ahmed in his sitting room about the prospect for his area being developed. Zahoor was the leader of Sheikhpur, a large village in the rural area of western Islamabad. Some years before, the village land had been expropriated by the city government, but the village remained undisturbed as disputes over compensation continued. Zahoor was recounting the many problems he had had with the Capital Development Authority. Capping his complaints, he declared that the CDA was not even planning mosques: "The CDA gets money for mosques, but this money is just eaten." He contended that even here, in I-14, where he expected to receive plots after the sector had been developed, they weren't planning mosques. I disagreed. At the time, the plan for sector I-14 had not been made public and I had not seen it, but I knew that the Islamabad Master Plan called for the construction of many mosques in every sector. In reply, he got up, walked over to a cabinet like those in government offices where files are stored, and pulled out a large roll of a blueprint. He said, "See for yourself," and, to my surprise, spread out a CDA map of I-14. Indeed, the map showed only one mosque, an existing village mosque that would be preserved as the sector was redeveloped.

I'll return to the intriguing absence of mosques on the I-14 map. But now I want to draw attention to Zahoor's possession of the map. Before the plan for I-14 had even been published, Zahoor had gotten hold of a copy and begun to press the CDA for more mosques. Maps like these set the terms of the organization of space. But they are also used to challenge the official spatial vision for the city. The circulation of maps as material artifacts is central to these challenges. As we'll see, maps have played an especially significant role in the conflict over the construction and sectarian allocation of mosques and, indeed, have contributed to sectarian strife in the city.

Before we get to Islamabad's mosques, let me first discuss its maps. The new capital was first seen in the map of Costantinos Doxiadis, a Greek modernist who was the project's architect-planner (see fig. 0.1 in the introduction). Versions of Doxiadis's map became ubiquitous in Islamabad. A billboard-size version welcomes you as you approach the city from Rawalpindi. Others are found on the office walls of planners and real estate agents, in newspaper advertisements, and on web sites. In the 1960s and 1970s, the first decades of the city's existence, Doxiadis's Master Plan of Islamabad was the object of numerous state rituals. Foreign dignitaries received tours of a museum enshrining the city maps in colored paper and clay. Afterward, such dignitaries were taken to Shakarparian, an overlook on a hill to the south of the city. The most eminent were invited to plant a tree next to its map of Islamabad in concrete and shrubs. On a high hill to the north of the city, the planners constructed another overlook, Daman-e-Koh, which commands a view of the whole city. Just below the level of the walkway, a large concrete slab juts out from the cliff with the city plan painted in bright white lines against a tennis-court green, which gives it the look of a giant, dangerous hopscotch game (fig. 5.1). Tourists and residents on outings, pointing from the map to the city, match its painted lines to the asphalt avenues below: On my own visits there I overheard, for example, a man, pointing from the map to the city, tell his wife, "See, on this side is G-6, on that G-7"; one young man exclaimed to his friend, "Wow, the roads are made completely straight [*sidhe sidhe*]!"; one resident explained to a visitor the meaning of the alphanumeric sector designations, "See, the whole city is divided into sectors and named."

Michel de Certeau (1984:91–93) portrays maps like these as the key to the perspectives and practices of planners. He contrasts the aloof, totalizing, panoramic visual perspective of overlooks and maps with the realm of practice "down below." By merging the grid of the Master Plan with the visual perspective of the city, the Daman-e-Koh overlook tries to fuse the abstract point of view with the situated perspective of an embodied viewer that de Certeau emphasizes. However, like

FIGURE 5.1. Daman-e-Koh overlook. (Photo by the author.)

de Certeau's walkers, planners are also "down below." Unlike the map at Daman-e-Koh, the maps most significant to the development of the Islamabad—the blueprints of houses, markets, mosques, and sectors—are also down below, in the realm of practice, on planners desks, on the walls of police stations, stuffed in files, clipped to petitions, even in the cabinets of well-connected villagers. These maps do not stand over against a reality they represent; rather, they are entangled in the prosaic practices through which the city is planned, constructed, regulated, and inhabited.

Approaching maps in this way suggests the limitations of modernist understandings of maps as the most basic technology and most fundamental metaphor of modern state surveillance and control. James Scott (1998:57), for example, not only describes the role of maps in modern regimes of control, but he also uses the map ("maps of legibility") as his image for state practices of documentation in general. The synoptic perspective is embodied in modern maps, whose order is most evident not at street level but from above, outside the social experience of most residents. Sumathi Ramaswamy (2003) cites Levin to place maps within a broader history of vision in modern social life: "the power to see, the power to make visible, is the power to control" (Levin 1993:7). J.B. Harley put it most succinctly: "to map the land was to own it" (cited in Andrews 2001:22). This emphasis on control is well justified by an overwhelming amount of scholarship showing the instrumental role of maps in governmental projects around the world from at least the nineteenth century. It should be noted, nevertheless, that synoptic state visions may also be mobilized against projects of state control.

Accounts of maps that emphasize instrumental control paradoxically often remain too focused on the imaginative constructs of visual representation. Rather than juxtaposing the abstraction of maps against the manifold qualities of the land and built environments they represent, we can examine what happens in between. From this perspective, abstraction is more than a logic of representation; it is a product of a dense network of connections with, rather than a separation from, what is represented. As we saw in the last chapter, a welter of people and things mediates the relation between documentary representations such as lists and their referents, opening opportunities for unexpected forms of participation. Only a map like Daman-e-Koh can be related to the built environment by nothing more than a pointing finger. Attention to the practices between maps and their representations highlights the complex temporality of the connections of maps with things they represent. Collectives of mediators shift, altering the epistemic status and political possibilities of map elements or maps as a whole. Such shifts often result from the movement of maps as material artifacts. It is precisely the sociomaterial mobility of maps as material artifacts that allows the separation from the perspective and projects of their makers.

The next two sections of this chapter trace the positions and activities of the CDA and Auqaf (or Islamic Endowments) Directorate of the Islamabad Capital Territory Administration as they responded to and unintentionally promoted contestation over sectarian allocation. The following three sections use different analytic approaches to maps to show the varying ways maps are consequential to the making and governance of the built environment of Islamabad, especially its mosques. Analyzing maps as graphic representations that articulate legitimate forms of sociality, I show how maps combine with state policies to enable new kinds of claims for the construction and governance of mosques. Next, I focus on the multiply mediated relations between maps and their material referents to show how maps work as instruments for the surveillance and control of mosque construction. Finally, I analyze the sociomaterial mobility of maps as material artifacts and the mosque locational politics in the undeveloped sections of western Islamabad that this mobility enables. These three approaches overlap, and I distinguish them by their emphasis rather than their discrete analytic difference.

Throughout the chapter, I pursue the ethnographic argument that in Islamabad official maps have been central to the organization of space, but they have not proven to be inexorable instruments of state control. As we'll see, maps have poorly served the government's struggle against illegal mosque building. In fact, maps have been very useful for groups attempting to build mosques, both in grounding claims for mosques and in facilitating the practical processes of unauthorized mosque construction and regularization. Although sectarian politics appear to many state actors to be an intrusion into the state arena, the history of mosque construction and allocation in Islamabad illuminates the complex role that Pakistan state documentary practices play in religious politics (Van der Veer 2002). Through involvement with mosque building in the city, the state literally mapped a new arena of competition and conflict between Islamic sects. Court cases and energetic public protests have led to the ad hoc authorization of many mosques, but have not fundamentally reshaped government policy on mosques. Islamabad bureaucracies have clung to long-standing policies, effectively leaving the mosque construction and allocation process in the hands of contending sectarian groups.

A MOSQUE FOR EVERY COMMUNITY

As I described in chapter 1, mosques in Islamabad were planned as part of a numbered and lettered hierarchy of "communities," from the smallest gathering of a few people to the city as a whole (fig. 1.1). Planners expected communities to grow around neighborly relations and the use of common, central facilities for educational, commercial, medical, recreational, and religious needs. The original planners envisioned the residential population of the city as differentiated only by age, sex, and income or rank. Religious divisions did not figure at all in their plans, beyond implicitly excluding Christians.

Only the skewed western orientation of mosques toward Mecca disturbed their seamless integration within the secular city grid. Like schools and markets, they were planned according to population projections and the catchment area, the area from which the mosque would draw *namazi*s or worshippers. Planners in the early 1960s projected that some 10 percent of the residents of an area would attend Friday prayers, and they should be expected to walk no more than one-quarter mile in ten to twelve minutes.[1] Class A mosques, sited at the center of sub-subsectors, were to accommodate 100 namazis; class B, focal in the subsector, 200–250 namazis; class C, at the center of the sector, around 1000 namazis. In one of many departures from the prevailing ideal-typical "Islamic City," with its central mosque-market complex, no mosque was planned for the major commercial artery, the Blue Area. A large national mosque, Faisal Masjid, was eventually built at the northern edge of the city at a remove from most commercial and residential areas, but as one planner told me, "it is a landmark, not part of the system." As we'll see, the absence of a planned mosque in the purely commercial Blue Area reflects the official vision of mosques linked to residents rather than markets and merchants, a vision that was subsequently codified in 1986 in the rules for forming mosque committees.

During this period, many people claimed that Islam was the "ideology" of Pakistan. There is much debate about what this means, and I will explore this more fully later on. Put simply, the claim was that the nation of Pakistan—with its separate west and east wings—was not grounded in a language, region, or culture, because none of these were shared by any majority of citizens in the new state. Rather, Pakistan was defined by a religion that gave rise to a distinct nation or community. However, it was less ideology than functionality that underlay the government commitment to the provision of mosques. Planners saw Islamabad not as an Islamic city but as a city populated by Muslims, that is, a city not to be designed and administered according to Islamic principles but a modern city that would serve the needs of Muslims.[2] Implicit in the official technical treatment of mosques was an ecumenical vision of Islam as a uniform "religion," all of whose followers could be served by the same institutional facilities, much as all the residents of a locality could be served by the same schools, fruit markets, and tailor shops.

In 1959, the area planned for the metropolitan region had over fifty-four thousand inhabitants spread over more than fifty villages, each of which had one or more mosques and usually a cemetery as well. The area was also dotted with shrines (*mazar*s), the graves of saints (*pir*s) or less venerated religious figures whom worshippers entreat to intercede on their behalf. The largest of these was the shrine of Hazrat Pir Syed Mehr Ali Shah at Golra Sharif, which was even then a major regional pilgrimage site. While development displaced the living, it left the dead in place, if not undisturbed. Cemeteries were simply leveled for development, but even humble shrines were preserved. The road near the center of F-8 narrows suddenly to accommodate a poorly tended shrine. Most of the village mosques were unceremoniously demolished as the land was redeveloped. Only those that were compatible with development plans were left intact, eventually becoming designated "old mosques" in CDA parlance.

From the early 1960s through the end of the 1970s, the CDA built new mosques and placed them in the care of groups of local residents and government servants and merchants who worked nearby. These groups assumed responsibility for funding and appointing the mosque staff. The testimony of records and of longtime residents suggests this allocation was very informal. The Auqaf Directorate and CDA files documenting mosques in this period rarely list the names of individuals charged with overseeing them.

The CDA originally planned to construct all the mosques in the city. However, from the early 1970s population growth created a demand for mosques that the CDA found increasingly unable to meet. Around this time, mosque committees of local residents began to fund and construct mosques, though the CDA continued to determine their locations. Mosques elsewhere in Pakistan were almost always built in this fashion, but in the context of a government plan to construct all mosques, the CDA described such mosques as "private construction," built on a "self-help basis." By 1980, only one-third of the some seventy mosques in the developed sectors of the city had been constructed by the CDA. This planning and ad hoc allocation process began to break down in the late 1970s with the complementary growth of state Islamization and sectarian politics. The increasing salience of sectarian religious identifications also accelerated the demand for new mosques, transforming the provision of mosques from a construction problem to a political problem for the government.

A MOSQUE FOR EVERY *MASLAK*

According to records and the testimony of residents and longtime CDA officials, through the end of the 1970s there was rarely any controversy surrounding the allocation of mosques or mosque sites to committees. Residents never petitioned the CDA for a mosque in sectarian terms, as members of one or another Islamic *maslak* (roughly, sect). Instead, petitioners to the CDA often identified themselves simply as officers of an association based on locality. For example, one petition was submitted by the president and general secretary of "The Welfare Committee of Sector G-6/4–1." As the name suggests, this association handled other neighborhood issues as well, for example, the leaky roofs of government quarters and irregular water supply.

There may have been informal understandings in official circles about the eventual sectarian affiliation of these mosques, insofar as they were seen to have one in this period beyond Sunni or Shia. But the CDA, oriented toward construction, maintained no records on the sectarian affiliation of mosques, reflecting its lack of open concern for such matters. I will have more to say about what constitutes a "sect" and a sectarian affiliation later, but it's worth noting here that by 1980, the CDA had constructed twenty-two mosques that came to be affiliated with the four major Islamic maslaks prevalent in the region. Among the Sunni sects, eleven became affiliated with the Barelvi sect, nine with the Deobandis, and one with Ahl-e-Hadith. One mosque became Shia.

In my examination of mosque files and my survey of all Urdu- and English-language newspapers distributed in Rawalpindi and Islamabad since the early 1960s, I found no controversy regarding mosque allocation until 1978, the year after Zia-ul-Haq took control.[3] Why did the affiliation of mosques become controversial at this time? To answer this question, we need to understand, first, the significance that mosques took on within the politics of religious community in the late colonial period and how this significance was transformed by the growing salience of political sectarianism generated by new state Islamization policies.

In a discussion of mosques in Islamabad published in 1995, Mohammad Ismail Zabeeh wrote, "In all times mosques have been a sign of the power and greatness of Islam" (1995:153). But as David Gilmartin (1988) argues, the mosque became a central symbol through a particular definition of the Muslim community that developed in early-twentieth-century India and led eventually to the formation of Pakistan (see also Devji 1993:77–78). The *ulema* (Islamic scholarly establishment) of several Islamist reform movements developed a "view of community defined not by political competition but by popular adherence to personal Islamic religious norms" (Gilmartin 1988:153). This view, however, was overwhelmed by a different conception of the Muslim community pioneered by the poet Muhammad Iqbal and popularized in the twentieth-century press, a conception that "tended not to be grounded in any particular form of organization or code of conduct, but, rather in the special inheritance—symbolized by the Prophet, the Quran, and the mosque" (153). The centrality of the mosque as a symbol of the Muslim community was dramatized in movements to defend mosques against regulation by the colonial state and encroachments from Sikhs and Hindus, most notably in Kanpur in 1913 (Freitag 1989) and Lahore in 1935.

This symbolic role of mosques was carried forward into what came to be called the "ideology" of Pakistan. The Constitution of Pakistan of 1956 directed the state "to enable the Muslims of Pakistan individually and collectively to order their lives in accordance with the Holy Quran and Sunnah" (Constitution of the Islamic Republic of Pakistan, 1956, part 3, para. 25), including the commitment to safeguard the proper organization of *zakat* (alms for the poor), *waqfs* (Islamic endowments, for example, a building or land for a school or charity), and mosques, a provision that has been included in all subsequent Pakistan constitutions. While this provision could be read as a matter of finance and organization, disputes over the Islamic status of the heterodox Qadiani sect in the 1990s led the Supreme Court and Lahore High Court to declare mosques "trademarks of Muslims" and "symbols of Allah" (Ahmed 2010). Compared to other Islamic institutions more strongly associated with a particular tradition, religious lineage, or figure, mosques have a "transcendental quality," an "ability to rise above particularities [that] made mosques the perfect site for the embodiment of the state's ideology, incomplete and implicated in the present but inevitably to be whole in the future" (Khan 2003:128). However, it is precisely this looser association with particular religious divisions that made mosques so contestable. Mosques remained a central symbol of religious community into the 1970s, but Islamization policies initiated by Zia led many Pakistanis to define religious community in terms of maslaks. As mosques once had to be defended from the central authority of the colonial government and the Sikh and Hindu communities, increasingly they were seen to be under threat from the Pakistan government and the challenges of other maslaks.

Islam played a central role in the movement for Pakistan and has continued to shape constitutional debates and political processes more broadly. Little, however, has been done to incorporate the teachings of Quran and Sunnah (the spoken and acted example of the Prophet) into the organization of the state or public policies (Ahmad 1998; Haqqani 2005; Malik 1996). Although Prime Minister Zulfiqar Ali Bhutto promoted Islam in the final years of his government as a way to bolster his increasingly unpopular rule, it was General Zia-ul-Haq who committed the state to Islamization. After ousting Bhutto in 1977 with the support of sections of the ulema, Zia proclaimed the establishment of a social order based on *Nizam-i-Mustafa* (the system of the Prophet Muhammad), with the ostensible goal of bringing society and the state in line with Sharia. As Mumtaz Ahmad argues, Islamic political groups in Pakistan saw Islamization as a "transfer of political power from the secular-minded corrupt elite to the *saleheen* [pious Muslims] who, by appropriating authoritative positions in various institutions of the state, would create the conditions conducive for the establishment of the complete *din* [religion]" (1997:103). Zia, however, did not carry Islamization to the point of threatening the political dominance of the military and civilian bureaucracy. Islamization measures included the institution of an Islamic penal code, federally administered zakat and *ushr* (agricultural tithe), interest-free counters at banks, moving the weekly work holiday from Sunday to Friday, the expansion of treatments of Islam in school textbooks, and the support of popular religious festivals.

Alongside such policies, the state appropriated a variety of Islamic institutions that had previously operated independently of state controls in order to undermine the autonomy of the ulema that had allowed it to criticize the government when it was seen to be acting against the teaching of Islam. Having surrendered much of the control of their institutions to the state, the ulema were given government positions in zakat and ushr committees, government-controlled mosques, madrassahs, and other newly created religio-political institutions, councils, and committees. As Jamal Malik (1996) has argued, Islamization in Pakistan is best understood as two complementary processes aimed at strengthening the state: the traditionalization, in an Islamic idiom, of state structures derived from colonialism; and the integration of relatively autonomous Islamic institutions into the state apparatus. Thus, on the one hand, federally administered zakat and ushr systems traditionalized economic extraction by the state. On the other, the regulation of Islamic education and nationalization of shrines and waqfs integrated these institutions into the state.

Although the growth of political sectarianism was a complex process, in most accounts it was a religio-political dynamic provoked by Islamization.[4] Islamization generated sectarian conflict as formerly autonomous and relatively unarticulated groups clashed in their efforts to project their particular vision of Islam within the state sphere. Sectarian politics has been promoted by hundreds of organizations—political parties, educational and welfare organizations, and militant groups—with stronger or weaker ties to the broad religious divisions of Islamic doctrine and practice particular to South Asia.

Although the particular political role that sectarian divisions took on at the end of the 1970s reflects the political dynamics of Zia's Islamization program, these divisions themselves have longer histories. The main division among forms of Islam in Pakistan is, of course, that of Sunni and Shia, stemming from conflicts in the early history of Islam.[5] There are three major Sunni maslaks emerging from the nineteenth-century reform movement in colonial India (Metcalf 1989).[6] The Deoband maslak formed around the seminary at Deoband in India established in 1866. They reject "popular" Islam and emphasize independent judgment, especially within the Hanifi school of jurisprudence (*fiqh*). Ahl-i Hadith, heir to the Wahabi movement, which originated in Saudi Arabia in the eighteenth century, rejects Sufism as un-Islamic and all schools of Islamic jurisprudence as accretions on the teachings of the Quran and the Prophet. The Barelvi, named after the madrassa founded in Bareilly, India, follows a "folk" Islam with emphasis on Sufism, veneration of saints, idolization of the Prophet, and popular festivals of syncretic rituals. As Islamization policies fostered the growth of politicized sectarian identifications, mosques became objects of contestation, both as symbols of religious community and, with the state funding for mosques in Islamabad, sources of state patronage. Although the bitterest sectarian conflicts in Pakistan have been between Sunni and Shia groups, competition for mosques has been sharpest among the less categorically differentiated Sunni groups.

The government response to increasingly acrimonious conflicts over the sectarian allocation of mosque sites in Islamabad exacerbated the problem locally. In 1979, Islamabad was made a district and given its own administration under the Ministry of the Interior. With a presidential directive in 1981, all the mosques of the city were nationalized and placed under the authority of the Auqaf Directorate of the new Islamabad administration. The Auqaf Directorate assumed operational control and financial responsibility for the mosques, and all mosque staff became state employees. In my discussions with imams (prayer leaders), Auqaf officials, and residents, they concurred that at that time many candidates for mosque posts welcomed the opportunity for state employment, and residents were happy to have the government assume financial responsibility for mosques rather than having to support them through their own donations as is the case in the rest of Pakistan. The measure enabled the government to control mosque activities by appointing what one internal Auqaf report called "non-controversial imams" (those who would not promote sectarian divisions or speak against the state) and by restricting the content of their sermons through the direct threat of official transfer.[7] Although direct administrative control over mosque staff ensured the obedience if not always the loyalty of mosque staff, the government mosque posts also became a state resource for sectarian groups to compete for.

Beyond administrative control, the nationalization aimed to renovate the position of mosques as symbols of a unified national community of Muslims, built upon local mosque congregations. According to the Auqaf Directorate policy described in a confidential report written in 1983, mosque committees of "local residents" were maintained to "provide participation" and were "entrusted with looking after the day-to-day affairs of the mosque and creating a spirit of unanimity and natural cohesion amongst the community."

Although the policies of the CDA and Auqaf were thus different, they each promoted a homogeneous vision of Islam. The technical policies of the CDA treated Islam in terms of sociospatial needs. The ecumenical Auqaf Directorate's Islamization policies reduced Islam to a uniform ideology and institution of sociopolitical cohesion. Both of these homogenizing approaches invited sectarian competition within the state arena while resisting policies that would directly channel the increasingly politicized heterogeneity of Islam in Pakistan.

CLAIMS ON THE MAP

Although the alphanumeric designations for neighborhoods, such as F-6/2 or G-7/1–1, do not generate the sense of bureaucratic alienation in residents that they might for readers of this book, a strong sense of neighborhood community has not grown up around these spatial divisions. Neighborhood residents join to petition the government, but both recent and longtime residents of the city often voice the same complaints about the lack of solidarity or even simple acquaintance among neighbors that are commonly made about American suburbs. However, if the spatial organization of Islamabad neighborhoods and its cartographic representations have not succeeded in generating community solidarity, they have officially linked mosque congregations to residence in a fashion unique to Islamabad. I am not arguing that maps have shaped the imagination of neighborhood community and mosque congregations, though this might be the case. Rather, I am arguing that maps made available to sectarian disputants a new spatial idiom to articulate claims to mosque governance and to the nationalization of mosques, as well as demands for new mosques with particular sectarian affiliations.

To understand these claims, we must understand what it means for a mosque to be affiliated with a maslak. This relationship is expressed through a variety of English and Urdu expressions: to be "for," "of," or "belong to" a maslak; to be "its" or "their" mosque; to be in its "possession" (*qabza*); or for a maslak to "to have" a mosque. The affiliation of a mosque is much more fluid and even uncertain, and therefore more contestable, than the affiliation of shrines (*mazars*) and madrassas, the other major forms of propertied Islamic institutions (Khan 2003).[8] Shrines that have not been nationalized are firmly in the control of the descendants of the original saint. The most prominent living descendant of the pir's lineage serves as the guardian (*sajjada nashin*) of the shrine and is seen to be an heir to the spiritual power and authority of the original pir. Madrassas, as educational institutions, maintain affiliation through their explicit propagation of the authoritative doctrines and practices of a particular maslak.

In contrast, mosques are open to all for prayer, and the affiliation (especially of Sunni mosques) is often much more an ongoing performance than an institutional fixity. Worshippers may effect affiliation through differences in worship practice (for example, certain hand gestures and saying certain prayers aloud or silently). Sectarian affiliation is also indexed in the practices of mosque staff: the doctrines and practices that the imam or *khateeb* (person who gives the Friday sermon) enjoins in the Friday sermon and the content and timing of the *moezzin's* call to prayer (*azan*), both broadcast over loudspeakers. Although signage and decorative elements of mosques can also index the maslak, there are few major architectural elements that fix the affiliation of the building in more permanent materials. The affiliation of a mosque, therefore, may often be uncertain, weak, divided, or provisional, open to change through alterations in the composition of worshippers or mosque staff.

Mosque committees, through their role in appointing mosque staff, exert a determining influence on the affiliation of mosques. In "private" mosques, mosque committees themselves appoint and financially support mosque employees. In government mosques, mosque committees shape the affiliation of the mosque through their influence over the government officials who generally defer to the desires of the committees in the sectarian affiliation of mosque staff, while maintaining exclusive control over which individuals are appointed.[9] For these reasons, mosque committees, rather than creating the "spirit of unanimity and natural cohesion amongst the community" that the Auqaf Directorate hoped for, became the focus of sectarian conflict in the early 1980s. Although conflicts over and within mosque committees are common elsewhere in Pakistan, CDA maps configured these disputes in ways unique to Islamabad.

The Islamic city discourse emphasizing the mosque-market complex has exaggerated the uniformity of urban form in the Muslim world. Historically, however, mosques in Pakistan are more often integrated with markets than residential areas, insofar as these are distinguishable. Mosques are often emblematic of particular neighborhoods, including their residential areas, but they are institutions open to participation by merchants. During the workday, when many residents are at work outside their residential neighborhoods, a large percentage of namazis who pray regularly in neighborhood mosques are merchants and their employees, who do so during the long hours in which they conduct business. Out of a desire to support their regular places of prayer and to build goodwill among their neighborhood patrons, merchants often contribute a major proportion of the funds for building and operating mosques. As regular namazis and financial supporters, they often take a leading role in mosque affairs.

As sectarian identifications intensified in Pakistan, disputants began to challenge this role by invoking the spatial logic of the Master Plan following the promulgation of a new Auqaf Directorate ordinance, "Mosque Committee Constitution, Functions and Dissolution Rules, 1986" (No. 1[79]-Law/86 [15 October 1986]). The aim of the ordinance, covering all government and nongovernment ("Auqaf and Non-Auqaf") mosques, was to "constitute Mosque Committees consisting of Pious, God fearing and practicing Muslims of an area to achieve/maintain sectarian harmony, peace and proper management of Mosques." The rules specified procedures for the Auqaf-run election of mosque committees consisting of a chairman, secretary, treasurer, and khateeb. "Only Pious, God-fearing and regular nimazees [worshippers] of the locality wherein the mosque is situated" were eligible for membership on the committee, and only "Resident Nimazees of the area" were eligible to vote.[10] According to Auqaf Directorate staff I spoke with and Auqaf records, there were no challenges to mosque committee members on the basis of piety. However, disputants immediately began to submit petitions to disqualify mosque committee members on the basis of residence. Significantly, although the exact meanings of "locality" and "area" were left unspecified by the rules, no uncertainty about the meanings of these terms is expressed in Auqaf Directorate records, and no petitions explicitly contest their meanings. Generally, parties adopted the spatial terms of CDA maps and assumed that "locality" and "area" meant the subsector, though petitions occasionally invoke the sub-subsector. Two disputes over the formation of mosque committees illustrate these processes.[11]

The mosque called Abu-Huraira in F-10/1, like many mosques in new sectors, began as what came to be called a "private" mosque built on a "self-help basis" in the initial period of the development of the sector in 1983. This was a Barelvi mosque at the start, reflecting the orientations of the majority of namazis. In the five years following the informal establishment of the mosque, according to Auqaf records, "people of the Deobandi maslaks" came to "inhabit in the subsector and desired to wrest control of the mosque from the original management." To do this, they enlisted the very Auqaf Directorate election apparatus intended to promote sectarian harmony. In July 1988, then again in late 1989, they submitted requests to hold elections for an Auqaf-sanctioned mosque committee, which would have replaced the existing unofficial Barelvi mosque committee. This move was resisted by the Barelvis in written representations from the "President (unofficial) Mosque Committee of Abu Huraira." The committee was "unofficial" because it was not constituted by Auqaf. Auqaf, "to keep the peace," chose not to proceed with an election so that the mosque could be settled informally with the Barelvis.

In the mid-1990s, unofficialized Barelvi control was again challenged, this time by a group of Ahl-i Hadith members of the congregation, who again attempted to hold an official mosque election. This time, the Barelvis resisted the move by vigorously invoking residence, understood as living in the subsector. In a letter to Auqaf, Barelvi namazis identified the Ahl-i Hadith with the earlier attempt to take over the mosque, claiming that "in 1988 these people tried to take possession of mosque then and make committee defrauding Auqaf and made committee though committee was there before." But the stronger argument of the letter was that there were "6–7 Ahl-i-Hadith who oppose majority" and none of them are residents of F-10/1: "1 is resident of Rawalpindi with a building in F-10–4, 1 is khatar/cashier in nearby mosque, 1 had recently returned from the US and is using his power and 3–4 remaining are not residents of area." Though these people were regular namazis of the mosque who owned or were employed in business in F-10/1, the letter portrays them as outsiders disturbing the sectarian harmony of the mosque. Their residence outside the subsector disqualified them as voters, and Auqaf summarily dropped consideration of a mosque election.

The translation of the spatial logic of CDA planning maps into mosque governance has been most significant in sectarian disputes such as the one in the Abu Huraira mosque. However, it has also shaped other sorts of factional disputes over mosque committees. By 1996, the mosque committee elections of Madni Masjid in F-6/3 had been postponed three times. According to Auqaf records, the official who was to conduct the election happened to get sick on each of the scheduled election days. This implausible claim was the Auqaf Directorate's delicate means of staying out of an ongoing dispute involving wealthy businessmen and powerful bureaucrats over the governance of what the chief commissioner of Islamabad himself wrote was "a prestigious mosque" in one of the city's most exclusive neighborhoods.

In this case, the dispute was not between sectarian factions but between what the Auqaf official dealing with the case called two "parties": residents of F-6/3 and businessmen of the large market where the mosque is located. The market "party" eventually pressured the Auqaf Directorate to hold a committee election for Madni Masjid in F-6/3 in September 1996. Soon after the election, the teacher of the madrassa attached to the mosque demanded that the election be set aside because two of the winners, the chairman and treasurer, were not "'resident namazis' of the area (namely F-6/3)." Assuming the subsector as the definition of locality under the rules, the teacher informed Auqaf that the chairman lived in F-6/1. The teacher did not give the chairman's exact address, but it might have been no more than one-quarter mile from the mosque. Additionally, the teacher claimed that "residents" were "mostly senior bureaucrats" and that the election was held on Sunday at time that made it difficult for bureaucrats at work in their offices to cast votes.

Both the winning chairman and treasurer ran stores in this market, and the majority of financial support for such mosques usually comes from businessmen, not residents. No one disputed that they were "regular namazis," perhaps more regular than their bureaucrat opponents, though neither the Auqaf Directorate nor mosques maintain any records of attendance (or piety). Invoking a long-standing understanding of participation in mosques that is also shared by many residents, the two elected businessmen complained that rules should be amended to allow regular namazis, irrespective of residence, to be involved. As Auqaf officials saw it, the residents clearly had the rules and map on their side, but the official dealing with the case most directly was sympathetic to the arguments of the businessmen: "The rules are there but the problem should be seen from a human point of view" (*insaniyat ke lihaz se*). In his view, this was after all a "market mosque" (*markazi masjid*), and the businessmen were also, as he put it, "concerned worshippers" (*mutaliqe namazi*), using the bureaucratic Urdu term used for talking about bureaucratic interest or responsibility (for example, a "concerned department").

The head official of the Auqaf Directorate was even more skeptical about the value of the rules it was his job to enforce. He told me that the program of limiting mosque governance to residents through official procedures, of integrating mosques into the spatial logic of the Master Plan, had greatly increased the disputes over mosque leadership. He was more in favor of leadership chosen by consensus among all who are involved in the affairs of a mosque: "it is not democratic but it is better." I asked him why "private" mosques request to hold official elections if they so often create strife. "Unless it is an officially registered committee," he replied, "it can't write to the CDA and Auqaf. Or rather it can, but the government doesn't have to act on it."

In addition to shaping the politics of mosque governance, the spatial order articulated by planning maps also led to sectarian demands for the nationalization of "private" mosques, which grew rapidly in number through the 1980s. The Auqaf Directorate tended to see the issue of sectarian balance in the number of government mosques in terms of the city as a whole, rather than with respect to particular areas. In response to a petition in 1989 by the mosque committee of the Barelvi mosque, Al-Huda, in F-10/3 to have the mosque taken over by government, the deputy director of Auqaf noted that there were forty-four Deobandi government mosques, thirty-six Barelvi ones, two Ahl-i Hadith, two Shia, and as many as ninety-five "non-Auqaf" mosques. In arguing against accepting the request, he wrote that the "Directorate is of the view that the proposed take-over of the mosque in isolation will result in unavoidable mud-slinging and criticism on the Directorate by the mosque committees of non-Auqaf mosques." He recommended that, if funds were available, Auqaf should take over five others that year, "preferably of Brelvi Maslak with a view to mitigating the sectarian unbalance between Deobandis and Brelvis." Representatives of national sectarian groups also counted government mosques throughout the city, but made direct demands on the basis of sector. The general secretary of the national Barelvi organization, Majlis Ulema Ahl-i Sunnat, excoriated Auqaf: "What Islamic system (*Islam-e-nizam*) and justice (*insaf*) is this that among Islamabad's 87 mosques, 45 be allotted to the Deobandi maktab and every year even more of this firqa's mosques are being constructed. When among the mosques in F-6, F-7, F-8, E-7, G-8, and G-6 only four have been given to Ahl-i Sunnat Jamat [Barelvis]."[12] Petitions for the government takeover of particular mosques always invoked the largest map-delineated area in which a particular sect had no government mosque. In some cases, this area was no larger than the sub-sub-sector (less than one-tenth of a square mile), as when the representative of an Ahl-i Hadith mosque buttressed his public demand for government control with his declaration that "this was the only mosque for 'ahl-e-Hadith' people in Sector G-7/3-1."[13]

Efforts to build mosques made use of both CDA maps and the socio-spatial vision they projected. For example, a petition for a mosque in F-6 included an image from a CDA map as proof that the CDA had no other plans for the requested location. In its petition for a mosque, the mosque committee of the yet-unbuilt Chishtia Masjid disguised its desire for a Barelvi mosque by eschewing sectarian references and instead invoking the spatial terms of the Master Plan, arguing that G-7/3-3 had no mosque, unlike contiguous sub-subsectors. Like other sub-subsectors, G-7/3-3 is barely a quarter mile by a quarter mile, with no distinct historical or ethnic character. Its definition and unsentimental name come only from maps.

TEMPORALITY OF MAPS AND ISLAMIC ADVERSE POSSESSION

But many people were not worried about writing to the CDA to request a mosque. From the late 1970s, without authorization from the CDA, competing sects erected numerous mosques on open land throughout the developed sectors of the city, particularly near markets, in parks, and in green spaces. These illegal constructions also needed maps. Groups consulted CDA maps to verify that the land was slated for no other purpose. If there were another designated use, it would strengthen the CDA's hand against them by providing a competing interest such as a property owner or neighbors upset that a school site is not available.

The CDA initially treated illegal mosques like any other illegal construction, such as commercial encroachments and misplaced residential boundary walls. After surveying the area to confirm that the structure violated the Master Plan as artifactualized in the relevant planning map, the CDA destroyed them. With its customary documentary meticulousness, the CDA photographed mosques before demolishing them.

FIGURE 5.2. Demolished Mosque in G-10/3 (*Pakistan Observer,* April 25, 1989).

Newspapers photographed mosques after they had been demolished. Figure 5.2 shows the "demolition" of mosque in G-10/3 in 1989. Note how the quotation marks around "illegal mosque" express criticism of the policy.

As in the case of the affectees of expropriation, the Urdu press was always closer to the sensibilities of illegal mosque builders than the English press. While English-language press described these events as "demolitions" of "illegal" mosques, Urdu coverage usually reported critically on the "martyrdoms" of mosques. The caption of an Urdu newspaper photo of the same demolition, for example, says the CDA "martyred" (*shahid kar diya*) the mosque (fig. 5.3). In this expression mosques themselves are figured as Islamic subjects."

While sects built their own illegal mosques, they sometimes used the CDA to destroy the illegal mosques of their rivals. The G-10/3 mosque was demolished on the complaint of a member of a competing sect, a

ا۔ لام أباد جی ٹمن تمری کے بلاکُس تعمیر شدہ مسجد جیسے سی ڈی ا ے نے شہید کر دیا۔ زفزہ مرکز ہی

FIGURE 5.3. Martyred mosque in G-10/3. The caption reads: "Under-construction mosque of G-10/3 Islamabad as the CDA martyred it." (*Markaz,* April 25, 1989).

sect that was building its own, equally illegal, mosque nearby. In chapter 4 I described how a person representing a widow who had invested in a dummy house came to the CDA to help get it back from someone who'd taken it over. Similarly, sometimes groups illegally building mosques petitioned the CDA to protect them from another group that was trying to take them over. This demolition in 1989 was exceptional, however. Two mosques along major roads were destroyed in January 2007 for security reasons on direct orders of the Interior Ministry.[14] But even as early as the mid-1980s, the CDA's bureaucratic machinery was no match for mosque builders. To understand why, we have to take a closer look at maps as a surveillance device, in particular at how they are generated and how they reference the built environment.

The referential function of maps has been sidelined by antipositivist approaches to maps. Christian Jacob (1996) distinguishes two broad approaches to maps: one treats maps as "transparent," the other as "opaque." The transparent map approach interprets maps as representations of material reality, a culturally neutral information device. In this approach, maps provide more or less accurate knowledge of the terrains mapped. Developed in reaction to the transparency approach, the opaque map approach, normal science for history and cultural anthropology, interprets maps as sociocultural constructions deploying semiotic conventions to articulate the sociopolitical ideologies of a nation, a religious group, a commercial practice, or a city government, much as I did in the previous section. In rejecting positivist approaches to maps, Harley nicely captures the basic thrust of this approach: a "non-positivist alternative entails looking not through the map to what it depicts but inwards or backwards to its maker and outwards or forwards to its readers" (2001:6). The stark choice between transparency and opacity, however, is a false one. While the transparent approach is only concerned with the relation of maps to their referents, the opaque approach largely cuts them off from their referents.

I suggest we take account of both how maps attach themselves to the world as well as how they are constructions, though not only social ones. First, we need to look at how ideologies and political processes are embedded in the practices that link maps to the realities they reference. And second, we need to look at how the referential functions of maps shape the sociocultural processes they mediate. As I discussed in the previous section, CDA maps embody powerful ideologies of sociality and space, in particular how residence should relate to mosque governance. But referential processes account for much of what maps do. While bureaucratic maps have their own logics, concepts, norms, and sociology, we need to account for how they engage (or don't engage) with people, places, and things to enact bureaucratic objects. So, I'll first describe cartographic referential practices before moving on to a discussion of how maps figure more broadly in mosque politics.

Much like the files in which they often move around offices, CDA maps are related to government functionaries and other graphic artifacts through elaborate bureaucratic procedures of authorization. Changes in maps follow the lengthy circulation of official comments up and down the organization hierarchy. As we saw in the case of files, authorization practices have grown more elaborate over the last four decades, expanding the bureaucratic practices through which all genres of graphic artifacts are collectivized. This expansion is most clearly seen in the circulation and inscription of files, but it is also evident in maps.

Consider first a Redevelopment Plan from 1995 for G-6 (fig. 5.4) whose only references to other bureaucratic people and things are the authorizing signatures (in the lower right). This plan is at an initial stage, produced by town planners on the written orders of senior offi-

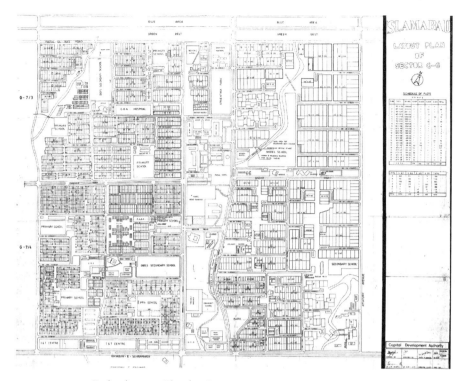

FIGURE 5.4. Redevelopment Plan for G-6, 1995.

cials who make decisions about what should be built in an area. One cartographic specialist in the planning division derisively described the process as follows:

> First comes the order, say, that 800 houses are needed, so they produce a plan with 800 houses, without going out to the site. They just take the maps and make the plans according to their own ideas, as if the land is flat, like the papers they are working on!

The basic maps the planners work with were produced fifty years ago by the Survey of Pakistan for the original Master Plan. Since the streams fed by tropical rains are always shifting, plots are sometimes placed in gullies, a fact sometimes discovered by the angry purchaser rather than the CDA. This is not a matter of incompetence. Rather, it reflects the fact that planners are more directly oriented to other planners than to the built—or natural—environment. Unlike a superior, no stream can ever fire a cartographer for misrepresenting its position.

As plans are revised and gradually become maps, documentary notes referencing other graphic artifacts are added to them, as we can see on a plan of F-7 (fig. 5.5) that was originally produced in 1989 and repeatedly revised through 1996. Crowding all around and even overwriting the image, the notes are added serially in a counterclockwise direction beginning on the right in a fashion resembling the "spiral texts" of Yemeni Arabic documents described by Brinkley Messick (1993:231–50). The notes overwhelmingly describe changes in the authorized bureaucratic status of elements of the built environment (fig. 5.6). For example:

NOTE: BOUNDARY WALL AROUND KATCHI ABADI [TEMPORARY SETTLEMENT] F-7/4 REGULARISED VIDE PARA 43/N DATED 27–8-96 FILE NO CDA/PLW-UP(137)/96

NOTE: SUBDIVISION OF PLOT NO 2 STREET NO 25 F-7/2 HAS BEEN APPROVED VIDE LETTER NO CDA/EM15–7(25) 1/55/1135 DATE 07.3.93.

One can even find such notes regarding issues as minor as the placements of dustbins.

What, then, do these maps represent? And, equally important, how do they represent? These are not straightforward questions. I suggest that the answers depend not only on which graphic elements of these maps we are talking about, but at what point in their careers we find them.

Helpful here is Bruno Latour's (1995:24) concept of "circulating reference." In approaching the problem of words and things in scientific practices, Latour suggests we think of reference as electricity flowing through a circuit of transformations, transmutations, and translations that link a representation to its purported referent. In correct reference, each translation in this circuit preserves an element of what it translates.

Let's first consider the topographical elements such as elevation lines and representations of rivers. At the time of their production, these elements of maps were clearly linked to material qualities of the landscape. As this landscape has changed over the last forty years, however, the circuit linking many of these graphic elements to the landscape has been broken. For example, the representations of rivers no longer preserve their shape or location relative to other land features (Verdery 1994). So then, how then do these lines represent rivers? I'll come back to this later on.

What of the notes we find, for example, surrounding the spatial dia-

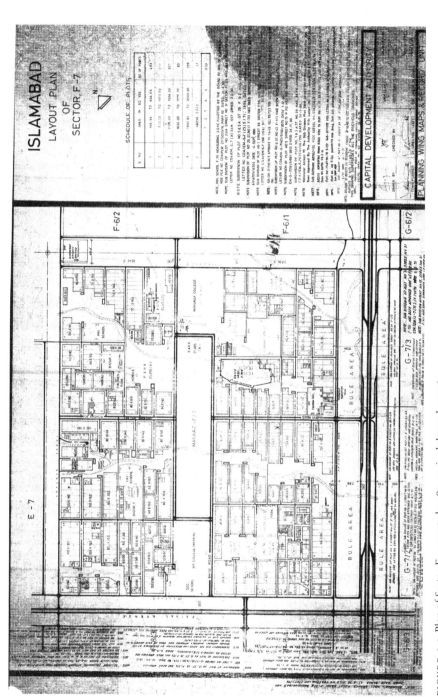

FIGURE 5.5. Plan of Sector F-7, created 1989, revised through 1996.

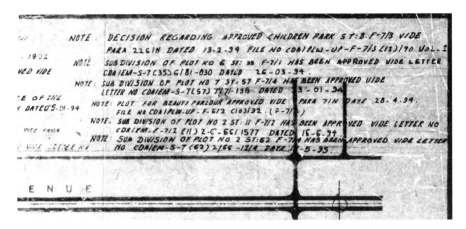

FIGURE 5.6. Detail of Plan of Sector F-7, created 1989, revised through 1996.

grams? Each note is normatively at the end of a chain of inscriptions on other graphic artifacts, stamps, signing hands, and so forth. An element of every note is a testimony to this chain, for instance, "vide file no. CDA/PLD" and so forth. The "vide" (meaning "see") invites you to see, refer, or consult this other artifact if you doubt. Of course, some notes are not translations that preserve the officially required elements of other inscriptions. This is another way of saying they are bureaucratically incompetent or perhaps fraudulent. These chains can also be interrupted by the destruction or alteration of one of the links (a file, for example), an event that is increasingly likely the older the map is. As I describe in chapter 1, a CDA town planner eliminated one section of a house from the official plan of the site of one of his private clients so that the unbuilt area of the plot would appear large enough for subdivision under CDA codes. This modified plan then became the basis for file-mediated authorization of the subdivision by several other officials, who unknowingly collectivized and secured the fraud.

Now we come to the major visual elements of the maps, those representing aspects of the built environment, such as buildings, plot lines, and roads. As the notes on older maps testify, these elements are altered in relation to inscriptions on other letters, memos, files, and so forth.

To go further in the analysis, we now have to distinguish between a map of an unbuilt sector and complete one. This is of course a relative distinction, since a built environment does not spring forth all at once. The transformation of the blueprint from representation of the proposed to representation of the existent, from utopia to ideology in Karl

Mannheim's (1985) sense, gives blueprints an ambiguous epistemological and political status. There is no well-defined moment in which this transformation occurs, when a plan becomes a map; it is rather a gradual or halting process that depends on construction and functionaries' knowledge of it, and, of course, it is rarely complete.

To understand the social role of blueprints in Islamabad, we need to understand not only the histories of particular artifacts, but the temporality of their genre. On maps of unbuilt sectors, the chains of translations back from diagrams end at other graphic artifacts, for example, the file ordering a town planner to draw eight hundred plots in a given sector. On maps of built sectors, the map diagrams might, but need not, be at the end of a chain of translations linking them to features of the built environment, via, for example, a survey of an existing plot line.

From my observations of the production and use of these maps in the CDA, the chains linked to graphic representations of the built environment often extend no further than another graphic artifact. If a physical survey is done whose results do not end up as a file inscription, no changes in the map will be made. New maps are redrawn only after inscriptions of critical number or importance have accumulated in files and letters. And they are redrawn for the purpose of visually representing those inscriptions.

So, what do these lines and shapes on a map represent? Clearly plots, roads, and so forth; but more proximately, they represent other graphic artifacts that mediate the relation between maps and the built environment. As they are regularly updated, CDA blueprints, like files, provide chronicles of their own production. Signs of their histories are inscribed upon the artifacts themselves, emplotting them within the human and artifactual order of the CDA.

Aspects of mediating artifacts are more certainly preserved than aspects of the built environment. This insight corresponds to the commonsense of planners. As the cartographic specialist I quoted earlier suggested, they are certain that diagrams represent the decisions of CDA officers inscribed elsewhere, but they will often doubt the accuracy of reference to the built environment.

References to files on maps link elements of the image to graphic elements of other artifacts that represent corporate decisions. The chain of translations producing maps leads not only from but to other inscriptions, since these maps are referenced in subsequent inscriptions. Maps and files can be like mirrors facing each other, reflecting each other in an infinite series of images. Blueprints are at the end of chains that include many utterances and graphic artifacts, but sometimes no plots, houses, buildings, streets, or mosques. In short, a map is a more trustworthy representation of bureaucratic process, more like an organizational chart than a photograph of the built environment. To summarize this sketchy history of CDA planning maps, we can say that, during the last four decades, the proximate referential anchors of maps have increasingly become other graphic artifacts rather than material features of the built environment, which have temporally and semiotically more mediated links with maps.

One aspect of this bureaucratic process is particularly important for mosque regulation: it is profoundly reactive. As we saw in chapter 3, casework proceeds as a response to an initiating petition from a citizen or written representation from another department. As I observed in chapter 3, files are rarely opened on the initiative of an officer alone. Officials often see illegal building or are informed of it through discussions with other officials. They usually do not, however, begin official site inspections on the basis of this knowledge, but wait until they receive some written representation, usually from a neighbor who would prefer not to have a mosque nearby, especially one of a particular sect. The reactive character of bureaucratic processes has hobbled the CDA in its efforts to deal with illegal mosques.

Here, we can see one of the consequences of the maps being generated more directly in relation to other documents than to the built environment: the maps function slowly as monitoring instruments. Until illegal mosques are documented, they are not officially cognizable and actionable. This is not a problem for the regulation of other kinds of illegal encroachments such as walls between housing plots or the expansions of shops. These are simply surveyed and torn down. But mosque demolitions have run up against a kind of extreme statute of limitations erected by the Federal Shariat Court and Council of Islamic Ideology. Rulings of these bodies invoked an adverse possession principle for mosques, making such official demolitions extremely difficult legally and politically.

The CDA's demolition solution to the mushrooming of illegal mosques was reviewed by the Federal Shariat Court in 1984. The Federal Shariat Courts are ambiguously parallel to the secular judiciary and handle what are seen as Islamic issues. In a public education campaign in 1981, the CDA declared, "building house of God on earth is certainly a blessed act, but at the same time no one could be allowed to ignore principles of Shariat and Islamic orders. The sanctity of the 'Khana-i-Khuda [house of God] is violated by constructing mosques in unsuitable places."[15] The Federal Shariat Court agreed with the CDA and ruled on religious grounds that mosques should not be built on land without permission of the owner, but the thrust of the ruling went the other way. The court all but invalidated mosque demolitions, declaring, as summarized in a file by one Auqaf official, "once a mosque always a mosque."

This Shariat Court ruling was reaffirmed in 1986 by the judgment of the Council for Islamic Ideology, a state advisory body on Islamic affairs. While there are passing references to the "sanctity" of mosques, the basis of the judgment was the common-law principle of adverse possession: rights to real property are acquired by some kind of continuous use over a specified period of time. Noting that a mosque takes months to build, the council found that a mosque must be considered to have been built with the tacit acceptance of government bodies charged with controlling illegal construction.

An official of the Council of Islamic Ideology explained to me that, in light of this ruling, every existent mosque is legal. He cited a colonial precedent from Lahore in the 1930s: a site was in dispute between Sikh and Muslim groups; before the final stage of the proceedings, the British magistrate declared his intention to inspect the site; that night, Muslims worked fervently and constructed a room complete with a roof; when the judge arrived the next day, he found a complete mosque and ruled in favor of Muslims that "it would not be expedient to demolish the mosque." He also told me that the principle of adverse possession applies not only to mosque structures but to prayer itself: "If an owner sees people praying but does not stop them, he cannot stop them later." If prayer is permitted on a site for some time, he said, then this site will be irreversibly dedicated to prayer.

The Council also made a much more expansive claim focusing on the religious needs of Pakistanis:

> The Pakistani public cannot be convinced that some road, or park, or market, and so forth, is more necessary than the mosque. The plan of any road, park, or market can be changed on account of a constructed mosque and there will be no objection from the public as a whole. . . . For religious demands and considerations and in view of public enthusiasm, all those mosques should be considered legal that have been built up to now on government lands. (Council of Islamic Ideology 1987,)

So, reactive bureaucratic processes and the Shariat Court and Council of Islamic Ideology rulings created a kind of catch-22. Mosques were not officially classified as illegal and subject to demolition until it was too late to have them demolished.

The positions of the Auqaf Directorate and the CDA were also complicated in 1981 by the Pakistan government's recognition of four maslaks (Deobandi, Barelvi, Ahl-i Hadith, Shia) in educational Islamization initiatives (Malik 1996:140–41). Officials saw this recognition of four maslaks as a way of limiting claims by other groups. Following this recognition, the Auqaf Directorate quietly acknowledged the claims of the four maslaks for mosques of their own in every locality. Auqaf continued to reject out of hand petitions for regional mosques, for example, one by a Baltistani religious leader. However, officials found it increasingly difficult to sustain their policy that a single mosque could serve all the residents of a locality.

In recognition of the need to coordinate CDA planning and Auqaf sectarian allocation policies, the "Special Mosque Committee" was formed in 1981, chaired by the Secretary of the Ministry of Religious Affairs, with representatives of the CDA and Auqaf. According to a confidential report prepared for the committee in the 1980s, the aim of this committee was to "meet the sectoral/sectarian balance necessary to maintain peace." The goals of the committee were framed by the spatial vision articulated in planning maps: uniform distribution of facilities for all residents. "Sectoral/Sectarian" balance was figured in terms of the relative number of mosques of each sect in a given subsector, independent of the sectarian orientation or size of the population. Neither the CDA nor Auqaf has ever gathered statistics on the maslaks of residents on the basis of which particular populations could be related to mosques, since such statistics would become very controversial. In any case, such a survey would not be a straightforward task. Identifications with maslaks are often diffuse or nonexistent. Many residents don't know the maslak of the mosque they regularly attend beyond whether it is Shia or Sunni.

In considering every petition for permission to establish a mosque, the committee received reports on the location of mosques and sectarian tensions in the neighborhood from the Senior Superintendent of Police. Here is a sample from a report in 1983:

> The proposed place for the construction of a mosque, exists between Kalsoom Plaza and Ali Plaza. The people residing in the surrounding area have to face problem to offer their prayers as the other mosque is situated far from that place. Hence, construction of a mosque is their necessity. Moreover, no sectarian issue is involved at present in the area. The place is suitable for the construction of a mosque please.

The overriding objective of the committee was to avoid violence among groups, or, in bureaucratic parlance, a "law and order situation." As Mohammad Waseem has observed, to many bureaucrats "politics has been just another name for instability, systemic disruption and disunity" (1989:163).

For several years, the Special Mosque Committee managed to keep the peace, but its decisions became largely irrelevant as sectarian groups increasingly occupied sites and then sought regularization. One CDA official told me, "There has been practically no involvement of the committee in mosque allocation since the early 1980s. After that it was mainly *qabza* [possession]. It's first come first serve, a fight on the ground." The regularization process itself has been regularized.

Many CDA officials consider the groups that occupy mosque sites just another kind of so-called qabza group. Qabza groups are land mafias that take control of public and private land in urban Pakistan through threats of force and payoffs to government officials. The director of Urban Planning summarized a view common among more senior CDA officials, that this mosque building is nothing more than a method of grabbing land. He noted how high the land values are in the areas of the illegal mosques, then said, "The mosque provides a residence and food for the imam. Sometimes there is a school too, filled with poor students, usually from the north, whose parents are happy to get rid of a son. Maybe he teaches them a little about the Quran too!" He described how he had once gone to a school where the students were washing the clothes of the imam and his family. He chuckled as he observed that the government then pays them money for the school, pays them to squat. Worse, he said, they are "using religion for politics, they incite the people in the name of religion. There is no difference, no strong difference among the sects in Islamabad, people don't care much, it is the qabza group who promotes." He cited the Shariat Court ruling that mosques must be built on legally acquired land but argued that no one cares about this law: "the mosques, which are supposed be the most disciplined, following religious rules, but instead they are the worst violators, look any place . . . and you will see that the buildings jutting out [into roads] are all mosques."

Although rival sectarian claimants to a site have occasionally clashed violently, they more often take possession of a site by praying there conspicuously five times daily. The petitions of groups requesting allocation of a site always include testimony to a history of regular prayer. One resident of F-6/1 who was a CDA officer described to me his own failing efforts to keep his neighborhood free of what he considered another unneeded mosque. One day he saw seven or eight men spread out reed mats and begin to say prayers on an open area behind his house. He interrupted them and asked them why they were saying namaz here when there was a mosque nearby. They apologized for disturbing him, and the next week returned to a spot fifty yards away. When he again questioned them, they moved another twenty-five yards away. "What can one say to them?" he exclaimed laughing, "They are not breaking the law, not doing anything wrong, not challenging your authority." Now seven or eight years later, they are "publicly recognized to have been saying their namaz there for years." They have cleared and leveled the spot, and there is a little rim of bricks. He sighed when he told me it is just a matter of time until they build a whole mosque.

SQUATTING ACCORDING TO PLAN

In undeveloped sectors, the illicit circulation of maps as material artifacts has played a significant role in shaping sectarian conflict. While maps in developed sectors of Islamabad, in conjunction with rules for forming mosque committees, embed mosques in residential neighborhoods, both sectarian representatives and the government are trying to use planning maps to wrest control of mosques from local neighborhoods. However, as in other spheres, CDA efforts to control activities are undermined by the very documentary instruments it uses.

We saw in chapter 1 how the record room for files on private houses acts as a kind of lending library from which plans are withdrawn and adapted for new houses, frustrating efforts of the CDA to have unique house plans drawn up for each house. The CDA has faced similar problems with the circulation of planning maps. One day, I went to see the official in charge of the planned redevelopment of the informal settlement in G-8 in order to see about getting a map of the area as it existed prior to redevelopment. Although he was willing, if a bit reluctant, to give me a copy, he stressed that it should not be given to anyone in the colony or even shown to them, since they would use it to sell plots or launch court cases. A week later, while sitting in the office of this same official, a man claiming to be from an NGO came looking for the same map to facilitate a survey of *katchi abadis* (informal settlements) in Islamabad. The official questioned him closely and repeated his concern that the map would provide the grounds for court cases or any other number of creative and unimaginable schemes to foil his efforts. In the end, skeptical that this man (unlike me) would not become a conduit to the wrong hands, he refused to give it to him. As the maker of the planning map, he had the power to set the terms for the reorganization of space in this area, but in his view this power depended on the material control of the map.[16]

The use of sector maps by mosque groups justifies his concern. To avoid clashes between sectarian groups, the minutes of a meeting in 1983 of the Special Committee recommended that the government build mosques in new sectors and appoint imams before the habitation of the area. While the government has never managed to do this, sectarian groups have successfully embraced the practice in their own fashion. Planning maps showing the future development of sectors, including the location of mosques, have played a major role in this process. Ironically, planning has facilitated the qabza operations of sectarian groups. Like Zahoor, the village headman in I-14, mosque groups or individual religious entrepreneurs obtain copies of planning maps before they are published from CDA officials who support their sect or mosque building in general. With the map in hand, they use surveyors to determine the planned location of mosque sites in empty agricultural fields of undeveloped sectors and erect shacks. Amplified by generator-powered loudspeakers, their calls to prayer establish a record of regular prayer by reaching the ears of residents too distant to come to pray. Figure 5.7 shows one such mosque in G-11, named Markazi Jama Masjid. Markazi means "central." When this photo was taken in 1996, though there was no center, the builders already knew its place in future development. Note the loudspeaker in the upper right of the picture. Figure 5.8 shows the same mosque in 2011, in its place at the center of a developed sector, loud speakers now mounted on a pole.

Built on sites planned for mosques but lacking official approval, the CDA designates these mosques "unauthorised planned mosques" until they are regularized by the Special Mosque Committee, when they become "authorised planned mosques." Unexpectedly, mosque groups make more conventional technical use of maps than the CDA. The CDA officials mostly relate maps to other graphic artifacts. The mosque groups relate them directly to the built environment. They squat according to plan; they literally honor the plans in the breach. It is important to note that mosque groups first use material tactics: they get hold of maps and possess the sites. These efforts literally lay the ground for their subsequent discursive efforts at regularization carried out through petitions.

FIGURE 5.7. Markazi Jama Masjid, G-11, in 1996 before development of the sector. (Photo by the author.)

The maps have enabled a separation between the processes of residential settlement and mosque building. There are often very high-level people—secretaries, federal ministers, even foreign ambassadors—involved in pressuring the CDA to regularize illegal mosques. As one CDA official put it to me, "The sectarian representatives stay in the background. They are often just fighting for the allocation. Sometimes after allocation, the group becomes silent, no one builds the mosque, beggars sleep there and say their prayers." A dispute over a mosque in I-8 eventually resulted in a gunfight. The ensuing investigation found that all the disputants were from outside the neighborhood.

In the western sectors of Islamabad, political and bureaucratic networks, more than neighborhood social dynamics, shaped the construction and affiliation of mosques. The Auqaf Directorate's main role became ascertaining which group first began to pray on a site rather than determining allocation with a view toward sectarian balance. For its part, the CDA, according to one town planner, clings to its policy of "no discrimination" among maslaks: "We examine such issues only from a technical point of view, catchment, capacity of mosque. . . . [W]e will not add [a mosque] to satisfy another sect." Without retreating from a resolutely technical policy, in the mid-1980s the CDA was able to incorporate sectarian demands into the Master Plan by raising the projected percentage of namazis in a population from 10 percent to

FIGURE 5.8. Markazi Jama Masjid, G-11, in 2011 after sector has been developed. (Photo by Faiza Moatasim.)

20 percent, thus doubling the number of mosques planned for the city. Under pressure from rival sectarian groups, the CDA and Auqaf sometimes duck responsibility by passing cases back and forth, each becoming an unexpected advocate of the other's allocation criteria. The CDA requests the Auqaf to make the decision based on sectarian allocation policy; the Auqaf requests the CDA to make the decision based on technical criteria.

Illegal mosque construction and sectarian conflict over control of existing mosques are not unique to Islamabad. Maps of new private developments are playing a similar role in Lahore, for example (Khan 2003:123). However, the statizing and graphic representation of mosques in Islamabad literally constituted sites of sectarian conflict. CDA officials clearly recognize this. They have responded by disguising planned mosque sites as schools and parks on planning maps of new sectors, for example, the I-14 map in Zahoor's possession I described in the vignette at the beginning of this chapter. As one planner explained it to me, "once the plan was prepared and we allocated plan for mosques, it was exposed to religious people, they would take a surveyor, just took possession of the area. We started avoiding allocation of mosque plot on the plan. We should not demarcate plot on the plan so people should not grab the plot in advance." CDA officials understand that these maps, their basic bureaucratic semiotic technology, have been turned against them. Their reluctant solution is to confine the knowledge of future mosque sites to oral channels they can control more effectively than maps.

The CDA's inability to wrest the land from the villagers of BQB brought about a reversion to the sort of urban development we see elsewhere in Pakistan. In contrast, the inability of the CDA to plan mosques in new sectors has created novel practices of mosque building and governance rather than a return to the way mosques are built and governed in other cities. Maps mediate new relations between mosques and locality. On the one hand, the construction of mosques in new areas is largely divorced from neighborhood settlement; on the other, governance of existing mosques is more tightly linked to map-defined areas as committee disputes disqualify nonresidents.

The use of maps in Islamabad cautions us about critiques of modernist practices that emphasize abstraction. As I hope I have shown, to understand the role of cartographic techniques of representation in government arenas, we need to see how these techniques work as embodied in artifacts. The abstraction of maps must be understood in their concreteness. It is here that the political ambiguity of state technologies is revealed. Mosque builders have never managed to alter the discursive terms of the Master Plan. But they have succeeded in part by turning the material artifacts through which this plan is implemented against the plan itself. Even uniform bureaucratic technical practices such as cartography do not range over uniform social and material terrain. Government technologies have unexpected engagements with the different actors, objects, and environments they aim to control. These engagements come into view when we privilege neither putatively hegemonic government representations nor the realities they aim to document, but rather look at the teeming masses of mediators that connect them.

Conclusion

Participatory Bureaucracy

It is important not to overstate the extent to which paper practices have undermined the Master Plan and the institutional operations of the Capital Development Authority. Through the 11-series of sectors, the main elements of Doxiadis's vision have been realized. The CDA employs thousands and, along with the Islamabad Capital Territory Administration under the Interior Ministry, controls municipal regulation, despite sporadic calls for a representative government for the city. However, the transformation of government housing allocation into an informal process, the return of mosques to the play of sectarian politics within the bureaucracy, and especially the astonishing halt to planned development in the west show that documents are not always the obedient tools of government. In *Government of Paper,* I have focused on certain events to make this apparent, not to portray the planning and regulation of Islamabad as dysfunctional. In many respects, the city works quite well. Rather, my purpose has been to use extraordinary processes to illuminate aspects of paperwork that are harder to see in the smooth flow of bureaucratic process when documents behave themselves.

Much work on state governance has focused on representations such as category schemes, measuring standards, and cartography. But as I've shown, the function of these forms of representation can be drastically transformed by the practices through which they are deployed, undermining them as techniques of bureaucratic control. The function of files in fixing responsibility, for example, is undermined through circulatory and discursive tactics that distribute authorship ambiguously. Material control of the lists and files used in the land expropriation process transformed these artifacts into means of manipulating the CDA. The temporality of mapping and the circulation of maps limited their utility as instruments to control illegal mosques.

The study of state representations has tended to underplay the difficult work through which representations are made to connect with other patches of the world, that is, the practices that deploy schemes on sociomaterial terrain to enact objects. Both realist and social-constructionist approaches to state representations recognize that these representations are partial as descriptions of their objects. But realism assumes records are unmediated traces (of some aspects) of people, places, and things, while social constructionism sees bureaucratic objects as the results of discursive positing and interpellation. Neither gives adequate attention to the mediations through which bureaucratic objects are enacted and consequently to the oblique relations documents have with that about which they speak. But as any bureaucrat will testify, these relations are a central concern. The specter of disconnect between documents and what they speak about, noncorrespondence in both philosophical and communicational senses, shapes the establishment of regimes of state representation; and noncorrespondence can have immensely important functions within representational regimes of presumptive correspondence.[1]

The British gave records the legal presumption of truth to seal the bureaucracy off from the divergent interests prevailing within the Company and, later, Indian society. It is precisely this regime of presumptive written truth that establishes the social possibilities of noncorrespondence, including fraud. In Europe, the practice of forging documents emerged in the twelfth century when governments began to establish written documentation as a basis of action (Clanchy 1979; Petrucci 1995). The very claim of graphic artifacts to transparency motivates their use to generate opacity or false clarity. In Islamabad, as elsewhere, the paper basis of regulation is widely recognized as central to activities characterized as corruption.[2]

As I have described, the response of some CDA functionaries to the use of graphic artifacts in fraud was a kind of inverted Bakuninism in which documents were partially rejected in the name of more effective government control. The expropriation process was the most dramatic example ("no fresh lists!"), but we've seen others. A financial officer refused to sign compensation checks in a late-stage effort to stem fraudulent claims. CDA planners stopped identifying mosque sites on maps.

Similarly, officers of the state utility corporation and the planners controlling a squatter resettlement project rejected the mediation of artifacts in their dealings with project residents. Residents pay regular fees for water and electricity to resident entrepreneurs who maintain illegal connections to the city electrical grid and water mains. The rates they pay are higher than those the Water and Power Development Authority (WAPDA) would charge, and residents press for legal provision of water and electricity. Likewise, WAPDA officers would like to gain revenue from the services they unwillingly provide already. However, at the urging of the CDA, WAPDA officers refuse to regularize utility services to these areas because residents would present utility bills in court to support claims to the land.

In the mid-1990s, the CDA began a project to demolish squatter neighborhoods in G-8 and reestablish them in the same locations on a "planned basis." Residents were to be granted ownership of plots on the redeveloped site, but initially the CDA steadfastly refused to produce any kind of title documents. CDA officials feared that titles, even with transfer restrictions, would enable residents to sell their plots (perhaps several times, creating legal problems for the CDA) and either remain where they are or squat somewhere else. The officer overseeing this project, picking up a scrap of paper, told me, "If you give even a chit with some names on it, you will not see that paper again. It will change hands four or five times. The selling begins at once." Residents were to receive ownership papers after five years of payments and documented habitation of the dwelling. By this time, officers hoped that residents would become so attached to their dwellings and neighborhood that they would no longer want to sell their houses.[3] The only graphic artifacts documenting tenancy were a computer list in English (carefully secured in a CDA office) and a large sign fixed in concrete at the entrance to the development, which listed tenants' names and plot numbers in Urdu. The plots were awarded to tenants in public ceremonies of ostensive reference. Officials called out each tenant's name and pointed out to each a plot outlined and numbered in chalk. Unlike discourse mediated by artifacts, discourse mediated by voice and gesture cannot be recontextualized in bureaucratically sanctioned form, a requirement for its use as documentation for market sales. In this case, as a medium of communication, sound gave government functionaries greater control than paper. While oral-gestural discourse can be neither authenticated nor circulated within the bureaucratic organization, it also can't be seized and repurposed by others outside the bureaucracy.

These actions reflect a practical understanding of writing at odds with most academic treatments of governmental documentation. Writing is usually seen to nail things down, but it can also set them in motion—often it does both simultaneously. Thus, state control can be extended not only through specification, but through ambiguity, by leaving matters undocumented.

The ad hoc rejections of documentation within the CDA were creative, even radical, measures for a modern government, which usually addresses the shortcomings of a documentary practice with new and more intensive forms. Initiatives within both India and Pakistan for the "'electronification' of information" and "e-governance" are more conventional responses to the recognition of the role of paper artifacts in corruption.[4] Discussion of electronic government systems in the region is saturated with the theme of "transparency," the watchword of a broad movement against state corruption. States, international institutions such as the IMF and the World Bank, multinational corporations, and NGOs see corruption as a major threat to domestic governance and the post–Cold War world order. Such systems have been broadly implemented in India but have yet to get very far in Pakistan, as the unhappy administrator of the empty CDA electronic land database I discussed in chapter 3 would attest.[5] Perhaps the most ambitious electronic records initiative in Pakistan was launched by the private consortium formed to build Islamabad New City.

It all started so well. On April 8, 1996, Pakistan's National Housing Authority, the Capital Development Authority, MG Hertz (a Pakistan conglomerate), and Asia Challenge Investments (a Singapore-based consortium) announced plans for Islamabad New City, a splashy high-tech city to occupy 12,500 acres to the southeast of existing Islamabad. The project brochure looked backward to the future, beginning with an Urdu translation of a saying of the Prophet (*hadith*)—"Don't expand your cities, settle new ones!"—and a line by Iqbal, the great national poet of Pakistan, declaiming, "The clear-sighted will settle new abodes." But Islamabad New City was to be the most modern of cities. A brochure declared, "Based on the most modern methodologies of town planning, infrastructure development and latest amenities ISLAMABAD N.C. will truly be a 21st century city, developing at a 21st century speed with 21st century standards."

Unlike the "old" Islamabad, the product of an aging mid-twentieth-century modernity, the new city would work with rather than ignore or obliterate the contours of the land. Large areas were to be reserved for spaces to be greened by the planting of five million trees. An elevated "intercity skyrail" running on air propulsion would whisk residents noiselessly to Islamabad. Broadband fiber-optic cable would be laid throughout, which would be the infrastructure for an "integrated city management and control" system that would, among other things, monitor security cameras placed at all the "gates" to the city. The city would have an "international standard country club," including a "5-star sports hotel," golf course, polo grounds, and area for rock-face climbing. Not the least of its twenty-first-century features was that it would be 100 percent financed by the private sector, though agencies of the Pakistan government would maintain strict financial and regulatory control. The project had the strong and highly public support of then Prime Minister Benazir Bhutto. It was widely publicized in Europe and the Middle East, and thousands of overseas Pakistanis subscribed to plots in the scheme. Planning and development would be done by the multinational Singapore-based management consultancy Meinhardt, the Japanese planning firm Fujita, and the Singapore construction corporation Asia-Link Construction. All these corporations and government authorities were grouped together as an entity known as the Joint Venture.

The plans were promising, but first they would have to get the land. Asia Challenge Investors did what most multinational real estate investors in South Asia do. It tasked its Pakistani corporate partners with land acquisition. MG Realtors would get hold of the land and the multinationals would take it from there.[6] Foreign investors interested in land development in South Asia frequently complain of the lack of transparency of the urban real estate market there.[7] Nontransparency is often just a way of talking about someone else's way of doing accounting. But the investors have a point. A tangle of bureaucratic authorizations and regularizations often creates a variety of de facto forms of land holding that are not comprehensible under multinational capital's concept of freehold property. Even without this overlay of bureaucratic complexity, however, ownership is often not a straightforward matter.

The Joint Venture's problems with land acquisitions were different from the CDA's. In Pakistan, every organization trying to acquire land is unhappy in its own way. But the Joint Venture's difficulties also turned on documents, particularly, as we'll see, the way ownership structures were represented in the material forms of the records. MG Realtors, the Pakistani partner, went forward with land purchases through the summer and fall. But less than a week after Benazir Bhutto's government was dismissed in November 1996, several top bureaucrats connected with the project were arrested, and the new Information Minister of the caretaker government, Irshad Ahmad Haqqani, declared that Islamabad New City was a "dubious scheme." Around this time, Asia Challenge Investments came to know of irregularities in the land acquisition scheme and brought in a fixer whom I'll call Greg Cooper, a New Zealand civil engineer with experience in large-scale development across Asia. It turns out that Asia Challenge was aptly named. Several people connected to the project estimated to me that the corporation had lost as much as several hundred million dollars through fraudulent and overpriced land purchases. The Pakistani partners were removed from land acquisitions, which was taken over by Cooper.

Cooper was a quick study. After just six months, he had mastered the technicalities of the landholding system and was even able to make sense of the land records, which are written in Urdu. Although he couldn't read Urdu, he learned to recognize the basic terms in written form. Cooper maneuvered the Pakistani partners to turn over records of its land purchases, which had previously been withheld from Asia Challenge. With the help of his assistant, who had served in the land acquisition department of the CDA, he set to work figuring out what had happened.

Cooper determined that land had been bought from the original owners for Rs. 1,000–4000 per *kanal* (one-eighth of an acre), then sold several times through dummy firms, at increasingly higher rates, until the Joint Venture bought it at the vastly inflated rate of Rs. 50,000 per kanal. At the highest level of the scheme was a man I'll call Zaffar Afridi, who had close connections at the apex of the Pakistan government. However, Afridi was hardly the mastermind. According to Cooper, Afridi and the people who worked for him knew nothing about the technicalities of buying land. So, while he defrauded Asia Challenge, he himself had been defrauded. As Cooper put it, it was fraud all the way down to village revenue officers, the *patwaris*: "The patwaris cheat the contractors. The contractors cheat the agents of Afridi. Afridi's agents cheat Afridi. Afridi cheats the company." Government servants, from the patwaris on up the chain, had taken generous bribes to carry out these transactions. This account was broadly corroborated by Pakistan government investigations in the 2000s, documented in files I examined in 2007.

But the purchase price wasn't the only problem with the land. Most of the land turned out to be common land surrounding villages. There are three broad kinds of village holdings: residential holdings, fields, and common land or *shamlat*.[8] Land held in common includes graveyards, mosques, and areas for communal activities, but the majority is land surrounding villages and fields is unsuitable for cultivation and therefore taxation. Since much of the terrain in the area projected for the new city is dry and rocky, a large portion of the land is in common holdings. Ownership of residential and agricultural holdings is often relatively clear, if only because the local official has to tax someone for them. Common holdings are another matter altogether. Common lands surrounding villages have complex ownership structures; thousands of shares in the smallest scrap of common land may be distributed among as many owners. Owners of agricultural holdings own a share of shamlat proportional to the percentage of the total area of the village they own.[9]

It is therefore as difficult to get a synoptic account of ownership as it is to make a synoptic view of the space. Since common lands are not taxed and are commonly held, they are rarely transferred. As a consequence, the land record system is not designed to clearly identify the owners of common plots. The single-page record of a common plot neither identifies the owners nor lists their shares; in the owner column, simply "shamlat" is recorded. Identifying all the owners of a particular tract of common land is a difficult task in aggregation since this information is dispersed on as many pages of the records as there are plots. Owners themselves, holding only titles to their freehold plots, have no documentation that attests their share of the village common land. Each owner's share of the shamlat, in the event of division and sale, can only be determined by calculating the share based on the proportion of the total village land he or she owns. Even this doesn't give a clear picture, because some transfers of property do not transfer rights to common holdings. In practice, the share of a common holding that every land-holder in the revenue estate can claim is undetermined.

Since MG Realtors hadn't bought the residential and agricultural plots of villages, they were still being occupied and farmed, making it impossible for the project to possess and develop the land. Owners had been willing to sell peripheral common land on easy terms, knowing it would remain in their possession so long as they didn't sell their houses and fields. Owners also knew that some relative certainly retained an unsold ownership share and could be counted on to tie up in court any effort to take possession of the property, on the basis of incomplete transfer. But at least such land existed. In some cases, patwaris transferred much more land than the whole village contained—in one village eighty acres more.

To set things right, Cooper had worked out an elaborate plan with politico-legal and sociotechnical components. He described this plan to me in a series of remarkably frank interviews. First, the politico-legal part. According to Cooper, there had been an unwritten arrangement with District Commission of Islamabad that if the project could acquire 70 percent of the land of a revenue estate (*mauza*), the district commissioner would claim the rest under the eminent domain provisions of the Land Acquisition Act of 1894, a colonial-era law still in place. Cooper ruefully noted that with the change of government and the transfer of the cooperative district commissioner, new legislation at the national level would be needed to enable such compulsory acquisition.[10]

He described why such compulsory acquisition was required with reference to an actual village he would only identify to me with a pseudonym. In this village, 17 percent of the people own 70 percent of the land. But 6,970 individuals are mentioned in the ownership record. He had determined that only around 30 percent of those owners lived in the area and a good number lived abroad. Without compulsory acquisition, every one of those owners would have to appear before a government land official or provide authenticated power of attorney.

The politico-legal part of his plan depended on his sociotechnical program to acquire land. He needed to overcome two problems that the fraud scheme had highlighted: first, the problem of identifying land for which a clear title might be obtained with the least effort; second, the problem of acquiring this land cheaply direct from its agricultural owners, rather than from speculators who would drive up prices. Cooper resolved these into the problems of knowledge and secrecy.

Even with the compulsory acquisition legislation in place, there was no getting around the need to purchase common holdings. In developing Islamabad, the Pakistan government, following British precedents, did not compensate individuals for common land, but simply expanded the scope of its "sharedness" to the entire nation and appropriated it as "public" land. As a private corporation, however, the Joint Venture would have to purchase these lands.

Cooper saw he needed a way to know who owned what and what their kinship relations were. His first goal was to translate the paper records for the whole area into an electronic database. The aggregate land record is not publicly available. But through backdoor channels, he got a full set of property records for all the villages in the target zone. The database Cooper built included not only ownership information but kin relations as well, preparing the way for negotiations with individuals influential within families who could persuade others to sell. The exact location of New City was not yet fixed, and Cooper planned to site it in areas owned by a few large landowners or by single lineages. The advantages of negotiating with a single owner are obvious, but he probably had an exaggerated sense of the unity of lineages and the capacity of elders to control them.

To help identify such areas, he was developing graphic projection software that would project three maps of the region with different areas using colors to code different information. The first map scheme would vary the color depending on the percentage of the property that the Joint Venture had already acquired in an area. The second would represent the complexity of ownership structure (calculated by the number of single owners per areal unit of land). So, for example, an area with a single owner would appear in red, an area with many owners in blue. Third, he planned a further refinement that would project areas in different colors depending on the complexity not of single owners but of kin-group ownership. So, for example, an area owned by one extended family would appear in red; an area owned by many unrelated persons in blue. Unlike the paper land records, this system would be able to identify effectively all the owners of common plots and represent both common and individual holdings in the same way.

But knowing what land to go after was pointless if others knew it too. To prevent speculators from purchasing land the Joint Venture would want to acquire and then charging exorbitant prices, it was essential to conceal the evolving location plans. The fraud had given Cooper an almost colonial distrust of the Pakistanis. He characterized the project as a contest between cunning and dishonest "locals" on one side, and naïve Singaporeans and himself on the other. The "locals" he was most concerned about were the Pakistani partners in the project; he told me he had an active disinformation campaign going on to fool them about his true intentions. He told me he trusted no one but his Pakistani assistant, whom I'll call Ahmed. He only trusted him, he said, because he had no choice: he could not directly control the whole process by himself, even with the aid of his technologies. This was trust more in the legal than the moral sense, since Ahmed was not above suspicion. One day while Cooper, Ahmed, and I sat together in the office, Cooper told me that he had come to know that Ahmed had refused an offer of Rs. 4 million (nearly $100,000 at the time) to turn over the topographic map of the project. Cooper somewhat hesitantly admitted this was evidence of Ahmed's loyalty. But he was quick to add that Ahmed would have known he would be immediately caught and that he might be waiting for an opportunity for a more lucrative deal further down the line.

Cooper translated the paper records into his database not only to generate new knowledge but to control it. He was running his database building and purchase negotiations, as he put it, "like a spy network." From Ahmed, who worked on land acquisitions in the CDA, he was well aware of how the poorly controlled circulation of documents had undermined the government efforts to acquire land. Cooper prevented his staff from gaining any general picture of New City plans by not permitting them to enter data from a particular file into the database for more than an hour or so. If more work remained, this file was then given to another individual on another day. While government file circulation procedures generate collective knowledge of cases, Cooper prescribed that every file move only between the individual working on it and himself or Ahmed. Cooper and Ahmed themselves maintained logs documenting work on the files, which were locked in a cabinet when not in use.

Files for areas of no interest to the project were given to the staff for entry to confuse them. The information entered by his staff was only integrated on two computers, which Cooper or Ahmed always kept in their possession. A rigid policy prescribed that no documents were ever allowed to leave the office, a residential house with only one working door. A security guard searched everyone for documents whenever they left the building. Cooper made a telling exception for me and my notebook. He said he intended to closely monitor real estate trading activity in the area and correlate it with work logs to catch leaks from his clerks. Cooper told me he'd already fired five or six people he thought he couldn't trust. Control over the files and database was to prevent the growth of the kinds of paper networks that had undermined government acquisition efforts, which Ahmed had told Cooper about. The database, constructed in accordance with Cooper's strict office procedures, was an electronic artifact that gave Cooper and his assistant exclusive access and comprehensive knowledge.

Cooper intended to use this instrument to obscure the activities of the Joint Venture. He said he intended to give the impression that the Joint Venture had packed up and gone home even as he opened a number of what he called "cells," small real estate offices, to purchase land. Organizing these real estate offices like cells of a spy network, Cooper hoped to conceal, even from the realtors themselves, that they were actually working for the Joint Venture.

We will never know if Cooper's elaborate program would have succeeded. In May 1998, Pakistan tested a nuclear device, jeopardizing its already troubled relations with world financial markets. The so-called Asian flu was still spreading, destabilizing currencies throughout the region Asia Challenge was investing in. In the face of these uncertainties, Asia Challenge pulled out of the project and abruptly dissolved itself.

Although the project ultimately collapsed, it has much to tell us about how land ownership and the sociomaterial possibilities of land are shaped by the material infrastructures of documentation. The project highlights the political ambiguities of the digitization of land records, a transparency project promoted throughout the world by a broad array of governments, international organizations, civil society groups, and corporations such as Asia Challenge.

Digitization aims to liberate landholders from the machinations of land registry officials. A recent report by a fellow at a leading Pakistan NGO stated:

> The prevalent system of land record management is an archaic paper based system whose complexity [along with] the control of state functionaries over its access has given rise to rampant rent seeking and deprivation of the weaker sections of the society. . . . Cumbersome processes and dependence on the *Patwaris* . . . lead to illegal annotations. Land records do not provide either conclusive proof of ownership nor are they linked to spatial data to perfectly identify the plot. (Qazi 2006:2, 5)

The "transparency of the land records" will, according to this view, spur investments for agricultural and residential development by facilitating transactions, credit, transfer, and mortgage and will "provide a chance to the smallholders to turn their fixed assets in the form of land, into dynamic assets to be integrated in the market" (Qazi 2006:5).

There is no doubt that the current system of paper records subjects owners to the sorts of serious problems highlighted in this report. We should in no way understate these problems. However, the story of Islamabad New City suggests that these same records protected village owners from the state-sanctioned coercive appropriations of national and multinational development corporations. Paper politics may be relatively inclusive when compared to e-governance. The very cumbersome paper processes condemned by transparency advocates require much wider participation in bureaucratic affairs, though I do not mean to suggest this participation is legal, just, or democratic.

The patwari or the bureaucrat may be a tyrant, but he is a petty one whose paper artifacts are hard to maintain and even harder to control exclusively. Stories of lands lost through the machinations of patwaris are common. But they must be seen in light of the massive dispossessions that the Joint Venture might have engineered with its database. The capacities of the database for dispossession were magnified by its control by a couple of individuals. But the public systems in place in India and being developed in Pakistan might serve the same ends. And the broad participation required by paper infrastructures of land records might prove a much stronger protection against dispossession.

This point can be extended to paper documentation more generally. If the Islamabad Master Plan stifled participatory democracy, the documents it required have promoted a participatory bureaucracy. The Master Plan succeeded in confining political participation to the bureaucratic arena itself rather than provoking successful opposition to it through the mechanisms of civil society—representative institutions, interest groups, and the press. And yet, over its five-decade history, the city did not separate the bureaucracy from "society" but rather drew that society within the bureaucracy itself.

It is no coincidence that I, like other scholars, have come to be interested by documents at what many observers see as the end of the paper era. While, of course, the heralds of the paperless office have proven famously premature, paper artifacts now share the field of graphically mediated communication with a variety of electronic forms. Roger Chartier (1995) credits his involvement with a French government project to examine the electronic future of the library with his insights on the importance of the material form of the book. Much as email has made us aware of previously unnoticed aspects of phone communication, my own use of electronic documents shaped my understanding of the specificities of the paper graphic artifacts I investigated. Alternatively, this point could be cast in terms of the concept of anthropological distance, which can be as relevant for the study of "technological" forms as it is for "cultural" ones. Against a familiar horizon of electronic media of communication in the United States, the paper documents I encountered in the Pakistan bureaucracy struck me as different.

The relation between electronic forms of communication and this study of paper, however, is not only historiographic but historical and theoretical. Electronic forms of representation build historically on discourse genres, means of distribution, concepts of authorship and ownership, and so forth that were developed through the medium of paper. An obvious example is the "electronic signature." The significance of any semiotic technology lies partly in its relation to previous and contemporary ways of achieving similar ends. An understanding of paper practices will help us recognize the genuine novelty and the continuity of electronic technologies, both of which are sometimes obscured by ahistorical rhetoric of technological revolution. Furthermore, historically, new communications technologies have supplemented and transformed rather than replaced older ones. As the "delay" in the arrival of the paperless office indicates, paper will be with us for some time (Sellen and Harper 2002).

Proponents of electronic documentation argue that new forms of access to information will reduce corruption. Equally salient to curbing corruption is an alteration in the means of producing the artifacts that will convey that information. Concerns about noncorrespondence shaped the semiotic regime of the East India Company and colonial bureaucracies that continues today. The solution was to give paper some of the qualities of discourse, people, places, and time through the use of signatures, dates, stamps, and interartifactual references. The deployment of electronic information systems can be seen as a development in this line. The object is to broaden the role of physical causation within the bureaucracy, or to give nonhumans greater agency in the human affairs of government. By generating sign-vehicles exclusively by physical mechanism, a greater range of graphic artifacts will become "natural signs," generated by what they would stand for without human mediation. Eyes, minds, and hands are to be replaced by satellites, computers, and printers in an attempt to restrict the human role in referential practices to interpretation.

It is still unclear how such systems will reconfigure the workings of bureaucracies in South Asia and elsewhere. Nevertheless, my account of graphic artifacts in Islamabad shows that whether transparency programs are pursued through intensified paper documentation or electronic records, the result will be neither transparency nor opacity, but a host of new forms of mediation that will invite unexpected forms of participation from beyond the office.

Notes

INTRODUCTION

1. What I term "graphic artifacts" have been called by various names: "textual objects" (Geisler 2001), "written objects" (Chartier 1995:10), "text-artifacts" (Silverstein and Urban 1996). My "graphic artifact" is most closely aligned with Silverstein's "text-artifact," a perduring object that is the "mediating instrumentality of communicative processes for its perceiver" (Silverstein and Urban 1996:2). The "text" of "text artifact" does not describe the composition of the artifact itself (inscribed with graphic forms functioning semiotically more or less like linguistic forms), but rather the kinds of semiotic process (entextualization and contextualization) that the artifact mediates. I use the term "graphic artifact" rather than "text-artifact" for a couple of reasons. First, many of the ongoing semiotic processes that involve artifacts are not well enough defined to be characterized as "texts." Second, I wish to define a certain class of artifacts, written materials, and to emphasize the non- and para-linguistic semiotic functions of this type of artifact. One last point about this term: the word "artifact" sometimes has the connotation of a secondary byproduct of some prior or primary process. As will be clear, I don't use it in this sense.

2. For accounts of the Pakistan bureaucracy, see the following: Braibanti 1966; Goodnow 1964; Hussain 1972; Jalal 1990; Kennedy 1987; Sayeed 1967.

3. Through the early 1970s, bureaucratic institutions maintained a high degree of autonomy, maintaining control over the selection, training, and posting of government servants in the name of administrative neutrality (Kennedy 1987:13).

4. Goodnow 1964:164; Hussain 1972:69. Alavi goes so far as to argue that the very creation of Pakistan was driven by the interest of this class in securing their government employment, which its members saw as threatened by a new Indian government that would favor Hindus in recruitment to government posts.

5. Munir 1964:36. The recruitment of American experts in pubic administration, Rowland Egger and B.G. Gladieux, to produce reviews of the Pakistan
administration in 1953 and 1955, respectively, reflected the growing influence of
the United States in Pakistan. Though the fact that these reports, highly critical
of the colonial character of the administration, were never released to the public
shows something of the limits of this influence.

6. In India one common quip about bureaucracy is, "The British invented
bureaucracy and the Indians perfected it." The system of regulation of business
and industry assembled in the years following Indian independence is often
called the "Permit Raj."

7. For works on documentation in the Company and colonial governments,
see Hejeebu 2005; Moir 1993; Ogborn 2007; Raman 2007.

8. Hejeebu 2005; Marshall 1976.

9. Of course, comparable documentary techniques have been underpinned
by different ontologies in South Asia and elsewhere

10. For accounts of these events, see Marshall 1976, 1987; Robins 2006.

11. The slips were colored as follows: white for "ordinary," "emerald" for
"early," "vermillion" for "urgent," and "sky" for "immediate." Communications
with the sky label were "only to be used in cases of *Extraordinary Urgency*
requiring instant attention;—such as Petitions for reprieve on the eve of execution, Military and Political intelligence of an unusually important description,
or other occurrences of great emergency" (Government of India 1891:38). Such
communications had to be "placed *at once* in the hands of the persons to whom
they [were] addressed, *whether by Night or by Day*" (38).

12. See Harper 1998:13–47 for an excellent review of the sociological literature on organizational documents.

13. Though some earlier anthropologists discussed the role of state documents in village and tribal life (Cohn 1987; Fallers 1950), Lévi-Strauss's account
of his encounter with the Nambikwara chief, whom he had given paper and
pencil, better captures a conventional anthropological view of the salience of
writing in such societies. The chief made a "list" of wavy lines and pretended
to read from it to inventory the objects the anthropologist was to exchange.
For Lévi-Strauss, this "farce" dramatized writing as an alien form, a form the
chief could use to show "he was in alliance with the white man and shared his
secrets" (1973:296).

14. This anthropological emphasis on everyday activities within structures
of rules and formal roles continued, and as late as 1980 Britan and Cohen
(1980) saw the task of an anthropology of organizations as laying bare the
informal structures of bureaucracy.

15. For anthropological treatments of bureaucracy through the early 1990s,
see the following: Haines 1990; Handelman 1981; Herzfeld 1992; Sampson
1983; Schwartzman 1992; Wright 1991. For an excellent review of more recent
anthropological writings on bureaucracy, see Hoag 2011. More recent anthropological work that highlights the role of documents in bureaucratic practice
includes the following: Boyer 2003; Brenneis 2006; Feldman 2008; Harper
1998; Holston 1991; Riles 2000, 2006; Verdery 2003.

16. As Annelise Riles puts it, "the problem of making documents a subject

of ethnographic inquiry is a problem of studying knowledge practices that draw upon and overlap with the anthropologist's own rather than serving as a point of analogy or comparison for the anthropologist's questions as ethnographic subjects usually do" (2006:79).

17. For discussions of these aspects of Saussure's theory, see Engelke 2007; Irvine 1989:30–31; Keane 2003.

18. The unrecognized abstraction of the concept of writing is part of what has fueled the debates about the "effects" of literacy. Studies of writing within the literacy framework have aimed to describe literacy either generally as a mode of communication (Biber 1988; Finnegan 1988; Goody 1977, 1986; Jahandarie 1999; Olson 1994) or as a heterogeneous phenomenon varying with different social domains in which a variety of written genres are used (Besnier 1995; Street 1984).

19. Clanchy 1979; Derrida 1974; Engelke 2007; Lewis 1999; Messick 1993.

20. The situation is somewhat different in the case of newspapers. While English-language norms have shaped the graphic organization of Urdu newspapers, the latter display their own distinctive features, most notably the inventive stylizations of headlines.

21. In some cases, utter disregard may be meted out to all documents written in a particular language. C.M. Naim recalls that in his days as a receiving clerk in Lucknow, India, in the 1960s, he was told simply to discard petitions written in Hindi. If the matter were important enough, he was assured, the petition would return in English (personal communication).

22. Johns (1998), for example, describes the ideological work that was necessary for the authorship of printed books to be widely perceived as reliable. The actual material likeness of all the books of a single edition was a minor factor.

23. For leading works on materiality, see Brown 2004; Gell 1998; Henare, Holbraad, and Wastell 2006; Latour 1999; Miller 1987, 2005; Strathern 1999.

24. Ilana Feldman (2008) beautifully describes the continuities of governance sustained by bureaucratic practices in Gaza.

25. Charles Hischkind (2006) has fruitfully developed this concept of the public beyond discourse, showing how an Islamic counterpublic is shaped not only by the circulation of discourses carried by cassette sermons but by the ways of listening they engender.

26. In his classic work, even Crozier (1967), who stressed the interdependence of "rationality and dysfunction" in bureaucratic organizations, saw writing purely in the service of organizational control. He observed that apathetic dependence on documented facts and adherence to written directives and rules could stymie the efficiency of an organization by intensifying superiors' control over subordinates. Thus, he concluded that writing may be dysfunctional by criteria of efficiency, but it nevertheless promotes formal organizational control.

27. Abrams 1988; Mitchell 1991.

28. When I had finished reading these files, I attempted to have them sent to the National Archives. The clerks and the junior officer above them pointed to their current appearance (and their previous disappearance) as evidence of their worthlessness and unfortunately had them taken out to be sold for scrap.

29. See Stoler (2010) on archives and Feldman (2008) for an excellent discussion of the differences between files and archives.

30. In India, however, the Right to Information Act of 2005, similar to the United States Freedom of Information Act, is bringing considerable change in public access (Roberts 2010).

CHAPTER 1

1. Syed Hashim Raza (1991:90) writes that in January 1948 he personally showed a draft of the plan to Mohammad Ali Jinnah, who approved it.

2. The Greater Karachi Plan, though, has been implemented, with the planned capital area replaced by a monument to Quaid-i-Azam (the Great Founder), Mohammad Ali Jinnah.

3. Quoted in *Pakistan Times*, July 7, 1959.

4. Ibid.

5. Ibid.

6. Ibid.

7. *Jang*, December 7, 1969.

8. *Pakistan Times*, January 4, 1970.

9. *Nida-i-Millat*, December 30 1969; *Jang*, January 3 1970.

10. *Pakistan Times*, January 29, 1970.

11. *New Times* (Rawalpindi), September 28, 1970.

12. See Spaulding 2003 for a concise biography of Doxiadis in relation to Islamabad.

13. As many have observed, there are continuities between this colonial tradition and the city-building activities of the Mughals, as exemplified by Delhi, Agra, and Fatepur Sikri. There are, however, significant differences. Important cities such as Karachi, Bombay, Calcutta, and Madras developed from isolated trading settlements, but the British more often developed settlements outside existing cities upon which they depended (King 1976).

14. For recent accounts of colonial cities in the subcontinent, see Glover 2008; Hosagrahar 2005; Legg 2007.

15. For one such reference to the "Presidential Palace," see "Construction of Islamabad/Work to Start in about 2 Months," *Pakistan Times*, August 8, 1960. For most of Ayub Khan's tenure, little more than a yellow flag topped this hill. The President's House was completed only in the late 1960s and Ayub Khan himself never occupied it, preferring to remain in Rawalpindi before moving into an undistinguished house in the elite residential area near the administrative area. In the mid-1990s, Ayub's house was unceremoniously razed for the construction of a new house by the wealthy owner of a major hotel, in what several observers described to me as a gesture of arrogance.

16. According to this official, Zulfiqar Ali Bhutto deployed the same height symbolism when he later insisted that a new prime minister's residence be higher than the President's House, "so you see it is on a higher hill" to the north of the President's House.

17. See Nilsson (1973) for a witty architecturally oriented account that captures the spirit of Doxiadis's Master Plan. Spaulding (1994) provides an excel-

lent and more thorough description and analysis of the Master Plan and the early years of its implementation.

18. In a departure from this alphanumeric austerity, the F and G series of sectors were given names, "Shalimar" and "Ramna" respectively. These names occasionally appear in writing but no one ever uses them in speech, inside or outside the planning offices.

19. Or, in the words of Richard Sennett, the grid "lacks a logic of its own limits and of form established within boundaries" (1990:272).

20. The hierarchy of communities also partly corresponded to modes of transportation: "Dynapolis is not built for man only. In it we are going to have a cohabitation of man and machines, of cars, trains, airplanes and helicopters and maybe rockets. And beyond rockets, what? . . . It is too early to predict what class of community is to have a rocket launching base" (Doxiadis Associates 1960b:136).

21. Doxiadis's reports try to accomplish this same feat on paper. Even reports devoted to the smallest element of the plan, for example, house designs, include a series of maps showing the series of communities in which the element is to be located.

22. In mohallas, the only location with a perceptible spatial relation to the mohalla as a whole is the entrance. A mohalla ends multiply in the blind alleys that form it; these end places can neither be placed on a single axis of depth nor directly related spatially through visual perception. The irregularity of the branching of galis prevents a "geometric deduction" of these spatial relationships. The spatial boundaries of a mohalla cannot be seen from the outside either, since a mohalla is usually backed by one or more other mohallas and cannot be directly circumambulated. It is interesting to note that this is reflected in the contrasting representational conventions of maps of Islamabad and mohalla areas. Maps of Rawalpindi mohallas produced in conjunction with the Master Plan of Islamabad define mohallas by networks of galis rather than by an outline of the space they occupy (Ahmed 1960).

23. It is unclear to me why, but a change in the allocation rules in 1993 reversed the classification of existing houses so that, for example, what was an A-type house for a BPS 1–4 occupant became an H-type house, an H-type house for a BPS 20 occupant became an A-type house, and so forth. These new rules also stipulated an entirely new five-category scheme (Classes I–V) for all government accommodation constructed in the future. Unlike the older classification scheme, the new one is given visual publicity: large signs on the exteriors of new quarters declare their classification. But outside of the CDA and the office that allocates quarters, the old classifications of houses built prior to 1993 have stuck.

24. More specifically, American planners, closely tied to social workers, reformers, and pragmatist philosophers, developed the neighborhood unit as a physical container and, more importantly, as a template for the imagination of the social interconnectedness made invisible by ethnic difference and the complex division of labor of the urbanizing American society (Hull 2011).

25. The potential for this originally egalitarian sociospatial form to promote hierarchical distributions had already been realized in the United States.

The policy of the Master Plan accorded with prevailing opinion among American sociologists, working in such diverse contexts as suburbs in the United States and Indian inner cities, concerning the social benefits and problems with "mixed" neighborhoods (Hull 2011).

26. "Master Plan for Islamabad," *Pakistan Times*, March 3 1960.

27. *Pakistan Times*, May 31, 1972.

28. One of the lesser-noted components of Weber's classic definition of bureaucracy is that functionaries are paid in money rather than in goods or other material benefits. The importance of this feature for Weber is that remuneration in money (rather than goods) is less likely to lead to appropriation of aspects of the office by the officeholder. While Pakistan government servants are given monetary salaries, they obtain a significant amount of their government income in nonmonetary forms. A senior officer of a powerful government division like the ICTA may receive facilities valued at four or five times his salary, including a car, a large house, phones, domestic servants, and so forth. At the other end of the spectrum, government servants receive modest quarters. This feature of the Pakistan bureaucracy owes less to notions of a welfare state than to the power of government servants and the continuities of contemporary bureaucracies with the East India Company, which was originally staffed by what we now call expatriate workers. The Company created "factories," settlements for its "factors" (employees), that included spaces for living, keeping records, and storing goods (King 1976). As the Company expanded and was transformed into a political entity, this practice of providing a range of facilities to employees continued, strengthened through its convergence with Mughal norms. New Delhi, built in the 1920s, included housing for all government servants from the Viceroy down to lower division clerks and peons.

29. Since the 1980s, renting part or all of a government unit has increased dramatically. A large percentage of houses in G-6/1–1 have one or more rooms rented out; the estimates of residents I spoke with ranged from 60 to 100 percent. The prospect of a rental income is one reason many residents add rooms in the rear courtyard. Such rooms allow the families of renters and allotees to remain somewhat separate, while sharing a bath and toilet. Male allotees living without their families, with no concerns about the purdah of their wives, often rent out even the rooms of the original house to as many as five or six other men. This pattern is similar in other sectors, though renting is somewhat less common because of the prevalence of apartments. The unavoidable threat to purdah in apartments usually prohibits everyone but men living without their families from renting rooms.

CHAPTER 2

1. The characterization of "face-to-face" interaction as unmediated has, of course, been criticized for decades (Goffman 1959).

2. Religious concerns also intrude into the bureaucratic order in more eccentric ways. One officer had made a habit of receiving a month of leave during Ramzan through an unorthodox means. For years, in the weeks preceding the beginning of Ramzan, he would approach his superior and recount a dream

of the Prophet he had had (a powerful sign among Muslims), in which the Prophet had told him that he should take a leave for the duration of Ramzan. One year, however, he encountered a formidable CDA chairman, a no-nonsense retired brigadier general. After his customary retelling of the dream, the chairman reportedly responded, "Well, isn't this strange. The Prophet came to me in a dream last night too. He told me you would come asking for a month of leave and that I shouldn't give it to you." Reportedly, the officer never tried the tactic again.

3. The gendering of drawing rooms, like other spaces of the home, is fluid, depending on a range of variables. For example, Laura Ring (2006) describes the complex gendering of the *zenana* in Karachi apartments. *Zenana* literally means women's space, but in Ring's account it is not a fixed physical space but a realm of women's sociality existing at the sufferance of men, expanding with their absence and contracting with their presence.

4. The extremely low number of women officers, staff, and, as I will describe later, clients accounts for my use of the pronoun "he" in reference to government servants and clients.

5. The class marking of toilets is evident in their distribution within houses and in the city more broadly. Asian WCs are always installed in servants quarters within residential houses. A bathroom fixtures dealer estimated to me that 80 to 90 percent of the toilets in the upscale F-10 and F-11 sectors are "English WCs," while in the more middling G-10 and G-11 sectors the split is about 50 percent for each.

6. One architect I talked with about this admitted he often neglected to observe this rule when designing bathrooms but clients always caught the mistake and insisted that the toilet be reoriented. CDA architects have also made this error. In 1978, for example, the worshippers of Markazi Masjid Shia G-6/2 asked to change the direction of a latrine to the proper orientation. Some young and bawdy Christian men I knew delighted in the petty sacrilege of standing up and pissing in the direction of Mecca.

7. *Banwae* is the subjunctive of the causative form of *banana* (to make or build).

8. *Tamir,* November 26, 1965.

9. Aitcheson College is the Eton of Pakistan and might be the most important institutional source of "old boy" connections after the Civil Service Academy, the elite civil service training institution. In explaining the strength and social significance of bonds among "Aitchesonians," one told me, "If there is someone who passed out [graduated] in 1960 and I have just passed out, and I just walk into his office and he says brusquely, 'Yes, who are you?' and I say, 'Sir, I am an Aitchesonian,' then he will greet me warmly and assist me in any way he can." I witnessed one such office encounter that followed exactly this script. On the rear windows of nicer cars, one occasionally sees a decal that says "Aitchesonian," adaptations of the decals of US colleges, with an even more direct identification of driver and institution.

10. "Martial Law Instruction No. 5," *Pakistan Times,* November 7, 1977.

11. *The News,* the prominent English-language newspaper in Islamabad, reported that Nargis Makhdoom denied writing the letter or even having such

letterhead. However, her personal secretary confirmed that the three mobile numbers on the letterhead belong to Nargis Makhdoom, her son, and her personal secretary. The home number is also correct. Such numbers are not in the public domain and not generally available. Usman Manzoor, "Gilani Warns His Family Members Not to Use His Name," *News,* November 11, 2008.

12. Ibid.

13. Ibid.

14. As Raman (2007) observes, this language of government fuses with appeals to gods in north India. *Ardas,* derived from *arzdasht,* is used in Hindi and other North Indian languages for prayer. Cody (2009:352) finds the same word in Tamil for entreaties to gods and government and notes the similarity of petitions to Kali and to its government.

15. C. M. Naim, working in the same bureaucratic tradition in India, recalled that in his days as a receiving clerk in Lucknow, India, in the 1960s, he was told simply to discard petitions written in Hindi (personal communication).

16. The signature portions of petitions include a signature and writing identifying the name and sometimes address of the signatory. These differ among petitions and are internally heterogeneous. They vary in script, language, and degree of stylization. For example, the name and address information might be given in English language rendered in Urdu script with a Roman script signature. The script used to produce a signature is sometimes indistinguishable from that used to render the main prose of the petition of the name identification, that is, completely unstylized. This is especially true of those using Perso-Arabic script to sign. Sometimes a thumbprint of the right hand is used rather than a signature (Parry 2004). Relative to other aspects of petitions, the signature portions of petitions seem to be relatively less ordered into genres. They appear to correlate with level of education, but do not to correlate with the three types of political subject I have described. Perso-Arabic script is used in signatures on English-language petitions and vice versa, especially when there are numerous signatories.

17. All nonstandard spelling, diction, and capitalizations in the original.

18. Jang, November 3, 1979.

19. Business Recorder, "CCPO Hold Open Kutchery," June 11, 2009.

CHAPTER 3

1. Sociolinguists have departed from this ultimately functionalist approach, but they are focused on externally oriented genres (mainly forms) that are either published or issued to so-called clients (Charrow 1982; Sarangi and Slembrouck 1996; Shuy 1998). While these studies provide important insights into how organizations represent themselves to those outside the organization, they have little to say about how writing shapes internal activities or the relations between internal and external activities.

2. Bakhtin (1986:61–62) was very interested in how "complex" speech genres absorb simpler ones, for example, how the novel incorporates genres such as letters, diaries, everyday dialogues, and narration. But despite his theoretical concentration on "concrete utterances," Bakhtin was not concerned

with the material form in which written genres were presented. He focused on linguistic devices of incorporation such as dialogism, direct quotation, and reported speech (1981:259–422). However, in addition to the linguistic devices he described, complex graphic genres use a variety of non- or para-linguistic graphic and nongraphic spatial means to incorporate other graphic genres. The Pakistani file may be characterized as a complex graphic genre, for its capacity to discursively and materially incorporate every other genre of writing in the bureaucracy.

3. See, for example, Government of India 1891:95.

4. I use the pronouns "he" and "his" in reference to CDA and ICTA functionaries because, as I described in the previous chapter, the overwhelming majority are men.

5. Each file "number" has four parts: the initials by which the directorate is identified, such as, in the example, "CDA/PLD" for the Planning Directorate of the CDA; the number of the "standard head" ("9")—an entry in the file index maintained by each directorate—to which the file was assigned; the serial number of the file under the standard head ("1"); and the year the file was opened ("62").

6. Although the alphabetical labels of sidebars are transcribed, the sidebars themselves are not represented on the note sheet. Sidebars function as "graphic deictics," that is, graphic signs whose basic significance depends on the context of their deployment and would be meaningless without a transcription of the unofficial discourse that they index. For the same reason, stamps are also not transcribed.

7. The technology of the autopen has brought into question the biomechanical fusion of person and signature. President Obama created a stir in 2010 when he authorized the use of an autopen to sign a renewal of the United States Patriot Act while he was away in France.

8. This difference in the basis of authentication systems clashed historically in 1930 during the League of Nations meetings when Western delegates contended that the Asian seals could not guarantee the authentic relation between image and individual (Harris 1995:82).

9. I use the term "ritual" to highlight action with particular formal properties and not as a label to exoticize and "anthropologize" bureaucratic practices in the manner of *Tribes on the Hill* (Weatherford 1981), an anthropological study of the United States Congress. More than two decades ago Sampson (1983) criticized a tendency of anthropological studies to transform formal institutions into "something exotic."

10. The status implications of initiating communication are illustrated by Zaffar Khan's story of his encounter with a high-court judge conducting a judicial inquiry into a high-profile crime in the city. The judge needed to speak with Zaffar Khan, who had authority over the police. But rather than calling him directly, which would have positioned him in an interactionally subordinate role, the judge had his personal assistant call the District Commissioner (DC), Zaffar Khan's immediate subordinate. When the DC informed Zaffar Khan that the judge wanted him to call, he replied disingenuously, "I have no business with the man, if he has work with me, he can just call me, I am here." Then the judge

himself called the Chief Commissioner, Zaffar Khan's immediate superior, who directed him to call the judge, but he again refused. Unwilling to be outdone, the judge then called the Deputy Secretary of the Interior Ministry, who called the Chief Commissioner (his subordinate), who this time successfully prevailed upon Zaffar Khan to call the judge. This maneuvering took several days. The judge ordered Zaffar Khan to appear before him. Zaffar Khan had, by his own admission, treated the judge badly when he was only a sessions judge (a district-level post) and was vexed by the judge's obvious intention to turn the tables. Zaffar Khan spent several days anxiously considering how he might avoid, as he put it, being "dishonored" by the judge. He couldn't simply claim to be busy and refuse to appear, since disobeying a judicial order could land him in prison for a day or two for contempt of court. He weighed going with large entourage of police "to show his strength," then decided against it. In the end. he sent the DC and a few police officers ahead to announce him while he was en route, one step away from just showing up directly.

11. The necessity of using pronouns is also reduced because many verbs that take an object complement in North American and British English don't require them in South Asian English. The suppression of pronouns is also evident in the use of transitive verbs whose direct objects are dropped, particularly when the object refers to the writer. Note how "inform," "confuse," "instruct," and "request" are all used without direct objects in the following examples.

> The case . . . has been discussed with Director (UP) who informed [∅] that Member planning has informed [∅] that during Chairman visit, Chairman agreed to extend the mosque in such a way that it looks a component of mosque design.
>
> Plan at f 'A' confuses [∅]
>
> Chairman instructed [∅] to extend the mosque.
>
> Later on DDG (Design) requested [∅] to review the case.

12. In her study of the relation of tense and narration, Fleischman (1990) shows how the use of tense not only shapes the portrayal of events but constructs a narrative subject as well. Summarizing her findings on the use of the perfective, Lee writes that "the perfective past, or preterit, is a nonexperiential grammatical form that objectively reports situations as they unfold in the past. As opposed to all the other tenses used in narration, it is the only one that does not imply an experiencing self as the reporter of the events it chronicles" (1997:291). In contrast to the nonperfective or simple past, the "perfect indicates the continuing present relevance of a past situation" (Comrie 1976:52). In narration of past events in CDA files, the overwhelming prevalence of the present perfect reflects the interest of officials in representing past events without implying an experiencing subject and in representing past events as relevant, even determinative, of present action. The subject of narrative file discourse is one whose actions are shaped by an objective past beyond the control of the current actor.

13. Though we have seen in recent years United States presidents diffuse their own responsibility for controversial directives on security matters by depending upon the opinions of the US Justice Department's Office of Legal Counsel.

14. The origins of the description are disputed, but it was popularized by the linguist Max Weinreich.

15. At the end of this exchange, the file becomes the vehicle for delivering the deputy director's reproach: "both officers have showed irresponsibility. Please convey them my displeasure and return the file." "Conveyed sir," wrote his assistant.

16. The "10 percent," of course, refers to his alleged customary "commission" on transactions and business profits. Reportedly, he was known as "Mr. Five Percent" during his presumably less ambitious first term as the prime minister's husband.

CHAPTER 4

1. Interestingly, some of the former officials I interviewed who had worked on land acquisitions in the early 1960s still usually referred to owners of expropriated land as "displaced persons." In English-language newspapers of the early 1960s, occasionally they were called "expropriated persons." Urdu newspapers from this period also sometimes referred to them as "about to be homeless people" (*beghar honewale log*).

2. The difference between the English and Urdu publics in Pakistan is much like what Rajagopal (2001) calls the "split public" of the Hindi and English press in India.

3. Used by government officials, the term expresses the authoritarian power of state institutions; it is invoked by the subjects of that power as a moral claim against it.

4. This approach can be compared to certain treatments of reference in analytic philosophy that see propositions referring in virtue of a sustained, though perhaps highly mediated, link to the object of reference. For example, Kripke (1980) sees proper names referring to an object after a "baptism" that links an object to a particular name; later uses of a proper name refer to that object because they are connected by transmission to that baptism. Gareth Evans (1982) argues that an "information link" is necessary for correct reference. However, unlike Latour, these philosophical approaches usually focus on the two end points, word and thing, and rarely go very far in empirically exploring how mediators connect them.

5. Unless otherwise noted, all my quotations of official writings in this chapter come from files of the Land Directorate and Planning Directorate. For a fuller discussion of sources, please refer to the introduction.

6. "Islamabad Development Body Soon," *Pakistan Times*, May 23, 1960.

7. When another 3,500 plots in I-10/1 and I-10/4 were reserved for owners of expropriated land, the CDA rigidly enforced a complete ban on the transfer of plots.

8. Those granted lands in other areas of Punjab often faced harassment from existing residents, who tried to prevent them from farming the new land in order to pressure them to sell the land cheaply.

9. *Nawa-i-Waqt*, July 20, 1970.

10. *Pakistan Times*, February 16, 1977.

11. The Urdu press was very sympathetic to the situation of displaced persons. An editorial in *Nawa-i-Waqt* supported the demands of displaced persons "for payment of compensation on the current market rate" and argued for a "mixed society" of rich and servants: displaced persons "should be allotted residential plots along with rich people to develop a mixed society of the rich and the poor, providing servants for the rich people." *Nawa-i-Waqt,* June 29, 1977.

12. In addition to losing countless cases in civil courts, affectees also lost their appeal to the Federal Shariat Court (FSC), a court that rules on issues from an Islamic legal perspective. The FSC ruled in 1985 that several controversial provisions of the original Capital Development Ordinance of 1960 were "not repugnant to Sharia" and ordered only a slight amendment of the calculation of the market value of expropriated properties (PLD 1985 FSC 221).

13. "Compensation Paid to D.P.s," *Pakistan Times,* September 11, 1971.

14. Although the CDA, under the Cabinet Division since 1981, has its own small police force, it relies for larger operations on the forces of the ICTA, which is part of the Interior Ministry. As might be expected, relations between the ICTA and the CDA have often been rocky. There has been little coordination between the two organizations, and the ICTA chief commissioner and the CDA chairman have often not been on speaking terms. The ICTA frequently refuses CDA requests to provide police support. The ICTA also frustrates the regulatory efforts of the CDA by issuing so-called No Objection Certificates (NOCs)—documents approaching permission—for activities the CDA prohibits. Because the chains of command of the two organizations converge only at the level of the prime minister, such disputes often go unresolved.

15. The obvious solution—to acquire both sectors over which a village spreads—would simply push the problem to the border of the next sector, where a different village would be bifurcated by the sector border. The problem could be avoided by acquiring all the sectors at once, thus reducing the number of villages straddling sectors. However, money for compensation is generated by the sale of developed plots, so there are not enough funds for such a comprehensive acquisition. Furthermore, the master plan called for the city to expand indefinitely, so total acquisition is theoretically impossible as well.

16. The Planning Wing has faced this problem more squarely in its resettlement of squatters in G-8, who are being awarded developed plots on the site of their current settlement. Possession of a house in the current settlement entitles the possessor to a developed plot. The awards of plots are based on a rigid physical definition of the house as a four-walled enclosure with a single door, and the CDA adjudicates competing claims of occupants to the award of the plot. This definition, of course, has led to the rapid proliferation of walls and doors!

17. The very title for headman, *numberdar,* an English-Persian hybrid, points to the inadequacy of the term "tradition" to capture the peculiar relation such figures have had to state authority under the colonial and postcolonial states. The most spectacular beneficiary of the expropriation process is probably the current *pir* (hereditary spiritual and temporal leader) of the Golra Sharif shrine. A descendant of the first pir and considered a saint by devout followers, the current and rather worldly pir has enriched himself through extensive land dealing and favorable CDA land exchanges and compensation packages. His

strong influence within the bureaucracy has also strengthened his influence over residents of the area.

18. Newspaper accounts confirm the outlines of these events: "Four Hurt as CDA Men, Affectees Clash," *The Muslim,* October 23, 1988; "Mutasareen Islamabad CDA ke daftar par dhawa 7 afrad khatmi," *Nawa-i-Waqt,* October 23, 1988; "Mutasareen-i-Islamabad ke multalbat," *Markaz,* October 24, 1988.

19. Reza Sajjad is a pseudonym.

20. "Approach" is a term of South Asian English referring to the ability to access influential people. The generative Hindi-Urdu suffix, *-wala,* can be added to almost any lexical unit to form a noun indicating a person who possesses something or does the action conventionally associated with the referent of the lexical unit. Common examples are: *taxiwallah, chaiwallah, policewallah, PPPwallah* (member of the Pakistan People's Party), *darhiwalla* (bearded person), even *competitionwallah* (those who sit for competitive civil service exams).

21. See the anonymous fictional account *Revelations of an Orderly* (Khan 1866) for a British view of how effectively even such lowly staff could shape bureaucratic activities during the colonial period.

22. He was later convicted of illegally allocating plots to friends, relatives, and himself. However, he was never charged for the likely much more remunerative activities under discussion here.

23. The accuracy of this claim is borne out by file notes one occasionally finds describing encounters with affectees. A memo written in 1969 by an accounts officer, for example, describes how, facing a shortfall of funds, he preferred to pay the maximum number of displaced persons with the amount at his disposal. One day, fifteen of them, "mostly ladies," came to his office for their checks. One "oustee" demanded the full Rs. 15,000 and was told the payment had to be delayed. In the accounts officers' words, "he began to shout at me. He was joined by a few others to hurl abuses at me. This unruly/undisciplined behaviour on their part led to the stoppage of payment."

24. The others were, Sihala, Bheka Sayyadan, Thatha Gujran, Dharmian, Koka, Madrassa, Korak, and Sheikhpur.

25. Ironically, most of the land of Zafar Khan's father had been expropriated by the federal government in the mid-1970s in "land reforms" enacted by Prime Minister Zulfiqar Ali Bhutto against his landed political opponents.

26. My account of the origin of these factions is taken from the history of this conflict in Sadiq (1987), which is based upon oral sources.

27. Of course, the lists are not "decontextualized" in the broad semantic sense that this term is sometimes used. That is, their significance does depend on the context of use.

28. This unique capacity of the list was highlighted in congressional hearings on the firing of United States attorneys by the Bush administration's Department of Justice. Here is Senator Diane Feinstein questioning Attorney General Alberto Gonzales:

> I may be very slow. But I don't understand how this list was compiled. . . . Kyle Sampson, your former chief of staff—I'm going to talk about the senior so-called leadership of the department—and the person you said you delegated this task to testified that he

didn't put people on the list. He said, quote, "It wasn't like that. It wasn't that I wanted names on the list. I was the aggregator." That's page 184 of his transcript. Mike Battle, director of the Executive Office of the United States Attorneys, said, "I had no input. Nobody asked me for my input." That's the interview, page 82. Bill Mercer, acting associate attorney general and number three at DOJ, said, "I didn't understand there was a list. I didn't keep a list. It was just that any time I had a particular concern, I made that known to different people." And you testified this morning that you didn't know the reasons U.S. attorneys were put on the list until after you decided to fire them. . . . And to this time, we do not know who actually selected the people to be put on the list. "Gonzales Testifies before Senate Panel," *Washington Post*, April 19, 2007.

29. "Rs340m Land Fraud Detected in CDA," *Dawn*, December 1, 2000.

CHAPTER 5

1. According to Markus Daechsel, Doxiadis drew the figure of 10 percent from projects he had done in Iraq and Egypt (personal communication).

2. The city has had a substantial Christian population since its beginning. There are several authorized churches and many more in the informal settlements of Christians. However, the CDA has never funded or built a church. The attempts of Christian groups to construct them on their own them have sometimes generated virulent protest. Opponents have portrayed their proposed proximity to mosques as an affront to a Muslim Pakistan and to Islam more generally.

3. Markus Daechsel (2012) documents sectarian conflicts over mosques in the early 1960s in Korangi, an area of Karachi also planned by Doxiadis, long before state Islamization initiatives. This suggests that state supervision of mosque construction in a comprehensive planning framework was enough on its own to provoke competition among different sects. He shows how, unlike in Islamabad, conflict in Korangi was as much between Shias and Sunnis as between Sunni groups.

4. Other important contributors include regional conflicts that brought financial support and organizational support from Iran, Iraq, Saudi Arabia, and the United States; the lack of opportunities for political participation; the weakening of state institutions of law and order in Punjab and Karachi; and the tactical use of sectarian discord by the civilian governments that succeeded Zia.

5. No reliable figures exist to answer the politically sensitive question of what percentage of Pakistanis could be characterized as Shia or Sunni, though estimates range from 15 to 20 percent for Shias. The percentages of Sunnis identifying with one or another sect are pure speculation, though Deobandis and Barelvis clearly greatly outnumber Ahl-i Hadith adherents.

6. In scholarly discourse, *maslaq* refers to a "path" within Sunni Islam rather than a distinct sect. However, in the Pakistan government arena, *maslak,* usually spelled with a *k,* is used interchangeably with "sect" to indicate one of the recognized subdivisions of Islam, three of which are Sunni (Ahl-i Hadith, Deobandi, Barelvi) and one of which is the Shia. I follow this usage rather than the scholarly one. In petitions, one occasionally finds Deobandis, Barelvis, and Ahl-i Hadith referred to as *firqas*, the more orthodox word for sect. Conflict among religious groups is generally referred to in Urdu as *firqabazi.*

7. A senior member of the Islamabad Administration told me that the administration has someone in the audience of every Friday sermon to monitor its political content, which, for this official, meant statements against the government and other sects.

8. The *imambara,* a congregational hall for ritual ceremonies, especially ones associated with Muharram, is a uniquely Shia institution.

9. Under the rules, Auqaf Directorate officially maintains that "the Community of the area is not involved in the appointment of Imam/Moazzin" (Auqaf Directorate 1997). Once a decision is made about which maslak will receive the allotment, candidates are interviewed by "the leading religious Scholar of that Maslak from which the candidate belongs" (Auqaf Directorate 1997). The maslak of candidates is determined by the affiliation of the religious seminary at which the candidate completed his Dars-e-Nizami, a standard curriculum used in a large portion of seminaries in South Asia.

10. The Auqaf Directorate, "with a view to maintain sectarian harmony," was given the right to dissolve the committee. The committee was also prohibited from inviting anyone but the officially appointed mosque khateeb from addressing the congregation in the mosque without the "prior consultation of the Khateeb and the express permission of the Auqaf Directorate." The committee was "to ensure that the forum of the mosque is not utilized for propagating any sectarian beliefs or views."

11. My accounts of these processes are based on the files on these mosques maintained by the Auqaf Directorate and the CDA and conversations with a variety of Auqaf Directorate staff involved in their resolution.

12. *Daily Wifaqi,* July 4, 1984.

13. *The Muslim,* November 28, 1982.

14. These mosques were located on the Islamabad Highway and Murree roads. Newspapers claimed intelligence agencies had reported to the Interior Ministry that these mosques could be used by terrorists to target VIPs and foreigners who use those roads to travel from the airport to Islamabad ("Two Mosques Demolished in Islamabad over Security Threat," *Pakistan Times,* January 21, 2007). It was widely rumored that United States security officials had insisted on the demolition. These demolitions were among the issues cited by students who occupied parts of the Lal Masjid (Red Mosque) complex in G-6, which eventually led to a very bloody battle between government forces and armed supporters of the leadership of the mosque in July 2007.

15. *Pakistan Times,* August 31, 1981.

16. Verdery similarly describes the efforts of local officials in Romania to keep exclusive possession of village maps. She recounts how a mayor became furious when one villager obtained a map from county archives because "he had lost his monopoly control" (2003:156).

CONCLUSION

1. Jeremy Bentham himself, an enthusiastic though ambivalent proponent of written documentation, noted the play of correspondence and noncorrespondence in the function of records:

A record is the very tabernacle of truth; let it say what it will, no man is permitted to dispute the truth of it, or any part of it. . . . [However such] is the matter of a record: everything is sham that finds its way into that receptacle, as everything is foul that finds it way out of Fleet-ditch into the Thames. (Bentham 1932:142)

2. In one encounter I witnessed, the identification of paper with corruption was rather more literal. I was riding in a car with a friend of mine when we were stopped at one of Islamabad's many police checkpoints. The policeman demanded to see my friends car documents ("Kaghaz!"). My friend immediately asked, "How many would you like to see?" "One hundred," the policeman replied. My friend handed over a hundred-rupee note and we were quickly on our way.

3. The CDA adopted this idea and tactic from the well-known Orangi Pilot Project in Karachi.

4. "'Electronification' of information" is the phrase of T.H. Chowdary, Advisor Information Technology, Government of Andhra Pradesh. "A Roundtable on IT Governance," January 12–13, 2001, Dehli. Retrieved from www.ima-india.com on March 15, 2002.

5. In India a large number of electronic systems have been established at the municipal, district, state, and federal levels to reshape the relation of government to its citizen-consumers. One Indian government information technology officer recently observed, "In many transactions, the government-citizen interface should be no different than that between a service provider and its clients. Historically, the relationship has been rather unequal." Information technology (IT)—which does not include paper documentation—will "bring transparency and balance into this relationship." The Chairman of the New Delhi Municipal Corporation, B.P. Misra, declared that with IT the government can achieve "participatory administration. . . . IT can break the stranglehold of government functionaries on information, through which they wield a lot of power" (Both quotations are from "A Roundtable on IT Governance.") Mazzarella (2006) discusses the aspiration for transparency in government in India.

6. MG Realtors was a separate legal entity from MG Hertz, but the officers and board of directors were the same as those of MG Hertz.

7. Searle 2009.

8. Technically, the village residential areas (*abadi deh*) are common holdings (shamlat) too, but residents have a bundle of rights to the land and houses they occupy that is close to ownership.

9. For example, an owner of 8 acres in a village of 4,000 acres, including 1,500 acres of shamlat, would be entitled to 3 acres (.2 percent of the shamlat) if a majority of village holders voted to divide up the shamlat land.

10. He argued that such legislation was not only in the interest of the project, but in the interest of good urban development. He noted how in Lahore, little 800 to 1,000 kanal schemes are tacked onto the city, drawing on existing infrastructure. Large projects, the sort compulsory acquisition would enable, would provide their own water, sewage, phone, and electricity infrastructures.

References

Abrams, Philip. 1988. "Notes on the Difficulty of Studying the State." *Journal of Historical Sociology* 1(1):58–89.

Ahmad, Mumtaz. 1998. "Revivalism, Islamization, Sectarianism, and Violence in Pakistan." In *Pakistan:1997*, edited by C. Baxter and C. H. Kennedy, 101–21. Boulder, CO: Westview.

Ahmed, Asad. 2010. "The Paradoxes of Ahmadiyya Identity: The Legal Appropriation of Muslimness and the Construction of Ahmadiyya Difference." In *Beyond Crisis: A Critical Second Look at Pakistan*, edited by N. Khan. New Delhi: Routledge.

Ahmed, Nazir Lt. Col. 1960. *Socio-Economic Survey Rawalpindi*. Central Statistical Office, Government of Pakistan.

Alavi, Hamza. 1983. "Class and State in Pakistan." In *Roots of Dictatorship: The Political Economy of a Praetorian State*, edited by H. N. Gardezi and J. Rashid, 40–93. London: Zed.

Ali, Sayad Fayaz. 1997. *Rahbar-i-Patwarian*. Lahore: Hamdard Kitab Khanna.

Andrews, John. 2001. "Meaning, Knowledge, and Power in the Map History of J. B. Harley." In *The New Nature of Maps: Essays in the History of Cartography*, edited by A. John, 2–32. Baltimore: Johns Hopkins University Press.

Appadurai, Arjun. 1986. "Introduction: Commodities and the Politics of Value." In *The Social Life of Things*, edited by A. Appadurai, 3–63. Cambridge: Cambridge University Press.

———. 1990. "Topographies of the Self: Praise and Emotion in Hindu India." In *Language and the Politics of Emotion*, edited by C. Lutz and L. Abu-Lughod, 92–112. Cambridge: Cambridge University Press.

Auqaf Directorate. 1997. *Islamabad Auqaf Directorate*. I.C.T. Administration.

Baden-Powell, B.H. 1892. *The Land Systems of British India: Being a Manual of the Land-Tenures and of the Systems of Land-Revenue Administration Prevalent in the Several Provinces.* Oxford: Clarendon Press.

Bailey, F.G. 1991. *The Prevalence of Deceit.* Ithaca: Cornell University Press.

Bakhtin, M. 1981. *The Dialogic Imagination: Four Essays.* Translated by Michael Holquist. Edited by Caryl Emerson and Michael Holquist. Austin: University of Texas Press.

———. 1986. *Speech Genres, and Other Late Essays.* Translated by Vern W. McGee. Edited by Caryl Emerson and Michael Holquist. Austin: University of Texas Press.

Bayly, Christopher. 1996. *Empire and Information: Intelligence Gathering and Social Communication in India, 1780–1870.* Cambridge: Cambridge University Press.

Bear, Laura. 2007. *Lines of the Nation: Indian Railway Workers, Bureaucracy, and the Intimate Historical Self.* New York: Columbia University Press.

Bentham, Jeremy. 1932. *Bentham's Theory of Fictions.* London: Kegan Paul, Trench, Trubner.

Besnier, Niko. 1995. *Literacy, Emotion, and Authority.* Cambridge: Cambridge University Press.

Biber, D. 1988. *Variation across Speech and Writing.* Cambridge: Cambridge University Press.

Bowker, Geoffrey, and Susan Leigh Star. 1999. *Sorting Things Out: Classification and Its Consequences.* Cambridge, MA: MIT Press.

Boyer, Dominic. 2003. "Censorship as a Vocation: The Institutions, Practices, and Cultural Logic of Media Control in the German Democratic Republic." *Comparative Studies in Society and History* 45:511–45.

Braibanti, Ralph. 1966. *Research on the Bureaucracy of Pakistan.* Durham: Duke University Press.

Brenneis, Donald. 2006. "Reforming Promise." In *Documents: Artifacts of Modern Knowledge,* edited by A. Riles, 41–70. Ann Arbor: University of Michigan.

Briet, Suzanne. 2006. *What Is Documentation?* Translated and edited by Ronald E. Day and Laurent Martinet, with Hermina G. B. Anghelescu. Lanham, MD: Scarecrow.

Briggs, Charles, and Richard Bauman. 1990. "Poetics and Performance as Critical Perspectives on Language and Social Life." *Annual Review of Anthropology* 19:59–88.

Brimnes, Neil. 1998. *Constructing the Colonial Encounter: Right and Left Hand Castes in Early Colonial South India.* London: Routledge.

Britan, Gerald M., and Ronald Cohen, eds. 1980. *Hierarchy and Society: Anthropological Perspectives on Bureaucracy.* Philadelphia: Institute for the Study of Human Issues.

Brown, Bill, ed. 2004. *Things.* Chicago: University of Chicago Press.

Bryan, Elizabeth. 1999. *Collaborative Meaning in Medieval Scribal Culture: The Otho Lazamon.* Ann Arbor: University of Michigan Press.

Burki, Shahid Javed. 1986. *Pakistan: A Nation in the Making.* Boulder, CO: Westview.

Burns, John F. 1998. House of Graft: Tracing the Bhutto Millions—A Special Report: Bhutto Clan Leaves Trail of Corruption. *New York Times,* January 9.

Capital Development Authority. 1984. Islamabad Displaced Persons Rehabilitation Policy. Government of Pakistan.

———. 1985a. Rules for the Conduct of Business. Islamabad: Capital Development Authority.

———. 1985b. Socio-Economic Survey of Unacquired Urban Areas, 1984–85. Directorate of Rehabilitation. Government of Pakistan.

———. 1996. Islamabad Displaced Persons Rehabilitation Policy. Government of Pakistan.

Caplan, Jane, and John Torpey, eds. 2001. *Documenting Individual Identity: The Development of State Practices in the Modern World*. Princeton: Princeton University Press.

Charrow, Veda. 1982. "Language in the Bureaucracy." In *Linguistics and the Professions*, edited by Robert J. Di Pietro, 173–88. Norwood, NJ: University of Delaware Press.

Chartier, Roger. 1994. *The Order of Books*. Translated by L. G. Cochrane. Palo Alto, CA: Stanford University Press.

———. 1995. *Forms and Meanings: Texts, Performances, and Audiences from Codex to Computer*. Philadelphia: University of Pennsylvania Press.

Clanchy, Michael. 1979. *From Memory to Written Record: England, 1066–1307*. Cambridge, MA: Harvard University Press.

Cody, Francis. 2009. "Inscribing Subjects to Citizenship: Literary Activisim, and the Performativity of Signature in Rural India." *Cultural Anthropology* 24(3): 347–80.

Cohn, Bernard. 1987. *An Anthropologist among the Historians, and other essays*. New York: Oxford University Press.

Comrie, Bernard. 1976. *Aspect*. Cambridge: Cambridge University Press.

Council of Islamic Ideology. 1987. *Salana Report, 1986–1987*. Government of Pakistan.

Crozier, Michel. 1967. *The Bureaucratic Phenomenon*. Chicago: University of Chicago Press.

Daechsel, Markus. 2012. "Seeing Like an Expert, Failing Like a State? Interpreting the Fate of a Satellite Town in Early Post-Colonial Pakistan." In *Colonial and Post-Colonial Governance of Islam: Continuities and Ruptures*, edited by V. Bader and M. Maussen. Amsterdam: Amsterdam University Press.

Das, Veena, and Deborah Poole. 2004. "State and Its Margins: Comparative Ethnographies." In *Anthropology in the Margins of the State*, edited by Veena Das and Deborah Poole, 3–33. Santa Fe, NM: School of American Research.

de Certeau, Michel. 1984. *The Practice of Everyday Life*. Translated S. F. Rendall. Berkeley: University of California Press.

Derrida, Jacques. 1974. *Of Grammatology*. Translated by G. Spivak. Baltimore: Johns Hopkins University Press.

De Rycker, Teun. 1987. "Turns at Writing: The Organization of Correspondence." In *The Pragmatic Perspective*, edited by Jeff Verschueren, 613–47. Amsterdam: John Benjamins.

Devji, Faisal. 1993. "Muslim Nationalism: Founding Identity in Colonial India." Ph.D. Diss., Department of History, University of Chicago.

Doxiadis Associates. 1960a. A Part of the Metropolitan Area, CDA 36. Capital Development Authority.

———. 1960b. Preliminary Programme and Plan, CDA 32. Capital Development Authority.

———. 1961a. Communities and Houses for Sector G-6, CDA 38. Capital Development Authority.

———. 1961b. Islamabad: Human Community Planning. Doxiadis Associates.

———. 1961c. On Architecture in Islamabad, CDA 56. Capital Development Authority.

———. 1961d. House Types, CDA 69. Capital Development Authority.

Doxiadis, Constantinos. 1963. *Architecture in Transition*. London: Hutchinson.

———. 1964. "Islamabad, The New Capital of Pakistan." *Ekistics* 18(108): 331–34.

———. 1965. "Islamabad: The Creation of a New Capital." *Town Planning Review* 36(1): 1–28.

———. 1968. *Ekistics: An Introduction to the Study of Human Settlements*. New York: Oxford University Press.

Du Bois, John. 1986. "Self-Evidence and Ritual Speech." In *Evidentiality: The Linguistic Coding of Epistemology*, edited by W. Chafe and J. Nichols, 313–36. Norwood, NJ: Ablex.

East India Company. 1621. *Lawes or Standing Orders, Made and Oredyned by the Governor and Company of Merchants of London Trading to the East Indies*. London: East India Company.

Eisenlohr, Patrick. 2011. "Anthropology of Media and the Question of Ethnic and Religious Pluralism." *Social Anthropology* 19(1): 40–55.

Engelke, Matthew. 2007. *A Problem of Presence beyond Scripture in an African Church*. Berkeley: University of California Press.

Evans, Gareth. 1982. *The Varieties of Reference*. Oxford: Clarendon Press.

Fallers, Lloyd. 1950. *Bantu Bureaucracy: A Century of Political Evolution among the Basoga of Uganda*. Chicago: University of Chicago Press.

Federal Capital Commission. 1960. Report on Preliminary Master Plan and Programme of Islamabad. President's Secretariat, Government of Pakistan.

Feldman, Ilana. 2008. *Governing Gaza: Bureaucracy, Authority, and the Work of Rule, 1917–1967*. Durham: Duke University Press.

Ferguson, James. 1994. *The Anti-Politics Machine: "Development," Depoliticization, and Bureaucratic Power in Lesotho*. Minneapolis: University of Minnesota Press.

Finnegan, Ruth. 1988. *Literacy and Orality: Studies in the Technology of Communication*. Oxford: Basil Blackwell.

Fleischman, Suzanne. 1990. *Tense and Narrativity*. Austin: University of Texas Press.

Foucault, Michel. 1977. *Discipline and Punish*. Translated by Alan Sheridan. New York: Vintage.

Freitag, Sandria. 1989. *Collective Action and Community: Public Arenas and the Emergence of Communalism in North India*. Berkeley: University of California Press.

Garfinkel, Harold. 1967. *Studies in Ethnomethodology.* Englewood Cliffs, NJ: Prentice-Hall.

Geisler, Cheryl. 2001. "Textual Objects: Accounting for the Role of Texts in the Everyday Life of Complex Organizations." *Written Communication* 18(3): 296–325.

Gell, Alfred. 1998. *Art and Agency: An Anthropological Theory.* Oxford: Clarendon Press.

Giddens, Anthony. 1984. *The Constitution of Society: Outline of a Theory of Structuration.* Berkeley: University of California Press.

Gilmartin, David. 1988. "The Shahidganj Mosque Incident: A Prelude to Pakistan." In *Islam, Politics, and Social Movements,* edited by Edmund Burke III and Ira M. Lapidus. Berkeley: University of California Press.

Glover, William. 1999. "Making Lahore Modern: Urban Form and Social Practice in Colonial Punjab, 1849–1920." Ph.D. Diss., Department of Architecture, University of California.

———. 2008. *Making Lahore Modern.* Minneapolis: University of Minnesota Press.

Goffman, Erving. 1959. *The Presentation of Self in Everyday Life.* Garden City, NY: Doubleday.

———. 1974. *Frame Analysis: An Essay on the Organization of Experience.* New York: Harper and Row.

———. 1981. *Forms of Talk.* Oxford: Basil Blackwell.

Gogol, Nikolai. 1985. *Dead Souls.* Edited by George Gibian. New York: W. W. Norton.

Goodnow, Henry. 1964. *The Civil Service of Pakistan: Bureaucracy in a New Nation.* New Haven: Yale University Press.

Goody, Jack. 1977. *The Domestication of the Savage Mind.* Cambridge: Cambridge University Press.

———. 1986. *The Logic of Writing and the Organization of Society.* Cambridge: Cambridge University Press.

Government of India. 1891. *Office Manual of Instructions for the Conduct of Business.* P.W.D. Secretariat, Government of India.

Government of India, Secretariat Procedures Committee. [1920] 1963. *Llwellyn-Smith Report.* Karachi: National Institute of Public Administration.

Gupta, Akhil. 1995. "Blurred Boundaries: the Discourse of Corruption, the Culture of Politics, and the Imagined State." *American Ethnologist* 22(2): 375–402.

Gupta, Naryani. 1981. *Delhi Between Two Empires, 1830–1931: Society, Government, and Urban Growth.* Delhi: Oxford University Press.

Haines, David W. 1990. "Conformity in the Face of Ambiguity: A Bureaucratic Dilemma." *Semiotica* 78(3/4): 249–69.

Handelman, Don. 1981. "Introduction: The Idea of Bureaucratic Organization." *Social Analysis* 9:5–23.

Hanks, William. 1990. *Referential Practice: Language and Lived Space among the Maya.* Chicago: University of Chicago Press.

Hansen, Thomas Blom, and Finn Stepputat. 2001. "Introduction: States of

Imagination." In *States of Imagination: Ethnographic Explorations of the Post-Colonial State*. Durham: Duke University Press.

Haqqani, Hussain. 2005. *Pakistan: Between Mosque and Military*. Washington, DC: Brookings Institution Press.

Harley, J. B. 2001. *The New Nature of Maps: Essays in the History of Cartography*. Baltimore: Johns Hopkins University Press.

Harper, Richard. 1998. *Inside the IMF: An Ethnography of Documents, Technology and Organisational Action*. New York: Academic Press.

Harris, Roy. 1995. *Signs of Writing*. London: Routledge.

Heidecker, Karl, ed. 2000. *Charters and the Use of the Written Word in Medieval Society*. Turnhout: Brepols.

Hejeebu, Santhi. 2005. "Contract Enforcement in the English East India Company." *Journal of Economic History* 65(2): 496–523.

Henare, Amiria, Martin Holbraad, and Sari Wastell. 2006. *Thinking Through Things: Theorising Artefacts Ethnographically*. London: Routledge.

Herzfeld, Michael. 1992. *The Social Production of Indifference: Exploring the Symbolic Roots of Western Bureaucracy*. New York: Berg.

Hirschkind, Charles. 2006. *The Ethical Soundscape: Cassette Sermons and Islamic Counterpublics*. New York: Columbia University Press.

Hoag, Colin. 2011. "Assembling Partial Perspectives: Thoughts on the Anthropology of Bureaucracy." *Political and Legal Anthropology Review* 34(1):81–94.

Holston, James. 1989. *The Modernist City: An Anthropological Critique of Brasilia*. Chicago: University of Chicago Press.

———. 1991. "The Misrule of Law: Land and Usurpation in Brazil." *Comparative Studies in Society and History* 33:695–725.

Hosagrahar, Jyoti. 2005. *Indigenous Modernities: Negotiating Architecture and Urbanism*. London: Routledge.

Hull, Matthew. 2011. "Communities of Place, Not Kind: American Technologies of Neighborhood in Post-Colonial Delhi." *Comparative Studies in Society and History* 53(4): 757–90.

Hume, L. J. 1981. *Bentham and Bureaucracy*. Cambridge: Cambridge University Press.

Hussain, Asaf. 1972. *Politics and People's Representation in Pakistan*. Karachi: Ferozsons.

Irvine, Judith. 1989. "When Talk Isn't Cheap: Language and Political Economy." *American Ethnologist* 16(2): 248–67.

———. 1996. "Shadow Conversations: The Indeterminacy of Participant Roles." In *Natural Histories of Discourse,* edited by M. Silverstein and G. Urban, 131–59 Chicago: University of Chicago Press.

Jacob, Christian. 1996. "Toward a Cultural History of Cartography." *Imago Mundi* 48:191–98.

Jahandarie, Khosrow. 1999. *Spoken and Written Discourse: A Multi-Disciplinary Approach*. Stamford, CT: Ablex.

Jalal, Ayesha. 1990. *The State of Martial Rule*. Cambridge: Cambridge University Press.

———. 1995. *Democracy and Authoritarianism in South Asia*. Cambridge: Cambridge University Press.

Johns, Adrian. 1998. *The Nature of the Book: Print and Knowledge in the Making*. Chicago: University of Chicago Press.

Kachru, Braj B. 1992. "English in South Asia." In *The Cambridge History of the English Language*, edited by R. Burchfield, 497–553. Cambridge: Cambridge University Press.

Kafka, Ben. 2009. "Paperwork: The State of the Discipline." *Book History* 12:340–53.

Kaw, M. K. 1993. *Bureaucrazy: IAS Unmasked*. New Delhi: Konark.

Keane, Webb. 1997. *Signs of Recognition*. Berkeley: University of California Press.

———. 2003. "Semiotics and the Social Analysis of Things." *Language and Communication* 23:409–25.

Kelly, John, and Martha Kaplan. 1990. "History, Structure, and Ritual." *Annual Review of Anthropology* 19:119–50.

Kennedy, Charles. 1987. *Bureaucracy in Pakistan*. Oxford: Oxford University Press.

Khan, Ayub Mohammad. 1967. *Friends Not Masters: A Political Autobiography*. New York: Oxford University Press.

Khan, Naveeda. 2003. "Grounding Sectarianism: Islamic Ideology and Muslim Everyday Life in Lahore, Pakistan Circa 1920s/1990s." Ph.D. Diss., Department of Anthropology, Columbia University.

Khan, Pauchkourie. 1866. *The Revelations of an Orderly: Being an Attempt to Expose the Abuses of Administration by the Relation of Every-Day Occurrences in the Mofussil Courts*. Benares: E. J. Lazarus.

King, Anthony. 1976. *Colonial Urban Development: Culture, Social Power and Environment*. London: Routledge Kegan Paul.

Kopytoff, Igor. 1986. "The Cultural Biography of Things: Commoditization as Cultural Progress." In *The Social Life of Things*, edited by A. Appadurai. 64–91. Cambridge: Cambridge University Press.

Kripke, Saul. 1980. *Naming and Necessity*. Cambridge, MA: Harvard University Press.

Kuipers, Joel C. 1990. *Power in Performance: The Creation of Textual Authority in Weyewa Ritual Spech*. Philadelphia: University of Pennsylvania Press.

Kula, Witold. 1986. *Measures and Men*. Translated by R. Szreter. Princeton: Princeton University Press.

Latour, Bruno. 1987. *Science in Action: How to Follow Scientists and Engineers through Society*. Cambridge, MA: Harvard University Press.

———. 1999. *Pandora's Hope*. Cambridge, MA: Harvard University Press.

———. 2005. *Reassembling the Social*. Oxford: Oxford University Press.

Latour, Bruno, and Emilie Hermant. 1998. *Paris ville invisible*. Paris: Institut Synthélabo pour le progrès de la connaissance.

Lee, Benjamin. 1997. *Talking Heads: Language, Metalanguage, and the Semiotics of Subjectivity*. Durham: Duke University Press.

Legg, Stephen. 2007. *Spaces of Colonialism*. London: Blackwell.

Levin, David Michael. 1993. "Introduction." In *Modernity and the Hegemony of Vision*, edited by D. M. Levin, 1–29. Berkeley: University of California Press.

Levinson, Stephen C. 1988. *Putting Linguistics on a Proper Footing: Explorations in Goffman's Concepts of Participation*, edited by P. Drew and A. Wootton, 161–227. Oxford: Polity.

Levi-Strauss, Claude. 1973. *Tristes Tropiques*. Translated by J. Weightman and D. Weightman. New York: MacMillan.

Lewis, Mark. 1999. *Writing and Authority in Early China*. Albany: SUNY Press.

Li, Tania Murray. 2005. "Beyond 'the State' and Failed Schemes." *American Anthropologist* 107(3): 383–94.

Lindstrom, S., and B. Ostnas. [1952] 1967. Report on the Greater Karachi Plan. Karachi: Merz Rendel Vatten for Government of Pakistan.

Malik, Asghar Javed. 1999. *Office Procedure Drafting and Noting*. Lahore: Umer Khurram Printers.

Malik, Jamal. 1996. *Colonialization of Islam: Dissolution of Traditional Institutions in Pakistan*. New Delhi: Manohar.

Mandelbrot, Benoît. 1967. "How Long Is the Coast of Britain? Statistical Self-Similarity and Fractional Dimension." *Science* 156(3775): 636–38.

Mannheim, Karl. 1985. *Ideology and Utopia: An Introduction to the Sociology of Knowledge*. Translated by L. Wirth and E. Shils. New York: Harcourt Brace.

Marshall, P. J. 1976. *East Indian Fortunes: The British in Bengal in the Eighteenth Century*. Oxford: Clarendon Press.

———. 1987. *Bengal: The British Bridgehead: Eastern India, 1740–1828*. Cambridge: Cambridge University Press.

Mazzarella, William. 2006. "Internet X-ray: E-Governance, Transparency, and the Politics of Immediation in India." *Publc Culture* 18:473–505.

Merry, Sally Engle. 1992. "Anthropology, Law, and Transnational Processes." *Annual Review of Anthropology* 21:357–79.

Messick, Brinkley. 1993. *The Calligraphic State*. Berkeley: University of California Press.

Metcalf, Barbara. 1989. *Islamic Revival in British India: Deoband, 1860–1900*. New York: Oxford University Press.

Miller, Daniel. 1987. *Material Culture and Mass Consumption*. Cambridge, MA: Basil Blackwell.

———, ed. 2005. *Materiality*. Durham: Duke University Press.

Misra, B.B. 1977. *The Bureaucracy in India: An Historical Analysis of Development up to 1947*. Delhi: Oxford University Press.

Mitchell, Timothy. 1991. "The Limits of the State: Beyond Statist Approaches and Their Critics." *American Political Science Review* 85:77–96.

———. 1999. "Society, Economy, and the State Effect." In *State/Culture: State-Formation after the Cultural Turn*, edited by G. Steinmetz, 76–97. Ithaca: Cornell University Press.

Mohiuddin, Momin. 1971. *The Chancellery and Persian Epistolography Under the Mughals: From Babur to Shah Jahan, 1526–1658*. Calcutta: Iran Society.

Mohsin, Hamid. 2000. *Moth Smoke*. London: Granta.

Moir, Martin. 1993. "Kaghazi Raj: Notes in the Documentary Basis of Company Rule 1773–1858." *Indo British Review* 21(2):185–92.

Mol, Annemarie. 2002. *The Body Multiple: Ontology in Medical Practice.* Durham: Duke University Press.

Mostert, Marco, ed. 1999. *New Approaches to Medieval Communication.* Turnhout: Brepols.

Munir, Ahmed. 1964. *Civil Servants in Pakistan.* Karachi: Oxford University Press.

Munn, Nancy. 1983. "Gawan Kula: Spatiotemporal Control and the Symbolism of Influence." In *The Kula: New Perspectives on Massim Exchange,* edited by J. W. Leach and E. Leach, 277–308. Cambridge: Cambridge University Press.

Nilsson, Sten. 1973. *The New Capitals of India, Pakistan, and Bangladesh.* Lund: Studentlitteratur.

Ogborn, Miles. 2007. *Indian Ink: Script and Print in the Making of the English East India Company.* Chicago: University of Chicago Press.

Oldenburg, Veena. 1989. *The Making of Colonial Lucknow.* Delhi: Oxford University Press.

Olson, David. 1994. *The World on Paper.* Cambridge: Cambridge University Press.

Ortner, Sherry. 1984. "Theory in Anthropology Since the 1960s." *Comparative Studies in Society and History* 26:126–66.

———. 1995. "Resistance and the Problems of Ethnographic Refusal." *Comparative Studies in Society and History* 37(1):173–93.

Palmer, F. R. 1986. *Mood and Modality.* Cambridge: Cambridge University Press.

Parry, Jonathan. 2000. "'The Crisis of Corruption' and 'the Idea of India': A Worm's Eye View." In *The Morals of Legitimacy,* edited by I. Pardo, 27–55. Oxford: Berghahn.

———. 2004. "The Marital History of a 'Thumb-Impression Man,'" In *Telling Lives in India,* edited by David Arnold and Stuart Blackburn, 281–317. Bloomington: Indiana University Press.

Peirce, Charles Sanders. 1986. *Writings of Charles Sanders Peirce: A Chronological Edition.* Volume 3. Bloomington: Indiana University Press.

Petrucci, Armando. 1995. *Writers and Readers in Medieval Italy.* Translated C. M. Radding. New Haven: Yale University Press.

Poole, Deborah. 2004. "Between Threat and Guarantee: Justice and Community in the Margins of the Peruvian State." In *Anthropology in the Margins of the State,* edited by Veena Das and Deborah Poole, 67–81. Santa Fe, NM: School of American Research.

Qadeer, Mohammad A. 1983. *Lahore: Urban Development in the Third World.* Lahore: Vanguard.

Qazi, Muhammed Usman. 2006. Computerisation of Land Records in Pakistan: A Comparative Analysis of Two Projects from a Human Security Perspective.

Qureshi, Sharif Al-Uddin. 1995. *Makan Khud Banwaen.* Lahore: Tajaran.

Raby, Namika. 1985. *Katcheri Bureaucracy in Sri Lanka: The Culture and Politics of Accessibility.* Syracuse: Syracuse University Press.

Rajagopal, Arvind. 2001. *Politics After Television: Religious Nationalism and the Reshaping of the Indian Public.* Cambridge: Cambridge University Press.

Raman, Bhavani. 2007. "Document Raj: Scribes and Writing Under Early Colonial Rule in Madras, 1771–1860." Ph.D. Diss., Department of History, University of Michigan.

Ramaswamy, Sumathi. 2003. "Introduction." In *Beyond Appearances? Visual Practices and Ideologies in Modern India*, edited by S. Ramaswamy. 1–32. London: Sage.

Raza, Syed Hashim. 1991. *Hamari Manzil: Walking with History*. Karachi: Mustafain & Murtazain.

Richards, John. 1993. *The Mughal Empire*. Cambridge: Cambridge University Press.

Riles, Annelise. 1998. "Infinity Within the Brackets." *American Ethnologist* 25(3): 378–98.

———. 2000. *The Network Inside Out*. Ann Arbor: University of Michigan Press.

———. 2006. "Introduction: In Response." In *Documents: Artifacts of Modern Knowledge*, edited by A. Riles, 1–38. Ann Arbor: University of Michigan Press.

Ring, Laura. 2006. *Zenana: Everyday Peace in a Karachi Apartment Building*. Bloomington: Indiana University Press.

Roberts, Alasdair. 2010. "A Great and Revolutionary Law? The First Four Years of India's Right to Information Act." *Public Administration Review* 70(6): 925–33.

Robins, Nick. 2006. *The Corporation that Changed the World*. London: Pluto.

Sadiq, Roohi. 1987. "Social Groupings and the Nature of Competition: A Case Study of Groups Prevailing in Badia Qadir Baksh with Special Reference to Golra Shareef." Master's Thesis, Department of Anthropology, Quaid-i-Azam University.

Sampson, Steven. 1983. "Bureaucracy and Corruption as Anthropological Problems: A Case Study from Romania." *Folk* 25:63–96.

Sarangi, Srikant, and Stefan Slembrouck. 1996. *Language, Bureaucracy, and Social Control*. London: Longman.

Sayeed, Khalid B. 1967. *The Political System of Pakistan*. Boston: Houghton Mifflin.

———. 1980. *Politics in Pakistan: the Nature and Direction of Change*. New York: Praeger.

Schwartzman, Helen B. 1992. *Ethnography in Organizations*. New York: Sage.

Scott, James. 1998. *Seeing Like a State: How Certain Schemes to Improve the Human Condition Have Failed*. New Haven: Yale University Press.

Searle, Llerena. 2009. "Constructing Legibility: Transparency Claims and the Internationalization of Indian Real Estate." Paper delivered at Annual Conference on South Asia, University of Wisconsin, Madison.

Sellen, Abigail J., and Richard Harper. 2002. *The Myth of the Paperless Office*. Cambridge, MA: MIT Press.

Sennett, Richard. 1990. "American Cities: the Grid Plan and the Protestant Ethic." *International Social Science Journal* 125:269–85.

———. 1998. *Corrosion of Character: The Personal Consequences of Work in the New Capitalism*. New York: W. W. Norton.

Shamil, Shehla Parveen. 1987. "Strategies for Female Subjugation in Patriarchal Family System of a Pakistani Village." Master's Thesis, Department of Anthropology, Quaid-i-Azam University.

Sharma, Aradhana, and Akhil Gupta. 2006. "Introduction: Rethinking Theories of the State in the Age of Globalization." In *The Anthropology of the State*, edited by A. Sharma and A. Gupta, 1–41. Oxford: Blackwell.

Shryock, Andrew. 2008. "Thinking about Hospitality, with Derrida, Kant, and the Balga Bedouin." *Anthropos* 103:1–17.

Shuy, Roger W. 1998. *Bureaucratic Language in Government & Business.* Washington, DC: Georgetown University Press.

Siddiqi, Majid. 2005. *The British Historical Context and Petitioning in Colonial India.* Delhi: Aakar.

Sieder, Rachel. 2001. "Rethinking Citizenship: Reforming the Law in Postwar Guatemala." In *States of Imagination: Ethnographic Explorations of the Post-Colonial State,* edited by T. B. Hansen and F. Stepputat. 203–20. Durham: Duke University Press.

Silverstein, Michael. 1979. "Language Structure and Linguistic Ideology." In *The Elements: A Parasession on Linguistic Units and Levels,* edited by Paul R. Clyne, William F. Hanks, and Carol L. Hofbauer. 193–247 Chicago: Chicago Linguistic Society.

Silverstein, Michael, and Greg Urban. 1996. "The Natural History of Discourse." In *Natural Histories of Discourse,* edited by M. Silverstein and G. Urban, 1–17. Chicago: University of Chicago Press.

Smith, Brian Cantwell. 1996. *On the Origin of Objects.* Cambridge, MA: MIT Press.

Smith, Richard Saumarez. 1985. "Rule-by-Records and Rule-by-Reports: Complementary Aspects of the British Imperial Rule of Law." *Contributions to Indian Sociology* 19:153–76.

———. 1996. *Rule by Records: Land Registration and Village Custom in Early British Panjab.* Delhi: Oxford University Press.

Spaulding, Frank. 1994. "The Gujars of Islamabad: A Study in the Social Construction of Local Ethnic Identities." Ph.D. Diss., Department of Anthropology, Ohio State University.

———. 2003. "Ayub Khan, Constaninos Doxiadis and Islamabad: Biography as Modernity in a Planned Urban Space." In *Pakistan at the Millenium,* edited by C. H. Kennedy, K. McNeil, C. Ernst, and D. Gilmartin, 351–75. Oxford: Oxford University Press.

Specht, Rabia Ahmed. 1983. *Islamabad/Rawalpindi.* Copenhagen: School of Architecture.

Spooner, Brian. 1986. "Weavers and Dealers: The Authenticity of an Oriental Carpet." In *The Social Life of Things,* edited by A. Appadurai,195–235 Cambridge: Cambridge University Press.

Star, Susan Leigh, and James Griesemer. 1989. "Institutional Ecology, 'Translations' and Boundary Objects: Amateurs and Professionals in Berkeley's Museum of Vertebrate Zoology, 1907–39." *Social Studies of Science* 19(3): 387–420.

Stock, Brian. 1983. *The Implications of Literacy: Written Language and Models of Interpretation in the Eleventh and Twelfth Centuries*. Princeton: Princeton University Press.

Strathern, Marilyn. 1999. *Property, Substance, Effect: Anthropological Essays on Persons and Things*. London: Athlone.

Stoler, Ann. 2010. *Along the Archival Grain: Epistemic Anxieties and Colonial Common Sense*. Princeton: Princeton University Press.

Street, Brian. 1984. *Literacy in Theory and Practice*. Cambridge: Cambridge University Press.

Tarlo, Emma. 2001. "Paper Truths: The Emergency and Slum Clearance through Forgotten Files." In *The Everyday State and Modern India*, edited by C. J. Fuller and V. Bénéï, 68–90. New Dehli: Social Science Press.

Torpey, John. 2000. *Invention of the Passport: Surveillance, Citizenship, and the State*. Cambridge: Cambridge University Press.

Van der Veer, Peter. 2002. "Religion in South Asia." *Annual Review of Anthropology* 31:173–87.

van Voss, Lex Heerma. 2001. "Introduction." *International Review of Social History* 46(9): 1–10.

Verdery, Katherine. 1994. "The Elasticity of Land: Problems of Property Restitution in Transylvania." *Slavic Review* 53(4):1071–109.

———. 2003. *The Vanishing Hectare: Property and Value in Postsocialist Transylvania*. Ithaca: Cornell University Press.

Vismann, Cornelia. 2008. *Files: Law and Media Technology*. Translated by G. Withrop-Young. Palo Alto, CA: Stanford University Press.

Volosinov, V. N. 1986. *Marxism and the Philosophy of Language*. Translated by L. Matejka and I. R. Titunik. Cambridge, MA: Harvard University Press.

Wade, Robert. 1982. "The System of Administrative and Political Corruption: Canal Irrigation in South India." *Journal of Development Studies* 18:287–328.

Warner, Michael. 2002. "Publics and Counterpublics." *Public Culture* 14(1): 49–90.

Waseem, Mohammad. 1989. *Politics and the State in Pakistan*. Lahore: Progressive.

Weatherford, J. M. 1981. *Tribes on the Hill*. New York: Rawson, Wade.

Weber, Max. 1978. *Economy and Society*. Berkeley: University of California Press.

Winner, Langdon. 1980. "Do Artifacts Have Politics?" *Daedalus* 109(1): 121–36.

Woolard, Kathryn A. 1998. "Introduction: Language Ideology as a Field of Inquiry." In *Language Ideologies: Practice and Theory*, edited by Bambi B. Schieffelin, Katherine A. Woolard, and Paul V. Kroskrity, 3–47. Oxford: Oxford University Press.

Wright, Arnold. 1891. "Petitions and Begging Letters." In *Baboo English as 'Tis Writ: Being Curiosities of Indian Journalism*. London: T. F. Unwin.

Wright, Gwendolyn. 1991. *Politics of Design in French Colonial Urbanism*. Chicago: University of Chicago Press.

Yakas, Orestes. 2001. *Islamabad: Birth of a Capital*. Oxford: Oxford University Press.

Yates, JoAnne. 1989. *Control through Communication: The Rise of System in American Management.* Baltimore: Johns Hopkins University Press.

Yates, JoAnne, Wanda J. Orlikowski, and Julie Rennecker. 1997. "Collaborative Genres for Collaboration: Genre Systems in Digital Media." In *Proceedings of the Thirtieth Annual Hawaiian International Conference on System Sciences.* Washington, DC: IEEE Computer Society Press.

Zabeeh, Mohammad Ismail. 1995. *Islamabad, Manzil-i Murad: Mazi, Hal, Mustaqbil.* Islamabad: al-Qalam.

Zaidi, S. Inayat A. 2005. "Introduction." In *The British Historical Context and Petitioning in Colonial India,* edited by M. Siddiqi, 9–16. Delhi: Aakar.

Zaret, David. 1999. *Origins of Democratic Culture: Printing, Petitions, and the Public Sphere in Early Modern England.* Princeton: Princeton University Press.

Index

adverse possession, legal principle of, 236–40

aesthetics, 5, 25, 26, 29

"affectees," 163, 164, 172, 270n12; built-up properties (BUPs) and, 174; CDA in conflict with, 187–88; compensation demands of, 182–83, 191; package deals and, 196, 198; politics of representation and, 207. *See also* "displaced persons"; village society/villagers

Afghan war, 182

Africa, West, 24

Afridi, Zaffar (pseudonym), 250

agency, 15, 33, 129, 130, 163; circulation of files and, 138; corporate/collective, 132, 133, 138, 150–51; hierarchy and, 144; nonhuman, 257; particular projects and, 150–60; passive verbs and, 140–41

Ahl-i-Hadith, 217, 220, 224, 226, 227, 272n6

Ahmad, Mumtaz, 219

Ahmed, Tariq, 182, 192

air conditioning, 73

Aitcheson College (Lahore), 77, 265n9

Alavi, Hamza, 6, 259n4

ancien régime, in France, 19

Angrezi WCs (English WCs), 72–73, 265n5

anthropology/anthropologists, 12, 13, 27, 129; cultural, 26; linguistic, 23–26

Appadurai, Arjun, 100

"approach-wallas," 188–89, 271n20

architects/architecture, 1, 4, 57, 61, 125

archives, 28, 273n16

Asia Challenge Investments, 248, 249, 250, 255

Asian WCs, 72–73, 265n5

Association for Islamabad Displaced Persons, 172

associations, 18, 20, 21, 25

Auqaf Directorate, 32, 111, 126, 159; passive verbs in writing of, 141; sectarian allocation of mosques and, 213, 220–26, 238, 241, 243, 273nn9–11

authentication/authenticity, 26, 169

authorship, 15, 130, 150, 261n22; circulation of files and, 138; corporate/collective, 132, 134, 135–36, 153, 203; printing as material technology and, 168; rituals' displacement of, 132

autopens, 267n7

Awami League, 42

Ayub Khan, Muhammad, 38, 39, 40, 41, 42; Doxiadis and, 43, 44–45; isolation of bureaucracy as goal, 44; President's House and, 262n15

Baba Parchi (film, 2003), 81

Badia Qadir Bakhsh (BQB), village of, 163, 175–76, 191, 244; aerial view of, 208; compensation paid to villagers, 164, 182; dummy houses in, 183, 185; fraud in compensation process, 189, 204;

languages influenced by, 141; status of, 16, 261n21; on surveyors' maps, 177; terms derived from South Asian languages, 81; on visiting cards, 83
ethnicity, 53
ethnography, 12, 31
Evans, Gareth, 269n4
eviction proceedings, 113, 157, 174

F-6 sector, 56, 122, 221, 225, 239
F-7 sector, 56, 122, 233–34
F-8 sector, 215
F-10 sector, 31, 122, 224, 265n5
F-11 sector, 122, 265n5
F-12 sector, 162
face-to-face meetings, 20, 66, 86, 102–3
"fair copy," 125
family, 1, 20, 53; compensation policies and, 185; housing of, 181–82; "joint family," 181, 182, 185
Federal Capital Commission, 44, 49, 55, 56
Federal Investigative Agency (FIA), 128, 153–54
Federal Shariat Court (FSC), 236–37, 270n12
Ferguson, James, 186
"feudals" (landed elites), 77
file note sheets and notes, 10, 15, 16, 17, 112–15, 120–22, 123, 124–25, 136–39, 143, 148–50, 159, 267n6
files, 15, 66, 70, 75, 115, 154; access to, 32; "current files," 28; destruction of, 32; "discussion" of, 137–38, 155; file numbers, 122, 267n5; generation process of, 119–21; history of, 116–17; identification of, 32; individual writers and corporate authority, 126–34; influence over files as sign of power, 151; maps and, 116, 234, 235; materiality cases, 115–26; misrouting or loss of, 151–53; predominance of, 161; receipts as components of, 122, 124; responsibility and, 245–46; state relations with populace and, 88; as time bombs, 129; as workhorse of bureaucracy, 113, 160
files, circulation of, 23, 121–22, 125–26, 132, 136–38, 146, 189–90; projects frustrated by, 154; slowed or stopped, 155–58; unauthorized persons and, 154, 155; theft of, 188; unauthorized possession of, 189
forgeries, 83, 170, 189, 200, 203–4; "chancery forgeries," 204; in European history, 246. See also corruption; fraud
Foucault, Michel, 114, 165, 180–81
framing, 24

fraud, 109–10, 193, 234, 246; in compensation process, 165, 184, 189, 190; government breakdown and, 164; land expropriation and, 170; lists and, 199, 202, 203. See also corruption; forgeries
French language, 16
French Revolution, 19
F sectors, 126
functionaries, 19, 22, 183, 247; alliance-making process and, 134; authorship of written discourse and, 127, 132–33; compensation lists and, 202; contest of graphic genres and, 161; denial or diffusion of agency by, 142–43, 146, 150, 153; files and, 114–19, 138, 154; in Germany (nineteenth cent.), 21; influence and, 106; movement of files slowed or stopped by, 153, 155; native functionaries in East India Company service, 9–10; passive verbs in writing of, 140–41; personnel changes and, 128; resident in Islamabad, 182; stamps and, 131; status among, 85–86; village society and, 187; writing communities and, 16; writing of, 129, 130. See also bureaucrats; CDA officers; civil servants

G-6 sector, 56, 211; as oldest sector of Islamabad, 31, 62; Redevelopment Plan for, 230–31, 231; subdivisions of, 51, 52
G-7 sector, 67, 154, 211; lack of community sense in, 221; petitions for mosques in, 98–99, 100, 103, 149
G-8 sector, 240, 247, 270n16
G-10 sector, 228, 229, 265n5
G-11 sector, 162, 175, 176, 184, 265n5; aerial view of, 208; CDA acquisition of land in, 181; fraudulent claims in, 204; map, 176; mosques in, 241; village leaders' influence in, 186–87
G-12 sector, 162, 175, 176, 176, 204
Gardezi, Syed Ali Nawaz, 196
Garfinkel, Harold, 166, 169
genre system, 10
Gilani, Yousuf Raza, 81, 83
Gilmartin, David, 217
Gladieux, B. G., 260n5
Glover, William, 48
Goffman, Erving, 146
Golra Sharif shrine, 176, 215, 270n17
Goody, Jack, 24, 113–14, 133, 146, 147, 200
gossip, 68, 74
Gournay, Jean Claude Marie Vincent de, 11
governance/government, 1, 5, 245; centrality of writing in, 7, 36; corruption as market-

responsibility, 107–8, 121, 132, 245–46; acknowledgment of, 152; agency and, 130; authorship and, 130; avoidance or diffusion of, 114, 115, 134–50, 267–68n10
"Revolution of Bengal," 9
Riles, Annelise, 26
ritual speech, 132, 138, 267n9
rivers, cartographic representations of, 232
roads, 3, 5, 6, 187, 211; British colonial government and, 47; on maps, 234
Romania, 174, 180, 273n16
Rules for the Conduct of Business (CDA manual), 69, 136

Sadiq, Roohi, 181, 182, 186, 199, 271n26
Sajjad, Reza (pseudonym), 187–88, 190, 191, 193
Saudi Arabia, 220, 272n4
Saumarez Smith, Richard, 205
schedules, 116
Schumpeter, Joseph, 158
science and technology studies, 18, 25, 27, 164
Scott, James, 4, 35, 165–66, 168, 207; on customary versus state measures, 167; on maps in regimes of control, 212
scribes, 92–93
semiosis/semiotics, 13, 18, 22
semiotic technologies, 5, 27, 130, 168, 257; maps as, 243; turned against government, 205
Senegal, 143
Sennett, Richard, 263n19
servants, domestic, 76–77
settlement reports (land tenure surveys), 11
Shah, Mehar Ali, 199
Shahan, Nurpur, 170
Shakarparian Park, 2, 45, 211
Shamil, Shehla Parveen, 181
shamlat (common lands), 251, 274n8
sharia (Islamic law), 219, 270n12
Sharif, Nawaz, 87, 106, 107
Sharma, Aradhana, 26
Sheikhpur, village of, 172, 178, 181, 188, 192; compensation list for, *201;* disputes with CDA, 210; package deal for, 194, *195, 196, 197*
Shia Muslims, 217, 220, 238, 272n3, 272nn5–6, 273n8
shopkeepers, 163
shrines (*mazars*), 32, 126, 215
Siddiqi, Majid, 104
sifarish (connection, "approach"), 81, 156

signatures, 10, 17, 23, 149, 159, 200; circulation of files and, 139; corruption and, 61; electronic, 256–57; on file note sheets, 124; forged, 189, 203–4; on G-6 Redevelopment Plan, 230, 231; graphic ideology of, 131; hierarchy of, 140; on petitions, 87, 93; as sanctioned indexes of individuals, 131, 267n8; on Sheikhpur Package Deal, 196, 197; signing as biomechanical act, 131, 267n7; thumbprints as, 131
signs, linguistic, 13–14, 131
Sikhs, 45, 48, 85, 218, 237
Sind, 37, 38
Siri Saral, village of, 189, 200
slips, colored, 11, 260n11
slums, 32
Smith, Brian Cantwell, 25
social networks, 21, 22, 136, 160, 165, 170
social sciences, 13, 25
Socio-Economic Survey of Rawalpindi, 54
sociologists, 12
South Asia, 28, 49, 219, 257; colonial government in, 7; dual cities, 35; kingly rule in, 105; kinship arrangements, 182; petitions used throughout, 88
Soviet Union: Afghan war and, 182; collapse of, 105
spatial organization, 15, 35, 46, 214
Spaulding, Frank, 38, 50, 53, 262n17
Special Commission for the Location of the Federal Capital, 38, 39, 40
Special Mosque Committee, 239, 241
speech, 16, 137–39, 147, 148
squatting, 53, 113, 194, 240–44, 247
stamps, 10, 70, 120, 121; "despatch," 125; as officially sanctioned indexes, 131; "receipt," 125; signatures and, 140
Star, Susan Leigh, 180
state, the: antagonisms with village, 20; European, 165; government breakdown, 164; as panopticon, 180–81; petitions and popular views of, 88; proceduralism and, 26; society's boundary with, 34–35, 36, 67; surveillance and control by, 212–13; translations and, 166. *See also* governance/government
statistics, 45, 61, 62, 164, 168
status: Basic Pay Scale (BPS) and, 54–55, 57; bathroom facilities and, 71–72; in CDA hierarchy, 69; of clients and visitors, 74, 75; divisions of labor and, 75–76; dress as indicator of, 86; judged by appearance, 84–85; of languages, 16;

TEXT:	10/13 Sabon (Open Type)
DISPLAY:	Sabon (Open Type)
COMPOSITOR:	BookMatters, Berkeley
INDEXER:	Alexander Trotter
CARTOGRAPHER/ILLUSTRATOR:	William L. Nelson, Krisztina Fehérváry
PRINTER AND BINDER:	Maple-Vail Book Manufacturing Group
COVER PRINTER:	Brady Palmer